Psychotherapy and
the Paranoid Process

Psychotherapy and the Paranoid Process

W. W. Meissner, S.J., M.D.

Jason Aronson Inc.
Northvale, New Jersey
London

Library of Congress Cataloging-in-Publication Data

Meissner, W. W. (William W.), 1931–
  Psychotherapy and the paranoid process.

  Bibliography: p.
  Includes index.
  1. Paranoia—Treatment.   2. Psychotherapy.
I. Title.   [DNLM: 1. Paranoid Disorders—
psychology.   2. Psychotherapy. WM 205 M515pb]
RC520.M45   1985   616.89'7   85-15614
ISBN 0-87668-752-4

Manufactured in the United States of America.

In memory of Rita,
a friend and counselor to many

Contents

Preface

The present work is an extension of theoretical formulations in *The Paranoid Process* (1978) to a variety of clinical applications. The most important area of application is that of the psychotherapeutic process. The original work, in which I advanced a conceptualization of the paranoid process and its constituent mechanisms, concerned itself almost entirely with a survey of the literature dealing with aspects of psychic functioning related to paranoid mechanisms and with the focusing of these processes in clinical material. While this approach offered the basis for a meaningful theoretical formulation, it provided little of a more concrete application to actual clinical work. My purpose in the present monograph is to remedy that shortcoming.

My orientation in the present work is decidedly less conceptual and more clinical. Readers who are unfamiliar with the conceptual framework may find it useful to peruse the previous volume. The most relevant section is Part III under the heading "Toward a Clinical Theory of the Paranoid Process" (Chapters 16–28). The theoretical material in the present effort is limited to little more than capsule summaries of the understanding of the paranoid process. The intention is much more to focus these ideas more immediately and practically in the clinical context.

A few comments regarding the organization of the material may be helpful. Part I is meant to provide a conceptual framework for the considerations that follow. My first purpose is to indicate the place of the paranoid process in the evolving context of psychoanalytic clinical thinking. A brief description of the major aspects of the paranoid process follows that I would hope provides sufficient understanding of what is involved in the paranoid process for the majority of readers. Some may wish to probe the matter more deeply by consulting the previous work. This first section is completed by the laying out of a psychotherapeutic schema based on the principles of the paranoid process. This schema is the product of my own years of clinical work and the supervising of psychiatric residents over the course of 15 years. I have found it extremely useful as a vehicle for the teaching of psychotherapy and as a helpful orientation in conceptualizing complex and often confusing case material. Of course, such a schema is no substitute for good supervision, but it may provide a helpful adjunct.

Part Two applies the ideas of the paranoid process to some of the major forms of psychopathology. The discussion of treatment of the psychoses aims at showing the role of the paranoid process in certain aspects of the psychotic process, particularly in its interaction with the schizophrenic process. The famous Schreber case, as described originally by Freud (1911), is used to illustrate certain aspects of this involvement. While the Schreber material is undoubtedly familiar to many readers, the approach in terms of the paranoid process tends to bring certain aspects of Schreber's psychosis into a somewhat different perspective that opens the way to a somewhat different therapeutic approach.

The chapter on borderline psychopathology introduces a somewhat divergent perspective on borderline diagnosis, which I have developed more at length in a previous work (Meissner 1984a). This encapsulated material provides the framework for some initial considerations regarding the psychotherapeutic treatment of patients in the borderline spectrum. I propose here an adaptation of the principles of treatment derived from the paranoid process to the understanding of borderline pathology and its therapy. Freud's experience with the Wolf Man offers a unique opportunity to study the vicissitudes of the treatment course of a typical and famous borderline patient in the hands of a master therapist. That therapy was undoubtedly a learning experience for Freud and continues to be such for us. I would hope to develop these ideas and this approach more at length in future work.

The treatment of the narcissistic personality (Chapter Five) is an area of considerable controversy and uncertainty. I have advanced here a consideration of the nature of narcissistic pathology and a conceptualization of a treatment approach that articulates the narcissistic aspects of the organization of the paranoid process to this problem. To my knowledge, the understanding and the psychotherapeutic approach are quite distinct from the approaches developed by Kohut and Kernberg. This section should offer readers another alternative in their attempts to understand and grapple with this difficult area of psychotherapeutic endeavor.

Part Three is devoted to the diagnosis and treatment of patients with a clinically paranoid disorder. Such patients are particularly difficult and trying for all therapists, no matter at what level of training or experience. Nonetheless, it is my conviction that many such patients are treatable and that the contextual framework provided by the paranoid process offers a significant model for understanding the nature of the pathology and for guiding effective therapeutic intervention. This section tries to bring these elements into useful and practical conjunction.

In Part Four, the problems of adolescent development and adolescent alienation (Chapter Eight) provide a unique context for the understanding of the implementation of the paranoid process as part of normal developmental experience. By the same token, the deviant course of such development offers a striking example of the complexity of the issues involved not only in the treatment of disturbed adolescents but also in that of the broader range of patients who reflect elements of social alienation as an expression of the paranoid process. The interplay of these issues is brought into dramatic focus in the case of a rebellious and alienated adolescent, and complexities of the treatment process unveiled.

The balance of Part Four is given over to the examination of several areas of clinical concern in which the resources of the paranoid process find a particularly telling application. Suicide, addiction, and aging are all areas in which the dynamics of the paranoid process come to play a central and determining role. My purpose here is to bring these aspects of clinical situation into clearer focus and to suggest that the understanding generated in the light of the paranoid process points in the direction of useful and specific clinical interventions.

Overall, my hope is that these formulations and understandings will contribute to and facilitate the efforts of clinicians to deal more effectively and empathically with a variety of difficult clinical conditions. The approach that I have described here in terms of the paranoid process is in no way a substitute or replacement for other approaches to these same problems. In my own thinking, it does offer a perspective, an alternative, a way of understanding, a basis for technical applications, that can complement, deepen, and enrich the approach to a variety of clinical problems. I would like to express my gratitude to those who helped me most in bringing these ideas to fruition—my students, supervisees, and patients. I have learned something from all of them. I would hope that if my efforts have been successful, the reader will have a similar opportunity.

W. W. Meissner, S.J., M.D.
Cambridge, Massachusetts

Part One

The Paranoid Process
and Psychotherapy

Chapter One

The Paranoid Process
as a Theory of Therapy

This chapter offers a conceptualization of the paranoid process specifically as a theory of therapy. The attempt to establish a meaningful bridge between the theory of the paranoid process and its clinical applications has a twofold intention: First, to articulate the paranoid process with the ongoing current of psychoanalytic thinking. And second, to provide a frame of reference that allows us to further focus on elements of the paranoid process as it enters the therapeutic situation and provides an additional basis for meaningful therapeutic intervention.

The Evolution of Theory and Therapy
in Freud's Thinking

It is useful in this context to review Freud's experience. Our concern is not particularly with the evolution in Freud's theory or in his understanding of technique, but rather with the interplay between them.

Early in his work on hysteria, Freud (1888) had considerable enthusiasm for hypnosis as a therapeutic technique. The rationale behind the use of hypnosis was fairly clear-cut. Hysterics suffered from reminiscences; that is, ideas based on past events, that were dissociated from conscious awareness and antithetical to the present intentions and expectations of the subject. Freud saw hypnosis as a form of intense suggestion which served therapeutically to reintegrate the conscious intentions with these dissociated reminiscences (1892–1893). But in the defensive (as opposed to hypnoid) hysterias, in which the hysterical dissociation was serving defensive purposes, Freud became aware of the need for diminishing the patient's resistances and working them through to a resolution. The resistance was seen to be in the service of defense or censorship. Freud commented that not knowing was often equivalent to not wanting to know, and it was the patient's not wanting to know that had to be overcome. In theory, when the patient's resistance had been diminished, it was possible to trace the associative links between the pathogenic ideas and the conscious ideas (1893–1895).

The shift in emphasis from the recovery of reminiscences through hypnotic suggestion to the overcoming of resistances through inter-pretation reflected one of the most significant alterations in Freud's theoretical thinking. The shift was generated and consolidated by the radical revision of Freud's seduction hypothesis. The realization that reported seductions in childhood memories did not always represent real events but, rather, were the products of fantasy and wishful imagining, represented a radical reorganization in Freud's thinking (Zetzel and Meissner 1973). It meant that the work of therapy involved far more than the mere recovery of dissociated memories. It meant, in fact, that the therapy had to deal with the mechanisms that gave rise to such fantasies and gave them meaning, as well as with the repressing forces which preserved them at an unconscious level and resisted therapeutic attempts to illumine them. Rather than suggestion, the primary tool of analysis became interpretation.

Along with this shift in Freud's basic theoretical understanding and in his technique, there was a growing awareness of the transference and its significance. In the basic therapeutic model the analysis was to be conducted under the rule of abstinence so as to maximize transference distortions (Stone 1961). Nonetheless, even in his early discussion of the psychotherapy of hysteria Freud stressed the importance of a positive relationship to the doctor as a sine qua non of the treatment process. He stressed that without this personal influence it would be impossible to overcome the resistances and that it was necessary to enlist the patient as a collaborator in the therapeutic task.

Freud came more and more clearly to understand that the early emphasis on understanding and insight was useful to a certain extent but that these were relatively powerless against the strength of the patient's resistances. Therapeutic change began to take place only when the resistances were overcome. Increasingly, Freud focused on the trans-ference as the major resistance. He commented:

The longer an analytic treatment lasts and the more clearly the patient realizes that distortions of the pathogenic material cannot by themselves offer any protection against its being uncovered, the more consistently does he make use of the one sort of distortion which obviously affords him the greatest advantages—distortion through transference. (1912, p. 104)

Thus, the transference represents the strongest and most effective weapon of the patient's resistance. It is important to note that the transference arises spontaneously after the work of undermining the resistances has progressed to a certain point. When the transference resistance has intensified, it can be approached and interpreted only after an adequate degree of rapport has been established between the patient and the analyst (1913).

Thus, the transference is at once the major form of resistance and the primary tool for overcoming resistance. It is, in effect, a repetition and acting out of the repressed past in relation to the analyst and thus serves the function of resistance. The patient's symptons acquire a new meaning, and his neurosis is replaced by a transference neurosis which becomes the object of therapeutic work. The tranference neurosis thus represents an artificial illness which is considerably more accessible to therapeutic intervention and which leads to the spontaneous awakening of memories through the overcoming of the transference resistance (1914). Freud (1916–1917) also described the transference neurosis as a new edition of the old conflicts where the decisive work of the analysis is to be done. The libido is equivalently forced away from the symptoms and concentrated in the transference. In the struggle now focused on a new object, libido is gradually liberated.

As Freud's theory and techniques changed, the transference remained both the most powerful therapeutic weapon and the strongest resistance to therapeutic progress. His more elaborate understanding of the ego as a part of the tripartite structure added to this point of view a more complex understanding of therapeutic resistances, particularly in connection with the defensive operations of the ego. Defense mechanisms which came into being as a result of previous conflicts and their associated instinctual dangers tended to recur in the treatment processes as resistances to recovery. Thus, the analysis of the ego's defenses led to an alteration of the ego in the therapeutic process.

There was thereby added to the process of id-analysis the more complex function of ego-analysis. The analytic process could then be understood in a more developed sense as shifting back and forth between these two levels of analytic activity—between the analysis of ego defenses in the service of resistance, and the recovery of id contents (Freud 1937). In addition, the role of the superego—deriving from an analysis of guilt and the examination of depressive reactions (Freud 1917)—took on an increasing prominence, particularly in terms of its relationship to unconscious guilt as an underlying motivation for the continuance of the neurotic process and as a motivating component for a negative therapeutic response. It was only Anna Freud's (1936) reformulation of the defensive functions of the ego and their relevance to the treatment process that the analysis of defenses achieved its rightful place in the analytic armamentarium.

The analysis of ego defenses and ego functions emerged as a more central aspect of the analytic process. It began to assume a focus that had much more to do with the corrective influence on the ego and with the modification and mollification of superego severity than it had simply to do with the diminishing of resistances and the recovery of unconscious content. It is important to note that Freud's shift from the topographic to the structural frame of reference was not accompanied by an abandonment of previous therapeutic insights. Rather, it introduced a new level of focusing of therapeutic intentions so as to deal more explicitly and effectively with aspects of the treatment process that had previously been dealt with only in vague or general terms.

Systematic Ego Psychology

The shift to a structural perspective facilitated the emergence and formulation of a systematic ego psychology. But as Kris (1951) pointed out, the emergence of an ego psychology did not provide the basis for a radical departure from earlier technical approaches, since Freud's early technique, particularly the principles of analyzing from surface to depth and of analyzing resistance before content, contained the rudiments of ego-psychological principles.

The new ego psychology brought with it certain emphases and understandings that had to have an impact on technical capacity. Among these were the increasing importance of the role of aggression and an understanding of preoedipal conflicts. Increased attention was paid to both present and later developmental experiences, but there was also a greater focus on autonomous ego functions (Loewenstein 1954). The emphasis here fell on the necessity of working with and maintaining the areas of autonomous ego function in the interests of promoting analytic work.

An important emphasis was added by Hartmann (1951) in his specification of intrasystematic correlations, such as those between the nonconflictual sphere of the ego and countercathexes, or between the autonomous and defensive functions of the ego, or the relationship of the ego to reality and control, regulation, synthesis, etc. Hartmann pointed out that it was necessary to deal with the patient's material in terms of its derivation from all systems. One could miss the structural implications of the material by correctly following economic principles, for example analyzing the quantitative aspects of a resistance without reference to its intersystemic or intrasystemic correlations.

The systematic view of the ego provided the basis for a more sophisticated approach to the problems of the emotional relationship between analyst and patient—that which took shape in the under-standing of the working alliance or therapeutic alliance (Greenson 1965, Zetzel 1970). Transference neurosis was essentially a repetition of past attachments to significant objects that was inappropriate to the present context. The working alliance was a reflection of the relatively non-neurotic and rational rapport between analyst and patient, and reflected the patient's ability to work effectively in the psychoanalytic setting. The alliance took place between the patient's reasonable ego and the analyst's analyzing ego.

Clearly the patient's capacity for such an alliance was a major requirement for effective participation in the analytic process. It required a significant capacity for object relatedness. If the patient's ego functions were sufficiently impaired, there would be danger of regressive trans-ference neurosis without the capacity to maintain the working alliance, or an inability to give up the attachment to reality and really testing in a temporary and partial manner so as to allow the partial regression of the analysis along with the emergence of an analyzable transference.

The correlative question, of course, was the part that the analyst played in shaping the alliance with the patient. From Greenson's (1965) point of view, an austere and rigid attitude in the analyst seemed incompatible with the establishing of a good working alliance. The rule of abstinence did not mean that the analyst was to be inanimate or cold or emotionally unresponsive. It was in fact, Greenson felt, the failure to meet the patient on this ground and to engage the patient in an effective working alliance that often led to therapeutic stalemate and the ultimate failure of the therapy.

We would emphasize that a more sophisticated psychology of ego functions allows for a considerably more effective conceptualization of the therapeutic process and particularly of the complexities of the relationship between analyst and patient that express themselves in the transference neurosis and the therapeutic alliance. Understanding of the therapeutic process has moved from a relatively naive level of insistence

on either interpretive-insight or corrective-emotive modalities of therapeutic effectiveness to a more complex and meaningful model of
therapeutic interaction in which essential integration of many aspects of
psychic functioning is called upon. The more broadly conceived model
does not abandon or trivialize previous appreciations of, let us say, the
therapeutic function of interpretations, but it articulates the therapeutic
context within which the analyst's interpretations operate and in terms of
which those interpretations gain their therapeutic efficacy. Particularly
relevant is the developmental model, which allows for an integrated
understanding of the levels of interaction and the complex patterns of
interpersonal relationship that evolve during the course of the psychoanalytic experience.

It is of interest that early, pregenital, object-related issues have
recently been brought into focus as essential components of the analytic
process. To some extent the basic theory generated from the systematic
ego context has drifted toward a consideration of such early, primitive,
and pregenital object relationships and has attempted to explore their
significance in the understanding of aspects of the therapeutic relationship. Thus there is a certain asymptotic congruence between the
therapeutic rationale of ego psychology and that of object-relations
theory.

The Object-Relations Point of View

The formulation of the structural theory set the stage for an emerging
emphasis on the role of internalized objects and an increasing awareness
of the significance in the transference of early object relations in the
development of both ego and superego. Thus, in the transference
neurosis the analyst serves not only as the object by way of displacement
for infantile attitudes and wishes but also as a substitute by way of
projection for the prohibiting parental objects. As Loewald (1960) points
out, the transference is also a new object relationship which makes it
possible for the patient to face the regressive crisis of the transference
neurosis and its attendant infantile anxieties—provided he can rely on
the potentiality of a new object relationship with the analyst. The
emphasis in therapeutic effectiveness shifted from matters of simple
interpretation to include concepts of the introjection of the analyst,
which resulted specifically in defensive modification as well as alteration
of the excessive severity of the neurotic superego (Loewald 1960).

Mutative interpretations (Strachey 1969) were seen as facilitating this form of analytic internalization and modification.

This variation between the ego-psychology and object relations schools is of particular interest because it reflects the impact of diverging theoretical perspectives on the therapeutic process. Considering the impact of therapeutic experience on theory, however, we suspect that ego psychologists tend to orient their thinking primarily toward higher levels of the psychopathological spectrum, namely toward patients whose psychic structure and functioning lend themselves more specifically to the ego-psychological approach, while object-relations theorists tend to drift toward the lower end of the psychopathological spectrum and think in terms of patients in whom the establishment of a working or therapeutic alliance is more problematic, and who presumably respond more effectively to their efforts to minimize primitive anxieties.

An interesting variant of the object-relations approach is that provided by Fairbairn, who seems to have trod a somewhat independent, although not totally unrelated, path. He postulates an original, integral ego at the beginning of life, which then undergoes various forms of splitting during the developmental experience. Therapy for his approach is essentially a process of modifying that splitting and thus regaining some of the integrity of the ego. He is critical of the emphasis on insight, since he feels this plays into the obsessional and even schizoid defenses of the patient, which are calculated to avoid significant emotional involvement.

Fairbairn's approach emphasizes the actual relationship between the patient and the analyst, a view which allows for a modification of the splits within the patient and the corresponding emotional development. He views other therapeutic factors in the analytic situation as dependent on the central relationshp to the analyst. He sees the interpretive approach as characteristically analytic and tries to shift the emphasis from "analysis" to "synthesis" of the patient's personality. This involves the diminution of infantile dependency and a modification of the intense hatred of the original libidinal object which was responsible for the early splitting.

The patient's greatest resistance is specified as his attempt to maintain as a closed system his internal world of internalized and split objects. It is only within such a closed system that the pleasure principle, based on the early Freudian notion of constancy, can operate at all. The therapeutic aim consequently must be to create a breach in this internal world of objects, this closed system, and to make it accessible to the influence of external reality. The reality principle, as opposed to the pleasure principle, is thus operative within the framework of an open system in which the inner and outer realities are brought into relationship. The transference neurosis operates within the framework of the closed system, so that the relationship with external objects is only possible as transference. Thus interpretation is not enough to promote therapeutic change; it is necessary for the patient's relationship with the analyst to develop to such a point that the transference neurosis can be replaced by a real relationship. The effect of this is equivalently to disrupt the patient's closed system and to replace it with a more open system of relationship and involvement with external objects.

Fairbairn's contribution is of interest because it is highly congruent with the contributions of other object-relations theorists. For example, Balint (1950) has discussed the significance of the transference as derived from earlier object relations and revived within the psychoanalytic setting. He emphasized the importance of understanding and interpretation in terms of object relationships, shifting the emphasis from the internal psychic economy to environmental influences.

We can reflect at this point that these approaches also seem in some degree congruent with the emerging concerns based on a more specifically ego-psychological theory. On the clinical level, both approaches have increasingly focused on the significance of early object-related experiences and their role in the analytic relationship. The object-relations theorists have made this a much more explicit and central aspect of their theory of therapy, while theorists espousing the ego-psychological approach have had to come to terms with these issues through understanding the basis of the alliance in the developmental aspect of one-to-one relationships deriving from early mother-child interactions. All of these approaches have gradually shifted their emphasis toward increasing concern with the analytic relationship and its constituents as the central problem in therapeutic effectiveness. Thus the basic concern with the transference and the correlatives of relationship with the analyst finds its natural theoretical and therapeutic extensions in these evolving points of view.

The Emergence of the Self

Starting from Hartmann's (1950) designation of the self as the proper object of narcissistic cathexis, and the consequent distinction between ego and self, there has gradually evolved a theory of the self within psychoanalysis. Needless to say, it is very much in flux at this time.

The exigencies for such a theory lie in several sources. First, there is a need to articulate and clarify the theory of narcissism, which was left by Freud in a relatively unsatisfactory state. Second, there are certain residual areas of unsatisfactory formulation left in the wake of the systematic reworking of psychoanalytic theory by the ego psychologists. Their emphasis on the ego as an aggregate of functions has left a vacancy in the theory, which does not account for the experiential sense of the ego as an originating and directing source of interapsychic activity. It is in part the theory of the self as a subjectively experienced source of intrapsychic activity that answers this need (Meissner 1985). This lack in the theory has also created a basic divergence between ego-psychological and object-relational theorists (Guntrip 1971). Finally, the theory of the self has been stimulated by a variety of clinical experiences with forms of psychopathology somewhat divergent from those found in the classical psychoneuroses, especially the narcissistic personality disorders and the schizoid and borderline disorders (Meissner 1984a).

Consequently, approaches to the problem of narcissism have been diverse. One view sees the maturation and therapeutic modification of narcissism in terms of the mitigation of primitive narcissistic impulses in the direction of object libido and object relationship. This view would see narcissistic cathexis and object cathexis as qualitatively differentiated (Freud 1914; Rochlin 1973). Another view, however, would see the developmental vicissitudes of narcissism more in transformational terms, so that the maturation and therapeutic modification of narcissistic impulses take place through the transformation of archaic infantile narcissism into more constructive forms of narcissistic expression and their integration with organized ego and superego functions. The main exponent of this latter position is Kohut (1971).

This later approach differentiates separate but related developmental processes, one the development of the self out of primary narcissism and the other the development of an organized system of ego functions out of the undifferentiated ego-id matrix (Levin 1969). Kohut (1971) sees this developmental differentiation in terms of the establishing of primitive images of the self. He comments:

> The equilibrium of primary narcissism is disturbed by unavoidable shortcomings of maternal care, but the child replaces the previous perfection (a) by establishing a grandiose and exhibitionistic image of the self: *the grandiose self*; and (b) by giving over the previous perfection to an admired, omnipotent (transitional) self-object: *the idealized parent imago*. (p. 25)

Further development of these narcissistic self-images involves a gradual transformation into an organized self whose relations to real objects emerge in proportion to the degree to which ego functions gain control over and integrate the basically narcissistic derivatives. In this sense, narcissistic libido is transformed into object libido.

The self becomes a structural entity within the psyche, intimately integrated with aspects of ego functioning. It is the locus of the narcissistic content of the ego, with its root in primary narcissism. But by transformation or modification it includes the secondary autonomous functions of the ego, ego qualities, the narcissistic aspects of other tripartite entities (including superego), and the basic libidinal components of a sense of identity. By implication, it becomes the structural seat of analytic resistance and gives rise to the economic problem of redistributing, modifying, and reorganizing narcissistic energies and structures of the self in the course of therapeutic modification. The resistance is specifically directed against the danger of trauma to the self in the context of an object relationship. This creates the experience of anxiety in the self and can mobilize aggressive countercathexes and flight/fight impulses to preserve the self (Rochlin 1973).

The emerging concept of the self has moved psychoanalytic concern toward the study of psychic states in which the impairment of reality testing reflects the underlying early genetic distortion in self-object differentiation and self-object relationships. This inevitably shifts the focus of therapeutic effectiveness toward self-object interrelationship, and the interaction between patient and analyst within the analytic setting. An increased emphasis is put on the analyst's experiencing self as an instrument of understanding and responsiveness, as an empathic receptive organ by which analyst and patient are able to be in relationship (Levin 1969). This emphasis seems to formulate in more specifically theoretical terms Freud's original notion of the analyst's use of his own unconscious as an instrument for responding to the patient's unconscious (Freud 1912). Thus Kohut (1971) emphasized the importance of the analyst's capacity to accept and not attempt to interpretively modify the patient's narcissistic transference distortion, either in the idealizing transference, in which the patient projects onto the analyst the idealized parental imago, or in the mirroring transference, in which the analyst becomes a reflection of the patient's grandiose self.

The countertransference vicissitudes of the narcissistic dispositions within the analyst himself then become more clearly focused. Ultimately, this begins to touch on what Levin (1971) refers to as ego-self disjunctions, specifically those lifelong intrapsychic conflicts which are distinct from, if nonetheless derived from, infantile conflicts, and which are reflected in the sort of age-specific crises expressed in Erikson's developmental stages. The emphasis here is on the countertransference strain and vicissitudes which are involved in the intimate object relationship with such narcissistic personalities. A closely related emphasis has been made in Balint's (1968) treatment of the "basic fault." The level of basic-fault impairment is not effectively modified by interpretations which function at a level of verbal, cognitive intervention—but must be met at a level of preverbal and affective involvement akin to Winnicott's (1965, 1971) "holding."

Kohut's problem—i.e., the analyst's need for interpretive impingement on the patient's narcissism—has been formulated in Winnicott's (1960a) notion of the "false self." The false-self pathology is a variant of the schizoid problem but in this regard has a certain degree of congruence with narcissistic vicissitudes, particularly in that the self is the locus of narcissistic cathexis. In the false-self situation, the patient tends to view the analyst's interpretive intrusion as essentially hostile and corrective. The danger is that the patient will react by compliant and evasive reinforcement of the false-self adaptation, with a stronger narcissistic investment of the hidden and isolated inner self, and a diminished capacity to relate to and utilize the analyst in therapeutically productive ways. The patient's retreat behind the facade of the false self presumably has the purpose of protecting an underlying narcissistic vulnerability. Thus the patient's inner self is closed off from the influences of real objects and the real world, which would serve to modify the inner grandiosity of the patient's self.

How can the therapist relate to the false self in order to establish meaningful communication with the inner true self? Or alternatively, how can he establish a meaningful relationship to the patient in order to somehow breach, in Fairbairn's terms, the closed world of narcissistic cathexis which is hidden behind the false-self facade? Here again, countertransference and the analyst-analysand relationship become the primary focus of therapeutic effectiveness.

Interpretation, in this view, is envisioned as a specific function of an object relationship. This point of view has been acutely expressed by Winnicott (1971) in his analysis of play within the psychotherapeutic relationship. He observes:

> The interpretation outside the ripeness of the material is indoctrination and produces compliance. A corollary is that the resistance arises out of interpretation given outside the area of the overlap of the patient and the analyst playing together. Interpretation when the patient has no capacity to play is simply not useful, for it causes

confusion. When there is mutual playing, then interpretation according to accepted psychoanalytic principles can carry the therapeutic work forward. This playing has to be spontaneous, and not compliant or acquiescent, if psychotherapy is to be done. (p. 51)

By implication, this capacity for playful involvement in the therapeutic encounter is based on an object relationship in which the creative self of the analyst and the creative potential of the patient's inner self are mutually responsive.

The widening scope of psychoanalytic intervention, whether through analysis itself or through derivative forms of psychoanalytically based psychotherapy, particularly with the therapeutically more difficult and challenging narcissistic and borderline personality disorders,* brings us to the thin edge of our theoretical and technical resources. Whether one thinks in terms of ego defects, narcissistic fixations and entitlements, or primitive defects in early object relations, such cases continually challenge the limits of our understanding and prevent us from achieving any easy complacency.

However unsuccessful or successful one would count experience with more challenging patients, the resources of theory make it relatively more possible to deal with them not in a blind, uncomprehending way but, rather, with a sense of the depth and complexity of the basic issues involved. While our understanding of what is involved at levels of primitive anxiety and in the context of extremely early and primitive object relationships is severely limited, it nonetheless allows us to respond to such vicissitudes of therapy in more sophisticated terms than merely making a pessimistic diagnosis and condemning the patient to unanalyzability. Theoretical sophistication allows for greater technical precision and depth in our ability to respond constructively and meaningfully to the difficulty of analyzing such patients.

The Paranoid Process

How does the theory of the paranoid process fit into this evolving framework of psychoanalytic understanding? The theory of the paranoid process builds on and extends three essential aspects of the psycho-

---

*See Chapters 4 and 5.

analytic perspective: systematic ego psychology, object-relations theory, and self psychology. The core elements of the paranoid process operate as ego functions, but they also both derive from and modify object relationships, and contribute core constituents to the organization of the self structure. The theory of the paranoid process is an extension of the theory of internalization (Meissner 1970, 1971b, 1972b, 1981b), particularly concerning itself with those forms of internalization that have pathogenic potential (Meissner 1978b). The core internalizations serve as the basis for the organization of the self and as the source of externalizations that influence and shape the nature of the individual's object relations.

Study has made it clear that the paranoid process is a quite general, even universal, process that comes into play in many aspects of human experience and personality functioning. It plays an important role in psychological development and in the formation and consolidation of personality structure. This is equally true whether that evolving personality structure is healthy and productive, terminating in the firm establishment of a mature and positive sense of personal identity, or whether the process takes a pathological turn to form personality structures that are essentially pathogenic and defective.

One of the criticisms of the theory of the paranoid process is that it attempts to explain too much and therefore explains nothing. Similar objections have been offered to the oedipus complex and to a variety of other psychoanalytic understandings. It has been argued that if every child is caught up in the dynamic conflicts of the oedipal situation, then there is no way to compare the effects of such influences with a control group of children who do not experience the oedipus situation. By the same token, if the paranoid process has such broad and general effects, it would be extremely difficult to find a control group that would give the argument greater force and specificity.

One must be careful of notions like "explanation" in any scientific endeavor but particularly in the psychological sciences. It is not enough to ascribe a certain set of personality features to the influence of the oedipal complex. One must know considerably greater detail and in particular must have knowledge of the mediating variables that have come into play in shaping the child's oedipal experience and the subsequent transformations that lead from that developmental context to the formation of later personality structures. In that sense, the oedipal situation explains nothing; but it does provide an orientation and a context within which important developmental influences can be examined and understood. The explanatory power does not reside simply in the fact of the oedipal involvement but in the nature and quality of that involvement, and the manner in which its various aspects were elaborated and worked through.

Something similar can be said about our understanding, however primitive and tentative, of the paranoid process. It is not enough to appeal to the existence of such a process. Rather, its explanatory potential derives from the qualitative and quantitative roles of various component elements of the paranoid process, and the vicissitudes of their interplay in whatever context of application may be in question. Thus, in the discussion of forms of paranoid psychopathology, it is in the interplay of aspects of the paranoid process, as they work themselves out and find expression in the paranoid pathology, that the contributing etiological factors can be focused and related in a fashion that allows for more substantial and penetrating understanding. The emphasis in such an approach is decidedly more descriptive and phenomenological than it is causal or etiological. The paranoid process, then, provides little more than an additional conceptual lens through which a variety of clinical phenomena can be brought into focus providing another perspective and another dimension to our current understanding of these phenomena. The elements of the paranoid process are nothing new but have been part of psychoanalytic theory from the time of Freud's understanding of the role of internalizations in development and personality organization.

Given that the paranoid process has a much broader connotation and application than merely the contexts of paranoid psychopathology, the question arises whether it is indeed advisable to continue to use the qualifying term "paranoid." The potentiality for misinterpretation in this usage must be acknowledged, since frequently enough we have found the paranoid process referred to and discussed as though it were more or less exclusively the mechanism underlying the pathology of paranoid conditions.

I would offer two reasons for persisting in using the term "paranoid process." First, the process itself and the mechanisms involved can be identified with the greatest degree of clarity and descriptive differentiation in frank paranoid pathology. Particularly in the extreme forms of paranoia, the pathology serves as a sort of *experimentum naturae* that permits a clear vision of the nature of these processes and their interrelationships. It is as though the effects of the pathology were to separate the various elements of the paranoid process and to display them each in clear and unequivocal isolation, providing us the opportunity for careful and detailed study. The paradigm is by no means alien to psychiatry or to medicine itself. The history of medical science is built on countless examples in which the study of disease processes sheds considerable light on and deepens our understanding of the natural physiology and functioning of the human body.

Second, use of the term "paranoid process," even referring to its nonpathological applications, highlights an inherent potentiality that is one of the more significant implications of the process itself in personality development and functioning. I refer specifically to the potentiality for the paranoid process, even in relatively better organized and better functioning personalities, to shift under appropriate eliciting conditions in the direction of paranoid pathology. This pathological expression tends to take the shape of either paranoid or depressive manifestations of varying degrees, and can be elicited by certain life stresses, alterations in the contexts of social and environmental support, changes in the physiological functioning of the body itself (as in the aging process, or in physiologically induced changes in mental capacity or functioning), and a host of other factors that have to do with the sustaining and the reinforcement of the capacity for psychic integration and inner psychic cohesiveness.

Frank paranoid psychopathology is merely the tip of an iceberg, the great mass of which extends into the vast reach of humankind. In fact, the impact of the paranoid process can be traced in social units, such as family systems, and even in larger social systems, in which some of the conditions under which more pathological forms of interaction can come into play can be studied and understood. To take a familiar example, the extent to which malignant prejudice can be found in otherwise normal and well-adapted populations, and the extent to which, given the proper eliciting conditions, prejudicial attitudes can be generated in otherwise reasonable and psychologically mature groups of people have been frequently documented.

Mechanisms of the Paranoid Process

The term "paranoid process" refers to a set of mechanisms that have both developmental and defensive components but which operate most critically in gradually delineating the individual's inner psychic world and his experience of an emerging sense of self. Correlatively, the paranoid process contributes to shaping the individual's experience of the significant objects in his experiential world. Consequently, the paranoid process contributes in important ways to the progressive individuation of a sense of inner cohesiveness and self-awareness, while at the same time it shapes and directs the progressive and continuing interaction with significant objects (Meissner 1978b).

The three core dimensions of the paranoid process that we will discuss are introjection, projection, and the paranoid construction. The terms "introjection" and "projection" are familiar to psychoanalysts, but in view of the variety of usages, it may be well to point out that in the present context the concepts have a somewhat broader significance.

Introjection

Mechanism. The concept of introjection is the central dimension of the paranoid process, insofar as projection may be regarded as a correlative, secondary derivative from the organization of the introjects. The paranoid construction serves consequently to bolster and articulate the projective system. The notion of introjection is based on Freud's (1917) original formulation of narcissistic identification, which arose originally in his analysis of melancholy and was later applied as the essential mechanism of internalization in the formation of the superego (1923). The mechanism of introjection implied loss of an object relationship and the preservation of the object intrapsychically through internalization.

Introjection must be distinguished on the one hand from more primitive and global incorporations, and on the other from higher-level, more differentiated, secondary-process identifications which serve as the basis for positive and constructive integration of healthy and adaptive personality functioning (Meissner 1970, 1971b, 1972b, 1981b). Between the level of psychotic incorporation, in which internalization of the object obliterates all differentiation between self and object, and more differentiated identifications, which maintain the differentiation between self and object and acknowledge the separateness and individuality of the object as such, introjections form an intermediate realm of internalization, in which the object is internalized (that is, becomes part of the subject's inner world) but at the same time retains some connection to the object realm. The introjected object never becomes completely integrated within the subject but always retains the potentiality for objectification, for the creating of an experienced distance between the content of the internalized object derivative and the subjective sense of self. Consequently, it retains a capacity for reexternalization, or transformation from the realm of self-representations to that of object representations.

This inherent quality of object connection of the introject is the basis for its potentiality for projection. In the sense we are employing the terms here, it would be accurate to say that identifications as such are never externalized, nor do they serve as the basis for any form of externalization. Projection, when and if it occurs, derives from some form of introjective organization.

The introject is the result of the operation of defensive mechanisms in that it reflects the inability to accept and tolerate the separateness of the objects of dependence, and requires internalization as a means of avoiding the threat of separation or abandonment. The introject thus comes to have a set of characteristic and interrelated qualities: it is subject to drive influences in varying degrees, it is defensively organized and maintained, it has an inherent regressive potential, and finally, it is susceptible to reexternalization by projection.

Development. Developmentally, the introjective configuration comes about by the internalization of elements provided primarily by the personality organization of the parents. The organization of the introjects consequently reflects elements combined from both parents in characteristic patternings. Most often, in family settings where pathological elements are at work, the patterns which serve as the basis for the pathological organization of the patient's introjects can be plainly seen in the relationship between the parents. The relationship between these patterns of parental interaction and the organization of the internalized derivatives in the patient's introjective alignment is often quite direct. In paranoid patients, for example, aspects of the patient's own sense of himself as victim or as destructive aggressor often reflect aspects of the personality functioning of his parents.

Reflection on the process of introjection in terms of the paranoid process has considerably broadened the meaning of introjection from the narrow focus of Freud's original formulations. Introjection has come to refer to that process of internalization by which aspects of objects or object relationships are taken in to form part of the subject's inner world. There is difficulty in illuminating how this process takes place. Jacobson (1964) saw the process in terms of the merging of the object images with self-images and regarded them as more or less psychotic phenomena. I think the process is more complex. While there is little question that the process of introjection plays upon and influences the organization of self-representations, this seems to be a secondary phenomenon. To envision the organization of the self simply in representational terms bypasses the obvious structural referents of the self-system along with the structuralizing aspects of introjection (Meissner 1971b, 1972b, 1981b, 1985). Rather, in terms of the paranoid process, introjection gives rise to the inner organization of the core elements around which the sense of self is formed. The process of introjection and the forming of the introjective configuration plays itself out in the developmental process and is expressed in an increasingly individuated and integrated sense of self.

The process is, of course, subject to all the vicissitudes of development itself: there is a progressive differentiation in the organization of the introjects and their economy. At the earliest developmental levels, the introjective configuration is relatively primitive, undifferentiated, and global. At progressive stages of development, it becomes more delineated, more specifically differentiated, and increasingly structuralized.

While the developmental aspects of introjection are of major significance, the fact remains that the mechanism functions basically in defense terms. Broadly speaking, the mechanism of introjection stems from the defensive need to salvage and preserve the residues of narcissism that are jeopardized by the developmental progression. The intimate involvement of introjection and the introjective organization with issues of narcissism and defense gives a characteristic stamp to the introjective organization. The introjects thus become the vehicle for the organization of drive derivatives and defensive configurations intrapsychically (Meissner 1978b).

Organization. The characteristic alignment of the introjects can be expressed as polar configurations of both aggression and narcissism. The aggressive polarities express themselves in the form of aggression versus victimization, while the narcissistic components express themselves as a sense of superiority versus inferiority. It is around one or the other or some combination of these introjective components that the individual structures his sense of self. In terms of the victim-introject, he sees himself as weak, ineffectual, inadequate, helpless, vulnerable, and victimized. In terms of the aggressor-introject, he would see himself as strong, powerful, domineering, controlling, sadistic, evil, hostile, and destructive. In narcissistic terms related to the superior-introject, he would see himself as superior, special, privileged, perfect, entitled, and even grandiose. In terms of the inferior-introject, he would see himself as inferior, worthless, valueless, shameful, and humiliated.

These configurations can be seen most dramatically in depressed and paranoid patients. The depressed patient usually lives in terms of the victim and inferior introjects. Usually, the aggressive and narcissistically entitled aspects of such patients' inner experience of themselves are either repressed or denied. Similarly, in the paranoid patient, the victim-introject tends to predominate in the patient's internal, subjectively aware sphere, while the aggressive aspects are projected to the outside in the form of hostile and destructive persecutors. The operation of these configurations is likewise seen with considerable clarity of definition in manic-depressive and borderline patients.* In these patients, the aggressive and superior configurations tend to cluster and alternate with the inferior and victim configurations. This alternation is often dramatically presented in the manic-depressive patient, who shifts back and forth between these polar introjective dimensions, especially the narcissistic ones, in the bipolar mood alternations.

The point should be strongly emphasized that in the clinical consideration of the organization of pathogenic introjects all of the introjective elements are pathologically involved. If a depressed patient is subjectively in touch with and expresses only the inferior or victim-introjective components, the therapist can presume that the opposite polarities are also operative, but in a repressed or dissociated fashion. Consequently, the therapist can be sure that he has not thoroughly dealt with the patient's pathogenic configuration of introjects until all of these elements have been brought to awareness and have been effectively dealt with. The depressed patient, for example, does not resolve his depression or bring about significant change in his depressive orientation to life and experience until he has become aware of, acknowledged, and accepted the superior and aggressive aspects of his own introjective organization. Similarly, the paranoid patient does not come to terms with the roots of his illness until he able to see that the aggression he perceives in threatening figures and forces around him is really his own. The same point can be made with regard to the narcissistic components. The fundamental appreciation of the nature of the introjective organization and its pathological expression has certain specifiable implications for the therapeutic approach to such problems. The broad outlines of such a therapeutic approach are developed in the discussion of the psychotherapeutic schema in Chapter 2.

There is a clear and direct relation between such introjective configurations and patterns of family interaction. More often than not, in the family of origin, the parents are caught up in a pathological interaction which acts out the aggressor-versus-victim and superior-versus-inferior patterns. In severely disturbed families, for example those in which there is a schizophrenic child, these marital patterns have been described as skewed and schismatic (Lidz et al. 1965). The patterns,

---

*See the more extended application of these concepts to borderline psychopathology in Chapter 4.

however, of parental imbalance, sadomasochistic interaction, emotional divorce, conflictual undercutting, and tension between the parents provide the rudiments for the organization of aggressive and victimized elements in the internalization of these object characteristics by the patient. Frequently enough in our own culture, the relatively domineering and controlling position of the father has been matched by the self-effacing, self-sacrificing, and relatively devalued position of the mother. This imbalance in the parental roles can serve as a significant developmental matrix out of which the child will internalize the aggressive and victimized aspects of the parental models. The more intense this overbalancing becomes, the greater the degree of pathology one can infer in the family system, and the greater the pathogenic distortion in the patient's introjective configuration.

Relation to the Self. With regard to narcissistic development, the critical notion is that intrapsychic development involves a progressive modification of infantile narcissism at sequential stages of the developmental process. At each stage, further modification of the original narcissism takes place so as to protect and preserve the emerging sense of self. Only gradually are the early infantile omnipotence and grandiosity modified and integrated. Kohut (1971) has described a first stage of this introjective organization in terms of the grandiose self. The preservation of such narcissistic remnants gives the introjective process, by which emergent self-components are formed, a defensive character. Later, the evolution of introjection leads in the direction of minimizing separation anxiety (loss of significant objects) or of defending against intolerable ambivalence.

The psychoanalytic literature has carved out certain introjective configurations and described them in terms of the aggressor-introject (Anna Freud's "identification with the aggressor," 1936), the victim-introject (Meissner 1978b), or even the grandiose self (Kohut 1971). Developmentally later and more structuralized introjective configurations have been traditionally described in terms of the ego-ideal or the superego. Clearly, the limited focus of the classic description of the introjective processes has not exhausted the understanding of this component of the paranoid process.

In any case, the introjective process must be regarded as organizing and expressing a specific configuration of drive derivatives and as serving specific defensive functions. By implication, the drive-and-defense organization of the introjects leaves them relatively susceptible to the regressive pulls of drive influences, and also allows them to serve as the point of origin for further defensive operations, specifically that of projection. Consequently, in a clinical frame of reference it is the inherent relationship of the introjective organization to drive derivatives—whether libidinal, aggressive, or narcissistic—its susceptibility to regressive pulls, and its propensity to projection that allows us to delineate and identify it (Meissner 1971b).

The question inevitably arises as to where this internalized, introjective organization is situated. Is it inside or is it outside? Is it internal or is it external? Is it in the mind? In the self? In the ego? The answers do not come easily, nor can the questions themselves be unambiguously posed. If we can agree that such introjected, internalized derivatives of objects are properly internal (as opposed to external) psychic formations, we are unavoidably confronted with a number of difficult metapsychological questions.

The critical questions have to do with the relationships between such introjective formations and the structure of the self, and consequently with the relationship of the self to the traditional structural components of the tripartite psychic apparatus—id, ego, and superego. In regard to the interiority versus exteriority of the introjective organization, the answer must not be yes or no, but rather more or less. The notion of "degrees of internalization" was introduced by Loewald (1962). Referring to superego introjects, he described them as being "on the periphery of the ego system" (p. 483)—that is, the introjective formations have a more peripheral character, as opposed to the more central character of components of the ego system.

Schafer's (1968b) clarification in terms of activity and passivity bears on the same issue. In these terms, the introjects are conceived of as imaginary, "felt" presences—Schafer elsewhere calls them "primary process presences" (1968a, p. 82)—by which the patient feels himself assaulted or gratified, and in relation to which he feels himself to be relatively passive. The passivity is a matter of degree and stands in contrast to degrees of activity, particularly the more purely self-originative and active quality of ego activities. Schafer (1968a) describes the peripheral quality of introjects in the following terms:

> An introjection is an inner presence with which one feels in a continuous or intermittent dynamic relationship. The subject conceives of this presence as a person, a physical or psychological part of a person (e.g., a breast, a voice, a look, an affect), or a person-like thing or creature. He experiences it as existing within

the confines of his body or mind or both, but not as an aspect or expression of his subjective self. (p. 72)

Both Loewald and Schafer are careful to exclude the introjective formation from any connection with the ego, and there are good metapsychological reasons for doing so. Attempts to dissociate the introjective organization and isolate introjects within the psychic realm do not meet with as much success, nor do such attempts find good theoretical support. The tension between the subjective and objective is reflected in Schafer's (1968a) further description of the introject as located within the subjective self, and yet not part of that self. Subjectively the person experiences internal objects or introjects as though engaged with something other than himself, yet within his subjective self.

In the light of these difficulties—namely, conceptualizing degrees of internalization and formulating the relationship between introjective formations as self-modifications and as influencing correlative ego structures—it makes greater sense to regard introjective organizations as part of the self-system. The degrees of internalization within the self-system, then, would reflect the extent to which a particular introjective configuration has been successfully integrated with components of the self-system. The "primary process presences," to which Schafer gives such discriminated and quasi-externalized status, reflect the separation of such introjective material from the rest of the self-content, against which it stands in relative opposition. Such primary process presences would have to be regarded as occupying a position on the periphery of the self-system.

At the same time, it has been my clinical experience that such primary process presences often evolve only as a result of extensive therapeutic clarification and delineation. Patients more often than not begin the therapeutic process in a condition in which the introjective formations are more or less undifferentiated from the main mass of the subjective sense of self. It is, in fact, only to the degree to which such patients are able to begin to put some distance between particular introjective formations and the rest of the subjective sense of self that therapeutic progress is made and the ground is laid for eliminating or revising such introjective configurations (Meissner 1976b, 1978b).* These formulations call for the further exploration and elaboration of complex metapsychological issues.

---

* This aspect of the therapeutic evolution of introjects is treated more fully in the discussion of the psychotherapeutic schema.

Projection

Mechanism. The mechanism of projection derives and draws its content from the introjective organization. In terms of the representational economy, following Jacobson's formula, projection can be described in terms of a transferral of elements from the self-representation to object representations, although the ultimate source remains the self-system. Consequently, the externalization involved in projection is an intrapsychic process—it involves a modification of object images or representations rather than of external objects. The role of projection in modifying object representations gives it a critical function in relation to object relationships. The correlative interaction of projection and introjection plays itself out throughout the whole of the developmental course, as we shall see later. Projection is a central dimension of the process of differentiation of objects in terms of which the quality of object relationships is continually being shaped and reworked.

Insofar as the projections serve to externalize elements of the introjective configuration, they bear the characteristic stamp of introjective components. Thus, the projective derivatives reflect the organization of drives and defenses inherent in the introjects. Projection influences the commerce between self-images and object-images, and correspondingly expresses the quality of differentiation and organization of these representations. Consequently, projection does not exhaust the limits of externalization. Externalization may also be based on relatively dissociated and depersonalized elements of the intrapsychic frame of reference. Thus, in certain forms of phobia, aggressive components may be externalized and experienced as external threats without the particular configuration of more personalized and organized qualities characteristic of projections as such. More often than not in the case of phobias, however, when such externalizations take place they do carry with them introjective derivatives. Thus, the analysis of phobic contents can be made through the externalized elements to their introjective derivatives and, in the therapeutic work, can be traced back to pathogenic object relationships. The classic paradigm for this process was established by Freud in his case studies of Little Hans (1909a) and the Wolf Man (1918).

In consequence, the effects of projection are experienced particularly in terms of object relationships. This is the primary area of expression of the projective function. However, the projective operation may play itself out in other nonhuman contexts. The mechanism may operate in any context in which human qualities can be attributed to external realities. This may take place in primitive animistic or magically superstitious interactions with the environment, but it also takes place in more mundane contexts of interaction with pets or in other forms of animal interaction, or even in determining the quality of interaction between the individual and his social environment—social organizations, institutions, business organizations, government, and so forth.

The operation of projection may or may not be accompanied by denial. If the projection is motivated by a defensive need to dissociate oneself from an intolerable or somehow noxious self-element, the projection will usually be accompanied by a denial. Thus, in the classical form of the persecutory paranoid projection, hostile and destructive intent is attributed to the object and at the same time denied in the subject. Further, the introjective components of helplessness and vulnerability serve to defend against the more destructive and threatening aggressive components. Where such defensive need does not operate, however, projection may take place without denial. This most usually is the case in the projection of more benign and tolerable attributes. The case may be somewhat similar where the combination of introjection and projection results in certain forms of empathic responsiveness.

It can be seen that projection is a highly complex phenomenon with many gradations and variations. Moreover, it can be readily seen that projection plays a critical part in the gradual elaboration of forms of introjection. The modification of object representations by projective components sets the stage for subsequent reinternalizations, which serve to modify the introjective organization. Thus, the interplay of introjection and projection provides a form of feedback process that can result in the progressive modification and differentiation of both introjective organizations and their correlative projections.

Development. The interplay of introjective and projective mechanisms weaves a pattern of relatedness to the world of objects and provides the fabric out of which the individual fashions his own self-image. His capacity to relate to and identify with the objects in his environment also develops out of this interplay, and it determines the quality of his object relations. This is particularly relevant in the relationships with significant objects in the course of development.

Projection and introjection must be seen in a developmental and differentiating perspective, which does not reduce them to mere defense mechanisms. They serve important developmental functions, particularly in the early course of development. They are intimately involved in the gradual emergence of differentiation between self and object.

The developmental and defensive aspects of introjection and projection are intertwined. As development progresses, however, intra-psychic differentiation and the differentiation between subject and object reach a point at which further developmental progression depends on the emergence of other, more highly integrated and less drive-dependent types of processes. The persistence of projection and introjection beyond this point suggests that they are employed in the service of defensive needs rather than facilitating the interaction between subject and object, which serves both to build the structure of the inner world through internalization and to qualify the experience of the outer world through projection. The persistence of introjective and projective mechanisms in the work of development extends at least through the resolution of the oedipal situation, since introjection and projection are involved in the formation of the superego and the ego-ideal.

It is difficult to say when their developmental function ceases. They may play a role in the reworking during adolescence of previous developmental crises. But beyond that they tend to be primarily defensive in nature. Introjective responses to loss, while they provide the matrix for adaptive change and personal growth in the course of the life cycle, are primarily defensive responses (Rochlin 1965). It may be most accurate to say that the balance between the developmental and defensive aspects of introjection and projection shifts in the course of the life cycle and that these mechanisms therefore undergo a change in function. They are continually at work adjusting the balance of instinctual pressures between the inner and the outer worlds. The process is always in some degree defensive and in some degree developmental, in that its effects involve the structuring and re-structuring of the internal world.

Correlation with Introjects. Introjection and projection are correlative. When we speak of projective mechanisms in paranoid states, we must remember that we are also speaking of their correlative introjects. What is projected is derived from inner introjects. Beyond the level of the most primitive primary projections, by which the differentiation between self and object is established, projection is a process of reexternalizing what has been internalized by introjection and internally modified by the influence of drive derivatives. Thus, the understanding of projection requires an understanding of the introjective mechanisms that have been involved in the developmental processes. To understand what comes from the inner world we must try to understand what comprises the inner world and how it got there.

Defense. Projection may be viewed as involving a partial dedifferent-iation, or fusion, of self-representations and object representations (Jacobson 1964). The infantile interplay between introjection and projection is involved in efforts to define and establish the boundary between self and object, and such fusion and confusion are undoubtedly part of the problem. In later defensive projections, however, such confusions are not apparent, and patients seem to be hypersensitive to differences between themselves and others, particularly the objects of their projections. Attribution to an object of characteristics that derive from aspects of the self does not necessarily connote fusion of representations. Rather, in the defensive use of projection, the distinct-ion between self and object is amplified in the interest of putting greater distance between the self and what it seeks to reject.

The defensive use of projection can take a variety of forms. An attribute or quality that lies wholly in the subject and not at all in the object is perceived as a quality of the object only. Conflict is resolved by ascribing to the other person or group the emotions, attitudes, or motives that actually belong to the self or one's own group. This use of projection involves a considerable degree of denial and a severe distortion of external reality. Projection may also take the form of an exaggeration or accentuation of qualities in the other that the subject also possesses, although the degree to which the subject is able to acknowledge the quality in himself varies. Allport (1958) called this the "mote-beam" projection. Freud (1922) pointed out that projection of this kind is often involved in jealousy, when one partner minimizes his own impulses to infidelity while accentuating the impulses of the other partner. Freud assumes the presence of impulses to infidelity in both partners, even though they may be unconscious impulses. Projection need not, however, take the form of either creating or exaggerating qualities in the other. It may simply provide an explanation and a justification for an inner state of mind by an appeal to external influences or the imagined intentions and motives of others.

Projection is a' defense that pertains primarily to object relations. The content of a projection derives from introjects, which are in turn derived from object relations. Moreover, projection is immediately caught up in the development of object relations. Jaffe (1968) pointed to the dualistic and conflictual role of projection in a persistent mode of ambivalence in dealing with objects. At one pole annihilation of the object is sought, whereas at the opposite pole identification with and preservation of the object is desired. There is a basic conflict between the impulse to destroy the object, to which some threatening subjective impulse has been ascribed, and the wish to protect the object, with which the subject has identified and which is thus invested with narcissistic cathexis. The ego is faced with a need to maintain inner stability in the face of structural regression, with its attendant threat of loss of control and instinctual discharge.

Paranoid patients are often terribly threatened by any attempt to confront them with their rage against and disappointment with significant (particularly primary) objects. The paranoid position often seems to be calculated to preserve these objects and to preserve the object relation. The ambivalence in the relationship is too difficult to tolerate, and the rage against the object cannot be faced. These relationships are often an important source of introjects, and the projection onto other objects provides a way of preserving the good aspects of the object relationship. On another level, projection onto such important introjective objects provides a way of preserving the relationship, albeit on desperate terms.

The duality of preserving and annihilating, of introjecting and projecting, is inherent in the full spectrum of paranoid states. What seems most significant in the operation of these mechanisms is their close relation to situations or circumstances in which the ego has suffered or is about to suffer a significant loss. At such points, the ego is confronted with its own inner sense of inadequacy and weakness. The mechanisms operate to preserve the inner elements that support self-esteem and its related narcissism. The complex of projection/introjection operates to rework the object relations involved so as to preserve the self in a meaningful context of relatedness. The analogue is the interplay of infantile projection/introjection in establishing the self and building its relatedness to objects. The operation of these mechanisms, therefore, cannot be regarded in isolation or as the result of intrapsychic dynamisms alone; it must be seen in the larger context of the subject's relatedness to objects and his embeddedness in a social context.

Self-Diminution. While the defenses are operating in an attempt to preserve the self, it is apparent that their capacity to do so is limited. The paranoid patient is under duress from within and from without. His defensive struggle is aimed at rejecting the painful and evil parts of his self—placing them outside (projection)—and affiliating unto himself the fragments of relationship that can enhance his own sense of self and his relatedness to the world of objects around him (introjection). But the attempt is abortive, since both projection and introjection bring about a diminishing of the sense of self. Projection preserves a relation to the object of a certain distorted quality, but at the expense of losing the projected parts of the self and compromising the capacity to relate in ways that facilitate the growth and integration of self.

Introjection preserves the relation to the object, but in so doing it creates an internalized presence that is subject to primary process influences and that preserves its derivative character. The cost to the self is the persistent infringement on its internal consistency and the reduction in its capacity to relate to objects more maturely. The defensive operation of introjection, therefore, attains some self-preservative compromise, but it interferes with the ego's capacity to integrate itself less in drive-derivative terms and more in terms of mature object relatedness. Introjection in its early developmental aspects allows the emerging ego to work through primary process types of organization and thus prevents the emergence of more autonomous secondary process forms of ego and self-integration (Meissner 1971b).

Superego Projections. Superego projections often serve as the basis for projective distortions. Superego projections are closely linked with the issue of autonomy. The autonomy of the paranoid personality is threatened both internally and externally. The internal threat derives from introjects, the most important of which are the superego introjects. The inner diminution of a sense of autonomy is closely tied to other effects of superego aggression. It calls forth feelings of inadequacy, diminished self-esteem, worthlessness, shame, and guilt (Freud 1916–1917). Projection serves to release some of this superego pressure. The paranoid projection can serve as a defense against the feelings of inner loss and futility that are associated with the internal threat to autonomy. If autonomy is threatened externally, at least the inner futility can be lessened and the external threat can be contested. Even if it cannot be avoided or overcome, one can preserve a false sense of rebellious autonomy in the face of an external threat. One cannot do this in the face of internal threat. Superego projection is really a special case of the overall problem of projection/introjection in paranoid states.

The projective system, whatever the degree of its complexity, does not stand on its own. Its components derive from the subject's inner world and are reinforced by the motivational components—the drive and defensive configurations—that characterize that realm of inner experience. But the projective elaboration cannot be sustained simply by means of drive-derivative exigencies. This is particularly true in the case of more or less pathological projective distortions, which unavoidably run afoul of other dimensions of the subject's experience of reality. Without some secondary considerations, one would have to anticipate that such projective distortions would be equivalently self-limiting and self-correcting.

Paranoid Construction

But clinically we know that such is not the case, particularly in the cases of the most severe projective distortion found in the forms of paranoid psychopathology. Here the projective system acquires a delusional fixity and a conviction that make it impermeable to therapeutic intervention and correction. In fact, the projective system is reinforced and maintained by what we have chosen to call the "paranoid construction" (Meissner 1978b). The paranoid construction is equivalently a cognitive reorganization of one's experience of reality in such a fashion as to include and integrate the elements of the projective system. The function of this cognitive organization is seen most dramatically in paranoid states where an elaborate system of beliefs, attitudes, and formulations serve to justify and sustain the projective components. These organizations may take the form of elaborate and extensive belief systems or may take the often more concrete form of what Cameron (1959, p. 518) has called the "paranoid pseudo community."

The paranoid construction thus plays a critical role in the operation of the paranoid process. Its immediate function is to sustain and reinforce the projective elements. However, the function of these projective elements, which are derived from and reflect specific aspects of the introjective organization, is related to the inner necessity for sustaining, to whatever degree possible, a sense of cohesiveness and integration within the experienced sense of self. Insofar as the introjective organization forms the core elements around which the sense of self focuses, the maintaining and the reinforcing of the introjective organization becomes a vital issue in this economy of self-organization and integration. Thus, the entire apparatus—paranoid construction, projections, and introjective formations—serves the overriding purpose of preserving and sustaining a coherent and integrated sense of self. This is the inner driving force and motivation behind the paranoid process. Moreover, this motivation not only operates in pathological aspects of the paranoid process, as in the case of severely depressive, paranoid, or other pathologies, but also plays itself out in the relatively normal and adaptive development of human personality and its maintaining of a mature and integrated sense of identity.

The paranoid construction can, therefore, be envisioned as providing a context within which the organization of the self finds a sense of participation, sharing, meaningful involvement, and relevance. We do not have to go far in our own experience to understand the importance of this dynamic in human experience. If the paranoid process operates in certain ways to separate and divide us from a sense of communion and belonging with our fellow humans, that same process creates pressures that drive us in the direction of establishing another context, another matrix, within which these needs can be adequately satisfied.

This inherent dynamic lies behind the shaping of social groupings and provides the inner dynamism for social processes. At its most pathological extreme, this same dynamism finds its distorted expression in the creation of a paranoid pseudocommunity. Even without such a persecutory confabulation on a larger scale, the persecutory bond, which is established between the paranoid individual and his persecutors or the terrifying forces that threaten him, serves as a form of paranoid construction that reinforces his projective delusions; these in turn serve to stabilize and consolidate the pathogenic sense of self that has formed itself around the core introjective configurations of victimhood and vulnerability. Thus, the victim-introject is a constant feature of these pathological expressions, yet it forms the core around which the individual's fragile sense of self is able to achieve some sense of perdurability and cohesiveness.

Developmental Aspects of the Paranoid Process

Object Representations

We have noted the role of the paranoid process in development. The critical influences of the paranoid process come to bear on the differentiation and articulation of both object and self-representations. Through the interplay of introjection and projection, the intrapsychic components around which the emerging sense of self takes place are gradually established. The commerce of these processes, in other words, contributes both to the organization of object representations and to the gradual internalization of object representational elements to compose the core elements of an intrapsychic substructural organization.

These inner structural modifications and the organization of object representations are in the beginning primitive, undifferentiated, and global. Only gradually does the process build up the residues, both internally and objectively, and increase the degree of differentiation between these elements so that the critical developmental step of the differentiation between self and object can begin to take place. Thus, it is the operation of these processes in the earliest stages of psychic development that lays the ground for the emerging distinction between what is internal and what is external.

Separation-Individuation

We can translate this process into the more familiar terms established by Margaret Mahler's (1975) research into the separation-individuation process. In Mahler's terms, the infant begins life in a state of autistic immersion within the mother-child unit. Within this normal autistic unity there is no differentiation, but rather a state of absolute merging, a condition of primitive hallucinatory disorientation in which need satisfaction belongs to the child's own global sense of omnipotent and primary narcissism. In this phase, there is no distinction in the child's experience between internal and external stimuli.

Within this omnipotent autistic orbit, the infant's waking experience centers around the continuing efforts to achieve physiological home-ostasis. The mother's ministrations are not distinguishable from the infant's own tension-reducing processes—including urination, defecation, coughing, spitting, and so forth. Little by little, however, the infant begins to differentiate between the pleasurable and the less pleasurable or painful qualities of his experience. Differentiation is achieved only in terms of levels of tension. Gradually, a dim awareness of the mother as a need-satisfying object begins to take shape in the child's experience, but the child still functions as though he and the mother form an omnipotent system, within which the duality is contained within a common boundary. Distancing emerges without separation. Gratification is sought from an emerging and distancing configuration ("nipple") that is not yet perceived as an object.

This marks the transition to a more symbiotic phase of the child's development, of which the essential feature is a delusional omnipotent fusion with the representation of the mother, as well as the delusional maintenance of a sense of common boundary between these two physically separate individuals. It is in terms of these primitive physiological affect states, governed by the experiences of pleasure and unpleasure, that the first differentiations begin to emerge. The cathectic attachment to the mother and the response to her ministrations are governed by the pressure of physiological needs. In the symbiotic phase, primary narcissism still prevails but in a less absolute form than in the first few weeks of life. The perception dawns ever so dimly that need satisfaction derives from a need-satisfying object—even though that object is still retained within the orbit of the omnipotent symbiotic unity.

Only to the extent that separation begins to take place does the infant begin to experience the receiving of milk that is not his own narcissistic (omnipotent) creation.

As these developments take place, there is a critical shift of cathexis from a predominantly proprioceptive-enteroceptive focus toward the sensory-perceptive and peripheral aspects of the infant's body. This is a major shift of cathexis and is essential for the development of a body-ego. At this juncture, the operation of projective mechanisms comes into play, not merely to contribute to the construction of a more or less separate need-satisfying object but also to begin to serve the specific defensive functions of deflecting more destructive and unneutral-ized aggressive impulses beyond the gradually emerging body-self boundaries.

As this developmental process works itself out, the organization of object representations not only is contributed to by external inputs, derived from external reality and, particularly and most significantly, from the primary objects of the infant's experience, but also is modified in some degree by the interplay between such inputs and objective elements. The organization of object representations becomes increas-ingly differentiated as the child's cognitive capacities become more developed and articulated. Thus, the capacity for the development of sensory and perceptual images, the gradual emergence of more complex forms of memory organization—shifting from more immediate and stimulus-bound forms of memory processing to the gradual emergence of more sophisticated and persistent forms of recognitional and finally evocative memory—the emergence of object constancies, and a variety of important influences from various forms of developmental learning, all contribute in meaningful and important ways to the gradual building up, differentiation, and organization of object representations (Meissner 1974b).

Internalizations

As the object representation is increasingly elaborated, its elements are correlatively internalized and introjected as parts of the infant's globally emerging and relatively undifferentiated sense of self. Even in the earliest phases of the symbiotic matrix, these internalizations are taking place, so that critical elements of the inchoate core of the infant's self are being shaped. At this point, we can only guess at the significance of the balance of pleasurable versus unpleasurable components and the contribution of maternal attitudes to these nascent stirrings within the child. Winnicott (1965) has stressed the importance of "good-enough mothering" and "holding" environment in the laying down of these primitive, yet crucial, early internalizations.

As these processes continue their interplay, the organization of elements of the self becomes more decisive and is more clearly and definitively separated from representations of the object. In the view we are proposing here, projection and introjection are the inner mechanisms which subserve the overriding process of separation-individuation. At each step of the process, there is a critical reworking of internalized elements that gradually allows the child to establish a more autonomous sense of self and to separate himself from the dependency on the parental object. In this sense, the individuation would seem to be related to the building up of an articulated sense of self through progressively differentiated introjections, while the gradual separation from the matrix of parental dependence is accomplished through the progressive projective modification and delineation of object representations.

The process is even more complex. The building up and integration of introjective components sets into operation critical identificatory processes that extend the processes of internalization and structuralization at a metapsychologically distinct level. These identifications have to do with the structural integration of the ego and with the transformation of superego (introjective) elements in terms of their integration with ego structures (Meissner 1972b). Reflexively, this further order of structural integration sustains and consolidates the organization and experience of the self. The degree to which such structuralizing identifications are brought into play is a function of the degree to which introjective formations are conflict-free, unambivalent, and not caught up in the pressures of drive and defense.

Separation Anxiety

The threat to the separation-individuation process is particularly that of separation anxiety. Mahler has described the various forms in which separation anxiety expresses itself, and the distortion that can work in the normal progression of separation and individuation. Separation as an inherent threat to development not only arises from the natural developmental impulse in the child and his burgeoning wishes for autonomous self-determination and expression but also can be reinforced and intensified by the reactions of the maternal figure. If the mother reacts to the child's bids for autonomy by excessive rejection and precipitant pushing of the child away from the comforting support of his dependence on her, the child is forced into a premature posture of self-sufficiency. On the other hand, if the mother is excessively threatened by the loss of the child as a dependent appendage, her efforts will be directed toward stalling his bids for relative autonomy and a prolongation of symbiotic dependence.

These varieties of maladaptive emergence from the state of maternal dependence can play upon the interaction of projection and introjection in a variety of ways. These distortions create defensive pressures, which make it necessary for the child's development to rely excessively on the utilization of these mechanisms in ways that are specifically and excessively caught up in defensive patterns. Thus, an excess of separation anxiety can lead the child to resort to an excessively regressive and global introjection of the parental image as a defensive means of preserving the contact with the need-satisfying, dependency-gratifying object, and as a means of preserving narcissistic integrity. The basic threat of separation anxiety at this level, after all, is the loss of the object. That object, in turn, is essential to the preservation of the infant's sense of narcissistic integrity and omnipotence. If the infant is allowed to make the separation from the maternal orbit without excessive stirring of separation anxiety, introjection will in fact take place, but not under the intense pressures of narcissistic need and defensive exigency.

Self-Constancy

As the developmental process advances, infantile narcissism is progressively modified, and the sense of self becomes more differentiated. These changes tend to gradually modify the quality and nature of the introjections involved at each phase and correspondingly change the quality of the defensive organization. At each phase of the separation-individuation process there is an increasing capacity for autonomous existence and a diminishing intensity of the child's dependence on need-satisfying objects. As the respective differentiations of object and self-representations and their inherent stability gradually increase, there emerges an enlarging capacity for toleration of the separateness of objects. The capacity to tolerate the separateness of objects is perhaps one of the primary goals of the development in object relationships. It implies that the object representation has been sufficiently developed so that the realistic qualities of the object are recognized and acknowledged, with a minimal complement of projective distortion. Thus, the discrimination between one's self and the object is clearly established and maintained.

In fact, the capacity to relate to the object in relatively realistic terms and to tolerate the separateness and autonomous independence of such objects is intimately related to the stability and cohesiveness of the self.

The capacity for realistic object relationships depends upon the organization of a sense of self that has at its core the internalization of a good and loving parent, which serves as the focal point for the integration of successively positive introjection elements. Modell (1968) has expressed this relationship succinctly in the following terms:

> The cohesive sense of identity in the adult is a sign that there has been a "good enough" object relationship in the earliest period of life. Something has been taken in from the environment that has led to the core of the earliest sense of identity, a core which permits further ego maturation. . . . It is a fact that these individuals who have the capacity to accept the separateness of objects are those who have a distinct, at least in part, beloved sense of self. If one can be a loving parent to oneself, one can more readily accept the separateness of objects. This is a momentous step in psychic development. (p. 59)

At the same time, correlative to the emergence and integration of increasing self-cohesion and identity, there is a process of integration and consolidation taking place in the organization of object representations that leads in the direction of object constancy (McDevitt 1975; Meissner 1974b). This process evolves not only the perceptual object constancy, which allows for the consistency and persistence of perceptual experience under the constant variation of stimulus conditions, but also the more complex forms of libidinal object constancy that contribute to and form the basis of stable and relatively consistent and mature object relationships. Thus, the differentiation and consolidation of object representations play their parts, along with the development of self-cohesiveness, in the articulation of important capacities to know and respond to external reality.

We are left, then, with a momentous conclusion—namely, that the capacity to know, recognize, and accept reality is a critical developmental achievement, and not a given or presumable quality of human cognition. Moreover, the attainment of that capacity depends upon the critical working through of developmental issues and the gradual consolidation of a cohesive sense of self, along with a differentiated and objectively articulated capacity for object representations. To the extent that object representations are contaminated by defensive needs, the capacity to know and understand reality is in that degree impaired.

Chapter Two

A Psychotherapeutic Schema

Relation of the Schema
to the Paranoid Process

The adaptation of some of the aspects of the paranoid process as a theory of therapy takes the form of a basic psychotherapeutic schema. The schema is organized around the principle that the externalized elements of the paranoid process—specifically, the paranoid construction with its component projections—must be traced back to the underlying organization of introjects from which they derive and on which they depend. The organization and supportive forces contributing to the shaping and maintenance of the introjects can then be effectively worked through.

The psychotherapeutic schema, like the theory of the paranoid process from which it derives, is not limited in application to paranoid forms of psychopathology but, rather, embraces a wide spectrum of clinical conditions (Schwartz 1963; Shapiro 1965). It is an organizing and guiding schema leading to an insight-oriented and interpretive form of psychotherapy.

The patterns of dynamic organization to which the schema addresses itself can be seen with greater or lesser clarity and impact in various forms of psychopathology. Perhaps the clearest and most striking expression of these dynamics can be found in more primitive forms of pathology, including schizophrenia, the manic-depressive psychoses, and the psychotic depressions.* In these the organization of the paranoid construction and its projective orientations can reach delu-

---

*See Chapter 3.

sional proportions and are driven by powerful underlying needs and dependencies. Such powerful needs may serve in these forms of pathology to maintain the paranoid construction and projective elements with a rigidity that creates considerable therapeutic difficulty (Polatin 1975; Frosch 1967a, 1983).

By way of contrast, the forms of borderline pathology function at higher levels of ego capacity and personality organization, but the rapid and often labile oscillation between projective and introjective alignments often gives such patients a chaotic and rapidly vacillating quality (Kernberg 1967). In such cases, the paranoid manifestations serve as important defensive alignments against the underlying depressive core rooted in the introjective configuration.

The interplay of projective and introjective mechanisms has a decisive role in the determination of psychopathology not only in the less organized forms of psychic impairment but even in the more elaborate and highly integrated forms of personality organization. Elements of the paranoid (projective) construction and its derivation from underlying introjects have important functions in the organization of the character disorders, including the narcissistic personality disorders (Kohut 1971) and the schizoid personality disorders (Guntrip 1969). Kohut (1971) has pointed to the archaic narcissistic configurations of the grandiose self and the idealized parental imago, which reflect the operation of introjective and projective mechanisms at quite primitive levels, in the differentiation of primary narcissism. Similarly, schizoid withdrawal can be seen in terms of an immersion in severely pathogenic introjects or, in Guntrip's (1969) terms, leading

> to the creation of an object-world that enables the ego to be both withdrawn yet not "in the womb," the Kleinian world of "internal objects," dream and fantasy, a world of object-relationships which is also withdrawn "inside" out of the external world. This, par excellence, is the world of psychoneurotic and psychotic experience. (p. 82)

A clear manifestation of the function of introjects can be found in the forms of neurotic depression, as well as in the more severe and incapacitating psychotic depressions (Jacobson 1971). Moreover, the same configurations can be identified even in relatively well organized and well functioning personalities, such as those with the more neurotic disorders, and the hysteric or obsessive-compulsive or phobic manifestations. Consequently, the mechanisms with which we are dealing in this psychotherapeutic schema are not limited to one or another form of psychopathology. Rather, they cut across all forms of personality organization and reflect the operation of basic mechanisms which play themselves out in human development and in the shaping of a variety of psychopathological manifestations (Meissner 1978b).

Nature of the Schema

The schema itself does not provide a paradigm of psychotherapy, nor does it offer a basis on which technical conclusions or directives can be made. Rather, it offers a more or less natural progression within which the therapist's thinking and orientation to the therapeutic process can be placed, based on an understanding of the mechanisms and dynamics of the paranoid process. The schema is in no sense univocal or prescriptive. Rather, it must be adapted idiosyncratically to each particular patient.

The aspects of the schema which come into play will vary in intensity, focus, and level of therapeutic difficulty from patient to patient, so that the therapist cannot dictate the course of therapy in terms of such an overriding schema. The schema can provide no more than a general orientation to the relevant therapeutic issues. Even so, it offers a logic of the progression and organization of the levels of pathogenic structure and the manner in which they play themselves out in the therapeutic process. It emphasizes the questions of priority of issues, with the implication that an important aspect of the therapy is the working through of prior issues and prior levels of function and organization before subsequent issues can be meaningfully approached in the therapy.

Consequently, there may be a shifting back and forth among the various aspects of the schema until successive issues are adequately defined, clarified, and worked through to the point at which their resolution allows for meaningful approach to and working through of subsequent issues. The schema not only provides a frame of reference for intensive and long-term therapy but also serves as a framework for conceptualizing and focusing the levels of difficulty involved in briefer and more short-term forms of psychotherapeutic intervention.

Establishing the Therapeutic Alliance

Necessity

The therapeutic alliance is a major part of any meaningful therapy, and it provides the more or less realistic basis on which the therapeutic work proceeds (Zetzel 1970). The therapeutic alliance forms between the working ego of the therapist and that part of the patient's ego which is relatively unembroiled in conflictual tensions, is capable of self-observation, and can join the therapist in the work of the therapy. It is this observant ego which enters the therapeutic contract and, together with the therapist, makes it a viable and vital reality (Greenson 1967).

The therapeutic alliance must be actively established and sustained. It does not simply happen but must be watched for, taken into account, worked at, and, at important junctures during the therapy, reinforced by the activity of the therapist. The more primitive, the deeper the level of the patient's pathology, the more difficulty there is in establishing and maintaining the alliance, and the more central it is to conducting the therapy. This is particularly the case with those patients in whom the developmental defect or deviation lies at an early level, and in whom trust and autonomy have not been adequately developed (Zetzel 1971).

In most neurotic patients, the therapeutic alliance happens to one or another degree. However, if the therapy makes effective inroads on a patient's neurosis, the therapeutic alliance is often threatened and disrupted, so that the further development of the therapy requires that it be sustained and reinforced or, if need be, repaired. In other, more primitive patients, the work of the alliance may form the central core of the therapy. This is very frequently the case with borderline and psychotic patients, in whom the therapeutic alliance remains fragile over extended periods of time and requires continual reinforcement and frequent repairs in the face of disruptions and formations of anti-therapeutic misalliances. Nonetheless, the alliance is essential for therapy with all patients (Langs 1974).

Therapist's Contribution

The question arises as to how the alliance is established and stabilized. Much of our knowledge about the alliance is as yet quite simple and undeveloped. The basic issues that we are able to define at this point center around the development of trust and autonomy within the therapeutic relationship.

The therapist's contribution to this development is not altogether clear. The most important elements generally have to do with empathic responsiveness on the part of the therapist to the idiosyncratic needs, anxieties, and inner tensions felt by the patient, such that the therapist responds to the patient in terms of the latter's individuality rather than in terms of the therapist's own needs or in terms of some preexisting therapeutic stereotype.

The therapist's patient and attentive listening to the patient's productions is crucial. This involves a sort of active presence within the therapeutic situation and within the therapeutic relationship. We are not referring here to activity, although in some cases, because of the patient's difficulties in relating to an object in a relatively unstructured context, activity on the part of the therapist may be desirable. Active presence is something different, more in the line of presenting the patient with a consistent, available, and "present" object.

The therapist's empathic understanding of what the patient experiences and feels is what Schafer (1959) has referred to aptly as "generative empathy." The therapist's being attuned to the patient's feelings in this way gives the latter a feeling of communication and response, a sense that he is being effectively understood, thus contributing meaningful dimensions to his experience of the relationship. The therapist's attitude is one of respectful unintrusiveness. It is difficult to operationalize such a concept in behavioral terms. It has to do with a central attitude on the part of the therapist which allows him to present himself within the therapeutic context with openness and availability, without forcing himself on the patient's attention or invading his inner world. Two elements of the description are extremely important: the therapist must be both respectful of the patient's individuality and the central core of his fragile identity, and unintrusive, in that the therapist does not violate the slender threads of the patient's fragile autonomy.

It is useful to recall Winnicott's (1963) notion of "holding" and its importance in psychotherapy. He commented:

> You will see that the analyst is *holding* the patient, and this often takes the form of conveying in words at the appropriate moment something that shows that the analyst knows and understands the deepest anxiety that is being experienced, or that is waiting to be experienced. (p. 240)

The "holding function" is all the more important in more primitive forms of psychopathology, but it plays a central role—explicitly or implicitly—in all psychotherapeutic interactions. Masud Khan (1972) makes this explicit in distinguishing two styles of relating to the patient: (1) Listening to the patient's communications and interpreting their *meaning* in structural and transferential terms; and (2) A psychic, affective, and environmental *holding* of the patient that facilitates certain experiences that cannot be anticipated or programmed.

Technical Aspects

In addition to such empathic responsiveness, there are certain technical procedures by which the therapist can contribute to the shaping of the therapeutic alliance. These include a definition of a therapeutic situation and the setting of the therapeutic contract in the very beginning of treatment (Langs 1973). It also may be important, not only in the beginning of therapy but from time to time at critical points during it, that the respective roles of doctor and patient be clarified. Another important technique is the therapist's attention to the patient's often implicit and minimally expressed distortions of the therapeutic alliance itself (Langs 1974). These may express themselves as fear of judgment or criticism from the therapist; as the patient's sense of helplessness or impotent dependence on the therapeutic situation; or finally, even, as a regarding of the therapeutic situation as a more or less confessional one in which the recitation of sins and defects is to be responded to by the therapist's curing absolution. In our own experience it is also not uncommon that students will respond to the therapeutic situation as though it were a school arrangement in which a certain standard of performance is expected and in which an evaluation or criticism is to be delivered by the therapist.

Another variant of alliance distortion is the narcissistic alliance (Corwin 1972; Meissner 1981b), in which the patient enters and submits to treatment with the (often unconscious) intent of gaining something from the therapist which will enable the former to attain a narcissistically invested and usually unrealistic objective. This usually represents some form of narcissistic wish fulfillment and may embrace omnipotent, grandiose, or magical fantasies. It impedes the establishing of any more realistic or meaningful therapeutic alliance.

Actions speak louder than words. The therapist must maintain a certain consistency between what he utters and the behaviors that express his attitudes and feelings. His task is to constantly work at building the patient's trust and to constantly encourage and foster his autonomy. Consequently, the therapist must do his best to engender trust in the patient by the way in which he manages his contacts with the patient, whether in or out of the therapeutic situation. Particularly with patients who cling to a helpless and infantile position in many of their behaviors, it is a constant temptation for the therapist to step into a parenting role and thus find himself unwittingly in the position of undermining his patient's trust and autonomy. The disparity between verbal formulations and specific actions is a rich field for the examination of the countertransference attitudes that may often be unconscious in the therapist.

The therapist must constantly remind himself that consistency is of the utmost importance in the establishing and maintaining of the therapeutic alliance, and that he must do nothing to further undermine the patient's sense of trust, autonomy, and self-esteem. This becomes particularly difficult when the therapist begins to work on the patient's resistances. The therapeutic task is, in effect, to analyze the resistances so that the therapeutic work can progress, but the risk is that, in contributing to the dissolution of resistances, the therapist may undermine the patient's fragile sense of self-esteem and autonomy. Consequently, the therapist's skillful interpretations of the patient's resistances must be accompanied by attention to alliance factors. This caution applies to other therapeutic interventions as well. Confrontations, whether routine or heroic, are effective only to the extent that they serve to establish or reinforce, or occur in a context of, a working alliance (Corwin 1972; Buie and Adler 1972; Adler and Buie 1972).

The patient is constantly confronted with the question of whether he can enter the therapeutic relationship and process without the loss of the minimal sense of self-esteem and fragile autonomy that he already possesses. In cases where the therapeutic alliance enjoys a certain solidity and stability, the task of entry is vastly simplified. But in cases where the alliance is fragile or contaminated by elements of misalliance, the task can be extremely difficult and tentative. In any case, establishing and sustaining and continually reinforcing the alliance must be a constant therapeutic preoccupation, since such alliance is the essential requirement for assuring the patient's capacity to do therapeutic work and to progress in the course of therapy.

Defining the Projective System

In the theory of the paranoid process, the patient's experience—both cognitive and affective—is seen as structured around three important constituents; namely, his introjections, the correlative projections, and the paranoid construction (Meissner 1978b). It is in terms of these three aspects that the patient organizes his experience, not only of himself but of the ambient world in which he moves and breathes.

Tactic

The projective process is in the service of confirming, reinforcing, sustaining, and validating the prior introjective constellation, around which the patient organizes and sustains his sense of self. At this level of working within the therapeutic schema, we are beginning to tune in on the elements of the patient's projective system. The general tactic is to identify the elements of the paranoid construction, and elicit and define within them the projective aspects, enabling us to shift back to an inner frame of reference and deal with the organization of the introjects as a central issue of the therapeutic endeavor.

In our first approach to the projective system, the task is primarily one of listening to the patient's account of his experience of himself and the world in which he lives. Equivalently, this provides a descriptive account of his paranoid construction. It is within that construction that we will be able to identify the projective elements. This tactic is essentially passive. There is no need to confront or refute the elements of the projective system. Our primary objective is to learn about that system, to find out what is in it, and to become as familiar with it as we reasonably can.

The patient tells us about his projective system and its related paranoid construction from the very first. There is little in his demeanor, verbalizations, and expressed opinions that does not provide us with data about his view of the world and himself. The student who tells us how anxious he becomes when he feels he might be called on in class, how he stutters and becomes confused in conversation with his professors, and how he becomes anxious and impotent when intimately involved with a date is telling us something about his image of himself and his perspective on the world around him. We are not surprised to learn that he was the baby of the family, anxiously and obsessively hovered over by an insecure mother, that he always felt he was a messy kid who would never grow up. Consistent with this is his persistent enuresis until about age 15. These details blend into a picture of a helpless child-victim lost in a hostile and threatening world of powerful grown-ups. His reaction to the therapist as threatening, intrusive, and powerfully controlling seems perfectly consistent.

Such a patient may present the world of his experience as fact; that is, as simply the way things are. A relatively attractive and very intelligent young professional woman maintained that she was worthless and inadequate because she did not have the sort of physical attributes that men find attractive. No amount of questioning or contrary evidence would dent her conviction. She was plainly displaying her construction of the social environment in such a way as to reinforce her own feelings of inadequacy and her perception of herself as unlovable and lacking as a woman. She saw the therapist as devaluing her in the same way; he was, after all, a man like any other man!

The critical elements in these organizations are the patient's projections. Projections, specifically, have to do with the modification of object relations (Meissner 1971b, 1978b). In the cases cited, relationships were contaminated by the patients' convictions, based on projection, that significant others were critical, demeaning, out to do them harm, put them in their place, and the like. In each case, these projective elements related to significant introjective components derived from parental imagos.

Techniques

There are certain defining techniques which can facilitate this descriptive accounting. First, it is important to get as much explicit concrete detail as possible. We want to know as much as possible of concrete events, actions on the part of various individuals, expressions of affect, and particularly the patient's own perceptions and feelings. Second, it is useful to elicit as many parallel accounts as possible, both those which deal with an interpersonal frame of reference in the present and those which may come from historical levels of the patient's experience. Again, the orientation toward details is important, since often in their eliciting the patterns of the patient's behavior and attitudes begin to emerge. Particularly helpful is the obtaining of historical accounts which suggest that similar patterns have existed earlier in the patient's experience, the earlier the better.

At this level of the schema we are not dealing solely with the elements of the paranoid construction; the patient may introduce direct expressions from the level of the introjects. He may tell us in a variety of direct and indirect ways how he sees himself, how he feels about himself, how he thinks others may regard him and react to him. Especially in eliciting the details of feeling, the hidden affects of depression, fear, shame, inadequacy, weakness, and vulnerability may become more manifest as direct expressions of the pathogenic sense of self.

Defining the projective system also requires a focus on the therapeutic relationship. The system operates in all spheres of the patient's experience, particularly those which are affectively important and in which the patient has some stake or investment. Thus, the projective system can be presumed to operate within the therapeutic relationship and as the therapy progresses will be manifest most dramatically within the transference neurosis. This is usually the most vivid and most dramatic manifestation of the patient's projective system and thus becomes the primary vehicle not only for the therapist's recognizing and defining the system but also for his beginning to deal with it.

The most important vehicle for the expression of these elements is the patient's affect. Affective channels of communication carry the weightiest information load. Also, the therapist may get signals from his subject's affect—sadness, bitterness, regret, anger, fear, etc.—but the therapist's own affective response to the patient may also provide important signals for identifying projective content. The therapist's feelings of boredom, irritation, incompetence, inadequacy—even hatred (Winnicott 1947)—can provide important signals for the reading of the patient's stance. In this realm of the transference/countertransference interaction the patient not only distorts his perception and representation of the therapist but frequently even works to elicit responses from the latter which will serve to confirm his distortions and misrepresentations.

Testing Reality

Tactic

The phase of reality testing, following the definition of the projective system, marks the first attempt to deal with the projective system therapeutically. It would seem obvious that the elements of the patient's projective system need to be tested against the hard stuff of reality, but the question is how this is to be accomplished. Our basic tactic here is to shift the focus of the therapy from the projective system back to the underlying introjective constellation from which it derives. The testing of the projective system is not usually best accomplished by challenging or confronting the system as a whole, or even explicit elements within it. This is not to say that any of the varieties of confrontation may not find their appropriate place (Corwin 1972), but in this context they run the risk of playing into the projective system. Rather, the undermining of the projective system, which carries within it so many of the residues of the patient's pathology, is undertaken by following the tactic established in the previous step of defining the projective system. The system is tested against reality by the process of detailed accounting. As the patient fills out the details of the picture, he is in effect confronting himself with more and more of the specifics or concrete elements of the reality. This tactic is obviously initiated in the stage of defining the projective system and carries over into the first stage of the testing of its reality.

Techniques

There are, nonetheless, some important specific techniques which are intended to call into question elements of the projective system, and to create some sense of distance between the projective elements as such and what can be seen to be an emerging reality perspective. The first important technique involves the tagging of feelings. When the patient expresses some content in terms of feeling, it is useful for the therapist to simply tag the content as one of feeling. Thus, when the patient says, "I don't feel that I could ever do anything right," it is useful for the therapist to tag not the specific content of the statement but the feeling quality of it: "That seems to be how you feel."

The tagging of feelings as feelings may need to take place over a long period of time and to embrace many concrete circumstances and details of the patient's affective experience. The tagging technique, however, has an intention and a direction. Its intention is to establish the distinction between feelings (and their intimate connection with fantasies) and reality. Thus, this technique forms an important aspect of the reality-testing phase of the schema. The direction of tagging is toward a gradual amplification of the patient's awareness of his feelings, as forming a coherent and consistent pattern of his experience of himself, and a gradual connecting of the organization of feelings to specific fantasies. Again, feelings tend to relate more directly to introjective elements, so that the direction of the tagging seeks to establish not only the fantasy proportions of the patient's perception of reality around him but also the fantasy proportions of his perception and appreciation of himself as a human being.

The second reality-testing technique has to do with defining the specific areas within which the patient's knowledge is lacking. The patient will frequently offer interpretations, explanations, conclusions, hypotheses, attitudes, etc., as though they were accepted fact. Frequently enough, these expressions tend to imply the patient's inadequacy or defectiveness, or are otherwise deleterious. The therapist's approach to such formulations cannot be by way of challenging the evidence or trying to refute the patient's expressions. Such approaches would only meet with staunch resistance and a rigidifying of his position. Rather, the therapist can tactfully point out the areas within which the patient's knowledge is uncertain. If the patient offers the opinion that people at work do not like him, the therapist's approach, following the schema, would be to elicit further details on the situation at work, particularly those which might suggest that, indeed, other people at work do not like the patient. When the latter fails to provide such details, as is usually the case, the therapist can point out that the patient feels unwanted, but that he really doesn't know whether people at work want him there or not.

The therapist's position is neither pro nor con. He is saying neither that people in the patient's work setting want to get rid of him nor that they don't want to do so but that the patient really doesn't know; carrying it a step further, that when the patient does not have real knowledge, his tendency is to fill in the blanks with something that comes from someplace else. By inference the therapist is carrying the therapeutic process a step further, making the point that what fills in the blanks in the patient's experience of his reality comes out of his own head; namely, out of the constellation of introjections which forms the substance of his inner world.

Defensive Reaction

The drift in this process is toward a progressively clearer and more discrete delineation of the realm of the patient's fantasy life—both in its external and internal referents—which had functioned by and large at an unconscious level. The further clarification of these introjectively derived fantasy systems and their role in early object relations, as well as in any current transference relations, helps to specify the introjective configuration and progressively delineate it from reality. Further steps of the schema elaborate these aspects.

The present schema does not represent a conflict-focused approach, although it remains conflict-based. Rather, it is concerned with the critical pattern of introjections which underlies, gives rise to, and reflects intrapsychic conflicts. Thus, the testing of the reality of the projective system, or rather its testing against reality, is an extremely important juncture in the therapeutic progression. As the elements of the projective system come increasingly under detailed examination, their stability and utility for the patient become diminished, and the patient's needs to defend and maintain the system are mobilized, often to an intense degree. The therapist has to deal not only with the systems as such but in important ways with the defensive responses which the patient throws up as the system is put under increasing pressure. The projective system is not simply there as a matter of chance. It is an intensely invested cognitive, affective, and defensive organization whose purpose is essentially the preservation of the patient's sense of self as well as of his narcissistic needs. These become focused on the issues of preservation of the introjects as core elements around which the patient's sense of self is organized. Consequently, the defensive titer in the face of the gradual undermining of the projective system can become quite intense.

Affective Shift

As the projective system is gradually modified, however, there is a progressive affective shift, so that the underlying (usually repressed) affects which motivate the system and against which it operates as a defense become increasingly available to the patient. Usually, the affects which are thus mobilized are depressive or have to do with the patient's underlying guilt and shame. Both in the working through of the patient's defenses and in the tolerating of the painful underlying affect, the therapeutic alliance remains a major consideration. These operations become possible only to the extent that the therapeutic alliance remains firm and intact, and allows the patient sufficient room and distance within the therapeutic relationship to engage with the therapist with a sense of alliance and supportive assistance.

Nonetheless, the therapist needs to be mindful that, in the face of such intolerable depressive affects, the patient may regress to a more projective defense and may reinvest the projective system or modify it to one which is more readily sustainable in the face of therapeutic pressures. The undermining of the projective system and the emergence of painful depressive affects carry the therapeutic process to its next stage, insofar as the depressive affects are intimately and dynamically related to the organization of the underlying introjects. It is these depressive affects which tend to bring the introjects into sharp relief and make them increasingly available for therapeutic intervention.

The Clarification of the Introjects

Shift to Inner World

If we recall the organization of the paranoid process, it becomes clear that the undermining of the projective system shifts the therapeutic focus from the projective system to the introjects. The projective system, including the paranoid construction, can be seen explicitly in terms of its defensive function in avoiding the impact of the pathogenic introjects and at the same time sustaining them.

When the undermining of the projective system leads to an unveiling of the introjects, the focus shifts from the external world to an internal one, and the patient begins to give an account of that internal world. Usually the content is depressive, in the sense that the patient sees himself in terms of overwhelming weakness, inadequacy, helplessness, inferiority, defectiveness, worthlessness, and vulnerability. Just as the therapist exposed the projective system through a detailed process of definition, here too the process of definition focuses on the inner world, the world of the patient's introjects, which becomes the focal part of the therapeutic process.

The therapist thus seeks to know the details, concrete and specific, of the patient's supposed inadequacy, helplessness, inferiority, etc. Again, the reality of these elements must be tested, moving toward the vital insight that, just as the elements of the patient's projective system had more to do with fantasy than reality, so the elements of the patient's introjective system have more to do with fantasies about himself and what he is than with reality. The presumption is that the patient does not know his own reality, so that the conclusions, attitudes, and feelings that he generates about himself are based on an unknown quantity.

The primary ground on which the introjective organization displays itself is the therapeutic relationship. The patient tends to play himself off against the therapist in a variety of ways. Most typically, within the therapeutic relationship the patient will see himself as weak and inferior, while he sees the therapist as powerful, strong, and competent. He may also see himself prominently as the therapist's victim; that is, as subject to the therapist's evaluation, criticism, and control.

Introjective Economy

Thus far, we have been addressing ourselves to only one half of the economy of the introjects. Frequently enough, patients will readily be in touch with the inferior and inadequate or the helpless and victimized aspects of their introjects. But if there is a part of the introjective economy which relates to the fantasy of the patient's weakness, we also know that there is a parallel part which stands at the opposite extreme and relates to the patient's sense of destructive power. If there is a part which expresses his worthlessness, we know that there is also a part that holds out for his specialness and entitlement.

What comes into perspective in this context is the inherent polarity of the introjects, the splitting of introjective elements on both sides of the middle ground of reality (Kernberg 1966). In relation to important objects, this polarity works in two ways. If the self is seen in narcissistic terms as inferior, the object is seen as superior; conversely, if the self is seen as superior, the object is seen as inferior. Correspondingly, if the self is seen as helpless victim, the object is seen as powerful aggressor; on the other hand, if the self is seen as powerful and destructive, the object is seen as victimized and helpless.

Thus, the polar aspects of the introjects tend to focus on one or the other side of the self-object differentiation and often shift back and forth. This vacillating of the introjective elements can be compared to an emotional seesaw. If my end is up, yours must be down; if your end is up, mine must be down. Latent in this polarization and the implicit seesawing are all the dynamics of narcissism, particularly envy. A similar patterning can be played out in terms of the aggressive determinants, which can be specified in terms of identification with the aggressor and identification with the victim. It is critical to this phase of the therapeutic process that both aspects of the polarity be seen as deriving from the patient's own introjects. Thus, the vacillation between the self as superior and special on the one hand and as inferior and worthless on the other is an intrinsic vacillation, both aspects of which derive from the patient's introjective organization. Hence, if one polarity of the introjective economy escapes repression and is available to the patient's awareness, the therapist can presume that the opposite polarity is lurking somewhere under the surface. Sooner or later it will show its hand.

Interpretation

The organization and the dynamics of the introjects are based on the patient's inherent narcissism, and the introjects tend to function in terms of the dictates of that narcissism. As the correlative and polarized aspects of the introjects become more and more clearly defined, it becomes apparent that they operate very much in all-or-nothing fashion. If the therapist is seen as superior, competent, and intelligent, the patient tends to see himself as totally inferior and abject, without any competence or worth at all. When the therapist comes to hear this unmitigated logic of extremes—the logic of all or nothing, black or white, either/or—he knows that he is closing in on introjective territory.

The polarized aspects of the introjects are locked together in a reciprocal defensive organization. Understanding this provides the basis for a critical insight into the patient's depressive dynamics. It makes no sense to cling with the intensity one often experiences to a perception of oneself as inferior, inadequate, helpless, vulnerable, and victimized. That intense clinging, which resists therapeutic intervention so stoutly, becomes understandable only in terms of the opposite polarity, which says that the patient is special, entitled, exceptional, et cetera. The critical point is that where one is allowed to see one aspect of the introjects, its polar opposite is irrevocably present and operative. The patient must come to see that the polarized opposites are linked, feed off each other, and are bound by the iron clasps of reciprocal defense and cannot be separated. The patient is in the position of accepting and integrating the whole package of the introjects, or of rejecting it and surrendering it as a whole.

As the introjects are more clearly defined, the process of testing can go on apace. Thus, for example, the patient's feelings of weakness, inadequacy, and helplessness can be repeatedly tagged as feeling elements, and the gradual understanding developed that such elements relate to a fantasy which reflects the organization of the underlying introjects. The patient knows only the fantasy, or he has accepted the fantasy as a part of his real self for so long that he no longer knows what the substance of his real self is like. The therapeutic relationship is the primary testing ground for distinguishing between these introjective fantasy elements and the reality of the patient's self, most specifically, directly, and powerfully in the distinction between transference neurosis and the therapeutic alliance.

The Derivation of Introjects

Object Related

The clarification of the pathogenic introjects—including the gradual delineation of the component elements, identification of the polarized aggressive and narcissistic dimensions, awareness of their reciprocal defensive involvement and the manner in which they form an integral whole within the subject's experience of himself, as well as progressive differentiation between elements of fantasy and reality—contributes to the delineation and undermining of the embeddedness of and investment in the introjects. However, this clarification rarely provides a sufficient ground for effective therapeutic intervention. An important procedure in determining the organization of the pathogenic introjects, and a logical and necessary next step, lies in exploring and establishing their derivation.

The introjects are internalized derivatives of object relationships, so that exploring their derivation involves establishing and clarifying specific ties to past and/or present objects in the patient's experience. The manner in which the therapist elicits this information and brings it to bear as a potential source of meaningful insight to the patient is a matter of technique. With some patients adequate exploration of this area of their experience can be done fairly actively, but this is not often the case. More frequently, this information must be acquired in more indirect and subtle ways, requiring a considerable degree of self-discipline and patience on the part of the therapist.

Therapeutic Task

Little by little, the picture of the patient's past relationships, particularly with parental figures, emerges more clearly. It often takes a considerable amount of time and amplification before reliable information about past experiences becomes available. Consequently, one cannot take the early reminiscences and the first or even second rendition of the patient's past experience as having unquestionable validity. The patient's first rough sketching of his past will be progressively filled in, resketched, refined, and recast as the therapy progresses. None of this recounting is simply the recapturing of a past reality. Rather, what is in question is the recapturing of the patient's experience, which may be overladen and permeated with elements of fantasy, wish, desire, and defense (Spence 1983).

The task at this level of the therapeutic schema is to retrace the patient's experience; to establish the links between the present organization and structure of the introjects, and the patient's past experience of object relationships. The critical objects in this context are the parents, though not exclusively. Other important figures may enter in, depending on the particulars of the patient's life experience. Often siblings play a vital role, and frequently other relatives, even nonfamily figures, may play a significant part.

One finds in time that the polarized aspects of the introjects are derived from the elements of ambivalent relationships to the significant objects of the patient's experience. The relative aspects of the primary polarities, organized around the dynamics of aggression and narcissism, can usually be related to specific objects in the patient's experience. Thus, in terms of aggression, the victim-introject derives from the patient's relationship with and attachment to a victimized object. In the typical form of sadomasochistic relationship between parents, this "identification with the victim" more frequently takes place with the mother, for both male and female children. The father, however, may not be excluded from this internalization. Frequently enough, when one examines the patterns of family interplay, particularly interaction between the parents, one finds that there are also aspects of the relationship in which the father alternately functions as a victim.

The aggressive aspects, the "identification with the aggressor," correspondingly derive from attachment to and dependence on a relatively aggressive object, and here the father tends to be the primary figure. Again, however, one frequently runs into aggressive, hostile, and destructive elements within the mother's character which can contribute to the child's emerging identification with the aggressor. Similarly, if we turn to the narcissistic elements of the introjective polarity, we find that the content of the introject derives from the narcissistic elements involved in the relationship with the same significant objects. Thus, the child may introject the depressive and devalued aspects of the parental object but at the same time internalize the parallel elements in the parents' own introjective alignment of aspects of narcissistic grandiosity, specialness, and entitlement.

At this stage, the progression takes its point of departure from the prior classification of the introjects within the patient. The question that is posed at this juncture is, "Where in the patient's experience have these elements been displayed within his relations with significant objects?" The introjective accumulation within the patient can be seen to represent a re-creation of elements derived from these important objects, so that the introjects come to represent a form of dependent, narcissistically motivated clinging to the infantile past, and they can be thus understood as serving to preserve the level of infantile fantasy and involvement with these objects.

This derivation of the introjective configuration was dramatically demonstrated in a young housewife who came into treatment for her chronic depression and dissatisfaction with life. Behind the feelings of worthlessness and inadequacy she felt not only as wife and mother but also as human being, there emerged the correlative feelings of special-ness, entitlement, and the feeling that she was different from other people, set aside by the fates to suffer and to go unrecognized and unrewarded for her extraordinary merits. Important determinants of these feelings were her intense penis envy, directed particularly at a much older brother who had been a brilliant student, concert pianist, and the apple of her mother's eye. Even more telling, however, was the relationship with her mother, a woman who saw herself as mistreated by the fates, who held herself apart as being different and superior to other human beings, who reveled masochistically in her victimization and suffering, and who jealously reviled the world for its failure to pay her her due and to acknowledge her superiority. The introjective con-figuration in the patient was derived directly and dramatically from the mother. Mother and daughter had formed a special magical bond, a union of narcissistic glorification through suffering, solidified by the constant expectation that true worth and superiority would have their day. The bond was motivated by the intense and continually frustrated yearning of this young woman for closeness, acknowledgment, and acceptance from a narcissistic mother whose own pathology allowed her to acknowledge little merit in her daughter, let alone in herself.

At times the parallels between the organization of the patient's introjects and the source objects are striking enough, but often they are more obscure. Introjection is, after all, a dynamic process. The introjective internalization is compounded not only of elements derived from the object but also of dynamic determinants from the patient's subjective inner world. Together these elements interact to constitute a realm of internalized object derivatives which remain essentially transitional (Modell 1968; Meissner 1971b).

Therapeutic Relationship

One of the most critical, vital, and forceful areas wherein the pattern of relating to significant objects manifests itself is the therapeutic relationship. A patient's increasing dependence on and involvement with the therapist give rise to regressive pressures which activate infantile projections, serve as the basis on which infantile distortions of the therapeutic relationship are organized, and represent the core elements in the organization of the transference neurosis. The patient, described in the elaboration of the transference, saw the therapist as a powerful and all-knowing wizard who would finally bring about a magical change in her life that would bring her the acknowledgment and admiration that she so desperately sought.

The exploration of the derivation of the introjects also serves to clarify the patient's understanding that the pattern of his experience of himself and, by derivation, of the world around him—particularly his relationships with other important figures in his environment—are dependent on a pattern of experiencing and responding that derives from his infantile past. The disparity between that past and his own present experience highlights the essential insight into the fantasy quality of the experience generated around the introjects, and clarifies the distinction between elements of that experience and the real world of the patient's present life and activity. It is in the transference neurosis, of course, that this understanding and realization are borne in upon the patient with particular force, since it is in that critical relationship that he can see most clearly and most vividly that the patterns of infantile relating play themselves out in inappropriate and unrealistic ways.

The Motivation of the Introjects

Resistance

The clarification and exploration of the derivation of the introjects lead
to the next logical question, namely, what is the patient's motivation for
retaining these introjects and in fact clinging to them with such dire
necessity? This is a critical juncture in the therapeutic progression and
often gives rise to the stiffest and most vigorous resistance. Up to this
point in the therapeutic process, the focus has been primarily on the
clarification of the elements involved in the patient's pathology and an
attempt to understand their organization along a number of important
parameters. Now, however, one begins to tap the patient's motivation for
the neurosis or other psychopathology.

This becomes a very difficult piece of work and is often the level at
which many therapies stagger. It is at this juncture that one begins to
approach not merely what is involved in the patient's pathology but his
own inner reasons for clinging to it. We say "clinging" because it is our
experience that one rarely finds a patient who is eager to surrender his
neurosis. Rather, the patient *clings* to his introjects in a variety of ways
and fights off the therapist's attempts to make any inroads on them. Why
are these introjects so intensely invested in and so important to the
patient? The answer lies in the inherent narcissistic dynamics of the
introjects themselves. They provide the essential core in many of these
patients around which the experience of the inner world and sense of self
as an individuated and in some degree coherent entity are organized. It
is the threat to the patient's organization of his sense of self that creates
the often rigid and intense barriers to therapeutic intervention.

Narcissism

The introjection represents an adherence to the now internalized
infantile derivatives of the patient's object experience, and serves to
prolong the infantile dependence on and attachment to those objects.
The most important parameter of this dependence is that of narcissism.
The introjection preserves the patient's sense of infantile narcissism and
is bound up in and expresses itself in the often repressed or split-off
feelings of omnipotence, superiority, and specialness. The dynamics of
the paranoid process operate in such a way that these patients, often in
hidden, subtle, and difficult-to-elicit ways, see themselves as exceptional,
in the sense in which Freud (1916) described the "exceptions." The
working through of this level of the patient's narcissism is absolutely

essential to the success of the therapy. This stage of the therapeutic work calls into play all of the difficulties of working with pathological narcissism that have been matters of such current concern and controversy.

Preservation of Objects

The introjects and the patient's clinging to them preserve not only the patient's infantile narcissism but also his sense of attachment to infantile objects. This clinging to infantile objects tends to prompt rehearsals of the elements of the patient's past experience with those objects. One frequently finds in such patients an unsatisfied and frustrated yearning for acceptance, love, closeness, and caring from objects that have been consequently introjected. The introjection thus serves as a sort of defensive repossession of objects that cannot be achieved in reality. At the same time, it serves as an important defense against the underlying sense of rage, disappointment, and disillusionment in the relationships with these same objects.

The paradox in this infantile involvement and its derivatives is that they serve to preserve and sustain the objects at the cost of the subject. This is true not only in the external relationship with objects but also within the patient's inner world, since these pathogenic introjects serve as a source of quasi-distortion and impairment within his own organization of himself, and inhibit or distort his capacity to achieve any real sense of autonomous self-identity. The cost, for example, to the depressed young housewife described above was monumental in terms of her chronic dissatisfaction, depression, and sense of tormented worthlessness and envy. She was willing to pay this exorbitant price to gain a golden fleece—a sense of specialness, superiority, moral hauteur, and entitlement. The idealized and aggrandized image of her mother was preserved at the cost of considerable neurotic impairment and unhappiness.

The dynamics also operate to preserve objects within the realm of the patient's external experience. For example, one frequently finds in the family involvements of such patients that there are hidden loyalties which operate in such a way as to reinforce and sustain the patient's introjective alignment, while at the same time they serve to protect the relationships within the family and the individuals involved in them. Often in this context, family myths will arise which represent forms of adherence to a family projective system, usually organized in such a way as to preserve the introjective alignment of all the family members and to maintain a delicate balance in the narcissistic equilibrium (Meissner

1978). Frequently, then, the introjective alignment within the patient actually serves as a vehicle for the preservation of elements of threatened parental narcissism. The young woman's adherence to the narcissistically embedded code of specialness and superiority through suffering was from this perspective calculated to reinforce and sustain the mother's highly vulnerable and fragile narcissism.

The Mourning of Infantile Attachments

Articulating the introjective configurations has led to a clarification of their elements and an examination of their derivation and motivation. This has involved focusing the intrinsic relatedness and unity of the introjective polarities, understanding that these polarities depend on each other and are locked together in mutual and reciprocal defensive interaction, so that they serve to reinforce each other and form such an inseparable unity that the patient is forced to a radical choice: either he must take both sides of the polarity together and work with them, or he must surrender both. He cannot have one side without the other.

This radical choice is quite dramatic in depressive patients who complain of their depression and are relatively willing to surrender the devalued, diminished, and depleted polarity of their introjective align-ment but are unwilling to surrender the specialness and entitlement of the opposite polarity. It remains, however, that they cannot surrender the one without surrendering the other. In addition, the work of articulation has brought into increasing focus the fantasy aspect of the introjects and their disparity from the real world of the patient's experience of himself and his environment.

The issue generated by these progressive insights is inevitably that of the surrender of the introjects. Accomplishing this requires some form of confrontation or working through of the infantile dependence and the narcissistic investment in the introjects. Not infrequently, as the narcissistic defenses are diminished, one begins to meet the intense rage against and envy of the significant objects, feelings which frequently have a highly oral character. This rage and envy often play themselves out in the relationship to the therapist, and this process becomes a significant phase of the therapeutic work. It is another manifestation of the narcissistic dynamics, which divide the world into haves and have-nots, and divide the distribution of goods in terms of either/or, or all-or-nothing. The patient's envy of the therapist and what he has—whether that be in terms of worldly goods, social position, intelligence, or even a penis—must be worked through in terms of the underlying narcissistic dynamics.

This working through sets in motion an important mourning process in which the attachment to the infantile objects is gradually given up and the loss of the objects accepted and integrated. As the mourning process proceeds and the potency and influence of the introjects diminish, one begins to experience with such patients a gradual and increasing emergence of autonomous ego capacities.

The Emergence of Transference Dependence

As the underlying determinants of the introjective economy become increasingly apparent and the mourning of the immature and largely narcissistic attachments takes place, the patient's infantile dependence on past objects gradually begins to wane. As that dependence wanes, however, the therapeutic dependence may begin to wax in important and problematic ways. The patient is often unwilling to surrender and resign infantile attachments but, rather, seeks to replace them and substitute for them by a dependent attachment to the therapist.

The motivation for this process needs to be clarified in the same terms as the patient's by this time explicit and recognizable narcissistic needs. Dependence on the therapeutic situation and on the therapist needs resolution on its own terms and quite independently of the working through of infantile attachments to past significant object relationships. Dependence on the therapist can be seen in the same terms of emotional vacillation or emotional "seesaw" as the previously explored attachments. Most typically, this emerging therapeutic dependence calls to mind the inferior, weak, vulnerable, and victimized aspect of the organization of the introjects—equivalently, the victim-introject.

The more powerful, superior, special, and entitled dimensions of the introjective economy remain latent in this condition. The residual dependent elements of the introjective dynamics express themselves in terms of the patient's feelings of inadequacy, difficulty in dealing with periods of interruption of the therapy or absence of the therapist, apprehensions over the apparent therapeutic progression, the looming possibility of termination of the therapy (thus being faced with doing without the therapist), and so forth. All of these issues must be worked through in terms of the therapeutic relationship and must be seen specifically in terms of the resolution of the residual aspects of the patient's introjective dynamics—particularly the narcissistic dynamics.

As the pressure of these dependency needs increases, drawing the patient into replacement of the objects of infantile dependence with the object of therapeutic dependence, there may be a defensive shift in the direction of a denial of such dependence and a retreat to a position of artifactual autonomy. This may take the form of a more or less narcissistic self-sufficiency, which defends against the pressure of dependency needs by a feeling of not needing the therapist or even of belittling or devaluing therapist and therapy. This may lead to the activation of the more powerful, superior, and even grandiose aspects of the introjective economy—leaving the more inferior, inadequate, and needy dimensions of the victim-introject out of the picture.

Underlying this narcissistic withdrawal and self-sufficiency or pseudoautonomy there may be operating residual defenses against the patient's sense of narcissistic affront, with accompanying feelings of rage and envy concerning the therapist. These may be accompanied by the patient's anxiety and guilt over such rageful and envious feelings, along with a longing for love and acceptance from the therapist. It is not difficult to see that these motivations are restimulations of infantile concerns and serve as important defensive maneuvers against the working through of immature attachments and dependencies.

Transference Resolution

What we have described thus far is a clarification of the introjective dynamics and the underlying motivations, particularly narcissistic, which support and drive them. The dynamics underlying the introjects are then shifted into the transference, where the issues of dependency are worked through again on a different level, hopefully with a therapeutic resolution. It is precisely this task which is now undertaken. When the patient's dependence on the therapist has become sufficiently intense, the next step involves working through and surrendering that infantile dependence. Thus, the mourning process, having previously to do with the surrendering of infantile attachments to past significant object relationships, is now extended and reworked in regard to the infantile attachment to the therapist. The patient must be helped to work through a variety of regressive infantile pressures which operate to keep him in a position of dependency and serve to satisfy underlying narcissistic needs. As these elements are gradually worked through, there begin to be established within the therapeutic relationship an increasing degree of autonomy and an increasing area for the exercise and expression of the patient's sense of initiative and industry. Finally, there is the clearer and more decisive emergence of the patient's own sense of identity (Meissner 1981b).

As the mourning process, which now deals specifically with the loss of the transference object, takes place, the therapist is gradually surrendered along with the patient's sense of reliance and dependence on him. The therapeutic relationship, particularly in regard to its transference elements, is gradually replaced with a more real relationship based on the more mature and autonomous aspects of the patient's developing personality. Thus, the mourning of the transference object is made possible by the gradual enlargement of the therapeutic alliance, which takes place through the increasing absorption, reworking, and reintegrating of the infantile aspects of the therapeutic relationship, most acutely the elements of the transference neurosis, into the therapeutic alliance.

Termination

The working through of the mourning of the transference object and the resolution of the transference elements set the stage for the final achievement of the therapeutic process, namely, the termination. As the infantile underpinnings and motivations for the organization of the introjects are gradually eroded, the potentiality becomes available for the introjection of aspects of the therapist and elements of the therapeutic alliance, which offer the possibility of a more reasonable, realistic, and adaptive organization of the patient's functioning sense of self.

These emerging introjections are considerably less susceptible to regressive drive influences and drive distortions. They are correspondingly less involved in defensive needs for projection, and sustaining of the patient's sense of narcissistic investment. Increasingly, the patient's capacity for modeling himself on the more realistic and adaptive aspects of the therapist opens the way for emerging identifications, which enhance the autonomy and structural capacity to resist drive derivatives in the patient's ego.* The termination work continues and enhances the critical internalizations which form the basis of inner structural changes,

---

*The role of the "analytic introject" and its influence in enlarging the scope of the patient's inner sense of identity and autonomy, particularly in the working-through process of termination, is developed more fully in Meissner (1981b).

specifically changes in the ego and superego, which serve as the basis for longer-lasting and adaptive therapeutic change. Thus, there is a shift from defensive to adaptive concerns, a refocusing of the patient's interest and investment from the past to the present and future, and, in general, an unleashing of developmental potential which leads in the direction of personality growth which is more reasonable, more stable, more adaptive and mature.

Part Two

Psychopathology of the Paranoid Process and Its Treatment

Chapter Three

The Paranoid and
Psychotic Processes

The subject of this chapter is the role of the paranoid process in the genesis of psychotic levels of psychopathology. At the most primitive levels of pathological functioning, more is involved than can be accounted for on the basis of the paranoid process alone. Other genetic and environmental determinants are involved that can interact with the developmental and structuralizing potential of the paranoid process to bring about a pathological result. This is particularly the case at the level of the psychotic organization of the personality. This discussion is intended to clarify the nature of the processes involved in schizophrenic disease when it takes on a paranoid form.

We are dealing with two separate, discriminable, and relatively independent processes that may manifest themselves relatively infrequently in the extreme expressions of psychopathology, but in great measure may be found intersecting and interacting in a relatively broad range of pathological conditions. Thus, the distribution of cases in the various diagnostic categories may be a factor of the nature of the processes involved. True paranoia is rare, if it exists at all. The relevant question regarding the pathology of true paranoia, as we shall demonstrate, is whether it is possible to have conceptual rigidity and underreliance on perceptual input, while maintaining perceptual integrity and an unimpaired capacity for perceptual intake and encoding.

At the opposite end of the spectrum, we are confronted by a condition or conditions in which the capacity for adaptation is based almost exclusively on current perceptual input, with little or impaired and distorted conceptual processing. The extent to which such a situation can occur may be quite limited and thus reflects the relatively

small number of patients who show an extreme and chronic schizophrenic deficit with minimal degrees of delusion formation, or with
delusions that are relatively disorganized or transient. In this spectrum
of schizophrenic conditions, the intermediate realm would reflect the
intersection of these relatively independent processes, the schizophrenic
and the paranoid. The varying expressions of symptomatology and
psychopathological impairment within this range of patients would
reflect the varying degrees of integration and the varying emphases on,
respectively, conceptual and perceptual processes in the integration of
experience and in the process of adaptation to environmental input and
demands.

We will discuss the nature of the schizophrenic process and its
interaction with the paranoid process. A concrete example that allows us
to examine this interaction in some detail is provided by Freud's classic
analysis of the case of Daniel Paul Schreber, perhaps the most famous
and influential case of paranoid schizophrenia on record.

The Relationship between
Paranoia and Schizophrenia

Rather substantial evidence is accumulating to suggest that a more
radical diagnostic discrimination can be made between paranoid illness
on the one hand and schizophrenic illness on the other than is presented
in the classic view, e.g., Kraepelin 1918. The basic issue is more than
merely descriptive or diagnostic. Beyond this merely phenomenological
level, there lies the question of our basic understanding of the nature of
the mental processes that lead to schizophrenia or to paranoia or to
some combination of the two. If it is true and can be demonstrated that
the divergence between forms of paranoid illness on the one hand and
forms of schizophrenic illness on the other is significant, the divergence
may reflect the differential operation of separate underlying psychological processes. By the same token, if paranoid schizophrenia could be
demonstrated to be of sufficiently different character and divergent in
the nature of its pathology from other, nonparanoid, forms of schizophrenia, we would have reason to think that we are, in fact, dealing with
different forms of pathology that reflect the operation of different
psychological deficits and different psychological processes, and that we
have to regard these diseases as separate and distinguishable entities
rather than grouping them in a common category.

Our line of argument leads to the conclusion that there is a
sufficient basis, on the descriptive clinical level and in terms of the
experimental study of forms of paranoid as opposed to schizophrenic

illness, to justify the separate treatment of these entities as different and distinguishable forms of psychopathology. In order to understand the underlying forces shaping these forms of mental disorder, we are forced to think in terms of two distinguishable and separate processes, which can operate in varying degrees separately and independently but which can also be found operating in conjunction in many patients to shape the form of their psychopathology: the schizophrenic process and the paranoid process.

History

While the discussion of the problem of paranoia dates from ancient times and can be found even in the Hippocratic corpus (Lewis 1970), the more modern history of the understanding of paranoia begins in the nineteenth century. The term was reintroduced by Heinroth as an affliction that predominantly affected the understanding as opposed to the will or affects. The question of the relationship between paranoia and what we now would think of as schizophrenia was raised in the middle of the nineteenth century by Kahlbaum, who posed the question whether paranoia was to be regarded as a persistent and chronic condition in its own right, or whether it was to be regarded as a rather late stage that occurred as a secondary feature in a deteriorating course leading to dementia. Kahlbaum's view tended to reinforce the understanding of paranoia as a primary delusional condition. His use of the term restricted it to a delusional condition characterized by persecutory or grandiose thoughts, which tended to be relatively stable and did not progress to dementia.

A more or less definitive cast was given to the diagnostic formulation of paranoia and its relationship to schizophrenia by Kraepelin. In his early work, Kraepelin followed Kahlbaum's lead on the subject, emphasizing the delimitation of disease entities on the basis of the analysis of cause, course, duration, and outcome. He emphasized that the term "paranoia" should be used restrictively to refer to a chronic, persistent, and incurable delusional condition which arose primarily on a constitutional basis. Thus, in the 1896 edition of his famous textbook Kraepelin defined dementia praecox, catatonia, and dementia paranoides as three degenerative diseases. Paranoia itself was distinguished as a further independent disease with a quite different course and outcome. However, in the following edition of 1899, the three degenerative processes were regarded as a single disease entity, dementia praecox. As Lewis (1970) notes, all of the various conditions, originally thought to be paranoia but which progressed quickly to dementia and took the course more characteristic of dementia praecox, were included under the term "paranoides."

By 1912, Kraepelin's views regarding paranoia and its relationship to dementia praecox had evolved. He then felt that paranoia should be dropped as a diagnostic category or that it should be used to denote only relatively insidious and endogenous delusional conditions in which the personality functioning remains intact. In such conditions, differential diagnosis from dementia praecox could be established by the presence or absence of the characteristic features of dementia praecox, that is, disordered thinking, apathy, rigidity of the personality, and volitional peculiarities. Other paranoid conditions, which develop later in life than dementia praecox and tend to be somewhat milder, Kraepelin designated by the term "paraphrenia." It seems clear in retrospect that Kraepelin was very much troubled and unable to resolve the very question that we are addressing, namely, the degree of diagnostic conjunction or disjunction between paranoia and schizophrenia. One of the major focuses of Kraepelin's orientation to dementia praecox was the question of outcome, namely, whether the patient followed a course of deterioration or nondeterioration. While observable clinical phenomena, such as hallucinations, delusions, and disordered affect, were a help in establishing the diagnosis, the clinician still had to wait for a course of deterioration to develop in order to establish a definitive diagnosis. This situation was complicated by the fact that Kraepelin himself recognized that a significant percentage of the cases of dementia praecox did not in fact so deteriorate.

The diagnostic impasse was resolved to a certain extent by the work of Bleuler, who discarded the term "dementia praecox" and replaced it with the term "schizophrenia." In Bleuler's view, relative incurability and terminal deterioration were not regarded as essential features of schizophrenia. Bleuler substituted an emphasis on the organization of symptoms which he described as either primary or secondary. The primary symptoms included disturbances of affect, association, and volition. Other features of the schizophrenic picture, such as hallucinations, delusions, negativism, and apathy, which had been the basis of Kraepelin's clinical description, were regarded by Bleuler as merely secondary manifestations of the disease process. He also introduced the important concepts of ambivalence and autism as significant features of schizophrenia. It is Bleuler's view that has come to dominate thinking about schizophrenia.

Recent Usage

More recent diagnostic usage tends to separate paranoid states and paranoid personality from schizophrenia. True paranoia is regarded as an extremely rare condition marked by pronounced delusions, which usually have been strongly systematized and which do not affect the organization and functioning of other parts of the personality. However, paranoid manifestations can be found not only in psychotic patients generally but in fact in the broad spectrum of psychopathology (Meissner 1978b). This complicates the differential diagnosis of cases of paranoia.

In general, the discrimination between paranoia and paranoid schizophrenic conditions hinges on the degree of preservation of the personality. When the personality structure remains relatively organized and intact in the presence of such delusions, the diagnosis is more likely to be some form of paranoia. Clinicians generally regard the delusions of the paranoid patient as better organized, that is, less bizarre, less fragmented, and more in touch with reality, than those of the schizophrenic. The secondary manifestations that may arise as, for example, hallucinations and changes in behavior, mood, and thinking, primarily arise from the patient's delusional system and can readily be connected with it. These same disorders tend to be primary in the schizophrenic patient and may not have any systematic connection with the delusional system.

Discrimination

The diagnostic differentiation between paranoid and nonparanoid forms of schizophrenia continues to be an area of controversy. Generally, the burden of recent studies is that paranoid schizophrenics have less impairment and better prognoses than nonparanoids. Among process schizophrenics, nonparanoids have earlier onset, increased length of hospital stay, greater degree of thought disorder, and a higher incidence of catatonic traits than paranoids (Tsuang et al. 1974). In addition, paranoid schizophrenic patients undergo briefer hospitalizations and experience fewer readmissions than do nonparanoid patients (Strauss et al. 1974).

Paranoid versus Hebephrenic

There is also a considerable amount of study contrasting the paranoid and hebephrenic subtypes of schizophrenia. The work of Winokur and his collaborators (1974) indicates the following differences: (1) the hebephrenic group was characterized by earlier onset of the disease process, more severe symptoms, and a greater degree of disruption of both social and family relationships than a comparison group of paranoid patients; (2) genetically, the families of hebephrenic patients included three times as many schizophrenic relatives as did those of the paranoids; (3) the schizophrenic relatives of the hebephrenic group were more often themselves hebephrenic than were relatives in the paranoid group; (4) by the same token, families in the paranoid group contained more paranoid disorders than did those in the hebephrenic group. The authors concluded that there may be at least two types of process schizophrenia, one basically hebephrenic but occasionally manifesting itself as paranoid schizophrenia, and a second type basically paranoid with a low degree of schizophrenic incidence in the family. In addition, the paranoid and hebephrenic subgroupings show little diagnostic change or shifting over time.

Separation of these subtypes was further supported by findings that hebephrenics show greater changes in affect, higher incidence of tendential thinking, more frequent blocking, and generally less delusional characteristics than do paranoids. The paranoids studied were older at age of onset and index admission than the hebephrenics. Half as many hebephrenics as paranoids were married, and even fewer had ever had any children. The hebephrenics were generally more seclusive and more distractable, and showed more frequent defects in memory and orientation, along with a higher incidence of psychomotor symptoms such as hyperactivity, agitation, pacing, and posturing (Winokur et al. 1974). They also had almost twice as many schizophrenic family members as did members of the paranoid group (Larson and Nyman 1973).

Premorbid Status

Additional information comes from the study of the relationship between premorbid status or social competence, and diagnosis. The first studies of this relationship found that state hospital patients with a good premorbid adjustment were more likely to be diagnosed as paranoid than if their adjustment had been poor (Goldstein et al. 1968). A subsequent study (Evans et al. 1973) indicated that paranoid schizophrenic patients more frequently have histories of good premorbid competence than nonparanoid schizophrenics, who may be equally divided between those having good and those having poor premorbid histories. Nonetheless, using a measure of social competence, Zigler and Levine (1973) were able to substantiate the relationship between paranoid status and premorbid adjustment in a population of state hospital patients but not in a population drawn from a Veterans Administration hospital.

To complicate matters, these findings, which seem to be selective in relation to the population studied, were not supported by other investigations (Johannsen et al. 1963; Sanes and Zigler 1971). Cromwell (1975) suggested that the inconsistency in the findings could be explained by differences in the samples of schizophrenic patients studied. He suggested that a relationship between premorbid competence and a diagnosis of paranoid or nonparanoid schizophrenia was more likely to be found either early in the course of the disease or in lower socioeconomic populations, such as those found more frequently in state hospitals. Support for this view was found in the fact that patients with good premorbid competence were more likely to be diagnosed as paranoid than patients with poor premorbid competence. There was also some support for the notion that the relationship was more frequently found in the acute phases of the illness than in chronic phases (Neale et al. 1972; Zigler et al. 1976). The same relationship was substantiated in a study of female schizophrenic state hospital patients, paralleling the findings based on populations of male patients (Zigler et al. 1977).

Although the relationship between premorbid status and diagnosis can be demonstrated and has been repeatedly supported, one should be cautious of placing too much weight on it. The supporting studies indicate that the samples studied contained a relatively high proportion of "poor" premorbid paranoids and "good" premorbid nonparanoids. Consequently, the relationship would seem to be less than robust, and the findings generally complicated by the heterogeneity of patient groups (Zigler et al. 1976).

Cognitive Style

Discrimination of paranoid and schizophrenic entities has also been supported by more experimental studies, particularly those focusing on differences in cognitive approach and cognitive style. Using a battery of objective tests of psychomotor speed, cognition, and social perception, Hamlin and Lorr (1971) found that the tests discriminated between groups of normal, neurotic, paranoid, and nonparanoid schizophrenic subjects. The conclusion was reached that the basic differentiation between the groups studied lies in the area of cognitive deficit; that is, the difference cannot be accounted for simply on the basis of bizarre associations, social isolation, or apathetic motivation.

Comparison of a group of paranoids with a group of paranoid schizophrenic patients on tests of visual scanning (Rod-and-Frame Test, Size Estimation Test) reveals little difference on either of these measures, indicating that visual scanning capacity and perceptual field articulation were similar for both groups. While the schizophrenic patients were somewhat more disorganized, the paranoid process seemed to operate in both groups in an equivalent manner, at least as far as perceptual functioning was concerned. Both paranoids and paranoid schizophrenics use similar modes of perceptual functioning and have similar perceptual styles (Tarter and Perley 1975).

Using a sentence verification test, Neufeld (1978) was able to compare the performance of groups of paranoid and nonparanoid schizophrenics with that of normal controls. The test allowed comparison of time lapse for operations of central scanning, and comparison of operations associated with response selection and execution. The results showed that the schizophrenic groups did not differ significantly from normals in latencies regarding noncentral aspects of processing (response selection and response execution) but did show a marked increase in latency measures for both central scanning and comparison. The findings are consistent with the view that a retarded rate of central processing is the primary source of cognitive deficit in the schizophrenic patient, and that the more global symptoms of thought disorder are secondary manifestations of this underlying deficit.

Cognitive Differences

Additional studies have emphasized the cognitive differentiation between paranoid and nonparanoid schizophrenics. The work of Magaro and his associates in this connection has been particularly useful. Using ambiguous slides of common objects in a visual discrimination task, Ross and Magaro (1976) were able to demonstrate a discrimination between the responses of paranoid schizophrenics and those of nonparanoid schizophrenics in that the paranoids seemed to follow dominant conceptual cues to a greater extent than did the nonparanoids. In addition, the paranoid patients seem to follow these cues and controls to a greater degree than nonparanoids even when the cues hindered successful performance of the task. Also, paranoids had more difficulty in changing the cues responded to, even when that was indicated for test success. As a result, the paranoid group tended to give more inappropriate responses where such dominant conceptual cues hindered rather than helped in the performance of the task.

Studies of field dependency likewise showed discriminable differences (Franco and Magaro 1977) consistent with the general view that field independents tend to have a more theoretical orientation and to be more socially detached (Witkin et al. 1954). This discrimination would reinforce the conceptual-perceptual discrimination between paranoids and nonparanoids.

As we have seen, there is considerable agreement, particularly among dynamically oriented psychiatrists, that schizophrenia and paranoia are separate disorders with different characteristic manners of onset, courses, prognoses, premorbid histories, and dynamics. The distinguishing characteristic that is usually emphasized is the level of integration, in terms of which the paranoid patient is seen as developmentally further advanced than the nonparanoid patient (Foulds and Owen 1963).

A considerable amount of empirical study of the cognitive differences between paranoid and nonparanoid schizophrenics has been summarized in a review by Magaro and McDowell (1981). We shall select and summarize some of the conclusions, insofar as they have reference to the present discussion. For example, various studies of symptom ratings using factor-analytic techniques seem to indicate that discriminable factors can be attributed respectively to paranoid, nonparanoid, and affective conditions. Paranoid factors have been identified as hostile belligerence, paranoid projection, and grandiose expansiveness. Nonparanoid factors would include conceptual disorientation and perceptual distortion. The work of Lorr et al. (1967) demonstrates two factors associated with paranoid symptoms. The first is a paranoid process factor which includes ideas of reference, delusions of persecution, conspiracy control and body destruction, ideas of grandiosity, and perceptual distortions, including auditory, olfactory, and kinesthetic hallucinations. The other factor is a hostile paranoid factor which includes perceptual distortions and verbal expressions of belligerence. The upshot of such factor-analytic studies is that paranoid patients generally differ from schizophrenics insofar as they are less confused and withdrawn, more openly hostile, and more likely to experience delusions. In contrast, nonparanoid symptoms tend to take the form of disorganized movement, bizarre motivation, and disordered thinking. The differences can be characterized as disorganization in the nonparanoid syndromes and hyperorganization in the paranoid.

Similar differences are identifiable on psychodiagnostic tests. On the Rorschach, for example, paranoids give less frequent color responses and show better form level, organization, and field articulation than do nonparanoids. On tests like the WAIS, paranoids generally show better intellectual functioning with less distortion than nonparanoids. Test data, therefore, suggest that paranoid conceptual capacity is better preserved, personality integration is more developed, and the perceptual field is better differentiated than in comparison groups of nonparanoid schizophrenic patients. As Magaro and McDowell (1981) note, non-paranoids often seem to be confused, or unmotivated to organize stimulus input sufficiently to be able to react to it effectively, and thus display a global approach that is marked by a general conceptual deficit. In general, on measures of cognitive and psychological functioning the paranoid group of schizophrenic patients tends to fall closer to the level of normal functioning than do comparable nonparanoid groups.

Overinclusion

One of the first cognitive characteristics of schizophrenic patients to be extensively studied was that of overinclusion. Cameron's (1951, 1959) early contributions in this regard were concerned primarily with paranoid pathology. Later studies have tended to reinforce the conclusion that overinclusion is unique to delusional (paranoid) schizophrenics. Some of Cameron's earlier studies may have been contaminated to a certain extent by the presence of manic patients in the delusional groups. The tendency of manics to show a high degree of overinclusiveness, even higher than that found in schizophrenics, has been demonstrated in several studies (Andreasen and Power 1974; Munschauer 1976). There is also some suggestion that overinclusion is related to the degree of psychiatric pathology rather than specifically to schizophrenia or paranoia as such (Harrow et al. 1972, 1973). Thus, conceptual overinclusion seems to be related to the degree of idiosyncratic thinking, suggesting that it reflects a more general dimension of psychopathology rather than being specific to any form of psychopathology. Thus, the more pathological the paranoid, the more inclusive he is, the greater degree of thought disturbance he manifests, and the closer he comes to the schizophrenic condition.

It seems, then, that on a number of empirical measures performance differences can be identified and substantiated between paranoid and nonparanoid schizophrenics. The evidence points toward the substantiation of the clinical differentiation between paranoid and nonparanoid schizophrenics, rather than supporting their grouping in a common category.

Levels of Function

Other studies have focused on the differences in levels of conceptual and perceptual functioning in paranoid and nonparanoid schizophrenic patients. For example, McDowell et al. (1975), utilizing a sentence completion task employing sentences of high- or low-probability completion, found that paranoids were able to identify the masked word with a greater degree of accuracy than nonparanoids when the task performance depended more on conceptual processes, that is, when expectation of the probable ending was high. When improbable endings were used, however, the performance levels tended to reverse; that is, the nonparanoid groups did better than the paranoid. Signal detection analysis showed that paranoids were biased toward high-probability responses, while the nonparanoids were similarly biased toward low-probability responses. The authors relate these findings to the difference in cognitive emphasis between the paranoid dependence on conceptual elements and the nonparanoid dependence on perceptual elements. When the expectation of a probable ending is high (cognitive factor), paranoid performance is maximal; when a lack of such expectation makes the performance depend on a more accurate discrimination of an ambiguous signal (perceptual factor), nonparanoid performance is correspondingly improved.

The data are used as a basis for comparison to the Chapman theory (Chapman and Chapman 1973). This theory suggests that schizophrenics exaggerate the normal response bias, so that they can be expected to make more of the most frequent errors made by normals on any given task. This seems to describe the paranoid performance quite well in that paranoids are much more strongly biased than normals in the direction of the high-probability response. The theory, however, does not describe nonparanoid performance. These patients did not make more high-probability response errors than normals, but made almost double the number of total errors and nearly six times the number of low-probability errors. These results were exactly the opposite of those predicted by the Chapman theory (McDowell et al. 1975).

Consequently, the paranoid style of attributing meaning according to relatively rigid conceptual expectations can operate adaptively when such an expectation is justified, but when it is not, this approach may be quite maladaptive. In his work on reaction-time experiments, David Shakow (1962) notes what he calls the paranoid's difficulty in forming a segmental set, or the "rigidity of set." The inherent rigidity of the paranoid conceptual orientation impedes his capacity to modify his set in any flexible or adaptive manner. As McDowell and Magaro (1981) note, delusions may be seen as extreme examples of set rigidity which serve to recast low-probability events in terms of high-probability expectations. The corresponding lack of validation is the mark of deviance.

Integration Theory

McDowell and Magaro (1981) summarize these various findings regarding the differences in cognitive style of paranoid and nonparanoid schizophrenic patients in terms of Magaro's integration theory. That is, paranoids function primarily in terms of conceptual processes with inadequate input of, reference to, and integration of perceptual data. In cognitive terms, then, the paranoid has difficulty with the encoding of information from perceptual processes. By way of contrast, the schizophrenic deficit falls precisely in the realm of conceptual processes. For the paranoid, situations requiring flexible cognitive schemata create difficulty because of his inability to take into account the sensory contexts of incoming stimuli. This can prove maladaptive when a certain flexibility of conceptualization is required. In the same context, the schizophrenic focuses on sensory aspects of stimuli to the defect of conceptual categorization. Thus, the paranoid's conceptual rigidity and lack of flexibility are contrasted with the excessive fluidity and lack of stable conceptual organization of the schizophrenic. Obviously, adequate adaptation in the variety of environmentally related contexts requires optimal functioning and integration of cognitive processes on both the perceptual and conceptual levels.

In terms of the diagnostic dilemma, while forms of paranoid pathology and schizophrenia share certain pathological characteristics when stated in relatively general and clinical terms, there seems to be ample evidence, as the preceding selective review suggests, for their separation on empirical, functional, and particularly cognitive grounds. Beyond the diagnostic question, however, there looms an additional matter that is more germane to the concerns of the present chapter. The question arises as to the nature of these differentiable conditions: differential emphases on perceptual factors, along with conceptual insufficiency, in the one condition, and a corresponding condition in which greater reliance is placed on conceptual factors along with relative perceptual insufficiency.

Schreber and Paranoia

The Schreber case is a landmark in the evolution of thinking about paranoia, since it provided the vehicle for Freud's formulations regarding the nature of paranoid illness and projection. Our examination of the case here, together with Freud's ideas about paranoia and the contributions of later analytic thinkers, focuses on the understanding of paranoid mechanisms and the paranoid process in the psychotic range of psychopathology. We will also examine more closely the interplay between aspects of the schizophrenic process, with its divisive and destructive influence, and the paranoid process, which gave the particular character and shape to Schreber's illness.*

Freud's Theory

Early Ideas

The basic elements in Freud's theory of paranoia were his definition of projection and his psychodynamic explanation of paranoia as a defense against repressed homosexual conflicts. Freud did not reach these conclusions by a simple intuition. Rather, his ideas underwent a complex and lengthy development.

His earliest writing on the subject was the unpublished Draft H which he sent to Fliess in 1895. In it Freud describes paranoia as an intellectual disorder which he groups together with obsessional ideas. Calling it an "intellectual psychosis," he emphasizes the analogy between hysteria and obsessional states on the one hand, and paranoia on the other, as modes of defense (Freud 1887–1902, p. 109). He describes the female patient who spared herself the reproach of seeing herself as a bad woman by projecting her badness to the outside. She was able to avoid accepting the judgment pronounced from within by projecting it to the outside and having it directed against herself from there. Freud observes: "People become paranoiac over things that they cannot tolerate" (p. 109).

The model Freud used to understand paranoia was the one he had developed in his study of hysteria: namely, the repression of a painful idea that was then allowed to return in modified form. The painful idea was regarded as a form of self-reproach. Freud also felt at this point that

---

*Shifting styles of diagnosis have brought Schreber's illness into question. While the diagnosis of paranoid schizophrenia might have been acceptable according to earlier, more broadly conceived criteria, there may be doubts in terms of the more restrictive and largely research-oriented criteria of DSM-III. Lipton (1984), for example, has recently argued that Schreber might be more appropriately classified under the DSM-III category of affective disorder. If one were to accept this diagnostic shift, granted the hotly debated and restrictive DSM-III criteria, the argument of this chapter might have greater relevance for the psychotic process more generally, rather than for the schizophrenic process specifically.

the mechanism of projection was one commonly experienced in normal life and arose as a result of a normal tendency to presume that internal changes are due to external causes. The process is relatively normal so long as we remain aware of the internal changes. It becomes abnormal when we lose sight of them.

In Draft K, written in 1896, he envisions paranoia as a pathological aberration of the relatively normal affective state of mortification. The primary symptom is distrust of or excessive sensitiveness to others. The mechanism of projection thus involves a refusal to believe in the self-reproach. The partial failure of this defense and the associated return of the repressed idea in its distorted form produces secondary alterations of the ego that can take the form of either melancholia, that is, a sense of the ego's smallness or worthlessness; or megalomania, in which the ego is completely remodeled by the more serious projective delusions of grandiosity.

In his famous paper, "Further Remarks on the Neuro-Psychoses of Defence" (1896), Freud discusses the case of a young mother who developed paranoid symptoms in a postpartum condition. He again emphasizes the defensive aspect of the symptoms and relates them to the repression of depressing memories. Here again, the burden of an intolerable idea is relieved through the mechanism of projection. The guilt derived from infantile sexual experiences returns in the form of accusations from hallucinated voices, and again we see a patient who has protected herself against self-reproach. In obsessional states, Freud notes, the initial self-reproach is repressed and replaced by self-distrust, but in paranoia the self-reproach is repressed and projected into a distrust of others. The return of the repressed in the form of delusional ideas nonetheless demands acceptance from the ego, and the preservation of the defense demands that the ego adapt itself to these ideas so that interpretive delusions end in an alteration of the ego as a secondary stage of defense (1896, p. 153).

Between these early papers and the study of the Schreber case, Freud made several important observations. He noted the transformation of affectionate impulses into hostile impulses, and the transformation of love into hate that are so characteristic of paranoid states (1905, p. 167). He also commented on the essentially sadomasochistic nature of paranoid fantasies (1908, p. 162). These early papers bring us to the threshold of Freud's treatment of the Schreber case, with the exception of the essential element, namely, the relation of paranoia to homosexuality. Aside from some cryptic suggestions in one of the letters to Fliess in 1899, in which he suggests a connection between paranoia and early levels of autoeroticism (Freud 1887–1902, Letter 125), paranoia is scarcely mentioned in Freud's early writings. Jones (1955) observes that Freud did present a paper on female paranoia at one of the meetings of the Vienna Society in 1906, but the connection with homosexuality was not mentioned even then (p. 281). It was just a little over a year later that he proposed the hypothesis to Jung and Ferenczi (Freud 1911, pp. 4–5), and presumably early in 1907, he also sent an unpublished memorandum on the subject of paranoia to Jung. But in none of these instances is there any hint of a connection to homosexuality (Freud 1892–1899, pp. 206–207). Thus, by the time Freud was ready to provide a more extensive analysis of the problem of paranoia and to express a more complete point of view on the subject, he had presented only a few straws in the wind. It was these elements that he assembled in his analysis of the Schreber case.

Schreber

The case of Daniel Paul Schreber and Freud's analysis of it are so well known that we need touch upon only a few central points. Schreber was a well-known jurist who had enjoyed a rather distinguished political career. He had stood as candidate for the Reichstag in the autumn of 1884, and quite soon after his election he began to experience hypochondriacal delusions and had to be hospitalized. He was discharged in the following year and then received an appointment in the Leipzig Landgericht. He functioned reasonably effectively in this office until 1893, when he was appointed to the court of appeals. In October of the same year he was appointed as presiding judge of the court, but in the month following he again decompensated and had to be readmitted to the hospital. Altogether, Schreber spent 13 of the 27 years following his initial breakdown in mental asylums. *Memoirs of My Nervous Illness* (Schreber 1903) is a remarkable document, written in the years 1900 to 1902, which recounts the developments of Schreber's illness and gives a graphic description of his elaborate delusional system. The *Memoirs* came to Freud's attention in 1910 and provided him with ripe material to which he could apply his germinating ideas about paranoia.

Schreber's delusions were bizarre and elaborate. His physician at the Leipzig Clinic had been Flechsig, the famous neuropsychiatrist. Schreber had originally admired Flechsig but later felt, as part of his persecutory delusions, that Flechsig was performing "soul murder" on him. Schreber never explained what he meant by "soul murder." Freud regarded the figure of the powerful persecutor as a substitute for an important figure in the patient's emotional life prior to his illness: a once loved and honored object becomes a hated and feared persecutor. In line with his libidinal hypothesis, Freud felt that the reason for the paranoid delusion was the fear of sexual abuse by Flechsig and that the precipitating cause of the illness was an outburst of homosexual libido. Later in the course of his illness, Schreber developed the delusion that he was being transformed into a woman by the power of God—that his genitalia were changing into those of a woman and that he was growing breasts.

The place of the divinity in these delusions was very special. Schreber thought that God consisted purely of nerves and that a divine influence was being exercised on his body by changes being brought about in his own nerves. The nerves of God had an unusual creative capacity in that, in the form of rays that emanated from the Deity, they could turn themselves into any kind of object in the created world. After the work of creation, God had withdrawn to an immense distance and left the world to its own meager devices. His activities were restricted to drawing to himself the souls of the dead. Schreber felt that he was selected by God for a special mission and that, consequently, God worked his power on Schreber's nerves to give them the character of female "nerves of voluptuousness," which thus transformed his body into a female body. Schreber was able to reconcile himself to this sexual transformation by seeing it as in harmony with the higher purposes of God. God demanded femaleness from him as part of his special mission in the world, in which he was to be God's special agent, to save and redeem God's creation. Consequently, Schreber developed an elaborate theocosmology which included ideas about God's special relation to the world and his own special relation to God.

It is not difficult to discern in these delusional productions the workings of the paranoid process. Our hypothesis would dictate that, in the face of disorganizing deterioration and decompensation caused by the schizophrenic process, Schreber's residual psychic capacity was able to mobilize paranoid mechanisms to salvage the residues of psychic functioning and to preserve a sense of psychic integrity—to whatever degree that remained possible in the face of psychotic deterioration. The outcome was a projective system that not only included persecutory projections but was bolstered and consolidated within a paranoid construction that was both theological and cosmic in its implications. Freud's discussion is concerned with the dynamic configurations that motivated and shaped the projective system.

Freud makes the point that Scherber's persecutor was divided into Flechsig and God—a paranoid reaction to a previously established identification of the two figures. Freud speculated that God stood for the patient's distinguished father and that Flechsig stood for his older brother, a man three years his senior who died in 1877.

Schreber's relation to the figure of God exhibited several curious features, including a mixture of blasphemous criticism and mutinous insubordination on the one hand, and reverent devotion on the other. He felt that God was incapable of learning anything by experience and that, since he knew how to deal only with corpses, he did not understand living men. Schreber also identified the sun with God, in the form of either the lower God (Ahriman) or the upper God (Ormuze). The sun thus became the symbol of the father, and the conflict with God could be constructed as representing the infantile conflict with the father whom the patient loved and to whom he was forced to submit. It was the oedipal threat of the father, namely, the threat of castration, that provided the basic material for Schreber's wishful fantasy of transformation into a woman.

Homosexuality

In Freud's conceptualization, the basic conflict in paranoia is that over homosexual impulses. He applied the model of symptom formation that he had developed in the study of psychoneuroses, particularly with regard to the role of the process of fixation, repression, and the subsequent return of the repressed in the formation of symptoms. The fixation in paranoia takes place at an early narcissistic level, intermediate between primitive autoeroticism, in which one's own body is chosen as object, and object love, in which the love object is a person of the opposite sex. The homosexual object choice and its related conflict are repressed. The subsequent failure of the repression allows for the return of impulses that then have to be dealt with by the characteristic mechanisms of paranoia. The return of the partially repressed object can be dealt with in a variety of ways: by delusions of persecution, in which the once-loved object is turned into a persecutor and the repressed love is turned into conscious hate; by erotomania, in which the repressed object is avoided by a flight to a heterosexual love object; by delusions of jealousy, in which the feelings of love for a homosexual object are transferred to a woman; or, finally, by megalomania, in which the love of any kind of object is rejected and the sexual overvaluation of the homosexual object translated into overvaluation of the ego.

Projection

Basic to the understanding of paranoia is the process of projection, by which an internal perception is suppressed and allowed to reenter consciousness in a distorted form as an external perception. Freud reminds us, however, that projection does not play the same part in all forms of paranoia and that it can be regarded as a much more general and even relatively normal process. Whenever we attribute the causes of internal sensations to external events rather than looking for internal causes, we are experiencing a form of projection.

One of the basic convictions of Schreber's delusional system was his belief in the imminent destruction of the world. Freud interpreted this conviction in terms of the withdrawal of cathexis from the environment, so that the expected end of the world becomes a projection for the patient's inner catastrophe—the end of his subjective world as related to the withdrawal of object cathexis. The delusional formation thus becomes an attempt at recovery—a process of reconstruction in which the patient attempts to recapture his relation to people and things. The repression, in the form of detachment of libido from external objects, is undone in the process of recovery that is carried out through projection. Thus liberated, the libido becomes attached to the ego in the form of self-aggrandizement and megalomania. Consequently, there is a regression from sublimated homosexuality to narcissism, which reflects the developmental fixation at the level of narcissistic object choice.

Cautions

Freud added several cautionary notes to his treatment of the Schreber case. He lamented the peculiar omission from the *Memoirs* of Chapter 3, in which Schreber apparently gave an account of the relation between his illness and his experiences in his own family. Such material would have been of the utmost importance in understanding the genesis of Schreber's paranoia. However, it has been possible to reconstruct a glimpse of it—even if only partially and indirectly—from other source materials, as we shall see. Freud also noted that social humiliation and feelings of inferiority often seem to have a role in the etiology of paranoia, but he discounted these as being secondary to the underlying homosexual conflict. Despite this emphasis on homosexual conflict, Freud (1911) makes an important qualification:

> In taking the view, then, that what lies at the core of the conflict in cases of paranoia among males is a homosexual wishful phantasy of *loving a man*, we shall certainly not forget that the confirmation of such an important hypothesis can only follow upon the investigation of a large number of instances of every variety of paranoic disorder. We must therefore be prepared, if need be, to limit our assertion to a single type of paranoia. (pp. 62–63)

It seems clear that Freud was quite aware that his thesis about the genesis of paranoia might have only a limited validity and that allowance must be made for other forms of paranoid disorders.

Post-Schreber

Freud did not significantly change his theory of paranoia in subsequent years, but he did add some important modifications under the influence of his evolving ideas on narcissism and the gradual emergence of the structural theory. In his paper on narcissism (1914), he spoke of the development of a special psychic agency whose task is to ensure satisfaction from the ego ideal and which, to this end, constantly watches and measures the ego vis-à-vis that ideal. He related this self-critical function to the common paranoid delusion of being watched. The delusion is thus a projection of this supervisory function of the internal criticizing agency, re-creating the situation in which the ego ideal and the critical agency of conscience were produced—specifically that of the critical influence of parents (Freud 1914, pp. 95–96). The same ideas on projection were presented, substantially unchanged, in the *Introductory Lectures* (Freud 1916–1917, pp. 248–249).

In 1922, Freud observed that in pathological forms of jealousy, impulses of infidelity are projected onto the partner. This use of projection, along with the implicit denial of repressed homosexual wishes, makes delusional jealousy one of the classic forms of paranoia. The delusion seems to be supported not merely by projection but by the patient's perception of the impulses to infidelity in his partner, even though these impulses are often unconscious. In a similar vein, paranoid patients cannot regard anything as indifferent in the behavior and attitudes of people around them, since they are often responding to the unconscious impulses of hostility in other people.

This addition was important in its acknowledgment that the paranoid process involves more than simply the mechanism of projection, and in its recognition that the role of hostility is more important than had previously been accounted. Early in his thinking about paranoia, Freud (1887–1902, p. 207) had acknowledged the importance of hostile impulses, but the role of hostility had been overridden by his interest in the libidinal aspect. He later (1931, pp. 227, 237; 1933, p. 120) commented that an important influence in the genesis of paranoia in females is the surprisingly common fear of being killed or devoured by the mother. Freud speculated that this fear may in part reflect the child's sensing of the mother's unconscious hostility. These considerations opened the way to subsequent formulations on the role of aggression in the genesis of paranoia.

Evaluation of the Freudian Formulation

Freud's formulations constituted the substantial basis for modern conceptions of paranoia. Nonetheless, they may be criticized on several grounds. First, Freud, as far as we can tell, had not had extensive experience with paranoid psychosis. The Schreber account was based on a written description by a patient Freud had never seen personally. Furthermore, his views on paranoia were an adaptation and application of his theory of symptom formation derived from the study of the psychoneuroses. This procedure ran counter to his normal methodology (Meissner 1971a) and seems to have been an exception to his usual pattern of clinical investigation.

Third, the role of aggression in Freud's theory remained inchoate. He seemed to acknowledge the role of hostility in his early treatment of paranoia, but later any consideration of it seems to have been overwhelmed by his libidinal preoccupations. This is particularly true of the writing up of the Schreber case, in which hostility received little mention. Some hints occur regarding the role of hostility in the later treatment of superego projections, but these are only passing references. Freud's preoccupation throughout was with the supposed transformation of love into hate. Fixating his thinking on this point forced him to consider hate as a defense against libidinal involvement. It is easy to see how his theory of paranoia as a defense against repressed homosexuality fits this pattern. It fails to recognize, however, that the basic problem may actually lie in the management of hostility.

This deficiency in Freud's approach to the Schreber case has been underlined by Rochlin (1973), who notes that Freud described the elements of hostility in Schreber but failed to regard them systematically as expressions of the vicissitudes of either aggression or narcissism. He writes:

> In Schreber's case, for instance, Freud recognized the judge's drive and his vulnerability, both somehow occasioned by and in his love for his father, as well as his desperate need to defend himself against his homosexual longing. Freud's single focus, as we have emphasized, was on the libidinal aspects of the case. His revision of the instinct theory ... didn't come till three years after the publication of the Schreber case. And neither Freud nor most of his followers evidently deemed it necessary or fitting to review the

old case material in the new theoretical and clinical light of ego psychology. (p. 117)

Post-Freudian Developments

Klein

One of the most significant contributions in post-Freudian considerations of paranoia was that of Melanie Klein (1960, 1964). Following Abraham's formulation of paranoia as a regression to the earlier phase of anal sadism and as involving a partial introjection of the love object (Abraham 1924, p. 490), Klein studied paranoid manifestations in young children. On the basis of her extensive clinical experience, she agrees with Abraham's basic position, believing that the period of maximal sadism in infantile development originated in the oral-sadistic phase of libidinal development and extended through the period of early anal sadism. She believes that the later development of paranoia could be understood in terms of fixation at this phase of maximal sadism.

The child's sadism is translated into fears of attacks upon itself on the part of both introjected and external objects. The excreta are given, in fantasy, a poisonous and dangerous quality and a power of destruction that arouses tremendous anxiety in the child and is defended against by delusions of reference and persecution. Klein proposes that behind the homosexual love that is regarded as transformed into hatred of the parent of the same sex is a deeper hatred and destructive wish. The child fantasizes an attack on the mother's breast and body, and their destruction by means of his own dangerous and destructive feces. Klein regards the homosexuality as a defense against the intense sadistic wishes to destroy the feared and hated parent.

Freud had hinted at the child's hostility to the mother and the fear of being devoured by her. Klein makes it clear in her formulation that this fear is due to the projection of sadistic impulses on the part of the child. She emphasizes that the sadistic fantasies of the omnipotent destructiveness of both bladder and bowels are closely connected with paranoid mechanisms. As she sees the process, the child projects his aggressive impulses onto the frustrating breast of the mother. The mother's breast thus becomes an internal persecutor. The ego struggles to defend itself against these internalized persecutors by processes of expulsion and projection. The resultant anxiety and the associated defense mechanisms form the basis of paranoia.

In Klein's view paranoid and depressive states are closely associated but can be distinguished by the direction of the persecution anxiety. In the paranoid, the anxiety is primarily related to the preservation of the ego, whereas in the depressive it is primarily related to the preservation of the good internalized objects with whom the ego is identified as a whole. The anxiety lest the good objects and with them the ego be destroyed is associated with continuous efforts—both internal and external—to save the good objects.

In the earliest phase of the child's development, the persecuting object and the good objects are kept widely separated. However, when the child moves from the introjection of partial objects to the introjection of whole and real objects, these aspects must be brought closer together. This is a major developmental step: now the child strives to bring the bad and good objects into conjunction, and his ego must resort over and over again to the splitting of objects into loved and hated, good and dangerous ones. If the child is able to gain more trust and confidence in its real objects and consequently in its introjected objects, the capacity for the tolerance of ambivalence—the capacity to relate to real objects—develops.

The child's capacity to move developmentally from the paranoid to the depressive position implies, therefore, the capacity to tolerate ambivalence and to achieve full identification with the good objects. Along with the capacity for love of and identification with a good object—at first the breast and then the whole person, particularly of the mother—an anxiety for its destruction and disintegration arouses feelings of guilt and remorse, and a sense of responsibility for preserving it against persecutors. Associated with these feelings is the sadness born of the expectation of the impending loss of the good object. It is the unconscious knowledge of the hate that exists in ambivalence alongside the love, and may at any point gain the upper hand and destroy the loved object, that brings about the feelings of sorrow, guilt, and despair underlying the depression.

According to Klein, the paranoid cannot, for a variety of reasons, allow himself this fullness of identification. The persecution anxiety is too great; a full and stable introjection of a good object is blocked by numerous suspicions and fantastic anxieties, which quickly turn the loved object once again into a persecutor. The paranoid cannot get beyond his early relation to internalized part objects and their sadistic accompaniments. Klein (1934) comments: "Where the persecution-anxiety for the ego is in the ascendant, a full and stable identification with another object, in the sense of looking at it and understanding it as it really is, and a full capacity for love, are not possible." (p. 291)

The paranoid is unable to tolerate the guilt and remorse that are implicit in the depressive position. Moreover, the depressive position is threatening because it limits his capacity to use projection. Projection carries with it the fear of expelling the good objects and thus the threat of losing them. But if the paranoid expels what is evil within himself, he runs the risk of injuring and destroying the good external objects. Klein thus presents, as a basic component of her position and as a fundamental insight, the idea that paranoid fears and suspicions operate as a defense against the intolerable anxiety and ambivalence of the depressive state.

Klein's views have been controversial from both methodological and conceptual points of view (Zetzel 1956a; Kernberg 1969). But it is not necessary to accept her theoretical suppositions to recognize that her descriptions of paranoia and depression have considerable clinical relevance and are important contributions to the study of these conditions. Her views have been of the greatest utility in refocusing attention on the issues of aggression and hostility in the genesis of paranoia; they have also redirected our attention to the considerable impact of the child's early life experiences on the development of later pathological states.

Aggression

Following Melanie Klein's work, the emphasis shifted from libidinal to aggressive aspects of paranoia. Schmideberg (1931) presents two cases in which she feels that the paranoid idea arose out of aggressive impulses and formed an exact mirror image of sadistic fantasies. Aggression was directed primarily against the copulating parents in the primal scene and was aroused by both homosexual and heterosexual wishes. She sees the projection of sadism from both attitudes as producing paranoid delusions. Her emphasis is on the instinctual or aggressive derivation of the paranoid content, even though she remarks on the harsh and sadistic treatment meted out to both patients as children. The punitive attitude of the parents left the children constantly feeling that they could never do anything right. The situations intensified the feelings of hate, anxiety, and guilt, and thus deprived these children of a normal outlet for their sadistic impulses and prevented them from testing out fantasies in reality. The aggression that was repressed and dammed up overflowed into the paranoid symptomatology.

Superego

Fenichel (1945) substantially agrees with Freud's formulation but adds some comments on the role of the superego in paranoid delusions. He suggests that these cannot be derived from a homosexual basis but may represent a relief, by way of projection, from aggression that has been turned inward in the form of shame, guilt, or feelings of inadequacy. Similarly, Knight (1940) discusses the element of intense unconscious hate in the paranoid by pointing out that he is caught up in an ever-present, excessive need for love in order to neutralize the intense unconscious hate. Hesselbach (1962) has emphasized the regression of the superego in delusion formation in paranoia. The original severity in the superego is determined by the severity of parental authority, by the projection of the patient's own aggressive impulses, and by the hostility resulting from repeated disappointments in them. In the regression, certain archaic introjects which had previously constituted the ego-ideal reemerge; these are then projected onto external objects which become endowed with all the aggression and sadism with which the superego was once endowed. The delusional persecutors thereby take on the terrifying, sadistic, devouring, and phallic qualities of the original parental introjects. The delusions of persecution permit the unbearably guilt-ridden person to become righteously indignant and to struggle against sadistic impulses in the legitimate form of self-defense.

While there were some progressive shifts in the development of thinking about paranoia, and an increasing emphasis on the vicissitudes of aggression, as we have seen, the situation was still such that MacAlpine and Hunter (1953) could complain that much of the literature was concerned with confirming Freud's formulations and that no open criticism of Freud's interpretation was to be found.

The Case against Schreber

Memoirs

The contemporary effort to critically reevaluate Freud's formulations of the Schreber case is a significant development. As we have seen, the impressions that the derivation of paranoia from homosexuality was not altogether adequate were not able to gain any solid footing until the text of the *Memoirs* was made generally available.

This was accomplished by the publication of the English translation of the *Memoirs* by MacAlpine and Hunter (Schreber 1903) in 1955. Surveying the literature at that time, they concluded that, by and large, the literature on paranoia had tended to uncritically endorse Freud's formulations. Basing their own analysis on the full text of the *Memoirs* and its associated documents, rather than on the extracts provided by Freud, MacAlpine and Hunter came to this conclusion:

We have interpreted Schreber's psychosis as a reactivation of unconscious, archaic procreation fantasies concerning life, death, immortality, rebirth, creation, including self-impregnation, and accompanied by absolute ambisexuality expressed in doubt and uncertainty about his sex. Homosexual anxieties were secondary to the primary fantasy of having to be transformed into a woman to be able to procreate. (Schreber 1903, p. 395)

They felt that the confusion and ambiguity in sexual identity should be clearly differentiated from the passive homosexual wishes implied in Freud's use of the term.

Since then, the Schreber case has come in for searching reevaluation and reformulation. Niederland (1951) points out that both of Schreber's illnesses were precipitated by his elevation to a position of power and influence, which aroused his dread of taking his father's position. The father was a primary figure in Schreber's psychosis, and Schreber's frustrated needs were primarily dependent ones. His delusional language was anal-sadistic in its origin, reflecting, rather than castration fears, the earlier pregenital fears centering around loss of the love object through the subject's own destructive rage. This reflected the intense ambivalence of the early libidinal object relationship, and it was this ambivalence that was defended against by projection. The projection involved a symbolization and condensation in which previous libidinal ties were condensed into the concept of God, and thus lost libidinal objects were replaced by a verbal abstraction that restored the primary dependent relationship in a less threatening form but at the sacrifice of reality. The *Memoirs* themselves represent a restitutive attempt to establish reality contact; this effort was evidently successful until the death of Schreber's mother and the illness of his wife, at which point he again relapsed—to die in an insane asylum four years later.

Schreber Père

Niederland also contributed a significant amount of information about Schreber's relation to his father, which has important implications for the genesis of paranoia. Dr. Daniel Gottlieb Moritz Schreber was a physician, lecturer, writer, and clinical instructor in the medical school at Leipzig. He had specialized in orthopedics and had written and lectured widely on the upbringing of children and physical culture through the use of what he called "therapeutic gymnastics." This comprised an elaborate series of compulsive and rigid ritualizations that were calculated to break the will of the child and subject him to a severe and inexorable discipline. Severe corporal punishment was recommended at the slightest infringement of any of these elaborate rules, even from the earliest age, because the rebellious and disruptive acts of the child's crude nature had to be weakened and brought under control through the greatest strictness.

Dr. Schreber rigorously applied these educative methods to his own children, and undoubtedly the infant Schreber was therefore subjected to a relentless mental and physical torment under the guise of medical and educational principle. The elder Schreber was thus pathologically concerned with the control of both masturbatory and aggressive practices in children, but he disguised this compulsive sadism and rationalized it within the context of his missionary and almost fanatical crusade for improved methods of physical culture and the moral formation of children. Schreber père's practices in child rearing, which Niederland describes in some detail, could be interpreted as compulsive-sadistic-projective experiences in self-control (Niederland 1959).

This radical crushing of the child's crude nature was accomplished from the earliest age by suppression of all strivings for independence and punishment of any failure to obey the elaborate rules required by the system. All indications of passion and bad habits had to be dealt with immediately and drastically by admonishment and mechanical restraints administered with bodily punishment. The elder Schreber maintained that, through proper administration, a state of complete submissiveness could be imposed on the child by the age of 5 or 6 years.

The father suffered a head injury and fell ill with a mental illness in about his 51st year. After the injury, he lived in partial seclusion and withdrew from many of his activities, as well as from personal contact with his children. He had violent outbursts of rage and fury, and often tolerated only the presence of his wife. He died in 1861 at age 53. The son too became ill for the first time at the age of 51, and his chief symptoms centered around complaints about his head—fears about a softening of the brain and impending death. Soon afterward, he was admitted to the Leipzig Clinic, where he made a suicidal attempt. Two years later, at age 53, he recorded a marked deterioration of his condition, which was reflected in the "signs" of transformation into a woman that characterized the course of his subsequent psychosis.

Niederland's material begins to shed considerable light on the kernel of truth that may have lain behind the psychosis. We can begin to understand the son's helpless longings for the father and his grievances when "God retired to an enormous distance." The complaint that God does not really understand living man is a reproach against the father, whose books were filled with lifeless drawings of anatomical representations. It also is a reproach against Dr. Flechsig, whose scientific work with corpses and whose therapeutic interest in castration were undoubtedly well known to the patient (Niederland 1959, 1968). Schreber's "little men" may very well refer to the drawings in his father's books, and the anatomical delusions that he entertained may also have referred to the illustrations of dissections in the same books and undoubtedly were related to castration anxiety and sadomasochistic fantasies stemming from his childhood.

MacAlpine and Hunter (1953) have also pointed out the strong feminine aspect of Schreber's delusional system, particularly his calling the sun a "whore," which was not consistent with Freud's view that the sun was a symbolic representation of the father. Schreber's mother was very closely associated with the father's theories and helped him carry them out, even assisting him in the writing, so that she became a participant in his compulsive-sadistic practices. The controlling and omnipotent figure of the deified power that controlled Schreber's life was undoubtedly a fusion of both maternal and paternal images. In addition, Schreber's father had elaborate ideas about attraction and repulsion as governing principles of the universe, and of the relation of God to the universe and his control over it, which may well have contributed to Schreber's elaborate delusional cosmology (Niederland 1963).

Schreber's Persecution

Freud concentrated on the erotic components of Schreber's illness to the exclusion of other, and perhaps more significant, dimensions. In a sense, Freud's formulations prescind from, even though they do not exclude, the possibility of real persecution as a part of Schreber's childhood experience. Freud's derivation of Schreber's paranoia from repressed homosexual conflicts must be set in relief from the additional determinants of the paranoid process that are detectable in Schreber's background.

Freud consistently ignored Schreber's constant complaint that he was being humiliated. Rochlin (1973) has observed in this regard:

Whether in the sense of being transformed from an active into a passive creature, subjected to violent abuses or otherwise cruelly used, he felt himself the helpless object of unremitting attack. The problem he presented to Freud (and presents to us) is not only that he felt threatened throughout his life by unaccountably intense, and consciously inadmissible erotic longing, but that he consistently viewed himself as a demeaned object of hard, hostile and aggressive intentions from those with whom he was (or wanted to be) most intimate. (p. 116)

Schreber himself (1903) commented on the humiliating bodily experiences he endured:

From the first beginnings of my contact with God up to the present day my body has been continually the object of divine miracles. If I wanted to describe all these miracles in detail I could fill a whole book with them alone. I may say that hardly a single limb or organ in my body escaped being temporarily damaged by miracles, nor a single muscle being pulled by miracles, either moving or paralyzing it according to the respective purpose. (p. 131)

Reading this statement out of its immediate context, we cannot be sure whether Schreber was referring to the humiliations he suffered as part of his illness at the hands of God, or to the humiliations imposed on him by the stern and rigorously demanding discipline at the hands of his father. The father's insanely sadistic and cruel series of physical torments were intended to train and discipline his children—literally with the purpose of breaking their wills so that they were completely docile and obedient to the wishes of their parents. Reading these accounts is like perusing a medieval manuscript of torture techniques.

But the persecution was neither straightforward nor open. The persecution could not be acknowledged as such, for this would have been offensive to the self-esteem and supposedly noble ideals of Schreber's father. Consequently, the sadistic breaking of a child's will and the attendant continual humiliation and physical torment had to be denied and perceived in the service of idealized motives (Schatzman 1971).

Hence, what permeates our few glimpses of Schreber's childhood experience is the realization that his emerging autonomy and self-esteem were under constant assault—undoubtedly the "soul murder" to which Schreber so mysteriously referred. Implicit in the father's bizarre theories is the assumption that the child is wicked, destructive, and evil, and that his dangerous qualities must be crushed and beaten out of him until he has no will of his own. A subtle collusion develops between the persecuting parent and the persecuted child. It is essential to the parent that the child see the parent's persecution as an expression of love. If the child does not accept this, if he should see the parent's persecution for what it is, the recognition becomes a form of rebellion that must be crushed by further persecutory action. Consequently, the child must conceal his persecution from himself, and in addition, he must conceal from himself the fact that he is concealing (Schatzman 1971). The pattern that thus evolves in the family system is similar to what has been described as pseudomutuality (Wynne et al. 1958).

White (1963) stresses the role of the mother in Schreber's pathology. He suggests that the primitive, destructive, dependent oral impulses toward the mother were of the most crucial importance and central to the pathology of the *Memoirs* (White 1961). The methods of child rearing employed by Schreber's parents produced the responses of rage, mistrust, and unresolved oral-destructive and dependent needs. Whereas these could be relinquished only through identification with the mother, they also had to be defended against by a more superficial identification with the father, wherein Schreber became competent and compulsively conscientious. Intense identification with the compulsive and rigidly restrictive father enabled him to weather the storms of puberty, helping him to manage the instinctual conflicts of childhood and adolescence. But he was left quite vulnerable to the conflicts of intimacy and isolation on an adult level of adjustment. His hypochondria and subsequent paranoia represented a response to a generativity crisis which developed in the context of his early political defeat and his stillborn children. Beneath the facade of compulsive masculine identification, he secretly remained the infant who wished to be the sole possessor of the wife-mother, and the delusional transformation into a woman may have been a psychotic way of symbolically merging with the mother. For an infant to destroy the mother is in fact to destroy the world, so that Schreber's world-destruction fantasies may have stemmed from primitive oral-destructive impulses.

Paranoia and Narcissism

Narcissistic Attack

We are left with a diversity of influences that may have had a profound effect on the shape and course of Schreber's paranoid pathology, over and above the basic Freudian consideration of repressed homosexuality. The illuminating data concerning Schreber's "persecution" at the hands of his father cast the whole question of the genesis of his pathology in a new light. If we try to locate the intrapsychic effects of these traumatic experiences, we are almost unavoidably forced to reconsider the problem of narcissism. Only recently have we come to a more profound understanding of the significance of the developmental vicissitudes of narcissism, as well as of the intimate connections between unresolved and destructive aggression and narcissistic deprivation (Rochlin 1973). Schreber's persecution at the hands of his father constituted a continual undermining and attack on his burgeoning narcissism. Consequently, at the very roots of his development was a distortion and impairment of his basic sense of self-esteem.

Self-esteem

Presumably, the emerging roots of a healthy and constructive self-esteem are nourished by those developmental experiences in which the child feels himself to be valued, loved, and cherished by the powerful and significant objects who form the matrix of his developmental experience. It is within this basic framework that Erikson has described the rudiments of basic trust and the emergence of autonomy. Basic trust can be seen as a fundamental form of self-regard that contributes substantially to the emerging sense of self-esteem. Basic trust, however, is rooted in that fundamental mutuality between the child and the mothering figure, which is in part the capacity of the mothering figure to recognize and respond to the unique needs of the child in a manner that is gratifying and comforting. Mutuality, therefore, involves the essential element of positive acknowledgment and responsiveness to the inner needs of the child.

Resting on this essential foundation, the later emergence of the child's autonomous self-expression presents a further challenge to the parental capacity for acknowledgment and positive responsiveness. Maintaining the mutuality in the parent-child relation depends on the parent's capacity to respond to the child's emerging impulses to declare himself against the wishes of the significant figures upon whom he is so critically dependent for recognition. If this emerging self-expression met with excessively punitive rejection or harsh restriction, the emerging sense of self is correspondingly injured. The result is often an abiding sense of self-doubt, shame, and inferiority or inadequacy. In the light of what we have learned about the unremitting "persecution" that Schreber suffered at the hands of his father, we can infer that his basic sense of self-esteem and the inherent narcissism related to it suffered severe impairment and mortification.

Relation to Father

The importance of Schreber's relation to his father looms large in this perspective. A consistent and constant feature, of male paranoids particularly, is an unsatisfied and frustrated longing for closeness with and positive acknowledgment from the father. Frequently, the father of such a patient either may have been a cold, detached, withdrawn figure in the child's experience, or have presented the picture of a harshly punitive and hostilely rejecting figure in the child's world. In either case, the availability of the father as a loving and affectively responsive figure in the child's developmental experience is lacking. Such patients, even in the later stages of the emergence of their pathology, demonstrate a continually frustrated and unrequited longing for closeness to and recognition and acceptance from the father figure or figures.

One begins to sense the extreme importance of the father figure in the development of the child, particularly with regard to the child's emerging sense of self-worth. The rejection and distance in some father-son pairs remain a source of continual disappointment and resulting erosion of self-esteem. Although this aspect of the child's development can be seen in terms of a negative oedipal attachment and associated homosexual longings for the father, it must also be viewed in terms of the narcissistic deprivation and the consequent undermining of the child's emerging self-image.

Aggression

The inevitable consequence of such narcissistic deprivation and mortification is an upsurge of humiliation and rage (Kohut 1972). The child mobilizes a variety of defenses, as well as aggression, in preserving and restoring his injured narcissism. It is this unresolved aggression that lies at the root of the child's ambivalence toward parental figures and interferes with the internalization and integration of parental introjects as the major contributors to the child's emerging sense of self and its corresponding developmental structuring of ego capacities (Meissner 1971b). The primary mechanism for dealing with such aggression is that of projection, which further contaminates the subsequent introjects that shape the child's emerging sense of self. Anna Freud (1936) described this process underlying the defensive constellation as "identification with the aggressor." From the point of view of the developmental pathology of narcissism, the quality of fixated and deprived narcissism embedded in the pathological introjects has been described by Kohut (1971) in terms of the grandiose self.

In the emergence of Schreber's adult pathology, it is apparent that his inner sense of worth and adequacy were under continual attack. The agony of his wife's bearing stillborn children and the disappointment connected with this must have put his own sense of masculine adequacy and potency under considerable pressure. Moreover, his acute decompensation in each instance proved to have taken place in the context of an appointment or election to some new and important public responsibility that would have presented a challenge to his sense of competence and worth. Again, the clinical phenomenon is not altogether unfamiliar—that patients decompensate in the face of apparent success. In such cases, it is frequently enough not simply the unconscious guilt motivation that is called into play but, in addition, the challenge of success or esteem from others to the patient's underlying sense of worthlessness and feeling of being undeserving and inadequate. A similar motivation has been described in certain cases of negative therapeutic response in which the patient feels underserving of therapeutic success. Modell (1971) has emphasized the unresolved envy in such patients. The dynamics follow the narcissistic dictate that if anything is received it must be taken away from someone else—the postulate of limited good. It is the paradox of narcissism that when it is challenged or threatened it becomes even more fragile. The more threatened and fragile narcissism becomes, the more ready is the embattled and endangered ego to bring destructive and unresolved aggression to its defense.

Consequently, we cannot simplistically view Schreber's pathology as a result of a childhood persecution at the hands of his severely punitive father, somehow extrapolated or generalized to fit the context of his adult experience. To rest our case there would be to ignore the essential dynamic basis for this projective distortion. The childhood persecution was a persecution indeed, but its dynamic impact was specifically rooted in the narcissistic deprivation and trauma associated with it. It is that deprived and pathologically distorted narcissism which provides the dynamic impulse and motivation for the defensive operation that gave rise to and determined Schreber's adult illness.

Implications for the Theory of Paranoia

Inferiority

The developments in psychoanalytic thinking about paranoia represent a questioning of and shifting away from Freud's early emphasis on homosexual conflicts in the etiology of paranoia. This has opened the way to considerations of other dynamic factors in the understanding of paranoid anxieties and conflicts.

Thinking about paranoia in terms of a defense against and compensation for feelings of inadequacy and inferiority was anticipated by

Sullivan (1953, 1956). He regards paranoid ideas of persecution and grandeur as complex processes which were intended to overcome or obliterate an irremediable sense of inferiority, unworthiness, and incapacity to awaken positive attitudes in others. He describes a process in which inadequate approbation in the child's early experience produces a prevailing negative self. This negative attitude interferes with subsequent securing of interpersonal satisfactions. Feelings of personal inferiority, unworthiness, and often loneliness are at times intolerable. The conviction evolves that the individual is not capable of being fully human, and this creates a sense of insecurity that makes it impossible to sustain any kind of adaptive effort (Sullivan 1953).

Security and satisfaction are obtained by the paranoid projection, in which the inferior person is turned into a victim of persecution. The feeling of worth is protected by the paranoid transference of blame onto others. Thus, the paranoid's security rests on his being persecuted. The transfer of blame, however, covers an insupportable weakness, so that the paranoid's self-system must continually draw into the protective system anybody who would be critical. The danger flags are continually flying, and relationships can be permitted only with people who do not present a danger of reminding the paranoid of what it is that really ails him (Sullivan 1956). The awareness of inferiority creates an unbearable anxiety that represents a fatal deficiency of the self-system, which is unable to disguise or exclude the underlying sense of inferiority and consequent rejection and insecurity.

Sadomasochism

Following Freud's (1908) lead, Bak (1946) focused on the sadomasochistic trends in paranoia. He sees the paranoid reaction as a delusional masochism in which the regression to masochism is accompanied by withdrawal of libido, along with increased hostility toward the previous love object, and sadistic fantasies. When mastery over the hostility fails, sadism is projected as a delusional restitution which enables the masochism to be reinstituted as delusions of mistreatment and persecution.

The link between paranoia and masochism has been strongly emphasized by Nydes (1963), who formulates the polarity between the masochistic and the paranoid character in the following terms: "The masochistic character appears to renounce 'power' for the sake of 'love'; and the paranoid character appears to renounce 'love' for the sake of 'power'" (p. 216). Thus, in the megalomanic phase of delusional paranoia, the patient renounces love and adopts the position of the powerful figure of God or one who is equated with God. The masochist projects his wishes for power onto another person and renounces his power for the sake of the love of the powerful figure. Nydes contrasts the paranoid orientation with the sadistic orientation and believes they must be distinguished even though they often overlap. The paranoid orientation is essentially defensive against the inner feeling of guilt. It involves identification with the victim, the one who is being persecuted, rather than identification with the aggressor, which is more characteristic of a sadistic orientation.

The power operation in paranoia is a kind of counterattack against an assumed accuser. The frequent effect of this is to provoke the punishment in reality of the very enemy against whom the subject is supposedly defending himself. The paranoid reaction simply affords a confirmation of his feelings that he is being persecuted. The paranoid equates power with invulnerability. He despises weakness in any form and will often endure excruciating pain. As Nydes points out, "To wish for love is to admit weakness, and to accept subjugation. It means yielding to castration and to homosexual degradation" (1963, p. 223). He sees Schreber's submission to God as a humiliating emasculation, a form of masochistic regression, allowing him some degree of safety and protection.

Nydes's position comes close to that of Ovesey (1954, 1955a, 1955b). But whereas Ovesey stresses the patient's failure to meet the demands of society, Nydes stresses the paranoid's selection of negative features of an otherwise positive social response. By reason of his punitive and infantile superego, the paranoid character expects to be punished rather than rewarded for success as is the normal experience. Paranoid-masochistic trends may have adaptive aspects, but they are basically motivated by the need to resolve underlying intrapsychic conflicts. Thus, both paranoid and masochistic types of characters fail to achieve a healthy identification with the same-sex parent, who is unconsciously regarded as omnipotent. They wish to replace that parent and at the same time dread retaliation in the form of annihilation or castration.

Any forms of self-assertion or real success are seen unconsciously as a defiance of and a transgression against the all-powerful authority figure. Success is played out in terms of the unconscious oedipal drama of incest with the parent of the opposite sex and murder of the parent of the same sex. Competition is particularly threatening, since it implies a desperate combat with the projected infantile superego figure, so that the paranoid individual must resort to a delusional form of magical control in which the behavior, thoughts, and wishes of others are secretly directed and controlled. Any independence of others, however benign and apparently innocuous, becomes a threat to the paranoid.

Depression

Closely related to this formulation is Schwartz's (1963, 1964) view of the paranoid-depressive continuum. The notion of responsibility provides the basis for this continuum: the depressive side is characterized by self-reference in regard to responsibility, and the paranoid side by object reference. In Schwartz's view, an introjection of feelings of blame or responsibility accompanies the introjection of good and bad objects. The child may experience deprivation as related either to himself or to the mother or to both. Insofar as he assumes the responsibility for his own deprivation, he develops the rudiments of the depressive orientation. If the source of the deprivation is experienced as an external one over which the child has no control for which he is not responsible, he develops the basis for a paranoid orientation. Melanie Klein's view of depression involves the guilt and remorse over destructive feelings directed to the bad mother, insofar as they also injure the good mother. The idea of responsibility is implicit in this formulation, consisting as it does of guilt and remorse. In the paranoid position, however, there is no concept of responsibility or guilt or remorse or anything except feelings referred to external objects.

Schwartz follows substantially Sullivan's point of view, that the paranoid person is faced with his own lack and his own unimportance or insignificance. His delusion is a denial of this intolerable idea and an attempt at compensation. He interprets deprivation as meaning that he does not matter to other people. His insignificance is due not to something he has done or something for which he is responsible but, rather, to the fact that nothing about him has any value to others. The sense of inferiority and lack of worth is based on a narcissistic fixation that is related to a narcissistic wound suffered in early infancy.

Because of the narcissistic wound, the patient needs to secure recognition from others, and he is hypersensitive and extremely vulnerable to the responses of others. Because his ability to relate to other people in the real community is impaired, the paranoid forms what Cameron (1959) describes as a "paranoid pseudocommunity." The pseudocommunity has the specific function of affirming the patient's significance and relevance to others. Unlike the autistic schizophrenic, who denies the meaningful existence of others, the paranoid in fact creates others in a meaningful context in which they have a special relation to him. As long as the paranoid delusional system functions adequately, the patient is able to carry on without undue impairment. But as the vulnerability to challenge in the delusional system is increased, the patient becomes more distrusting, suspicious, guarded, and even angry.

Salzman's (1960) view of paranoia, in which he sees the denial of low self-esteem as central to the syndrome, is similar. To Salzman, the primary consequence of the paranoid's denial of low self-esteem is his grandiosity, which then produces rebuffs from the environment secondarily. The projective transfer of blame through the delusional structure is then organized to deal defensively with this threat to the primary grandiosity. It is not clear that grandiosity plays such a primary role in all cases. Nonetheless, the effort to compensate for the sense of inferiority or the loss of self-esteem seems to be a relatively constant feature.

In Modlin's (1963) study of paranoid states in women, he found that in women with adequate life adjustment and satisfactory marital relationships a specific stress precipitated the phase of depression that was expressed in the sense of reduction and loss of self-esteem. This was accompanied by significant alterations in the husband-wife relation and an actual reduction in frequency or a complete cessation of sexual intercourse. Regression followed the loss of self-esteem, and projective delusional mechanisms appeared. Successful treatment of these women focused on the reassertion of the woman's feminine social role, on the regaining of her lost self-esteem, and finally on the reestablishment of the marital relationship.

The relation between depression and paranoia has also been stressed by Allen (1967). These two states may substitute for one another, and in the treatment of a paranoid patient one frequently finds an underlying depression. The depression is primary, and the paranoia is an attempt to deal with the implicit suicidal impulse. The paranoid patient is extremely sensitive to the suicidal impulse and can deal with it only by projecting it. When the impulse becomes too strong to be handled by mechanisms of denial and projection, a serious suicide attempt may be made. Thus, the paranoid defenses take their place alongside the manic defenses as major strategies to avoid and diminish the pain of depression and lowered self-esteem. The paranoid resorts to mechanisms of denial and projection, whereas the manic resorts to mechanisms of denial and flight into activity. At their pathological extremes, the paranoid psychosis and the manic-depressive psychosis are often difficult to differentiate.

Hostility

In discussing the sources of anxiety in paranoid schizophrenics, Searles (1965) points out that the paranoid sees his world as filled with sinister meanings and with malevolent intentions toward himself. He cannot ignore the persecuting figures, because they actually represent the projection of his own unconscious feelings and attitudes, and if he renounces his concern over them, he is in fact renouncing part of himself. Yet he cannot come to terms with them because he cannot accept the abhorrent qualities that he has projected onto them. The alternatives are desperate because the price is loss of identity and disintegration of the self. The psychotic person seeks safety and protection by placing his self outside all experience and activity. It thus becomes a vacuum, constantly threatened with being overwhelmed by the malevolent reality outside. Alongside the dread, however, he experiences an intense longing for participation in the world. Thus, the deepest longing of the self becomes its greatest weakness and the source of its greatest dread, since to participate in reality is to run the risk of obliteration, of what Laing (1965) has called "engulfment." The same dilemma is addressed by Bychowski (1966, 1967) in terms of the interpenetration of the archaic object and primitive image of the self—the self as ultimately vulnerable and helplessly victimized, and the reality as somehow powerful and relentlessly overwhelming:

> This interpenetration of hostility contributes to the formation of archaic object representations, which become an important depository of primitive destructive hostility. In a predisposed psychic organization these distorted representations of the original love-hate objects remain split off and isolated from the rest of the ego, and therefore may at some future time become the source of serious psychopathology. In such formations hostility is externalized and projected onto the original love-hate objects or their derivatives, which then assume the status of an arch enemy and persecutor. (1966, pp. 190–191)

The issues of paranoia and depression lie very close together and in fact seem to share some of the same genetic roots. On the clinical front, the therapist is constantly faced with the problem of helping the paranoid patient to surrender his delusions; to face, to bear, and to resolve the underlying depression which is so theatening and which involves the loss of self and destruction of all personal value. Often, the way in which the paranoid expresses what Winnicott (1965) calls the "false self" is apparently normal—he becomes the obedient child, the ideal husband, the industrious worker. But in his compliance the individual does not have a sense of his own autonomy and thus is unable to experience his separateness on the one hand, or his relatedness on the other, in a normal way. The sense of reality of his own selfhood is bound up in the other, and he is thus placed in a position of ontological dependency on the other. Indeed, that dependency on the other for one's very existence becomes so threatening that the slightest indication of hostility or rejection from the other becomes a threat to the very existence of one's self. The alternatives are utter detachment and isolation, and the struggle becomes a struggle for one's lifeblood, for one's very survival.

The Schizophrenic Process

Psychoanalytic Theories

The basic hypothesis on which this discussion is based is that in Schreber's pathology the paranoid process was a response to and a compensation for the disorganizing and disruptive effects of an underlying schizophrenic process. Our quest to understand the schizophrenic process can be assisted by a review of recent psychoanalytic formulations. London (1973a, b) has described two separate lines of thinking in Freud's theory of schizophrenia, each of which is represented in contemporary debates. The first, the unitary theory, emphasizes the continuity between schizophrenia and neurosis, both of which are viewed as intrapsychically motivated behaviors determined by instinctual drives and defenses. Within this framework, both decathexis and the disturbance in reality contact are regarded as defensively motivated, and transference is considered as fundamentally the same in both schizophrenia and the neuroses. Freud developed the unitary or conflict theory as a way of providing a unified psychoanalytic account that would embrace both the neuroses and the psychoses. But, as London observes, this theory has failed to provide a satisfactory basis for research into the nature of the schizophrenic process and is more oriented toward the maintenance of a cohesive theory than toward the exploration of unique schizophrenic phenomena.

Freud's second theory, however, the specific theory, presents schizophrenic phenomena as reflecting unique psychological deficiency states. London views the psychological deficiency in question as primarily a decathexis of the mental representations of objects. Decathexis in this context refers to a basic disturbance in mental representation, and the loss of reality contact is regarded as secondary to this primary deficit. Also, the capacity for transference in schizophrenics comes to be regarded as limited or nonexistent. In our present state of knowledge, the ultimate understanding of the schizophrenic process, whether it is essentially a condition of pathological defense or of deficiency, remains unsettled.

London himself opts for a modified version of the specific theory. In place of the much misunderstood term "decathexis," he suggests the following formulations:

> A disturbance in the capacity to organize memory traces into mental object representations and to sustain mental object representations. . . . It is rooted in developmental factors which are superordinate to the development of instinctual drives, is linked biologically to withdrawal responses, and is regulated by the unpleasure principle. (p. 182)

Thus, the schizophrenic scans his environment for patterns of stimulus organization that would normally be provided by a stable representational system interacting with and integrating itself with the ongoing flow of perceptual experience. Even when sufficient structure is provided by the pattern of stimulus input and the attempt is relatively successful, the integration with reality that results may appear to be adequate and adaptive, but it is relatively inefficient and brittle. The schizophrenic has effectively relied on an organization of stimulus input that is not reinforced by a complex organization of patterns of past experience, which is implicit in a stable representational system. London (1973b) comments:

> The environment, being limited by the dimensions of time and space, cannot provide the consistency, the symbolic condensations or the range of patterns afforded by a representational system. When the environmental patterning fails to organize -ongoing experience, then the chaotic behavioural disturbances characteristic of acute schizophrenia ensue. (p. 185)

The view of schizophrenia as reflecting an underlying psychological deficiency state rather than a form of conflict-based and defensively motivated behavior is more consistent with other contemporary approaches to the study of the schizophrenic process. In this sense, the primary intrapsychic disturbance is in the capacity to organize memory traces into mental object representations and in the ability to sustain these object representations. Thus, schizophrenia is viewed as qualitatively different from the psychoneuroses. This primary disturbance extends to the formation and maintenance of self-representations, as well as to object representations (Frosch 1983). This representational defect limits the capacity to regulate environmental stimulation, so that schizophrenic subjects are particularly vulnerable to either insufficient or excessive degrees of stimulation. The disturbance of reality relations is secondary to the intrapsychic deficit and may reveal itself paradoxically in either excessive dependence on the environment and/or excessive interference with reality integration (London 1973b).

With regard to the specific theory, two points are worth focusing on. The first is that the formulation in respect to a deficiency in the forming and sustaining of mental representations again focuses the understanding of the schizophrenic process in terms of cognitive deficiency states, here more broadly conceived in terms of representations. Hence, failure of representational systems leaves the schizophrenic unable to organize and integrate the flow of perceptual input from the environment, as we have seen in the previous discussion of perceptual-conceptual integration defects and the disorganization of response hierarchies.

The second point is that London's argument, consistent with a current trend in psychoanalytic theorizing, puts the emphasis on representational phenomena. However, it seems to me that the understanding of the schizophrenic process is more far-reaching and profound than can be reflected in merely representational terms. I would agree that the deficiency in the formation and sustaining of self-representations is an important area of disturbance, reflecting the influence of the schizophrenic process. But instead of emphasizing the representational components, I would prefer to envision the process in more specifically structural terms, that is, in terms of the specific patterns and forms of internalization deficit and structural vulnerability that are involved in the schizophrenic process.

The debate between proponents of these various models persists, and each has its own particular consequences for the understanding of the underlying processes and for the course of therapeutic intervention. Based on the deficiency model, the treatment aims at repair of the underlying deficit with restoration of internal object representations. Hence, technical measures, which are the basis of psychoanalytic work, may be not only nontherapeutic and inappropriate but even antitherapeutic. Such measures as the use of the couch, free association, and therapeutic neutrality may only increase the void of separation and reinforce the sense of object loss. Rather, the therapy will aim at creating and maintaining contact with the patient, working to keep channels of communication open, and continually fostering identification with a caring and concerned therapist. As Greenson and Wexler (1969) observe, "Whatever will advance the 'real' relationship, at least with disturbed schizophrenic patients, takes precedence over transference considerations and ultimately opens the way for effective interpretive intervention" (p. 37).

In the defensive model, based on the view of schizophrenia as a disorder of conflict and as not differing qualitatively from neurosis, the loss of internal representations and the deformation of the ego are regarded as consequences of an active defensive operation warding off intolerable affects. These may be related to what Frosch (1983) describes as the "basic anxiety," namely the fear of the disintegration of the self. The difference between psychosis and neurosis lies in the degree of instinctual regression, the prominence of aggression and disturbances in both ego and superego functions. Proponents of the defensive view would regard psychoanalysis as the treatment of choice and would regard therapy based on a deficiency model as basically harmful. The danger of such therapies, based on notions of object replacement, is that they ignore the inherent aggressiveness and destructiveness of the schizophrenic condition. Thus, the analytic method, which is viewed as harmful by deficiency theorists, is viewed by conflict theorists as a necessary and indicated approach (Aronson 1977).

A somewhat different approach to the understanding of the schizophrenic process is provided by Grotstein (1977a, b). Following a basically Kleinian line, he essentially redefines schizophrenia as a splitting off of a part of the personality which undergoes a separate course of development and which is cut off from the normal developmental unfolding. The split-off portion centers around a form of infantile psychosis which consists of the paranoid-schizoid and depressive positions. The paranoid-schizoid position becomes the locus of fixation, which impedes the development of key maturational functions and thus disposes to schizophrenia. Schizophrenia as a core disturbance, then, is a separate part of the personality that is distinguished from psychosis, which is a clinical state to which schizophrenia may predispose or that it may precipitate. In this view, psychosis may be treated by a number of modalities, but schizophrenia itself may be responsive only to psychoanalysis, the preferred mode of treatment.

The schizophrenic portion of the personality originates in a constitutionally (genetically) determined, inadequate threshold barrier to incoming stimuli, along with a constitutionally precocious sensitivity to perceptions which predispose the infant from birth to a perceptual catastrophe due to inadequate filtering. The potential for terror in these infants at risk for schizophrenia remains unbuffered and becomes registered as a nameless dread due to the failure of primal repression. The perceptual emergency precipitates desperate defensive maneuvers in which perceptions and perceptual objects are attacked and the very capacity to perceive such objects is undermined, probably by interfering with the capacity to integrate perceptual inputs. Thus, Grostein's view reestablishes the vicissitudes of the integration and organization of perceptual input as central to the understanding of the schizophrenic process. However, his view of the process ultimately originates in Kleinian assumptions regarding the role of primitive and unmodified aggression and its effects in the undermining of stimulus thresholds, with the inevitable consequences of perceptual disorganization, and an undermining of the developmentally normal progression both in the formation of the structure of the self and its correlated self-representations, and in the capacity to conceptually organize and integrate perceptual experience.

Levels of Organization

The material presented here, admittedly partial and selective, nonetheless seems to point in a relatively consistent direction. The conclusions from several avenues of inquiry point to a general cognitive deficit in the organization of the schizophrenic's intrapsychic experience. On the level of the processing of stimulus input, there seems to be an identifiable disparity in the schizophrenic's capacity to integrate, regulate, and organize the ongoing flow of perceptual experience. This is thought to be due to a conceptual deficiency that is reflected in a limited capacity to organize perceptual material in terms of conceptual categories.

At another level of cognitive organization, the schizophrenic deficit can be seen in terms of an incapacity to organize representational schemata, whether of objects or of the self. It is not clear whether the conceptual incapacity previously described is a by-product of the incapacity for representational organization and integration, or whether both of these identifiable deficits stem from a further underlying deficiency state. In focusing the nature and the central deficit of the schizophrenic process, as we have previously indicated, we would prefer to place the emphasis on the primacy of the failure in self-organization.

Rather than emphasizing the merely representational aspects of this phenomenon, that is, the incapacity to form and sustain coherent, integrated, and well-differentiated self-representations, we would prefer to shift the emphasis to a structural frame of reference. That is, the deficit is specifically the structural one to which the disorganization in self-representations refers and which presumptively underlies them (Meissner 1972b). In these terms the schizophrenic process pertains to a developmental deficit, which contributes to a failure to organize, integrate, and stabilize the inherent structures forming the core of the individual's self-organization. Thus, the schizophrenic process impinges specifically on the patterns of internalization which give rise to pathogenic introjects. It is through the internalization of such introjective configurations and their progressive developmental modification that the rudiments of a sense of self are acquired, integrated, and formed into an integrally functioning personality (Meissner 1979a, 1980a, 1981b). In this frame of reference, self-representations are secondary manifestations of the underlying self-structure and are derived from them. Consequently, the central deficit in terms of these theoretical formulations lies at the level of structural deficit rather than at the level of secondary representational derivatives.

By the same token, there is no basis currently available on which we can discriminate between such structural deficits as the primary area within which the pathogenic effects of the schizophrenic process are manifested and inherent conceptual-perceptual deficits. It is entirely plausible that such cognitive deficits, interacting at the border between the environment and the experiencing individual, reflect the underlying structural deficits. By the same token, keeping in mind that the nature of structural formations is dependent on internalizations from the very beginning of the individual's infantile experience, and that the quality of such internalizations reflects the patterning of object relationships and the experience of such objects, distortions on the level of the functioning of these cognitive processes may play a role in determining the ultimate quality and nature of the crucial internalizations which give rise to psychic structure.

In any case, we can make a plausible case for the impact of the schizophrenic process on these three levels of psychic organization and functioning, which seem to be so closely allied and interwoven. On the level of the organization of cognitive processes, on the level of the formation and integration of representational systems—both of objects and of the self—and on the level of structural integration of the self-system, the schizophrenic process seems to exercise a profoundly disturbing and destructive influence. Its effects are to produce in a destructive manner states of disorganization and dysfunction which impede the adaptive processing of cognitive inputs and the organization of response capabilities, to allow for the defensive distortion and instability of representations, and to lay the basis for the introduction of structural impediments which reflect varying degrees of structural disorganization, discontinuity, instability, and dysfunction.

The Projective System

Relation to Narcissism

The major emphasis in Freud's consideration of Schreber's pathology fell on the projective system. Moreover, as we have seen, later studies exquisitely documented the relation between specific elements in Schreber's projective delusions and detailed aspects of what he must have experienced as a child—particularly the persecution at the hands of his father (Niederland 1951, 1959, 1960, 1963). In a sense, Schreber's projective system preserved and extrapolated the relationship to the father. The persecutor relation, however, was the only one that Schreber could attain with his father. The price of the relation with the father, therefore, was subjugation and submission, just as the price of becoming the special agent and instrument of God's divine purposes for redemption of the world was his transformation into a woman. Schreber's projective system allowed for recognition and acceptance by, and special relationship to, the projected father figure of God.

The projective system, consequently, can be viewed as an attempt to redeem and salvage Schreber's damaged narcissism. Within the delusional system, he retained a somewhat grandiose and narcissistically embellished position as the agency of divine purpose. His self-esteem and his impaired sense of inner value and worth were generously restored. The important element, however, was the transformation into a woman. On one level, the transformation offered the potentiality for redeeming the narcissistic loss experienced through his failure to generate healthy children. On another level, the transformation into a woman established and consolidated the underlying identification with the mother. In exploring the dynamics of this aspect of the delusional system, we are at somewhat of a disadvantage, since the little we know of Schreber's mother can be based only on inference. Nonetheless, as we shall see, this identification forms an essential and central part of paranoid pathology.

The function of this projective system can be made more specific. The dynamics of narcissism are particularly related to establishing and preserving a sense of self. Insofar as the projective system contributes to a salvaging or redeeming of injured narcissism, it must contribute to the sustaining of the self. Part of the effect of the schizophrenic process is to interfere with those elements that constitute an integral sense of self. For Schreber, the underlying sense of rage, humiliation, and vulnerability fueled the schizophrenic disorganization and created a situation of instability and fragile integration in his internal world. The formation of a sense of self requires that it be embedded in a context of objects. In a sense, the self is defined in relation to objects, even as it derives its constituents out of relations with objects.

Self-preservation

Establishing and sustaining a sense of self requires a meaningful context within which the self can be defined and in relation to which it can be articulated. Within this context the self can find a sustaining sense of belonging and meaningfulness. In the normal course of development, the emerging self achieves this context of meaningful belonging through real relations with significant objects, in which it finds itself acknowledged, accepted, valued, and recognized. But this emerging context of belonging and meaningful relatedness can be distorted by pathological influences. Particularly where destructive impulses and intense unresolved ambivalence permeate the relationship, the sense of belonging and meaningful integration with the object context are undermined. The meaningful contexts of human relatedness in Schreber's life experience were distorted and permeated by rage, hatred, disappointment, and loss. His ties with the object world were shattered. In such circumstances, it is unavoidable that the emerging self should seek to provide, by a process of construction, the missing or impaired context. The projective system, thereby, provided him with a substitute matrix within which his reconstituting self could define and articulate itself.

The projective system has a correlative and derivative relation to the patterning of introjects around which the emerging self is organized. The roots of the projective system are in the patterning of introjects, even as the structure of the projective system is a response to the undermined and deprived narcissism embedded in the introjective economy. Schreber's early developmental experiences left him with a crippled sense of his self as valueless, humiliated, evil, unlovable, and ultimately worthy only of sadistic subjugation and cruel restraint. Around this nuclear formation was erected a context of object relatedness defined by the emerging sense of self based on the central introjects.

The introjective economy is derived in crucial ways from the introjects received from both parental figures. Closest to our historical scrutiny, and dominating the traditional view of the Schreber case, is the introjection of the aggressive and primitive father figure. Identification with the aggressor, which takes place around this paternal introject, forms the basis for the persecutory projection. Other elements are also present. Although we have very little direct knowledge of Schreber's mother, we can infer that she was a woman whose character contained strong depressive and masochistic elements. To sustain a relationship with her sadistic and authoritarian husband, she must have carried strongly masochistic elements in her own character structure.

In a powerful and convincing manner, Schreber identified himself with the castrated figure of the mother-victim. His delusional system realized the ultimate in victimized subjugation to the power of the father-God. Close and extensive study of paranoid pathology indicates that the combined elements of identification with the aggressor and identification with the victim are persistent and central in the introjective economy of paranoid patients. In one aspect at least, the paranoid process can be seen as a reinforcement of the victimized introject as a means of defending against the aggressive and victimizing introject (Meissner 1978b).

Permutations in the dynamics of these introjects provide the basis for the complex manifestations of the paranoid process. Invariably, paranoid patients—either alternatively with paranoid manifestations or often detectably in conjunction with persecutory anxiety—will become depressed, often severely depressed. At such points, the victim-introject has come to dominate the intrapsychic economy, and the undermining or failure of externalizing defenses leaves the pathological introjects in a dominating position, which then issues forth in dysphoric and often depressive affect. The externalizing or paranoid defense in turn offers the opportunity of relief from the pain of depression and the associated sense of worthlessness, inadequacy, and vileness.

Consequently, the projective system can be seen as serving an important function in the preservation and maintenance of a sense of self. The sense of self in the paranoid individual is derived from the pathogenic introjects that do not allow for the establishment or organization of an authentic sense of self as meaningfully related to the context of real objects. To sustain the pathological sense of self related to these introjects, the ego must organize a projective system that allows for the substitute relatedness of the pathological self and provides it with a sense of meaningful belongingness within the system of projective relations.

Conclusions

We are considering two psychological processes which operate relatively independently in the forming or deforming of human personality. Both serve as the focus for varying aspects of genetic, physiological, metabolic, interpersonal, and sociocultural influences. Each has a genetic history and developmental patterning that is unique to the life history of the individual personality in which it operates. The schizophrenic process impedes internal structural organization, differentiation, and integration. It has the effect of impeding the progression through normal psychological development toward an integrated and harmoniously functioning personality organization.

Schizophrenic Process

The schizophrenic process is precipitated by a genetically determined diathesis of varying degree, in combination with an infinite range of factors involving environmental stress. Individuals who are afflicted with the full potential of the genetic diathesis will develop schizophrenic pathology almost regardless of the degree of environmental stress. Individuals whose affliction is less can become schizophrenic as a result of greater degrees of environmental stress and pathogenic interaction with significant others in their environment, or through other stress-inducing pathogenic factors. There is at present no substantial evidence to suggest, nor is there any reason to suspect, that individuals who lack the genetic diathesis and who are subjected to extreme degrees of malignant and stressful influence will develop the disease, however pathogenic those influences might be or pathological the resulting personality organization.

It seems best, in terms of the current state of our knowledge, to envision the effects of the schizophrenic process as being fairly diffuse, affecting multiple levels and multiple aspects of psychic integration and functioning. Thus, the integration of psychic capacities is disorganized at multiple levels, and, to the degree that the schizophrenic process is operating, reflects the failure of organization and integration of inter-related capacities and functions. Consequently, there is an identifiable relative disorganization and lack of integration between cognitive and affective capacities, and within cognitive capacities similar disorganization and disequilibrium are found between conceptual and perceptual functions. There is a relative failure of the formation of well-differentiated and stable psychic structures, which allows for a failure of personality integration, a high degree of vulnerability to regression, even under slight degrees of stress, and a need for resorting to more infantile levels of regressive organization and more primitive defenses which interfere with and distort the individual's capacity to maintain reality contact and to respond adaptively to environmental input. Consequently, individuals in whom the schizophrenic process operates in its purest and most malignant form are the most chronically afflicted and regressive schizophrenics.

Paranoid Process

In contrast, the paranoid process involves certain specifiable mechanisms that have to do with the organization and integration of internal personality structure. From the beginning of life the paranoid process operates to provide, by way of various forms of internalization, the shaping and internal patterning of the personality. It is the paranoid process, by means of its interacting mechanisms of introjection and projection, that shapes the individual's self-organization and thereby contributes to the quality and patterning of the subject's interaction with external significant objects. If the paranoid process operates with adequate genetic endowment and significant object relationships of sufficiently good quality, personality organization can follow a relatively normal, healthy, and adaptive course of development leading toward a meaningful, purposeful, and constructive sense of self and capacity for psychological functioning.

By the same token, the paranoid process can have a pathological outcome, depending on genetically influenced patterns of instinctual endowment in interaction with the relatively healthy or malignant quality of object relationships during the period of growth and development. To the extent that the developmental experience is excessively colored by ambivalence, the resulting introjective configurations can fail to achieve a full measure of structural coherence and integration, and may serve as the basis for internal pathogenic formations that can express themselves in varying forms and degrees of psychopathology.

Such pathogenic outcomes can be readily identified in forms of paranoid pathology. In such cases, the mechanisms and dynamisms of the paranoid process are shunted into the service of maintaining the pathogenic introjects and the corresponding pathological sense of self and self-organization that lies at the heart of the patient's pathology. Projection and the paranoid construction become the vehicles for the organization of a threatening, generally hostile, and pathological view of the world, which colors the patient's interpersonal relationships and his ability to deal with the world of his experience. At the same time, it serves as a buffer to facilitate the stabilization of personality structures and functions that maintain the patient's capacity to organize and integrate stimulus input in a consistent and realistic way, even though the construction carries within it pathological distortion and malicious intent.

Interaction

In cases of paranoid schizophrenia or paraphrenia, we can see evidence of the combined effects of the separate processes and their interaction. The undermining of psychic structures and the disorganization of psychic functioning call into play forces of compensation and re-integration. In the face of the ravages of the schizophrenic process, the paranoid process can be brought into play to achieve these objectives and to provide the patient with a semblance of inner coherence and stability, even though the price of such stability is high in terms of the effect of the resulting paranoid pathology. In a sense, then, the paranoid schizophrenic is willing to pay the price of the sacrifice and distortion of his relationship to the outside world in order to gain some degree of inner organization and coherence, even though that integration itself be pathological. Thus, in cases of paranoid schizophrenia, we can see the positive integrating and constructive aspects of the paranoid process at work, even within the limiting confines and destructively undermining potential of the schizophrenic process.

The Schreber case would presumably fall within this category. We can conjecture some degree of genetic diathesis, interacting with the profoundly pathogenic influences of his family and particularly his father, as contributing elements in the schizophrenic process. The resulting state of inner disorganization and disintegration brought with it the threat of annihilation and disintegration of Schreber's sense of self. At the same time, his personality resources were not completely overwhelmed or destroyed; rather, the inner catastrophe called into play the resources of the paranoid process. The mechanisms of projection and the paranoid construction made it possible to salvage some degree of meaningful relatedness to the world and reality, while the operation of introjective mechanisms salvaged the residues of his fragmented inner world in terms of pathological introjective configurations—primarily centered around the victim-introject, but clearly without excluding other complementary configurations.

However, it is entirely possible that forms of paranoid pathology—for example, the so-called true paranoia, which as we have noted is rare enough to allow some doubt as to the validity of such a diagnosis—may in fact be expressions of the paranoid process in relatively pure culture, expressing itself in its relatively pathological form. One need not think that such a pathology can only be defensively compensating for an underlying or latent schizophrenic process. The paranoid process on its own terms, given the proper malignant and pathogenic influence, can turn in the direction of pathological expression. Moreover, the expression of paranoid pathology, reflecting varying degrees of deviation and distortion of the paranoid process, can be found in a broad range of forms of psychopathology, and even in somewhat regressive aspects of normal psychological functioning where there is no suspicion and no suggestion of the operation of the schizophrenic process.

When the schizophrenic process itself can be identified, those patients become paranoid who have preserved a capacity for mobilizing the resources of the paranoid process in an effort to modify and counter the ravages of the schizophrenic process. Consequently, such patients must be counted as relatively healthier and as having an inherently greater potential for therapeutic response and recovery. This understanding of the interaction and interplay between the schizophrenic and paranoid processes also has implications for the treatment process. It would suggest, at a minimum, that the optimal resources for correcting, modifying, and countering the effects of the schizophrenic process lie in the direction of our increasing understanding of and ability to make effective therapeutic use of aspects of the paranoid process.

Chapter Four

The Paranoid Process and Borderline Psychopathology

Development of the Concept

Neurosis versus Psychosis

The borderline diagnosis arose when the classic dichotomy between the psychoses and the neuroses was broached by particularly troublesome, intermediate forms of psychopathology that seemed to lie securely and consistently in neither category. The patients involved seemed to show in one or other degree, or at one or other time, evidence of an underlying psychotic process, but would in other contexts and other phases of their life experience seem to present a reasonably well-functioning personality organization characterized by neurotic mechanisms and behaviors. The problem was how to conceptualize these intermediate forms. Many authors regarded these cases as "formes frustes" or milder expressions of an underlying schizophrenic process. Regardless of the uncertain relationship of these forms of pathology to schizophrenia or other psychotic processes, they generally came to be viewed as lying between the borders of psychosis on the one side and neurosis on the other, and sharing, in some way difficult to specify, in the characteristics of both.

For some years, the decision as to how to describe this relationship and the interaction of psychotic and neurotic mechanisms remained in a limbo of uncertainty. Efforts to define and delineate the dimentions of this nebulous realm of psychopathology each seemed to catch some part of the picture and to emphasize different aspects of a complex phenomenon. These efforts were thus only relatively successful, limited as they were by various theoretical perspectives and methodological approaches.

Borderline Personality

This confusing picture gained clarity and resolution through the work of Kernberg, who in the mid-1960s developed his formulation of the borderline personality organization. Kernberg's (1967) contribution emphasizes a number of important points. First is the understanding that the so-called borderline personality is neither neurotic nor psychotic, but represents a distinct category of mental and emotional disturbance from the earlier classical categories. Secondly, Kernberg postulates that fundamental defining issues in borderline pathology are not behavioral or phenomenological but that they essentially are underlying structural issues that lay the foundation for borderline pathology.

As a result, the diagnosis cannot be made on the more superficial terms of the patient's behavior, affects, or other phenomenological manifestations, but has to be made in terms of evaluation of the patient's personality structure and organization. The emphasis in this approach falls on the primitive organization of the patient's ego, the relative weakness of the ego, and the primitive characteristics of the typical defenses the borderline ego utilizes, namely splitting, projection, primitive idealization, and projective identification. In addition, reflecting the underlying structural deficits in the organization of the ego, Kernberg emphasizes the role of splitting as an intrapsychic defense which creates shifting and unstable dissociated ego states. One result of such structural fragility is the vulnerability of such patients to the loss of self-cohesion and the correlated sense of identity. Consequently, splitting, the diffusion of identity, and the predominance of primitive and unresolved aggression became the hallmarks of Kernberg's borderline concept.

While Kernberg's contribution was immensely clarifying and helped to resolve many of the uncertainties regarding borderline pathology, his approach may well have been too encompassing and clarifying. His thinking had a major impact on the subsequent currents of research into borderline conditions. Starting from Kernberg's conceptualization, for example, Gunderson and his associates tried to gain more precise definition of the borderline syndrome by identifying more reliable and precise research criteria for the diagnosis. In this vein, Gunderson and Singer (1975) determined a list of criteria that would characterize the core borderline syndrome. The list included:

1. the presence of intense affect, usually hostile or depressive;
2. a history of impulsive behavior, comprising episodic acts of self-destructiveness (self-mutilation, drug overdoses, et cetera) and more chronic behavior patterns, such as drug dependency or promiscuity;
3. social adaptiveness, reflected in good work or school achievement, and generally socially appropriate behavior;
4. brief psychotic experiences, which often have a paranoid quality and may be precipitated in periods of stress or as a result of drug intake;
5. a psychological testing performance in which the performance on structured tests is more or less normal but reveals bizarre, dereistic, illogical, or primitive responses on unstructured or projective tests devices, suggesting the possibility of underlying thought disturbance; and finally,
6. interpersonal relationships that vacillate between transient and superficial relationships, and relationships that tend to be intense, conflictual, dependent, and reflect varying degrees of manipulation, demandingness, and devaluation.

Continuing attempts to lend a greater degree of refinement and definition to the characteristics of the borderline syndrome have led to the relative concretization of diagnostic characteristics in the formulations of the DSM-III regarding borderline and schizotypal personalities. While these formulations have lent a greater degree of specificity to the diagnostic evaluation of borderline conditions, they have done so at the risk of limiting the range of patients to whom the diagnostic labels can be applied. The result is that there may well be patients who can be classified as clinically borderline but do not fit neatly into the more research-oriented diagnostic categories.

Heterogeneity

Returning to Kernberg's notion of the borderline personality organization, several qualifying points can be made. Kernberg apparently uses a lumping strategy, trying to include many aspects of the clinical descriptions of pathological entities occupying the obscure terrain between the borders of psychosis and neurosis. While such an approach has its advantages, it also carries with it certain disadvantages. From a clinical point of view, it seems fair to say that few patients fit the full scope of Kernberg's description of the borderline personality. Rather, some parts of the description seem applicable to some patients, while other aspects fit other patients. It may be that the borderline conditions involve a certain degree of inherent heterogeneity that Kernberg's description tends to gloss over. In addition, Kernberg's description seems to put greater weight on the more primitive aspects of borderline functioning, particularly on aspects of ego weakness, identity diffusion, and the more primitive defense mechanisms. Clinical evidence suggests that there may indeed be some category or categories of borderline patients to which this emphasis does apply, but there may be other categories of borderline patients to whom it does not. There is the possibility that we have to deal with more than one kind of borderline patient.

Certain borderline patients come to professional attention in a state of regressed crisis and turmoil. These are the patients who are usually seen in emergency clinics, or who may be hospitalized for severe regressive episodes, including suicidal or other self-destructive acting out. But another group is rarely seen in such contexts. Such patients may get into treatment for a variety of life issues or conflicts, and seem relatively well functioning and competent. But in the course of the treatment experience they undergo a gradual regression, so that in time and with the proper, less-structured context, these patients can increasingly manifest borderline characteristics. We are thinking here particularly of the common experience of the evaluation of patients for psychoanalysis in which the patient presents with a relatively well integrated and well functioning facade, such that the experienced analyst judges the patient to be good material for analytic work. Nonetheless, when the patient becomes involved in the analytic process and as the gradual pull of the analytic regression takes hold, more and more borderline features become available to observation.

Clearly, these two populations would give rise to two quite opposite views of borderline functioning. The former fits the profile of borderline pathology in terms of more primitively organized borderline personalities or in terms of borderline patients who may be seen in a relatively severe regressive state. These patients are quite different from those who normally function at a relatively well integrated level and whose underlying borderline features can be exposed only under the inducing effect of some regressive influence, whether that be life circumstances, developmental crises, drug experiences, or even psychoanalysis. These latter patients enjoy a greater degree of ego strength, a higher-level psychic structural organization, and a better level of defensive organization and functioning.

One could say that the Kernberg view offers a caricature of the borderline personality rather than a clinically accurate characterization.

However, it can also be argued that subsequent attempts to better define and clarify the borderline description have also tended to focus on this more primitive, less well organized, and less well functioning level of borderline pathology, precisely because it is those characteristics that lend themselves to description and evaluation.

These considerations force us to think more seriously about the possibility that we have to deal with some degree of inherent heterogeneity in the borderline diagnostic picture. That impression is supported by the classic contribution of Grinker and his associates (Grinker et al. 1968), who made an empirical attempt to systematically evaluate the borderline conditions. Grinker's group studied 51 young adults of both sexes, who were evaluated as not schizophrenic but who showed borderline characteristics, including anger as a dominant affect, defective object relationships, identity failures, and depressive features, usually expressed as emptiness or loneliness. Cluster analysis of a wide range of behavioral and observational measures delineated four groups of patients: (1) a severely disturbed group with occasional psychoticlike features and seemingly bordering on psychosis; (2) a "core borderline" group characterized by chaotic interpersonal relations, acting out, and loneliness; (3) a group, comparable to Deutsch's (1942) "as-if" personalities, with difficulties in establishing and maintaining identity; and finally (4) a group of less disturbed patients who seemed to be generally better functioning and closer to a neurotic picture. A follow-up of approximately three and a half years found that only two of the patients in the most severely disturbed group developed a more frankly schizophrenic outcome.

Subsequent studies have refined and clarified Grinker's findings but have not altered the basic thrust, namely that the borderline conditions represent a spread of pathological conditions that encompass more severely disturbed and pathological forms, as well as forms that are considerably better functioning and better organized. Patients in the latter category fall into a borderline regressive state only under certain kinds of stress or regressive induction. For the most part, such patients do not look, feel, or act in a borderline fashion. It is usually only in the regressive states that the borderline features can be identified.

The Borderline Spectrum

This line of thinking has led us to attempt to formulate the borderline conditions in terms of the borderline spectrum (Meissner 1984a). The borderline spectrum can be thought of as a range of pathological conditions that stretch from the border of psychosis, marked by the loss of reality testing, to the border of better psychological functioning, set not by the neuroses, as had earlier been the case, but in the wake of Kohut's (1971) contributions, by the narcissistic personalities. The spectrum runs from the more labile, disorganized, and frequently chaotic forms of personality functioning—in which one finds patterns of emotional lability, dissociation of ego states, higher levels of regressive vulnerability, marked ego deficits, tendencies to act out, a high titration of anger and rage, and object relations that remain on an impoverished level, reflecting poor developmental achievement and the persistence of need-satisfaction and both narcissistic vulnerability and demanding-ness—to better-organized personalities whose ego strengths are relative-ly intact, who often function on a high level socially, who tend to reveal none of the regressive or vulnerable features that we frequently associate with borderline personalities, but who under certain regressive stresses or in certain contexts of interpersonal conflict tend to react in a fashion that suggests underlying borderline issues. This phenomenon comes most vividly to attention in the context of psychoanalytic treatment where presumably healthier and well-functioning patients react to the analytic regression with identifiable borderline manifestations. This can occur even in candidates undergoing analysis as part of their training to become themselves psychoanalysts.

The Hysterical Continuum

We have divided the spectrum of borderline disorders into the hysterical continuum and the schizoid continuum. The hysterical continuum represents a series of disorders of decreasing pathological severity, extending from the most primitive forms of character pathology, bordering on the schizophrenic, to more highly organized and inte-grated forms of disturbance bordering on the narcissistic and hysterical. The more severe levels of disturbance within this continuum are marked by increasing affective lability, diminished tolerance for anxiety and/or frustration, increased ego weakness, greater tendencies for external-ization and acting out as a means of releasing tension, greater instability or fragility of introjective configurations and a corresponding vulner-ability of self-cohesion, higher levels of primitive pregenital aggression, increasingly primitive defensive organization, greater tendency to regressive states and functioning, and increasing tendencies to clinging dependence on objects, constantly threatened by fears of abandonment and loss.

Pseudoschizophrenias

The first group of patients reveal primary symptoms which they share with schizophrenics, even though they may be less striking and intense; these include thought and association disorders, both of process and content, disorders of affective regulation, and even disorders of sensorimotor and autonomic functioning. The anxiety is diffuse, chronic, intense, and pervasive. The neurotic symptoms are usually multiple, shifting, and confusing; they include obsessions and compulsions, phobias, hysterical manifestations, hypochondriasis, depression, depersonalization, and a variety of apparently neurotic defense mechanisms occurring simultaneously or successively. The obsessions and phobias may often reach delusional proportions. This pan-neurotic picture may include tendencies to acting out and dramatic or histrionic behavior, or even antisocial and drug-dependent behavior. Sexual organization and functioning are chaotic, both in fact and in fantasy.

These patients, if not basically schizophrenic, live on the very border of psychosis. The fragility and vulnerability of the ego is reflected in the constant susceptibility to drive influences, and the intolerance of and inability to bind anxiety, which teeters on the brink of traumatic and even catastrophic anxiety. They often manifest severe degrees of annihilation anxiety (Adler 1985). While the defensive organization and symptom-patterning can often look neurotic, the symptomatology is generally more severe than would be expected in a neurotic pattern of organization (Dickes 1974) and is not at all effective in binding the underlying anxiety.

There is little cohesiveness or stability in the organization of the self, so that whatever tentative configurations are achieved cannot be maintained or stabilized over any significant period of time. Correspondingly, these patients have considerable difficulties in object relationships, which tend to be intensely ambivalent, covering a diffuse and intense primitive rage, and are chaotically caught up in the flux of the dilemma of intense need and paralyzing fear.

Psychotic Character

These patients may never actually develop psychotic symptoms, but they have a significant capacity for psychotic decompensation under certain circumstances. Such transient regressions may be accompanied by a loss of reality testing, but patients retain the capacity for ready reversibility of the regression, so that psychotic episodes remain transient. Unlike the pseudoschizophrenics, these patients have a higher capacity to maintain their functioning on a more or less consistent level during nonregressed periods, so that they remain in reasonably good contact with reality and are relatively more capable of adaptive functioning. However, the propensity for transient regressions, even though relatively brief and reversible, remains a marked aspect of this form of character pathology.

These patients generally have a vulnerable ego but are in a stronger position than the pseudoschizophrenics, who have little capacity to organize a consistent pattern of defensive organization or neurotic symptomatology. Psychotic characters can achieve this level of organization, but it remains susceptible to regressive pulls. The maintenance of an integrated and cohesive sense of self is a constant difficulty, in that the self is continually threatened with dissolution and disintegration and is plagued by the need to cling to objects, as well as the fear of fusing with them. Where such ego boundaries become porous and uncertain, there is often a preoccupation with identity problems; this is often the case in analysis, where regressive pulls tend to increase the dedifferentiation and defusion of ego boundaries. As Frosch (1970) notes, in the analytic situation this may result in tenuous identifications with the analyst which have an "as-if" quality, as well as in attempts to increase the sense of differentiation and separation from the analyst, which may take the form of negativism or even of paranoid distortion.

In regressive phases, the intensity of these fears is buffered by a variety of primitive defenses of a psychotic kind. But even at levels of better functioning, the object involvement of these individuals is highly qualified by active use of projective and introjective mechanisms, which tend to lend a paranoid discoloration to object relationships and to intensify the inner feeling of vulnerability and victimization.

The object relations in such patients are generally on an intense need-gratifying basis, often leading to unrealistic demands. The frustration of these demands leads to intense rage, which often takes a paranoid form. Thus, the relationship with objects is often highly conflictual and intensely ambivalent. Moreover, the superego remains poorly integrated; superego components have undergone little depersonalization or abstraction. Rather, superego functioning is carried out in terms of often regressed and archaic precursors, which remain highly susceptible to forms of externalization and projection. Superego integration is highly irregular and reflects multiple lacunae, so that there is a propensity for impulsive acting-out behavior, side by side with hypercritical and harshly punitive superego attitudes. There is a capacity for guilt and depression, but this seems fragmentary and inconsistent.

The psychotic character comes closest to the more familiar description of the classic regressive, disorganized, acting-out, and intensely tempestuous borderline patient, particularly those assessed and treated in the hospital setting. The psychotic character is closely related to the Borderline Personality Disorder as described in DSM-III. By the same token, the pseudoschizophrenics resemble the Schizotypal Personality Disorder. These categories encompass what are being designated in this study as lower-order borderline disorders. The lower-order borderlines tend to show the basic picture of emotional lability and more or less regressive functioning as a chronic or characterological feature of their personality organization. In higher-order borderlines, these features emerge only in regressive crises and borderline states, and are not an aspect of the patient's more usual and better integrated states.

Dysphoric Personality

The dysphoric personality represents a more disturbed form of higher-order borderline condition. There is a peculiar quality to these patients' subjective experience of interpersonal situations. They seem extraordinarily sensitive and responsive to the unconscious fantasies and impulses, as well as the primitive superego contents, in the significant objects around them. The conscious and intentional ego activity of people around them is beheld with abiding suspicion and mistrust, as though they were somehow deceptions or malicious tricks, while the id and superego elements seem to them somehow more genuine. There is also a tendency to feel that the elements of enduring character style, self-organization, and ego functioning in themselves are somehow unreal or phony (Krohn 1974).

Correspondingly, the dominance of the oedipal phase is not so clearly seen in these patients (Frijling-Schreuder 1969), with the result that, as in Kernberg's (1967) infantile personalities, there can be a mixture of pseudohypersexuality with sexual inhibition, sexual provocativeness which is rather direct, crude, or inappropriate mixed with orally determined exhibitionism and demandingness. The failure to achieve oedipal phase dominance means that in the pathology of these patients libidinal material can be detected from all phases of libidinal development, leading to an often confused and disturbed picture. Phallic trends are interfered with, so that there is a faulty relationship between the operation of the drives and the ego, and the bulk of the libido remains fixed in the oral and anal phases.

The general fluidity and lack of phase dominance are related to the propensity to acting out in borderline conditions. The more flamboyant and particularly destructive forms of acting out are found in borderline states and may represent an attempt to restore a sense of reality by creating a situation of intense feeling or pain. This counters the emptiness and feeling of unreality related to the acute diffusion of identity in the regressive state (Collum 1972). This regressive form of acting out is more related to the functioning of the psychotic character than to that of the dysphoric personality. On a more general level of adjustment, however, acting out in the dysphoric personality may take the form of externalization, by which the patient transposes his inner conflicts and difficulties to the outer world and develops a more or less exclusive preoccupation with dealing with them in that external realm. There is a constant tendency to blame forces outside the self for one's problems, and to assume little or no responsibility. This takes the form of subtle projections, particularly in the therapeutic setting (Giovacchini 1972).

When seen in a regressive crisis, dysphoric personality patients, unlike potentially healthy neurotics, are unable to easily establish a confident relationship with the therapist. Rather, magical expectations, the diminished capacity to distinguish between fantasy and reality, episodes of anger and suspicion, and fears of rejection dominate the therapeutic interaction for an extended period. Gradually, however, such patients are able to respond to good therapeutic management and, at least partially, to relinquish their unrealistic and magical expectations as well as their fears and suspicions, and to establish a workable therapeutic alliance (Zetzel 1971).

Although the therapeutic alliance is often difficult for the dysphoric personality, he is able to retain a relatively good level of functioning and adaptation to reality. The regression in these patients is more typically seen either as the result of progressive involvement in the therapeutic relationship and increasing susceptibility to regressive pulls, usually in analysis but also frequently enough in psychotherapy, or in particularly intense relationships with significant objects outside the therapy.

It is in these regressive states that intense affects are often unleashed, usually hostile and destructive or depressed (Gunderson and Singer 1975; Kernberg 1967). The destructive impulses may be turned against the self in forms of self-destructive cutting, self-mutilation, or impulsive suicidal gestures. Such regressive destructive manifestations reflect the organization at a primitive level of the themes of victimization and aggressive destructiveness, which reflect the inner organization of the victim-introject and the corresponding aggressor-introject (Meissner 1978b; Robbins 1976). Although Kernberg relates such self-destructive tendencies to the predominance of pregenital and oral aggression, these self-destructive tendencies can be manifested by or organized into pathological character traits which reflect a more or less self-destructive etiology (Kernberg 1971).

It has been customary in the descriptions of borderline pathology to refer to ego defects (Blum 1972; Maenchen 1968; Masterson 1972; Brody 1960) or to ego weakness (Kernberg 1967). Such defects are quite evident in regressive borderline states, but we wish to focus the question of ego functioning on a more specifically characterological level. On that level, the dysphoric personality is capable of maintaining a quite adequate functional capacity, but ego apparatuses remain vulnerable and reveal a characteristic instability (Rosenfeld and Sprince 1963). We would prefer to reserve the terminology of defect and weakness for the lower orders of borderline pathology.

The ego of the dysphoric personality reflects a certain passivity, which is manifested in more or less passive or masochistic behaviors, a sense of ego helplessness, and a difficulty maintaining a sense of control or capacity to achieve goals. Such individuals often anticipate defeat and may adopt a posture of passivity. This takes a minor and often quite subtle role in the patient's more characterological level of adjustment, and becomes a marked characteristic of borderline states in periods of regression. Thus, the primitive defenses (Rosenfeld and Sprince 1963; Kernberg 1967) are identifiable but cannot be said at this level of organization to be distinguishable from similar defenses in neurotic personalities or the higher-order character disorders. It is only in regressive crises that the full flowering of the primitive defenses, including splitting, primitive idealization, projection, denial, omnipotence, and devaluation, as they have been described, for example, by Kernberg (1967), are in evidence. In general, dysphoric personalities tend to function with fairly high-level neurotic or near-neurotic defenses during nonregressive periods. During regressive states, however, they tend to shift to the level of immature or narcissistic defenses (Meissner 1980b).

Anxiety tolerance is compromised in the dysphoric personality but not to the degree found in the psychotic character and even more extremely in the pseudoschizophrenic. In these, anxiety tends to be pitched at a level of severe separation anxiety or even a catastrophic or annihilation anxiety level. The issues for these entities, then, tend to be psychotic in proportion, and the anxiety is pitched at a life-and-death level. In the dysphoric personality, the issues tend to be generated more on the level of castration and separation anxiety. Such patients may express castration fears and castration motifs, but, particularly in a meaningfully productive and gradually regressive therapeutic context, the issues rapidly become those of loss of love and fear of loss of the object. The description of intense, traumatic, overwhelming fears of disintegration, annihilation, the panicky fear of merging or engulfment, and the fears of inner disintegration and loss of identity (Maenchen 1968; Rosenfeld and Sprince 1963; Frijling-Schreuder 1969) are more closely related to lower levels of borderline pathology or are found more explicitly in transient regressive borderline states, even in the dysphoric personality.

The object relations of dysphoric personalities require careful delineation. The dysphoric personality shares in the need-gratifying quality of object relationships in general. Object relationships also tend to reflect the influence of relatively intense narcissistic needs. However, in the therapeutic context, the more typical picture with the dysphoric personality is for these needs to emerge gradually as the therapeutic relationship develops and as the more regressive aspects of the relationship mature and emerge. The rapid, precipitous, and intensely ambivalent involvement with objects is not characteristic of the dysphoric personality, as it might be of the psychotic character or the pseudoschizophrenic.

In addition, object constancy is relatively well maintained but remains vulnerable (Rosenfeld and Sprince 1963; Frijling-Schreuder 1969; Kernberg 1970, 1971). Generally, as the intensity of the involvement with a given object increases, the dysphoric personality's capacity to tolerate and integrate aspects of increasingly intense ambivalent feelings becomes more and more tenuous. Thus, even at levels of characterological functioning, there is a certain instability in object relations, a diminished capacity for empathy (Kernberg 1970), or a peculiar quality of the experience of meaningful relationships in which the subject is considerably more responsive to the instinctually derived aspects of the object than to the more enduring and consistent character traits or ego qualities (Krohn 1974). The need-fear dilemma in such patients on the level of characterological functioning remains an unexplicit but subtly pervasive concern that runs as a constant counter-melody under the more predominant themes and day-to-day concerns; when there is a significant involvement with objects, the entire tenor of the relationship is pervaded by a subtle and often implicit, but also often relatively conscious and explicit, fear of abandonment.

These factors point to what we think is the predominant area of pathology in the borderline personality, and that is the pathogenic organization of introjects. We would not regard the primary defect in the dysphoric personality as a defect in the structure of the ego, as might be the case in lower-order borderline forms. Rather, the impediment is in the organization of constituents of the self. The identifiable pathogenic configurations of introjects in borderline personality include the victim-introject and the aggressor-introject, as well as the narcissistically determined and impregnated configurations of grandiosity and inferiority.

Primitive (Oral) Hysteric

The primitive hysteric often presents with more or less marked hysterical symptomatology, but the character organization tends to be somewhat more infantile. Prominent hysterical characteristics that are included in the description of the hysterical personality might also be included in a list of characteristics of the borderline personality, particularly emotional lability, strong suggestibility, easy disappointment, alternating idealization and devaluation of objects of dependence, compulsive needs for love and admiration, intense feelings of inadequacy, strong dependence on others, a need for approval for maintaining self-esteem, and a tendency to dramatize or act out feelings. The discriminable differences that distinguish the primitive hysteric from the hysterical personality are the level of pregenital (particularly oral) libidinal elements, the prominence of narcissistic elements in the personality organization, the lesser degree of cohesiveness in the self-organization, the greater degree of regressive potential, and the relatively less mature level of defensive organization.

Long-lasting or significant involvement with objects frequently shows a progressively more regressed, childlike, oral, demanding, and frustrated aggressive quality, which is not characteristic of the hysteric. The need to be loved, to be the center of attention and attraction, functions on a less specifically sexualized level, has a quality of greater helplessness and inappropriate demanding, and reflects more primitive narcissistic trends. The hysterical tendency to pseudohypersexuality in combination with sexual inhibition turns into a sexual provocativeness, which is often more crude and inappropriate, and reflects more orally determined exhibitionism and demandingness than in the sexualized hysterical approach. When this takes the form of promiscuity, it has a more drifting quality, with little stability of object relationships. There may also be a tendency to conscious sexual fantasies of a primitive polymorphous-perverse character in the infantile personality, which is generally missing in the more diffuse repression of the hysteric.

The primitive hysterical personality, then, shares in the basic borderline characteristics and has some that are distinguishing. The transient attachment and involvement with objects and the alternation between idealization and disparagement are reminiscent of the as-if personality, but the primitive hysteric maintains a better-integrated and more cohesive sense of self without the as-if characteristics that define the as-if personality. At a more primitive level of organization, the primitive hysteric can look like the dysphoric personality, but here again the dysphoric personality is distinguished by its inability to maintain a cohesive sense of self and the tendency to alternate between a variety of introjective configurations. The primitive hysteric, even at its lowest level of character organization, tends to articulate itself around the victim-introject, thus assuming some of the qualities of a depressive structure. Moreover, it must be remembered that the primitive hysteric retains the capacity to mobilize hysterical defenses and a hysterical style in the interest of defending against underlying conflict.

The Schizoid Continuum

The schizoid continuum is a rather loosely organized group of character pathologies which represent a variety of resolutions of the basic schizoid dilemma, a form of the need-fear dilemma in which the intense need for objects is countered by the fear of closeness or intimacy with the same objects. The schizoid defense counters this fear of involvement (which in its more severe manifestations becomes a fear of engulfment) by withdrawal or minimization of the need for objects. The schizoid continuum includes the schizoid personality, the as-if personality, the false-self organization, and finally the condition of identity-stasis.

Schizoid Personality

The schizoid dilemma and defense are seen most characteristically in the schizoid personality. The schizoid patient complains of feeling isolated, shut out, out of touch, strange, or he complains of life seeming futile and meaningless, empty, leading nowhere and accomplishing nothing. External relationships seem to be affectively empty and are characterized by an emotional withdrawal. Vital and effective mental activity has disappeared from sight into a hidden inner world, so that the patient's conscious self is emptied of vital feeling and capacity for action and seems to have become unreal. Glimpses of an intense activity in this inner world can be captured in fragments of dreams or fantasies, but the patient merely reports these as if he were a dispassionate and passive observer not involved in the inner drama and turmoil. The attitude to the outer world is one of noninvolvement and mere observation, without any feeling, attachment, or sense of participation.

Such an individual often lives by himself, characteristically has few or no friends, has few meaningful interactions in the community of his fellows, is withdrawn, is usually hypersensitive and shy, and is often eccentric. He is unable to express any feeling or to show any anger, and he responds to conflict with relative detachment. These patients may also show paranoid characteristics manifested in extreme sensitivity, suspiciousness, and guardedness. These patients often complain of depression and of a diminishing interest in things, events, and people around them, feeling that life is futile and meaningless, and often expressing suicidal ideation.

The schizoid personality is able to maintain a position of reasonably good functioning in the real world, even as he holds himself emotionally aloof. The defenses are so rigidly maintained that the character structure is quite stable, and disruptive states are relatively uncharacteristic of this entity (Pine 1974).

Patients having this condition are all preoccupied with the central problem, namely, that of the ever-present danger of the potential dissolution of nuclear structures. In these terms, the narcisstic vulnerability of the schizoid stands in marked contrast to that of the narcissistic character (Kohut 1971). The schizoid withdrawal results from intense narcissistic vulnerability and the fear that narcissistic injury will initiate an uncontrollable regression. The retreat from real objects, then, does not serve as a protection of what is vital in the self against unappreciative or threatening objects but occurs because of the danger inherent in the frustration of narcissistic needs. By contrast, the narcissistic character seeks out and is involved with objects as sources of needed and sought-for narcissistic sustenance.

The quality of emotional withdrawal, in any case, should not mislead us into a belief that the schizoid individual is uninvolved or unaffected by object relationships. Indeed, his contact with objects is intense, highly ambivalent, and subject to the torments of the schizoid dilemma we have described. His commerce with objects is intensely colored and distorted by projections which turn these objects into threatening, persecuting, engulfing objects. The basic organization of the schizoid self, then, is formed around an internal victim-introject which provides the core of the personality organization. It is the protection of this vulnerable and victimized core of his self-organization that the schizoid withdrawal is intended to effect. The basic defect of the schizoid character lies at an extremely early level of the introjection of primary objects. The schizoid condition is based on the internalization of hostile, destructive introjects. These internalized unconscious objects are locked away within the psyche, where they remain always rejecting, indifferent, or hostile. The result of this negative introject is that it becomes a focus for feelings of inner worthlessness, vileness, inner destructiveness, evil, and malicious power. We have already come to recognize these introjective configurations as the victim-introject and its correlative aggressor-introject (Meissner 1978b).

False-Self Organization

The false self is essentially a schizoid condition which is marked by a turning away from interpersonal relationships, motivated more by the need to preserve a sense of inner autonomy and individuation than by a specific anxiety from intimate contact with objects. The idea was originally introduced by Winnicott (1960a), who describes a split between the false self, that part of the personality which is related to and involved with the external environment and real objects, and the true self, which inhabits the inner core of the personality and is hidden away from the scrutiny of observers. The real self is the true self, and that part of the personality related to external objects or to the physical body is false.

The false self is erected to protect and preserve the true self and to guard it against losing its sense of subjectivity, vitality, and inner autonomy. Thus, the dilemma is essentially a schizoid dilemma in that the inner autonomy and authenticity of the true self is threatened by engulfment in its relationships to objects. The reality of these objects and the relatedness to them are impingements, similar to the infantile impingement of the "not-good-enough mother," which may threaten to overwhelm or obliterate the self.

The narcissistic vulnerability underlying the false-self organization relates to the persistence of an infantile grandiose ego-ideal or grandiose self. The false-self individual feels that his early caretakers and later significant objects do not appreciate or accept his grandiose attempts to preserve a sense of inner spontaneity and integrity, and he thus retreats to an inner world to preserve this sense of vitality and spontaneity. It is a retreat to a kind of grandiose self-sufficiency, which is characteristic of schizoid states (Modell 1975). The need to maintain this grandiose self-sufficiency is often what motivates these patients to seek treatment. The goal of the treatment for them is to be able to achieve and maintain such isolation and self-sufficiency without the stigmata of loss or abandonment.

The other important component of the false self which Winnicott delineates is the element of compliance. There is a compliant aspect to the true self in any healthy personality which derives from the infant's ability to comply without fear or the risk of exposure or vulnerability. Thus, the socialization of the child involves compliance and adaptability, but even here Winnicott notes the capacity to override this compliance at crucial points or periods, for example, adolescence. The compliance of the false self, however, forms a substitute way of relating to objects and dealing with the external environment which is fallacious, unreal, and fragile. The operations of the false self seem false, often empty, lacking in vitality or significance, and may be a source of inner desperation and hopelessness.

The false self may appear quite normal and adaptive. It may even provide the individual with at least a partial sense of "identity." The same tendency to counter identity diffusion through adherence to causes, groups, leaders, and the like, may also apply to the false-self organization. Nonetheless, trouble arises when authenticity and real object involvement are called for. When the false self cannot measure up to or sustain itself in the face of such pressures or demands, the outcome may be a severe regression into a borderline state. At its most pathological, the false-self organization may cover an underlying schizophrenic process, so that when the false self begins to fragment, the schizophrenia emerges, often in the form of acute disorganization and decompensation.

As-If Personality

Deutsch's (1942) original description of the "as-if" personality focused on the patient's impoverishment of emotional relationships. Such patients may be unaware of their lack of normal affective involvements and responses, in which case the disturbance may be perceived by others or may first be detected in treatment; or they may be keenly distressed by their emotional defect, which may be experienced as transitory and fleeting, or as recurring in specific situations, or which may persist as an enduring distressing symptom.

The patient's relationships are devoid of warmth, expressions of emotion are formal, the inner experience is excluded. Deutsch compares the situation to the performance of an actor who is well trained to play the role but who lacks the necessary spark to make his enactment of the role true to life. She takes pains to distinguish this inner emptiness from the coldness and distance of a more schizoid adjustment: in the latter there is a flight from reality or defense against forbidden instinctual drives, while the former seeks external reality in order to avoid anxiety-laden fantasies. The as-if personality involves loss of object cathexis rather than repression. The relationship to the world is maintained on a level of childlike imitation, which expresses an identification with the environment and results in ostensibly good adaptation to reality despite the absence of object cathexis. The results are passivity to the demands of the environment, and the highly plastic capacity to mold oneself and one's behavior to such external expectations. Attachment to objects can be adhesive, but there is a lack of real warmth and affection in the relationship that creates such emptiness and dullness that the partner often breaks off the relationship precipitously. When the as-if person is thus abandoned, he may display a spurious ("as if") affective reaction or a total absence of affective reaction. The object is soon replaced with a new one and the process repeated.

The as-if personality reflects a certain quality of borderline compliance, which in turn reflects the underlying dynamics of the victim-introject (Robbins 1976; Meissner 1976b, 1978b). It represents a resolution of the problems related to the victim-introject, as well as of the dilemmas of narcissistic peril and object-relations conflicts through the vehicle of transitory and superficial as-if involvements and their associated internalizations. The issues of compliance are shared with other borderline patients, particularly cases of identity stasis, schizoid personality, and false-self organization. The discrimination between these states lies in the manner in which these conflicts are dealt with— whether by diffusion of identity, by as-if imitative attachments, by schizoid withdrawal, or by the organization of the false self. The as-if personality resolves these underlying conflicts by a transient, often superficial, imitative, and idealizing attachment to an object. This attachment is paralleled by a modification of the self in terms of imitative and introjective mechanisms which, because of their defensive vicissitudes, lead to no further or more meaningful internalizations (Meissner 1974c). Thus, these patients do not present with a significant deficit in ego functioning as a general rule; rather, the pathology lies in the realm of the organization of the self, which achieves a transient cohesiveness through such as-if mechanisms. Deficits in structural organization not only of the ego but more particularly of the superego are thus secondary to this basic dynamic.

Identity Stasis

We are indebted to Erik Erikson for the notion of identity diffusion, which he describes as a problem that presents itself in borderline and adolescent patients, frequently as a life crisis (Erikson 1956). As Erikson envisions it, a state of acute identity diffusion arises when developmental experiences demand a commitment to physical intimacy, occupational choice, competition of various sorts; in general, to a specific form of psychosocial self-definition. The necessity of choice and commitment gives rise to conflicting identifications, each of which narrows the inventory of further choice; movement in any direction may establish binding precedents for psychosocial self-definition. The result is an avoidance of choice, a lack of inner definition of self, and an external avoidance, isolation, and alienation. The same difficulties in establishing an adult identity can be found in the more enduring form of personality disorder we are describing as identity stasis.

Engagement, whether in terms of friendship, competition, sex, or love, becomes a test of self-delineation. Engagement carries with it the constant threat of fusion and loss of identity. Confrontation with it may result in various forms of social isolation, stereotyped or formalized interpersonal relationships, or even the frantic seeking of intimacy with improbable or inappropriate partners. Such attachments, whether as friendships or affairs, become simply attempts to delineate identity by a form of mutual narcissistic mirroring. Such patients have a characteristic difficulty in committing themselves to any line of action or career choice. Particularly difficult is a commitment in the areas of work and love: they find themselves unwilling or unable to make a definitive choice of life partner, just as they find it extremely difficult to decide upon and commit themselves to any line of life endeavor such as a profession or career. At times these difficulties in self-definition and commitment are found in one area but not in others. The patient may have a well-defined worklife or career but be unable to make the defining commitment in an intimate love relationship.

These patients may resort to intense and devoted attachment to a set of ideas or ideology, a group, a cause, or even a leader—all of which, by implication, involve repudiation of other causes, groups, and leaders. Attachment to such causes or groups may take on some of the as-if characteristics or even evolve into a false-self configuration. The attachment to and repudiation of groups, leaders, causes, and ideologies may attain an almost paranoid flavor (Meissner 1978b). The failure of these devices, however, may lead such individuals to withdraw to a position of constant self-questioning and introspective uncertainty, a need for constant self-doubt and self-testing, which can result in an almost paralyzing borderline state in which there is an increasing sense of isolation, a loss of a sense of identity, a deep sense of inner uncertainty and shame, an inability to derive any sense of accomplishment from external activities, and a feeling that one is the victim of circumstances and forces beyond one's control, without any sense of initiative or responsibility for the direction of one's own fate.

There may be in fact a retreat to an identification with the victim-introject as a convenient escape from the uncertainties and emptiness of identity diffusion. Moreover, the narcissistic aspects of this configuration should not be missed. There are protests of potential greatness, missed opportunities, a need to cling omnipotently to a sense of the availability of all possibilities, and an unwillingness to sacrifice any possibilities or limit any potentialities in the inevitable determination and self-limitation of specific choice. There is a fear of engagement, a reluctance to compete or assert oneself as separate and individual, a fear of time and its passage, and a constant vacillating, doubt, and uncertainty, an unwillingness to choose that often looks obsessional but is in fact drive by motivations of a different order.

Identity stasis involves an impairment of meaningful identifications and an inability in self-definition. The pathology does not reside in the ego or even superego as much as in the organization and delineation of the self. There is a complex interplay with object-relations conflicts, related to the incapacity to define or commit oneself. On a primitive genetic level, however, the underlying fears have to do with the threat imposed in separation and individuation and the surrender of infantile objects and one's dependence on them. Ultimately, commitment to a life, whether of work or of love, means acceptance of limitations and change, the surrender of infantile omnipotence and narcissistic entitlement, and the ultimate acceptance of the finitude of human existence and death. Maintaining the self in a posture of persistent uncertainty, lack of definition, and lack of commitment, is to maintain a condition of continuing possibility and a denial of the necessity to ultimately come to terms with the demands and expectations of reality.

A Borderline Case: The Wolf Man

Pathology

The case of the Wolf Man holds a primary place in the history of psychoanalysis. In the present context it provides an opportunity to examine the dynamic and structural issues connected with borderline psychopathology and to explore some of the treatment issues from the perspective of the difficulties encountered by Freud and, later, Ruth Mack Brunswick. From the point of view of later theoretical and clinical developments, we can recognize that the Wolf Man's pathology falls within the borderline spectrum (Frosch 1967b; Blum 1974) and that the treatment problems recounted in Freud's and Brunswick's discussions are not unfamiliar in the therapy of borderline patients. In the diagnostic schema described earlier in the chapter, we would regard his pathology as possibly a form of dysphoric personality.

The Wolf Man had originally been in treatment with Freud from February 1910 until June 1914. He returned again for several months of treatment in 1919. However, when he again decompensated and returned to Freud for consultation in 1926, Freud referred him to Ruth Mack Brunswick, who conducted a brief second analysis lasting five months.

At the time of his treatment by Brunswick, the patient developed a delusional paranoid psychosis with hypochondriacal features (Brunswick 1928). These dimensions of the Wolf Man's pathology lend themselves quite readily to reanalysis from the perspective of the paranoid process (Meissner 1978b). Our immediate concern is with the organization of pathogenic introjections which formed the nucleus of the patient's self-system and the core of his pathology, and which found their ultimate expression in his paranoid delusional projective system. Correlative to and derived from this introjective configuration, we can delineate the patterning of projections around which the patient organized his interactions with the world, and then define the paranoid construction that provided an overall framework within which he could organize his projective system into a set of coherent and sustaining beliefs.

Freud's Case

Phobia

The first expression of the Wolf Man's psychopathology came in the animal phobia which appeared just before his fourth birthday. This phobia unveiled the infantile neurosis, in which libidinal paths were fixed in such a way as to influence the course of the adult neurosis. The onset of these phobic symptoms came in the context of feelings of abandonment and loss, together with the sadistic and tormenting onslaught he felt from his sister and his governess. The phobic symptoms were paralleled by the emergence of sadistic tendencies directed toward both animals and his Nanya. The picture of the threatening wolf shown him by his sister terrified him, but the phobia extended to other animals as well, including butterflies, beetles and caterpillars, and horses. When he saw horses being beaten, he would cry and scream; once he had to leave the circus for this reason. Yet at the same time, his own sadistic wishes were expressed in the enjoyment he felt in beating horses.

It can be easily seen, as Freud explains in great detail, that the childhood animal phobia was multiply determined. Some of the factors were the intensification of the Wolf Man's separation anxiety together with the narcissistic trauma it conveyed, the emergence of genital impulses and the threats of castration, and the regression to anal-sadistic levels of libidinal fixation. As Rochlin (1973) notes with regard to the Wolf Man's phobia:

> He enjoyed tormenting small insects. Or, at the circus, he vacillated between excited glee at witnessing the animals seemingly being beaten into obedience and then shrieking terror at the sight which suddenly became so intolerable to him that he had to be taken home. It is the ambivalence of this early identification with animals which is so potent—as children project onto other living creatures their divided sense of themselves as both attacker and victim of attack. (p. 74)

The important elements in this phobic alignment are the splitting of the aspects of the young Wolf Man's ambivalence and the consequent externalization of sadistic and destructive impulses into the phobic objects. Thus, he becomes the helpless and fearful victim of externally derived destructive and powerful forces represented by the threatening wolves of his dream. At the same time, he becomes himself the tormenter and aggressive destroyer. These parameters of the infantile neurosis point in the direction of significant internalizations that contribute to the organization of the child's inner world and the patterning of his pathology, and also set the terms of later pathological developments.

Obsessional Neurosis

The patient's anal-sadistic organization and its accompanying phobic symptoms were transformed in the child's fourth year into an infantile obsessional neurosis that lasted until he was about ten. The replacement of obsessional symptoms for the previous anxiety symptoms was initiated by the patient's mother, who determined to teach him about the stories of the Bible as a means of distracting him from his phobic concerns. He became very pious in his attitude and indulged in a variety of obsessional rituals of a religious nature. He would feel obliged to pray for a long time, making an endless series of signs of the cross before going to bed. He had to kiss all the holy pictures in the room, recite prayers, and so on. During this period the "naughtiness" did not altogether disappear, but gradually diminished.

The Wolf Man's obsessional neurosis did not remain limited to the childhood experience. The tendency to vacillation, to self-doubt and ambivalence remained characteristic of him for a long time. He recalls that, when he was about to begin lectures at the university, he was unable to make up his mind about what department he should enroll in. His obsessional doubts turned into tormented brooding that also seemed to feed his depression. Decisions reached with agonizing tentativeness were immediately overthrown with bitter self-reproach and remorse. He was often reduced to a state of paralyzing indecision and profound depression in which he was incapable of making any decisions or following through on any lines of activity whatever.

It was in this state of apathy, depression, and total paralysis of will that the patient came to Freud's attention. Freud notes the extension of these obsessional traits into his own analysis of the Wolf Man, particularly his propensity to ambivalence and the tenacity of fixation, along with the power of maintaining simultaneously quite obvious and contradictory libidinal cathexes. This produced a characteristic posture of constant ambivalence and vacillation, which formed a predominant characteristic of his work in the analysis.

Depression

In addition, the Wolf Man manifested a lifelong propensity toward depression. The severity of his depression had led at one time to his hospitalization and to a diagnosis of manic-depressive psychosis.* We know that at critical periods the Wolf Man was afflicted with severe depressions, particularly after his sister's suicide and again after his wife's suicide years later.

Hypochondriacal Paranoia

Another important part of the Wolf Man's pathology was his severe hypochondriacal preoccupation. After leaving Freud, the Wolf Man developed a series of hypochondriacal delusions having particularly to do with his nose and his teeth (Frosch 1967b). Brunswick (1928) describes in some detail the Wolf Man's preoccupations with his nose at the time of the beginning of his treatment with her. He had been treated for obstructed sebaceous glands by electrolysis and complained that the treatment had left his nose permanently damaged, leaving a gaping hole

---

*The Wolf Man's father had also carried a diagnosis of manic-depressive psychosis. In addition, the father's brother was probably paranoid schizophrenic. The data suggest a heavy genetic loading at the root of the Wolf Man's pathology. See the further discussion of these issues in the Wolf Man's case (Meissner 1977) and in borderline pathology more generally (Meissner 1984a).

and a scar. He was in a state of despair because he had been told that nothing could be done for his nose since nothing was wrong with it. The nose became the focus of a constant preoccupation in which he was continually looking at himself, examining his nose in a pocket mirror, powdering to conceal the defect, and then again repeating the process a few minutes later.

The Wolf Man was obsessed with the hole in his nose and felt, in a paranoid fashion, that everyone was staring at it. Brunswick described the patient's disorder as a form of hypochondriacal paranoia, noting in addition that the hypochondriacal idea served as a cloak for more persecutory fantasies. This hypochondriacal preoccupation again placed the Wolf Man in the position of being the vulnerable and castrated victim, in this instance of the castrative attack by Dr. X., the dermatologist who treated his pimples. Thus, the motif of vulnerability and victimization links up with the more aggressive components embedded in his persecutory ideas.

The reactivation of the Wolf Man's illness, which precipitated his return to Freud and the referral to Brunswick, had a decidedly paranoid cast. Freud himself noted the paranoid character of the unresolved transference (1937). When he came to Dr. Brunswick, the patient had formed a delusional hatred toward Professor X., who had treated his nose with electrolysis, leaving the delusional gaping hole. Brunswick points out that the patient's relationship with doctors had always been colored by distrust and that in a variety of situations he either abused his medications or found countering opinions from other doctors which would allow him to place his physician in a position of blame. This distrust also affected his relationship with Freud, whom the Wolf Man blamed for the loss of his fortune in Russia. Although the Wolf Man could on the one hand half admit that Professor X. was an obvious substitute for Freud, on the other he would deny any implication that Freud's advice could have been intentionally malicious. This tendency to place blame on others was a persistent characteristic of the Wolf Man, as it is generally of the paranoid.

Vulnerability

Although the motif of vulnerability appears early and its determinants can at least be suggested at an early infantile level, there are other indications in the Wolf Man's later career of the persistence of the issue. One such indication was the patient's rather neurotic attitudes about money. Mondy was of the utmost importance to him, and, by his admission, he ascribed power and influence to its possession. However, if the possession of money represented power to him, the threat of being without money represented a state of intolerable vulnerability. Frequently, and without reason, he accused his mother of trying to appropriate his father's inheritance. The loss of the family holdings in the Revolution was a particularly devastating blow.

The story of the passion of Christ allowed the patient to sublimate his masochistic attitude toward his father. He identified with Christ—an identification facilitated by the fact that he and Christ shared the same birthday. This not only satisfied his narcissistic wishes but also gave expression to his repressed homosexual attitudes and his fear that he himself could be used by his father like a woman—that is, like his mother in the primal scene. He could also become the victim of the sadistic and brutal beating (castration-crucifixion) of the father-god. Once again, the heir to the throne, the son of the father, was being beaten, particularly on the penis, in a position of sacrifice and suffering, the prototypical victim.

The twofold identification was manifested in his identification with the sadistic father (aggressor-introject) and with the victimized and castrated son (victim-introject). Edelheit (1974) has specifically analyzed the connection between such double identifications (introjections) manifested in crucifixion fantasies based on the primal-scene schema. In the Wolf Man, the religious obsessions served to sublimate the sado-masochistic sexual organization, and the wolf phobia vanished.

Narcissism

Freud notes the connection of the Wolf Man's castration anxiety and the underlying homosexual wishes to the narcissistic affront. The investment of his libido in the preservation of genital integrity was threatened by these basis anxieties. In the later development of his illness his conviction that he was the special child of Fortune was severely damaged by a gonorrheal infection, which was, more than a form of castration, a narcissistic insult. The motif of threatened narcissism repeated the pattern dictated in his original phobic anxiety. The fantasy of invulnerability and omnipotent grandiosity was shattered.

However, the narcissistic current obviously did not abate after his analysis with Freud. Brunswick (1928) draws attention to his preoccupation with his appearance in the exaggeration of the nasal symptoms but also mentions that the Wolf Man had undertaken to paint his own portrait, an exercise that required many hours of looking at himself in the mirror. The links between the mirror image and the processes of projection and introjection, the dynamics of narcissism through the prolongation of parental and narcissistic omnipotence, as well as the relation to voyeurism, exhibitionism, castration motifs, and the primal scene have been discussed by Shengold (1974).

Whatever the Wolf Man's residual difficulties as he advanced into his twilight years, it seems plain that his involvement with psychoanalysis had served him in important ways in the restitution and maintenance of his narcissistic integrity, and in gratifying the demands of his grandiose self (Kohut 1971). Various requests that he recall his experiences with Freud, and his recountings of his life story as "the most famous psychoanalytic case" obviously gave him a sense of purpose and meaning in his life. It was through this means that he was able to reassure himself: "I can now assure myself that not everything I have done has been in vain" (Gardiner 1971, p. 342). Moreover, Gardiner comments that the Wolf Man told her repeatedly that "writing gave a point and purpose to his life" (p. 343). He wrote to her that he was overjoyed about his first publication in a psychoanalytic journal, and that he "began to feel that his life now had a purpose" (p. 346). This aspect of the restitution of the Wolf Man's narcissism is of considerable significance, since it indicates a primary outcome of the paranoid process in the restitution of injured narcissism and the maintenance of self-cohesion (Meissner 1977, 1978b).

The Wolf Man and the Paranoid Process

Introjections

The critical introjections, around which early strata of the Wolf Man's personality formed, seemed to create a sense of weakness and vulnerability, susceptibility to injury and attack. These introjections, of course, derived primarily from relationships with the parental figures but also, in no insignificant measure, secondarily from his relationship with his depressed, self-denigrating, preschizophrenic, and suicidal sister.

One stratum of the introjective organization consisted of the correlative pairing of victim-introject and aggressor-introject. Both of these elements could be identified in the father's introjective organization but were undoubtedly complemented and made more complex by introjective components derived from the Wolf Man's mother. His sense of victimization and its correlative vulnerability took the form of hysterical bowel preoccupations and fears of anal attack, which undoubtedly reflected maternal introjective components. Both these introjective components were reflected in the primal-scene schema, either deriving from or generating the reciprocal elements, but nonetheless taking the form of this double "identification."

It was these introjective configurations, forming the core of his own emerging sense of self and the organization of his personality, that provided the underpinnings for the Wolf Man's marked depressive tendencies, as well as for his capacities for cruel and sadistic behavior. This patterning of the victim- and aggressor-introject can be identified clearly in the Wolf Man's early nightmare, in his phobic anxieties, and in his later paranoid illness. In the dream, the aggressive components were externalized in the figures of the wolves (the father substitutes), and the victim aspect was played out in himself. In the phobia, the castrating, aggressive and hostilely destructive components were externalized into various animals, whereas the sense of vulnerability, weakness, impotence, and terrorized helplessness was maintained internally. Finally, in the paranoid distortion of his later illness, the aggressive, hurtful, powerful, and destructive elements were again externalized in the form of projections which took the shape of specific persecutors—concretely, the doctors who were supposedly taking care of him but were felt to be conspiring to do him damage—whereas the sense of vulnerable victimization was again sustained as an internal referent.

Narcissistic Configuration

The dynamics of narcissism play a central role in the genesis of the paranoid process. Not only is the introjective configuration organized around and structured in narcissistic terms, but the correlative function of the projections operates equivalently as a narcissistic defense. Even more, the interplay of the introjection and projection in the developmental working through of narcissistic concerns is a central influence on the shaping and internal organization of the self. Thus, the introjective configuration forms the critical core of internalizations around which the self-system is organized and in terms of which the sense of self takes shape. Similarly, the interplay between introjective and projective aspects of this process provides the matrix within which the child's emerging differentiation between self and objects, self and others, takes place (Meissner 1978b).

These narcissistic components played themselves out in the Wolf Man's adult experience as well as in the course of his treatment. His relationships with the critical persons around him seem to have had the quality of transitional object involvements rather than that of more objective forms of relationship. His dependent relationship to these objects was based on his inherent need to stabilize his inner narcissistic equilibrium and give his otherwise fragmented self a sense of coherence. This was apparently the case with his wife, with whom he developed an extreme passivity and dependence. It was also the case in his idealizing relationship with Freud. It also seems apparent that his experience with Freud and psychoanalysis served as an important supportive context within which he was able to maintain the sense of narcissistic grandiosity that Brunswick recognized so well.

The narcissistic components of the introjective organization played themselves out in a typical narcissistic polarity. We can identify both aspects of this introjective organization in the Wolf Man: his inherent grandiosity, his sense of specialness (particularly in relation to Freud and the analytic movement), his sense of entitlement, and the feeling that he was a specially endowed and privileged child of destiny. The opposite component is also clearly reflected in his propensity to depression, often suicidal in proportion, his sense of worthlessness, and his chronically impoverished self-esteem.

Dysphoric Personality

The composite picture offered by these aspects of the Wolf Man's pathology reflects the particular vulnerability to the vicissitudes of object relations and the distorting influence of the interplay of projections and introjections that characterize the dysphoric personality. The introjective configuration casts its shadow on his interpersonal relations through projection. His object relationships thus undergo shifting patterns of variability that affect not only his personal relationships but the transference relationship as well. The overall pattern is marked by generally good maintenance of reality contact and the sense of reality but periodically punctuated by regressive episodes that bring him to treatment. The most severe such regressive state is the paranoid psychotic regression precipitated by the threatened loss of his idealized and sustaining relation to Freud.

Treatment Approach

Some of the difficulties in maintaining a psychoanalytic process can be gleaned from Freud's attempt with the Wolf Man. Not only was there great difficulty in sustaining the analytic process but the nature and intensity of transference distortions created particular problems in moving the analytic work forward and in stabilizing an effective and meaningful alliance. From the more developed perspective of a contemporary analytic assessment, the Wolf Man would have to be regarded as questionably analyzable, and would preferably be evaluated more extensively in a course of preanalytic psychotherapy before any commitment to the analytic process and its rigors was made.

Keeping in mind the diagnostic framework sketched on pages 121 to 136, and the inherent complexities and difficulties of the treatment of borderline patients, we outline here a treatment approach based on the paranoid process. Within the therapeutic process itself, the issues take shape with varying degrees of intensity at different levels of the borderline spectrum. We will discuss three major components of the treatment process, namely, the therapeutic alliance, the transference, and the countertransference.

Therapeutic Alliance

Difficulties

The therapeutic alliance remains a troubling difficulty in the psychotherapy of all borderline patients. Some authors (Adler 1979, 1985) have offered the opinion that the therapeutic alliance with borderline patients is either nonexistent or extremely fragile. For the most part, that assessment is based on the therapeutic difficulties with lower-order borderline patients, particularly the pseudoschizophrenics and psychotic characters, whose capacity for alliance is primitive and limited at best. This, however, is fortunately not the case with all patients in the borderline spectrum. But observation highlights the systematic bias in much of the literature on the therapy of borderline patients, derived both from the history of the concept and from more recent attempts to focus the borderline concept in terms of its more primitive forms or in terms of borderline regressive states (Meissner 1984a).

Given the structural impairment or the regressive potentiality that limit the patient's capacity for alliance, the therapy must be structured so as to maximize whatever capacity for alliance may exist. In the initial phases of the therapy of borderline patients, it is essential that the therapeutic framework be structured in such a way as to provide room for the patient's available ego strengths and capacities to contribute to a meaningful working situation within which the therapeutic effort can take place. For many borderline patients, particularly those who are not caught in the throes of a regressive state, this does not particularly present a problem. Such patients can involve themselves in the therapeutic situation and engage in the therapeutic relationship without any immediate or significant turmoil. The problems in setting the routine structure of the therapeutic framework for such patients are minimal. Arrangements regarding the therapeutic regimen, the time and place for therapeutic meetings, tardiness, missed sessions, payment of fees, and the negotiations regarding issues of confidentiality can often be matters of routine discussion.

For patients whose level of functioning is more primitive, the mere setting of the therapeutic framework can be a source of considerable difficulty. Not uncharacteristically, the more primitive borderline patients may engage the therapist from the onset of the therapy in a struggle to control, manipulate, and/or violate the therapeutic context. With some such patients, there is a powerful tendency to act out around the therapeutic arrangements or to find a variety of ways in which the therapeutic regimen can be violated. This may take the form of missing appointments, coming late, seeking extratherapeutic contacts with the therapist by way of telephone calls, seeking extra visits, or even arranging chance meetings with the therapist outside of the therapist's office. In order for the therapeutic work to progress and for the necessary basis to be laid for an emergent therapeutic alliance, the therapist owes it to the patient to move in the direction of gaining control over such acting-out tendencies and of gradually and firmly establishing a meaningful therapeutic situation. Telephone calls between therapeutic hours must be gradually diminished in frequency and duration and finally reduced simply to matters of essential communication or to occasions of real emergency. Other channels of extratherapeutic communication should be gradually minimized and ultimately eliminated. All of this is in the interest of establishing the therapeutic situation, which requires that the therapeutic effort be confined within the actual therapeutic sessions in the therapist's consulting room.

Opening Phase

There is a particular difficulty that arises in the opening phases of the treatment of lower-order patients. The therapist is caught between the need to establish the therapeutic context as described above and the demand on the part of the patient for a reassuring and secure holding environment. Adler (1985), for example, insists on the open availability of the therapist and the encouraging of telephone contacts and extra visits. From the point of view of the present approach, the dilemma requires clinical judgment as to how far and in what terms the therapist should go in balancing these needs. At some point, however, the need for providing reassuring availability and support must give way to the need for structuring the therapeutic context in appropriate ways. To the extent that the therapist senses the necessity for accommodation to the patient's needs, he must also keep in mind the further necessity for constructing the therapeutic frame.

Confidentiality

Obviously, confidentiality is an important aspect of the therapeutic work with any patient, but with many borderline patients the issue is particularly sensitive, especially when the patient has a tendency— common enough in borderline patients—toward paranoid reactions and defenses. The issue of confidentiality should be explicitly addressed with all patients, and considered and discussed in as much detail as seems advisable in terms of the patient's ability to address the issues and to gain some meaningful understanding of them. It may be necessary with some patients to take up in detail the specific arrangements for any forms of communication that may impinge on the therapeutic process. Arrangements for dealing with insurance companies, with employers, with family members, with telephone calls, all may be explicit areas of the patient's concern about confidentiality (Meissner 1979b).

It is also more often than not the case that such a discussion does not lay to rest the patient's anxieties about the confidentiality of his communications to the therapist. This is particularly the case when paranoid tendencies are in play. When actual occasions arise for contacts or communications with the outside world that may impinge on the patient's therapy, these issues may have to be addressed in detail once again. If a request comes from an insurance company, for example, for some information about the patient's treatment, it is immensely relieving and facilitating of the alliance for the therapist to take the time to go through the steps of response with the patient, including the writing of the letter, the patient's reading and approving or correcting it, and the patient's seeing and approving the final typed copy, sealing the envelope, and mailing it himself. The basic principle is that nothing should transpire between the therapeutic situation and the outside world without the patient's full knowledge, cooperation, and approval.

Alliance Distortion

Once the therapeutic context has been established, the therapist cannot take it for granted but must constantly monitor and tend it as the therapeutic process moves along. The tendency for borderline patients to create problems, misunderstandings, contexts for subtle or even more flagrant acting out, and misalliances is immense. The tending, fine-tuning, and correcting of the therapeutic alliance is an effort that persists continually through such patients' treatment and, particularly with lower-order borderline conditions, may provide the major focus and vehicle for the therapeutic work. The potentialities for distortions of the alliance in even the best-integrated and well-functioning of borderline patients must never be lost sight of. For example, with primitive hysterics the therapist must remain alert for subtle innuendos that would point to a subtle yet pervasive distortion of the alliance. Most frequently, of course, the alliance can readily be distorted in such patients by the permeation with transference components.

The burden of the treatment with borderline patients tends to fall within the alliance sector, particularly when dealing with lower-order borderline pathology or in the face of regressive states and crises. One of the major points of discrimination between the therapy of healthier, neurotic and/or narcissistic patients and borderline patients is the constant fragility and vulnerability to distortion displayed by the borderline alliance. That alliance can never be presumed or taken for granted but must be constantly focused in the therapeutic work as a pervasive area for therapeutic exploration and adjustment.

By the same token, the therapeutic alliance is neither univocal nor static in its form and implication. In any form of intensive and meaningful therapy, including psychoanalysis, the therapeutic alliance undergoes progressive modifications as the therapeutic process moves forward (Meissner 1981b). The same progression through phases of initial trust, leading to gradually increasing autonomy, initiative, et cetera, play themselves out in the psychotherapy of borderline patients. But in the case of the borderline patient they can often be cast as progressive issues of struggle and conflict requiring greater degrees of therapeutic exploration and work than are required for healthier patients. One reason for this is that the inner world of the borderline patient is so pervasively and intensively dominated by pathogenic introjects that there is little capacity for the development of relatively autonomous ego functions that are required for the stability and progressive growth of the therapeutic alliance.*

The typical pattern with such patients is that even when they attain a certain level of progress in the development of the alliance, it remains

---

*Adler (1985) refers in this context to the development of a "holding introject" as an essential element in the opening phase of the therapy.

vulnerable to regression and to the undermining by distorting influences, particularly from the side of the transference. Consequently, any ground that can be won in the alliance sector is hard-fought and can easily be lost in the face of regressive pressures. An important index of the progression of the therapy is the extent to which the patient has increasing facility to gain such footholds in the alliance and to regain them in the wake of regressive retreat. Again, as one moves from the lower orders of borderline pathology to the higher levels, these vulnerability factors become increasingly muted and subtle, reflecting both the greater capacity for autonomous functioning and the greater potentiality to develop autonomous functioning in the better-organized borderlines.

While the disruptions in lower-order borderlines are often dramatic and pathological, so that the therapist is much more likely to be in touch with them, the disruptions in higher-order patients can often be masked by a variety of forms of compliance or idealization, either of the therapist or the therapeutic process, that can mislead the therapist and lull him into a comfortable disregard for persistent distortions of the alliance.

Wolf Man's Therapeutic Alliance

In reassessing Freud's treatment of the Wolf Man, it seems clear that there were difficulties in the alliance from the beginning. When the Wolf Man came to see Freud, there seems little doubt that he came with the highest expectations. He had been through countless attempts at treatment of various kinds and had defeated the efforts of some of the most famous psychiatrists of Europe. Even the world-famous Kraepelin had had to confess failure.

The Wolf Man commented on his first meeting with Freud:

> Freud's appearance was such as to win my confidence immediately. . . . Freud's whole attitude and the way in which he listened to me, differentiated him strikingly from his famous colleagues whom I had hitherto known and in whom I had found such a lack of deeper psychological understanding. At my first meeting with Freud I had the feeling of encountering a great personality. (Gardiner 1971, p. 137)

The Wolf Man believed that he had finally met a psychiatrist whose genius was adequate to the task of completely understanding everything he had experienced. The transference seems to have been instantaneous and idealizing.

Almost immediately, the Wolf Man placed himself in the position of submissive compliance with and dependence on Freud; he thus assumed a position of submission to the father-substitute. Although the Wolf Man found the satisfying and idealized relationship with the good father of his yearning, the position of submissive compliance in which he placed himself carried inherent risks.

The relationship with Freud seemed to fill a void that was left by the recent death of the Wolf Man's father. As the Wolf Man saw it, he had now found himself a benevolent and understanding father to whom he was able to become a favorite son. This feeling that he was a favorite son to Freud remained even after his analysis and provided a focus of resistance in his later treatment. His craving for gifts from the good and loving father was reflected in his wish to have gifts from Freud, in his acceptance of financial support from Freud, and in his anticipation of an inheritance from Freud after his death. The yearly sums of money that Freud gave him seemed to reinforce the unconscious passivity which remained unresolved after his analysis. Freud, wittingly or not, provided a kernel of reality to support the Wolf Man's narcissistic illusion.

One of the important aspects of the analytic experience which Freud was careful to note was the Wolf Man's resistance to the analytic process. Freud commented that he seemed "unassailably entrenched behind an attitude of obliging apathy" (1918, p. 157). Much of Freud's effort was directed toward helping the patient take up a more independent role in the work of the analysis. When the Wolf Man began to experience some relief from his symptoms, he would immediately retreat from any effort in the analysis in order to avoid further change. The Wolf Man apparently successfully evaded Freud's efforts by taking refuge in his obsessional defenses, obscurities, intellectualizations, et cetera, and by avoiding any independence, self-sufficiency, or responsibility in the analytic work.

In the face of this resistance, Freud finally reached an impasse and decided upon his famous, and at that time revolutionary, maneuver. He decided that, in order to break through the patient's resistance and mobilize the work of the analysis, he would set a termination date. Under the pressure of this time limit, the Wolf Man's resistance gave way, and the work of the analysis could proceed. The possibility remains, however, from what we know of the later developments in the case, that the apparent breakthrough of the resistances and the subsequent flood of material may have represented another level of compliant submission of the Wolf Man to Freud's insistence. Freud may have unwittingly settled for compliant suggestibility rather than a meaningful therapeutic alliance.

Transference

Forms of Transference

The protean quality of transference manifestations in borderline patients is well known. In borderline patients on a higher level of psychic integration, the transference manifestations differ little in quality from those found in narcissistic or even ordinary neurotic patients. As such patients verge toward a regressive inclination or when they are in the throes of a regressive crisis, the transference manifestations can take on a qualitatively different coloration. A discrimination here can be made between transference by displacement, in which the transference manifestation rests on the displacement from an object representation reflecting an earlier developmental object relationship onto the therapist, and transference by projection in which the transference material is projected onto the analyst out of an introjective configuration of the patient's inner world.

The difference in these patterns of transference reaction is that the first deals only with the displacement of content from an object representation from an older context to a new object representation in the present therapeutic context. The projective transference material, however, implies that the projected content has been internalized by the patient in the form of a pathogenic introjective configuration and reflects some important dynamic and structural issues taking place within the patient's internal world itself. When borderline patients verge toward the more primitive level of borderline organization, whether regressively or characterologically, the influence of projective transference tends to take precedence over that of displacement transference. When these shifts take place, the transference coloration changes into the hues dictated by the underlying introjective configuration based on the pathogenic integration of narcissistic and aggressive components. The more primitive the regression, the more the aggressive components come to dominate the transference paradigm, particularly in the form of the aggressor- and victim-introjects.

Projections

The regressive emergence of such projective transference elements carries with it a number of implications. The projective distortion of the therapeutic relationship frequently takes on a paranoid quality that qualifies such patients in regressive phases as, for all practical purposes and for varying periods of duration, paranoid. The observations regarding the therapeutic approach to paranoid patients in Chapter 7 would become pertinent to the approach to these patients. By the same token, the regressive and paranoid trend may reflect some inner fragmentation of the patient's self-organization and an increasing permeability of ego boundaries, setting the stage for a transference psychosis. In the face of such regressions, the therapeutic outcome often depends on the inherent capacity of the patient to sustain or recapture an adequate footing in the alliance to allow for a buffering of the regressive process and its reversal to a more effective level of ego functioning. The therapist plays a critical role in maximizing or minimizing the effectiveness of such recuperative processes by his capacity to provide sufficient structure and limit setting, along with the reinforcing of the patient's available ego resources, to bring the therapeutic process back in line.

For patients who function at the lower-order borderline level, the elements of projective transference tend to predominate as a matter of course and create comparable difficulties in the therapeutic relationship. In terms of the aggressive vicissitudes, such patients often adopt a position of victimization, undergirded by the victim-introject, and correspondingly project the aggressive elements onto the therapist, so that he becomes the aggressor to their victim. This constitutes the frequently observed paranoid stance in lower-order borderlines or borderlines in regressive states. But frequently, in such lower-order patients, the position of the patient can shift rapidly from one introjective configuration to another, reflecting the underlying lability and instability of the organization of the patient's inner world. Such patients may often shift rapidly from a victim stance to one in which they become the aggressor, in a defensively motivated attempt to turn the tables and make the therapist the victim in their stead. This shift often takes the form of angry outbursts, hostile and hateful stances directed against the therapist, forms of acting out and resistance to any attempts at effective therapeutic intervention, all of which serve to frustrate the efforts of the therapist to do his job effectively. Behavior such as coming late for appointments, missing appointments, being dilatory or refusing to pay the fee, threatening to stop treatment, and even, at a high pitch of escalation, threatening suicide or self-mutilation, can play out this introjective reversal.

Pathological Narcissism

All borderline patients are caught up in the vicissitudes of pathological narcissism in varying degrees, usually of a more severe and incapacitating kind. As a general rule, the more primitively organized the patient's personality, the more primitive, archaic, and infantile are the narcissistic configurations. Parallel to the organization of aggressor- and victim-introjects, are the narcissistically superior and inferior introjective configurations around which borderline patients tend to shape the vicissitudes of their pathological narcissism. These give rise to patterns of idealization and devaluation, narcissistic omnipotence and impotence, severe difficulties in the maintenance and regulation of self-esteem, and often pervasive problems with a sense of shame, inferiority, and inadequacy. Again, particularly in the lower-order forms, the propensity for a rapidly shifting lability between these narcissistic configurations is often a marked aspect of the clinical picture.

Whatever the pathological alignment, it provides the basis for the projective transference reaction. If, in terms of the internal economy of the introjects, the patient shifts to one or the other pole of the introjective configuration, the opposite pole tends to be projected onto the analyst or therapist and to shape the transference experience. Some of the most central work of the therapeutic process has to do with the gradual identification of these patterns, and particularly with the identification of projected elements in the patient's own introjective configuration. Most patients will express the various aspects of the introjective alignment gradually as the treatment proceeds, and the alert therapist gradually acquires a familiarity with the patient's repertoire of ways in which these configurations are expressed in his interaction, both within and outside of the therapy. As these patterns are increasingly clarified, the therapy inevitably moves to more meaningful questions regarding their genesis and inherent motivation.

The Wolf Man's Transferences

The Wolf Man's transferences are interesting in this regard. Insofar as the transference to Freud was based on the patient's passive and complaint relationship with his father, we might also expect from what we have seen that it was not without ambivalence. The clear evidence for this comes not directly from Freud's account so much as from the reconstructions provided by Brunswick (1928). We have already discussed the patient's delusional hatred for Professor X., who had treated his nose. The Wolf Man was readily able to admit that Professor X., who had been Freud's friend and to whom Freud had referred the Wolf Man, was about the same age as Freud and obviously a substitute for him. But, at the same time, he staunchly denied any antipathy to Freud. He gave the lie to this in his delusional thoughts that X. had mutilated him, that the only just recompense would be to kill him, or at least to expose him by bringing litigation for the purpose of obtaining financial recompense for his mutilation. Just as he held Professor X. responsible for his physical condition, he held Freud responsible for his present mental condition. Brunswick recalls that he had also held his father accountable for his mother's illness. It is perhaps in terms of his fantasy of making Freud responsible for his illness that he felt justified in accepting recompense from Freud later on.

In fact, the ambivalence to Freud extended even further and embraced the paranoid core of the patient's illness. Brunswick (1928) was able to uncover this core so that the full impact of the persecutory content became apparent. X. had intentionally disfigured him; and now that he was dead, no means of retribution remained. All his doctors had treated him badly, and since he was again mentally ill, Freud too had treated him poorly. The whole medical profession was against him and had abused and mistreated him from his youth. He compared his situation to the sufferings of Christ, whom a cruel father-god had permitted to be tormented and crucified (p. 290). In the course of his psychotic raving he even threatened to shoot both Freud and Brunswick. At least he could retaliate against them and kill them, even though he could no longer kill X. Nor, we might add, could he kill his father.

The narcissistic elements seem to shine through the Wolf Man's own accounts of his analysis with Freud. He regards himself "less as a patient than as a co-worker, a younger comrade of an experienced explorer setting out to study a new, recently discovered land" (Gardiner 1971, p. 140). He comments on Freud's recognition of his excellent understanding of psychoanalysis and of his "unimpeachable intelligence." Seeing a picture of the Egyptian statute he had given Freud at the end of his analysis, he is reminded that Freud called him a "a piece of psychoanalysis." He carried these ideas of having a special and intimate relationship with Freud, more friendly and personal than professional, into his second analysis. His narcissism was fed by the yearly gifts of money he received from Freud and generated his expectation that he would receive an inheritance after Freud's death. Thus, the possibility exists that Freud's treatment of the Wolf Man foundered on a rather powerful narcissistic transference in which the patient's grandiosity was left essentially unanalyzed and unresolved.

Countertransference

Transference/Countertransference Interaction

The therapeutic interaction with most patients in the borderline spectrum tends to take the form of a transference-countertransference interaction, which can take place on varying levels of intensity and awareness (Meissner 1982–1983). As a general rule, whatever aspect of the introjective configuration the patient may be projecting, there is an inherent pull to draw the therapist into responding and behaving in a fashion to support and reinforce the projection. Part of the counter-transference mechanism is the unavoidable and inherent human tendency for the therapist, in the context of such projective induction, to internalize in some part the patient's projection so that it becomes, at least transiently and peripherally, part of the therapist's own introjective alignment. In the subsequent interaction with the patient, there is a subtle, and sometimes not so subtle, tendency to take a position that fulfills the expectations of the patient's projection. In addition, there is a counterprojective element that enters the picture, such that the therapist begins to view the patient and to deal with him in terms dictated by the previous projective-introjective interaction.

An example may clarify this process. We were recently supervising the work of an advanced resident with a patient possessing a rather high-level borderline personality, probably a primitive hysteric. The patient, for some time, had been utilizing the therapy to present her tale of woe, piteously presenting herself in a variety of contexts in her life as taken advantage of, as suffering from the slings and arrows of outrageous fortune inflicted on her by all kinds of people in her environment. The therapist's reaction was to feel sorry for the patient, to pity her, to see her as an unfortunate victim of unfeeling, uncaring, and exploitative individuals around her, and to inject this feeling into the interaction with the patient by comments like, "Oh! you poor thing!" or, "What a terrible thing to have happened to you!" The therapist thought that she was being understanding and empathic, but the tone of the communications to the patient was pitying, condescending, and to a certain degree infantilizing. What was missing were the real elements of understanding and empathy, which would have allowed the therapist to deal more productively and effectively with the patient's posture rather than to reinforce the patient's victim position both by supporting her sense of victimization and by generating an attitude of pitying condescension within the therapy itself.

Lower-order Transference/Countertransference

While such interactions can remain somewhat subtle in dealings with higher-order borderline personalities, in lower-order borderlines the interaction tends to be much more on an explicit and affectively intensive level (Meissner 1982-1983a). The therapist may find himself feeling frustrated, angry, resentful, helpless, and impotent in the fact of the patient's adopting the posture dictated by the aggressor-introject. Conversely, when the patient is in the victim position, the therapist may find himself feeling urged to intervene, to control the patient's life, to move excessively or precipitously in the direction of setting limits, to take over areas of responsibility from the patient, et cetera. Thus, the therapist can be drawn into adopting the position of the aggressor to match the patient's victimization and its inherent pull.

Similar vicissitudes evolve around the narcissistic configurations, so that the therapist may find himself feeling and acting in omnipotent fashion, feeling at times that he has special therapeutic skills or resources, or that he is the only one who can deal effectively with this particular patient. Conversely, he may find himself feeling inadequate, worthless, and inferior in the face of the patient's resistance or lack of therapeutic progress. With more primitive patients, these counter-transference experiences often have an intensely affectively toned quality, in which the therapist finds himself reacting with strong emotions to what is happening in the therapeutic relationship. Such affects are a strong signal to the therapist that he is caught in a transference/countertransference interaction and that he needs to take steps to remedy this situation.

Thus, the therapeutic work with borderline patients concerns itself in intense, unremitting, and central ways with the countertransference vicissitudes within the therapeutic relationship. The therapist must constantly monitor and adjust his own countertransference reactions so as to avoid the pitfalls that are constantly being laid at his feet by the transference dynamics coming from the patient. Inevitably, these interactions are pathological, express the pathogenic aspects of the patient's introjective configuration, and are quite effective in under-mining the alliance and frustrating the work of the therapy.

Countertransference in the Wolf Man's Case

It is important to consider the countertransference elements that may have played into the Wolf Man's analysis. We know that Freud conducted the second segment of analysis in 1919 without charging the Wolf Man and that he undertook to provide the Wolf Man with sums of money for his support. We also know that, at the end of the first analysis in 1914, Freud had arranged for the Wolf Man to give him a gift of a female Egyptian figure. Freud's rationale was that such a gift would lessen the patient's feeling of gratitude and dependence on the analyst.

Doubtless, Freud regarded the Wolf Man as a special and favored case in which he took an unusual interest. Offekrantz and Tobin (1973) point out that the special status of the Wolf Man as an object of Freud's research interests may have created problems in the establishing and maintaining of an effective therapeutic alliance. Freud himself noted that his interest in the case was related to the pressure he felt to respond to the attacks of Jung and Adler. He felt that the case provided a decisive refutation to any denial of infantile sexuality. Moreover, the special relevance of the case focused on the dream of the wolves, which was related quite early in the course of the treatment.

In his excellent review of the Gardiner book, Kanzer (1972) adds some significant insights. He notes that Freud, as early as 1912, appealed to his colleagues for reports of similar dreams which might reflect early sexual experiences and their consequences. Moreover, the case holds a pivotal position in psychoanalysis as a critical reference point for hypotheses about the primal scene, primal fantasies, et cetera. Kanzer argues further that the entire analysis with Freud was influenced by a tacit triangle that was created by Freud's acquiescence in the Wolf Man's proposed but postponed marriage with the sister-substitute Theresa. Kanzer further argues that Freud's special interest in the Wolf Man was prompted by his own need to work out primal-scene residues and particularly to repress aggression against his own father. The Wolf Man played a substitute part for Freud himself in the pursuit of forbidden areas of his own self-analysis. It is also noteworthy in this context that Freud backed away from analysis of the Wolf Man's negative transference elements.

The upshot of these factors was that the Wolf Man left his first analysis with Freud with a considerable residue of unresolved trans-ference elements. When he returned to Freud in 1919, despite his optimistic outlook and relative emotional stability Freud recognized the residue of unanalyzed material and advised a brief period of analysis to deal with this. Freud later remarked that these were specifically unresolved transference issues (1918). Even the later attacks that necessitated a further analysis and the referral to Brunswick had to do with residual portions of the transference. Freud (1937) commented as follows:

Some of these attacks were still concerned with residual portions of the transference; and, where this was so, short-lived though they were, they showed a distinctly paranoid character. In other attacks, however, the pathogenic material consisted of pieces of the patient's childhood history, which had not come to light while I was analysing him and which now came away—the comparison is unavoidable—like sutures after an operation, or small fragments of necrotic bone. I have found the history of this patient's recovery scarcely less interesting than that of his illness. (p. 218)

The Second Analysis

Paranoia

Other unresolved transference components were reflected in the subsequent analysis by Brunswick. She recorded the patient's illusion that she was in constant communication with Freud about his case; when she told him that she had not talked to Freud since the referral was made, the patient was shocked and outraged—incapable of believing that Freud could show so little interest in his famous case. As Blum (1974) notes, the Wolf Man's paranoia was not manifested in the original transference to Freud but, rather, was expressed as a post-termination regressive decompensation triggered by Freud's illness. He argues that this suggests the borderline nature of the Wolf Man's pathology and the typical inability of borderline patients to terminate therapy. Rather, they require continuing contact with and support from the therapist to maintain ego integration. Thus, Freud may have served as an idealized parental object in the Wolf Man's narcissistic transference (Gedo and Goldberg 1973). The threatened loss of that object created a severe narcissistic disruption and disequilibrium which had to be redressed. The Wolf Man's continued attempts to idealize Freud, his inability to acknowledge or resolve his negative transference feelings toward Freud, and his maintenance of a special and favored position in relation to psychoanalysis (and therefore Freud) served important functions in the narcissistic integrity and the maintenance of his sense of self-esteem and self-cohesion.

Analytic Difficulties

The analysis with Ruth Mack Brunswick took place from October 1926 until February 1927. The Wolf Man was referred to Brunswick by Freud, with the stipulation that his reanalysis would be conducted without a fee. Thus, the same elements that made him a special case, an object of special interest and investment, continued to play themselves out in his experience with his new analyst.

He approached the analysis with considerable resistance. Brunswick (1928) made the following observations:

In the analysis his attitude was one of hypocrisy. He refused to discuss his nose or his dealings with dermatologists. Any mention of Freud was passed over with an odd, indulgent little laugh. He talked at great length about the marvels of analysis as a science, the accuracy of my technique, which he professed to be able to judge at once, his feeling of safety at being in my hands, my kindness in treating him without payment, and other kindred topics. . . . When it finally came to dealing with the subject of the nose itself, I became acquainted with the patient's firmness in all its ramifications. (p. 280)

Brunswick likewise noted his hostility, manifested first in a dream in which she appeared as a gypsy woman to whom no one listened since gypsies are essentially liars, and later in his frank paranoid expressions of murderous wishes toward both Freud and herself.

We can certainly read in these expressions the Wolf Man's embattled and staunchly entrenched narcissism. We have already noted the narcissistic stress to which the Wolf Man was subjected by the threatened loss of his idealized object (Gedo and Goldberg 1973). He may well have taken his referral to Brunswick as a rejection on Freud's part, a further loss of the idealized object, and an abandonment to a poor substitute, much like the abandonment he had suffered as a child at the hands of his parents. Unable to express his narcissistic rage and unable to tolerate the threat to his vulnerability posed by this loss and abandonment, he apparently tried to restore the loss by making Brunswick an extension of Freud. We hear little, however, of what it must have meant for him to be abandoned and left in the hands of a woman. Who did Brunswick come to represent—the patient's mother? his sister? his old Nanya? the sadistic governess? or all of these?

Brunswick decided to take the course of attacking the Wolf Man's narcissistic defenses and grandiose illusions, tearing down the fantasy by confronting him with the reality of his relationship to Freud. This tactic had a dramatic effect. The attack was followed by several dreams. In the first, a woman appears wearing trousers and high boots and driving a sleigh in a masterful fashion. In the next dream, the Wolf Man is in front of the house of Professor X., who is analyzing him, and an old gypsy woman is there hawking papers and chattering at random to herself. Brunswick took the dream to mean that the Wolf Man regretted his choice of analysts and wished to be back with Freud.

This led to a further confrontation, in which he expressed disappointment that she was not in continuing contact with Freud about his case. In a subsequent dream, the patient pictured his mother taking holy pictures from the wall and smashing them on the floor. Brunswick interpreted this in terms of the patient's mother who took on the role of destroying the patient's religious beliefs and particularly his Christ fantasy. The mother-dream was followed the subsequent day by a reworking of the original wolf-dream in which the patient was looking at a benign and lovely landscape. The branches of the tree where the terrifying wolves had been were now empty and entwined in a beautiful pattern. Offenkrantz and Tobin (1973) reinterpret this material to mean that the breaking of the pictures by the analyst-mother was followed by a disappearance of the wolves in the manifest dream, thus suggesting the magical belief that Brunswick was powerful enough in her own right, and not as an extension or agent of Freud, to rid him of his unresolved transference entanglements. She thus became a new object for a narcissistic transference.

Narcissistic Transference

But the quality of this transference involvement seems to have differed from that of his involvement with Freud. Freud had served as an idealized object in an idealizing narcissistic transference. Moreover, the Wolf Man's preoccupations with the mirror may have represented a regression to magical mirror self-object ties and set the stage for the development of a narcissistic mirror transference to Brunswick (Blum 1974). In this sense, his rapid recovery in the few months of this reanalysis may reflect the formation of a narcissistic object relationship with fantasies of protective narcissistic omnipotence and a retreat to a narcissistic transference cure. We have already noted the emergence of a powerful feminine psychotic identification in the Wolf Man's paranoid regression. Thus, in both the pathological identification and the narcissistic transference, he was on the verge of merging with the maternal object. The use of the mirror, then, may have served to buffer him against this reengulfment by the maternal object and diffusion of self-object boundaries. The displaced castration anxiety served both as a screen for and a manifestation of the underlying anxiety of disintegration and engulfment.

Assessment

In the light of these formulations it becomes apparent from Freud's account of his therapy with the Wolf Man that Freud was struggling with what we can now recognize as a narcissistic transference. In retrospect, it seems that the analytic process was feeding the patient's infantile grandiosity while his facade of lethargic apathy and ambivalent compliance kept Freud at arm's distance. The rigidity of these defenses, the unyielding resistance to Freud's attempts to deal with them, and Freud's sense of frustration and impotence in the face of these narcissistically embedded defenses shine through the material quite clearly.

Freud finally reached the desperate point of resorting to the extreme measure of arbitrarily setting a date for the termination of therapy. The Wolf Man's response to this maneuver is in some sense surprising, since his apparently unyielding and distancing defenses seemed to crumble and be swept away in a remarkable therapeutic turnabout. Freud saw this as a therapeutic breakthrough which unearthed many of the memories of the infantile neurosis. In retrospect, however, the possibility presents itself that Freud's technical intervention equivalently threatened the Wolf Man with the deprivation of the idealized object that had become essential to the maintenance of his narcissistic equilibrium. In response, the Wolf Man merely dropped back to a second line of defense—namely, to the presentation of a compliant and analytically productive false self that served to satisfy Freud, yet left the inner realm of introjective grandiosity untouched. The Wolf Man gave Freud what he was looking for, and in return he received the benign accolades and approval from Freud that a part of him, even behind the rigidly defensive facade, had continually yearned for. This false-self maneuver thus settled several critical dilemmas and satisfied narcissism at both ends of the analytic couch.

Misalliance

It seems that Freud was never able to successfully establish an effective alliance with the Wolf Man. The alliance was from the very start a narcissistic alliance. That is to say, the unexpressed yet operative assumption, unconsciously maintained in the mind of the Wolf Man, was that the psychoanalysis with the genius-wizard Freud would somehow enable the Wolf Man to preserve his sense of being a special child of destiny, to reconstitute and redress his fragile narcissistic equilibrium, and to preserve the rudiments of the grandiose self. That narcissistic disequilibrium was effectively responded to by Freud's satisfying the Wolf Man's inherent need for idealized objects. Freud spontaneously stepped into the role of such an idealized and powerful object by his manner of approaching the patient and the way he assumed the power of deciding on the Wolf Man's visits to his mistress (Gedo and Goldberg 1973). The narcissistic need for sustaining the inner integrity of the grandiose self was answered subsequent to the analysis with Freud by his becoming Freud's special and famous patient. Thus, any attempt on the part of his analyst to gain a foothold on the plane of alliance was frustrated by the overwhelming dimensions and the power of the Wolf Man's rather primitive and archaic narcissistic transference.

A central question in dealing with such cases would focus on the patient's capacity for therapeutic alliance. If the transformation from a narcissistic alliance to a more effective therapeutic alliance can be accomplished, then there is hope for the patient's analyzability. This crucial discrimination distinguishes the analyzable narcissistic personality disorders from more primitive and archaic narcissistic formations that cannot be touched by the analytic process. In other words, the forms of idealizing and mirror transference described by Kohut (1971) are analyzable to the extent that the self-cohesiveness and autonomy of psychic structure are sufficient to allow for the establishing and maintenance of a therapeutic alliance. The combination of narcissistic transference with unmodifiable narcissistic alliance vitiates the possibility of effective analysis.

Chapter Five

Narcissistic Disorders and
the Paranoid Process

The working definition of narcissism we will utilize follows the lines suggested by Hartmann's (1950) clarification of narcissism as a libidinal investment in the self. Hartmann's usage has often been perverted to imply that whatever is involved in the organization or functioning of the self is to be regarded as narcissistic, an approach elaborated on in the work of Kohut (1971, 1977; Meissner 1981c). Nonetheless, whatever is included in the organization of the self may become the object of a narcissistic investment. Joffe and Sandler (1967) conclude their sorting out of the conceptual difficulties regarding narcissism by observing that the narcissistic disorders involve enduring affective value cathexes attached to object and self-representations. The self-representation can be the object of an enduring affective value-cathexis of love or hate. Like objects, the self may be ambivalently loved and hated, along with the extensions of self in the individual's life experience. In the present consideration, narcissism is not regarded simply in terms of its cathexis of self-representations, as is the common psychoanalytic usage (following Hartmann, Jacobson, Sandler et al.). The self here is proposed and regarded in structural terms, particularly insofar as the structural component is required to complement and complete a representational understanding. In other words, the self-representation cannot stand alone but must be a representation of something that precedes it in the substantial realm. Consequently, when we speak of the narcissistic introjects in the following discussion, these do not refer simply to representational phenomena but are intended to connote structural formations within the subject's internal world.

We will first discuss the pathology of narcissism, then take up some of the diagnostic issues, and complete our consideration with some comments on the treatment process.

Pathological Narcissism

Pathology

The manifestations of pathological narcissism are protean. They include infantile and neurotic wishes to remain the protected and defective child; the hidden conviction that one is a special and privileged person to whom love and consideration should be paid regardless of the cost to others; grandiose delusions that one could be a powerful and invincible godlike figure; embattled and hostile confrontations with the world in which one sees oneself as constantly watched and believes that countless people are taken up with the important project of working some evil effect on one; and the continual rage at parents for not having given one what one always expected and continues to expect from them.

In each of these cases there is a substratum of pathological narcissism. Often, the narcissistic core is well concealed and well guarded. It takes long periods of intense therapeutic effort to penetrate the layers of defense to the narcissism which lies at the heart of them and for the protection of which all the rest is stoutly maintained. This narcissistic core is expressed in a basic conviction that life should not have been as it was or is, that the world should treat these patients with greater consideration and kindness, that their parents and family should be held accountable for what they were deprived of. These patients are all victims of the inexhaustible tyranny of narcissism, with its unending and uncompromising demands. Theirs is a narcissism that has been traumatized and brutalized, deprived and dishonored. The pathology is an elaborate attempt to redress and redeem this sense of loss and deprivation.

Self-esteem

We should not allow ourselves to be deceived into thinking that narcissism is limited to such pathological manifestations. Rather, narcissism is a fundamental human concern from the cradle to the grave. From earliest childhood to the last gasp of dying breath, human beings are caught up in the preservation of a sense of self-esteem which remains highly vulnerable and fragile. Whatever threatens our status in life, whatever throws into question our accomplishments and attainments, whatever defeats us or limits us, or prevents us from attaining the object of our desires, all these and more are forthright assaults on our narcissism. They bring our self-esteem into question and make us feel vulnerable and defeated and humiliated. We must struggle to find ways to sustain a threatened sense of selfhood within us and to preserve in whatever way possible the diminished sense of self-esteem which accompanies such attacks (Rochlin 1973).

From birth the child is dependent on his relationship with significant others for the building and maintaining of his sense of self. The child's ontological security rests on a fundamental commitment to others, along with a basically sensed and realized commitment of others to him. Whatever the subsequent developmental history of such relationships, we nonetheless cling to them as to a taproot of our existence. As Rochlin (1973) has commented:

> To lose them would mean to give up our demands for imperishable relationships, and to acknowledge the transience of all things and therefore of ourselves. It would signify, too, a willingness to forego denials of vulnerability and thereby relinquish our religious beliefs, renounce our expectation of altering reality, and thus in consequence abandon wishes for fulfillment. (p. 3)

The force that opposes any such relinquishment is narcissism. Any separation from the things or the objects which we value is poorly tolerated. One way in which the child clings defensively to his objects is through the process of introjection. The loss of the loved object inflicts a deprivation upon our narcissism that places self-esteem in jeopardy. Patients with personality disorders are highly susceptible to the fear of loss of objects and of love, or of the symbolic losses of castration anxiety. But in the narcissistic disorders, the fear of the loss of the object takes first place (Kohut 1971). A narcissistic investment of self in objects sets the stage for the susceptibility to loss. The result is a narcissistic disequilibrium which disrupts the sense of self-cohesiveness and self-esteem which has come to depend on the presence, the approval, or other narcissistic gratifications derived from the object. The diminution of self-esteem is a major parameter and signpost of narcissistic injury.

Development

According to Kohut's (1971) schema, the disturbance of the original narcissistic equilibrium, produced by the unavoidable defects in maternal care, leads to replacement of the original narcissism with a grandiose and exhibitionistic self-image (the grandiose self), or alternatively, to attributing the narcissistic perfection to an omnipotent object, the idealized parent imago. These antithetical narcissistic configurations serve to preserve a part of the original experience of narcissistic perfection. Optimally, the exhibitionism and grandiosity of the grandiose self can be gradually integrated into a more mature personality structure, thus coming to supply the narcissistic basis for an emerging sense of healthy self-esteem. The idealized parent imago can be similarly integrated by way of introjection as the ego-ideal or the idealized aspect of the superego. Under the burden of narcissistic disappointment, however, the archaic narcissistic self retains its grandiosity, and the idealized imago remains an unassimilated introject which is required for narcissistic homeostasis. These relatively stable configurations can become highly cathected with narcissistic libido and can thus contribute to a degree of cathectic constancy toward particular objects. Such stable configurations, when attached to the analyst, can become the basis for narcissistic transference.

One of the most significant disappointments that a child suffers comes with the termination of the oedipal period. His expectations come to naught, and the experience of failure of his oedipal wishes serves as a template for subsequent losses and disappointments. The depression which follows subsequent losses in life reflects unconsciously back to the loss suffered in failure of oedipal ambitions. As Rochlin (1973) points out, there is no reason to suppose that when such longings or wishes are thwarted, the result is ever resignation or abandonment of these wishes. The disappointment of the oedipal situation is accompanied by a serious loss of self-esteem. This condition provides the stimulus for the recovery of lost narcissism. The child is thrust into a latency period of development, in which the heroes of myths and fairy tales serve as a means of retrieving some sense of power and high-minded worthiness. Similarly, the child's immersing himself in the rigors of learning and attainments, both mental and physical, serves to channel his energies toward the restitution of the narcissistic injury he has suffered.

Not the least of the narcissistic assaults to which all men must submit is the threat of death. The struggle between the acceptance of the fact of death and the wish to repudiate and overcome it is lifelong. Facing the inevitability of death leaves us with a sense of helplessness and ultimate vulnerability. Primitive man turned to magic; contemporary man turns to religious beliefs, which find their most profound motivation in restitutive attempts to overcome this fundamental narcissistic assault. Man can also turn to less realistic and more pathological forms of restitution as well—particularly fantasies of omnipotence and invulnerability.

Primary Narcissism

Freud originally postulated a state of primary narcissism which is gradually altered as, in the course of development, the infant becomes aware of and attached to significant figures around him. This dependent and infantile attachment is never completely satisfying and is always discolored by human limitations. The greater the dissatisfaction and the less the infant's demands are met, the more he will cling to his original narcissism and its attendant egocentricity. Further failures in the form of losses or disappointments serve to further injure his sense of self. Such narcissistic defects only serve to turn the infant back toward his self-contained primary egocentricity. Such deprivations are narcissistic injuries, and in the early years of childhood, when the sense of self-esteem is delicately forming, such deprivations are experienced as a loss of self-esteem. Rochlin (1973) writes:

> The paradox is that the indulged child tolerates any deprivation poorly and is affected by it even more severely than one who has been less generously cared for. The more narcissism is indiscriminately satisfied, the less strain it bears. As the egocentric character of early childhood is extended through excessive gratification, it shows as an unconscious resistance to change with less and less effort to accommodation to others. (p. 50)

It is this disturbance in the equilibrium of primary narcissism produced by the shortcomings of maternal care, and its associated disappointments and deprivations, that leads the child to establish the exhibitionistic grandiose self or to attribute the previous perfection to an omnipotent self-object, the idealized parent imago (Kohut 1971). From the earliest moment of infantile existence throughout the rest of life, our unfulfilled needs and wishes compel us to relieve the sense of deprivation. The experience of deprivation, moreover, is intimately linked with the diminishing of self-esteem. The child's reach inevitably exceeds his grasp. His feeble efforts to enforce his will and the frustration in not getting what he wants leave him both unsatisfied and threatened.

These are significant blows to the developing child's sense of self-esteem. It is only when the child begins to attach itself to another person, and to invest that other with interests and importance, that the primary state of narcissism begins to erode. Should this process fail or meet with obstacles, narcissism suffers. Frustrated narcissism responds not with resignation but with an intensification and obstinate clinging to its infantile and self-centered demands. The more frustrated and deprived, the more stubbornly do patients cling to their narcissistic expectations.

As the growing child comes to know reality, his narcissism is inevitably and profoundly affected by it. He is forced on countless fronts to accept limitations, to give in to the insistence and convictions of others. The child must learn that his capacities are limited, that his existence is finite, that choice and determination are fraught with anxiety and uncertainty. Through all of his painful learning experience, there runs the thread of the child's continuing sense of helplessness and weakness. Children manage to transcend the real world and its limitations by the forces of imagination, active and vivid fantasy, a belief in magical power and omnipotence, and a capacity for imitation and assimilation of the powerful figures around them. The young child's tendency to identify with the aggressor, which Anna Freud described so vividly, is a striking example. It is through such devices that the child gradually turns from the precarious weakness of passivity and victimhood to the relative activity and striving for mastery which is dependent on psychic growth.

Forms of Narcissism

Kinston (1980, 1982) has introduced the useful distinction between "self-narcissism" and "object-narcissism." Self-narcissism aims at preserving a self-representation which is integrated and achieves a sense of positive value. We can extend that definition to any aspects of the self-structure or organization. The pathology of self-narcissism is expressed in terms of negatively valued self-images and their associated narcissistic vulnerability. In contrast, object-narcissism refers to a defensive mode of object relating, which allows the needy and emotionally dependent part of the patient to isolate him from potentially meaningful and gratifying relationships. As Kinston (1982) develops this notion, it implies the denial of separateness from the object, and the destruction of the object of dependence so that the emotional and needy aspect of the personality is deprived of any attachment to the object. Such patients tend to manifest characteristic attitudes of self-sufficiency, and a denial of any need for attachment to or dependence on another human being.

In the analytic situation, object-narcissism may appear as confusion about the relation of one's self to the analyst, or as a form of indifference to that relationship. It may express itself in forms of dishonesty, in hypervaluation of the patient's role in the analysis, or in the adoption of a false-self facade. In contrast, self-narcissism may manifest itself in perceiving the experience of the analysis and the person of the analyst as highly significant, even vital for the patient's well-being. Such patients remain extremely vulnerable to even minor changes in the analytic routine or even minor and transient failures of empathy and understanding in the analyst. Such patients require regularity and constantly seek the analyst's attitude of benevolent regard, respect, and even admiration.

The roots of these forms of pathological narcissism can be found most significantly in childhood rejection, either as a fear of rejection and self-rejection in self-narcissism, or as rejection of others and/or by others in object-narcissism. Kinston (1982) lists the components of rejection in the following terms: (1) rejection by the parent, either implicitly or explicitly, of forms of authentic self-assertion on the part of the child, (2) internalization of the rejecting attitudes of the parent, (3) a primary form of self-rejection based on the infantile tendency to rid the self of what is bad or unpleasant, (4) a second form of self-rejection based on the perception of one's own inadequacy, immaturity, or incompetence (that is, the failure to meet parental ideals of functioning and performance), and (5) mobilization of defenses against any of the preceding elements.

There are some elements of narcissism which are basic to understanding it. Narcissism is incapable of self-sustaining action and continually requires fresh gratification. It is by its nature uncompromising. It is not self-limiting. It has no inherent stability and has a quality of insatiability. Pathological narcissism can allow no allies. It can tolerate only enemies. The struggle with reality convinces the child, undoubtedly quite correctly, that but for reality he would not be deprived and would have what he wished. The very nature of his wishes precludes their realization, and it is this that is at the basis of his deprivation. It is in this regard that we can begin to grasp the inner links which forge the tie between narcissism and the paranoid process. The paranoid process is thrown into the service of narcissism. It seeks to separate and divide; it seeks to find and establish enemies. It is uniquely the process by which deprived and threatened narcissism is sustained and restored. And we must not forget that the operation of the paranoid process has as its purpose the defense and preservation of the self.

Depression as a Pathology of Narcissism

Narcissistic Introjection

Depression is *par excellence* the clinical expression of pathological narcissism (Rochlin 1961, 1965). The basic insight into the nature of depressive states was provided by Freud in his *Mourning and Melancholia* (1917 [1915]). The basis of the pathology in Freud's formulation lies in the narcissistic (introjective) identification by which the ambivalently regarded object is internalized. With the shift in libidinal cathexis from an exterior to an interior direction, there is a redirection of aggressive and destructive energies. Consequently, the resentment and hateful components of the original ambivalence come to be directed against the patient's self. Freud emphasizes the redirection of aggressive impulses, but nonetheless the involvement and derivation from a basically narcissistic libidinal distribution is an evident and primary part of the pathology. The introjective mechanisms were later adapted by Freud to his concept of superego formation, so that the superego came to provide the basis for understanding unconscious guilt mechanisms and also became the vehicle for the understanding of depressive states.

Diminution of Self-esteem

The understanding of depressive phenomena and their intimate involvement in narcissistic dynamics was clarified by Edward Bibring (1953). Bibring points to the theme, common to a variety of depressive states, of the undermining or diminution of self-esteem. In depressive states, patients feel helpless in the face of superior forces or in the grip of organic disease. Or, on a more psychological plane, they feel incapable of controlling or directing an inescapable fate—loneliness, isolation, a lack of love and affection, or other apparent evidences of weakness, inferiority, or failure. They are without hope—they are helpless and powerless. Bibring consequently defines depression as "the emotional expression (indication) of a state of helplessness and powerlessness of the ego, irrespective of what may have caused the breakdown of the mechanisms which established his self-esteem" (p. 24).

Paradoxically, in the face of feelings of helplessness, these patients tend to strongly maintain a set of goals and objectives which are highly narcissistically determined and pertinent to the individual's self-esteem. The depressive patient aspires to be worthy, to be strong and powerful, to be loved and appreciated, to be valued and esteemed, to be thought superior or talented or especially gifted. He wishes to be felt good and loving; he wishes not to be thought hateful or destructive. It is the disparity between these highly charged narcissistic aspirations and the acute awareness of the ego's helplessness and inability to attain them that lies at the heart of the depression. There is a haunting fear of failure, and whenever the fear of inferiority or defectiveness comes into play, the patient begins to feel hopeless. He feels that he is doomed to be a victim of overwhelming powers, or he feels himself to be hateful and evil in the face of his latent aggressive tendencies.

Whatever shape the narcissistic aspiration takes, the resulting mechanism of the depression seems to follow a common path. It is, in Bibring's (1953) terms, "the emotional correlate of a partial or complete collapse of the self-esteem of the ego, since it feels unable to live up to its aspirations (ego ideal, superego) while they are strongly maintained" (p. 26). As long as the ego maintains its investment in longing for the narcissistically invested object, and as long as it is confronted with its inability or inadequacy to obtain the object or to undo the loss, the conditions of the depression persist. Thus, depression must be regarded as an affective state which is characterized primarily by a diminution of self-esteem, along with a more or less intensely felt state of helplessness and/or hopelessness.

Helplessness

In Bibring's view the basic mechanism of depression, namely, the ego's awareness of its helplessness in relation to excessive or unattainable aspirations, represents the core of the depressive state, whether the depressive response takes place on a normal, neurotic, or even psychotic level. Bibring feels that the tendency to depression is related to early childhood fixation of the ego to the state of helplessness, and that this original state is regressively reactivated in situations of later frustration of narcissistic wishes.

The claims of narcissism on us must not be restricted to a more or less pathological concept of orally fixated and infantile helplessness. Rather, the claims of narcissism are universal, and its demands for satisfaction are inescapable. As Rochlin (1973) has recently observed:

Neither the beloved child nor the fabled heroes of legend, any more than a people chosen by God, are spared outrageous trials. The flaw and the virtue in all is in the peril to self-esteem. Its defense may bring the highest honors and justify the lowest violence. But its loss risks our extinction. (p. 216)

Grandiose Self

Narcissistic fixation in the form of the grandiose self, usually a consequence of pathogenic enmeshment with a narcissistic mother and a consequent traumatic disappointment, leaves the exhibitionistic and grandiose fantasies isolated and disavowed, or repressed, and consequently inaccessible to the more realistic and adaptively functioning ego. The persistence of the grandiose self involves a damming up of primitive

narcissistic-exhibitionistic libido which can be symptomatically manifested in an intensification of hypochondriacal concerns, or of self-
consciousness to the point of shame and embarrassment.

The persistent grandiose self, even when repressed and disavowed,
also carries with it the capacity for undermining self-esteem. This is a
direct consequence of the linking of narcissistic expectations to the
unrealistic, though disavowed and unconscious, grandiose fantasies and
primitive exhibitionistic wishes involved in the repressed grandiose self.
Such fantasies and impulses remain unavailable to the realistically
modulating activity of the realistic ego.

Reich (1960) relates the problem of narcissistic fixation to conditions of quantitative cathectic imbalance, i.e., when the balance between
object-cathexis and self-cathexis has been disturbed in the direction of
excessive self-cathexis, or to the persistence of infantile forms of
narcissism in which self-cathexis is fixed at a level of incomplete ego
differentiation and self-object differentiation. Such fixation often results
in the resort to magical devices to achieve satisfaction of needs or to
attain some degree of mastery over reality. However, the growing ego is
always confronted with its own weakness and limitation and is continually challenged to accept these limitations. The persistent infantile wish
to attain the impossible thus reveals a lack of ability to face both inner
and outer reality. The injury to self-esteem is often compensated by
narcissistic self-inflation and grandiosity. When this attempt at compensation fails, however, severe symptoms may result.

Thus depression is the underside of states of narcissistic enhancement, particularly grandiosity. The connection between grandiosity and
depression has been well described by Miller (1979). She describes the
grandiose person as being in desperate need of admiration: Whatever he
undertakes must be accomplished brilliantly; he stands in admiration of
his own exceptional qualities, particularly when they are supported by
success and achievement. But if one or other of these supports to his
fragile narcissism should fail, he is plunged into catastrophic depression.
The need for admiration in such a personality is insatiable and
consuming: It is his curse, his tragic flaw, the mark of the tyranny of a
narcissism that demands total admiration and leaves no room for
admiration for any others. Credit, acknowledgment, or praise given to
another is perceived as taken away from him, and gives rise to intense
envy. He can even be envious of healthier people around him, who do
not have such a need for admiration and do not have to exert themselves
constantly to impress others and to gain their acknowledgment. As
Miller (1979) notes, the grandiose person can never really be free, not
only because he is excessively dependent on others for their admiration

and acknowledgment but because his own precarious narcissistic equilibrium depends on qualities, capacities, and achievements which are inherently vulnerable and can at any point in time fail. In such personalities, depression looms whenever grandiosity is undermined as the result of sickness, injury, or simply aging (see Chapter 11). As the narcissistic support and the continual reinforcement of the sense of self-importance and specialness are eroded, depression looms as a desperate alternative.

Grandiose fantasies, along with depression, form the primary aspects of pathological narcissism. The persistence of grandiose fantasies is described further by Reich (1960) as forms of primitive ego-ideals related to primitive identifications (introjections). The degree of pathology depends on the capacity of the ego to function adequately on a realistic level and on the availability of or capacity for sublimation in the service of partially realizing or transposing the fantasy ambitions into realistic attainments. Often, the grandiose fantasy is overcathected due to the intensity of inner needs, and the distinction between wish and reality becomes obscure.

Such unsublimated and relatively grandiose fantasies easily shift to feelings of utter dejection and worthlessness, or to hypochondriacal anxieties. Often the narcissistic affliction takes the form of extreme and violent oscillations of self-esteem. Periods of elation and self-infatuation are followed almost cyclically by feelings of total dejection and worthlessness. The infantile value system knows only absolute perfection and attainment or complete destruction and worthlessness. The shift can be precipitated by the most insignificant disappointment or experience of failure. In the logic of such extremes, there are no degrees or shadings. The situation is all or nothing, black or white, all good or all bad, omnipotent or impotent. Any failure to attain perfection is translated into terms of absolute failure.

Inadequacy/Rage

Patients experiencing narcissistic and exhibitionist urges are attempting to overcome feelings of inadequacy by seeking attention and admiration from those around them. But their failure to attain these leads to the feeling that the attention they receive is more negative than positive. They fear that others will see through the facade they present and will recognize the inferiority and defectiveness within. There is defensive contempt for those whose admiration is nonetheless sought. Contempt turns to self-contempt and is experienced often as shame. These patients feel themselves to be constantly evaluated or judged by outside observers who in effect play the role of the reexternalized superego. The narcissistic defense, therefore, is in the form of projection.

Primitive Narcissistic Personalities

As Kernberg (1970) points out in describing the pathology of narcissistic personalities, the grandiose and coldly controlling behavior of such patients can often be seen as a defense against the projection of basically oral rage which forms a central component of the psychopathology. This aspect of narcissistic pathology points to the primarily introjective component, with its primitive, destructive, and depressive aspects. This is reflected in the clinical dialectic of introjection and projection, and in the sometimes difficult-to-detect distortion in object relations. Where the introjective aspects come to dominate the inner realm of the patient's experience, there are often strong conscious feelings of inadequacy and inferiority.

These feelings—caught up as they are in the narcissistic polarization of extremes—may alternate with grandiose and omnipotent fantasies. Frequently enough the omnipotent fantasies. Frequently enough the omnipotence and narcissistic grandiosity of such self-demeaning patients is long and laborious in coming to the surface. The pathological organization of such personalities may ofter approach a borderline constellation. They may resort regressively to primitive defense mechanisms of splitting, denial, projection, omnipotence, and idealization. Usually they are able to preserve areas of adequate social functioning—often to the point of being able to mask the underlying pathology quite effectively. In addition, they often demonstrate a remarkable capacity for consistent and effective work in some areas of their lives, which provides them with significant amounts of narcissistic reward and gratification.

Such a personality organization by no means excludes creative capacity in professional fields of endeavor. These individuals are often outstanding leaders in areas of professional and academic life and may be distinguished performers in the arts. More often than not, their insistence in living at the extremes and the depressive impact of the failure to live up to the demands of their narcissistic expectations serve as greater impediments to their professional and artistic attainment. There is a failure to integrate ego-ideal precursors and idealized self-images; consequently, the grandiose self on the one hand and the unmodified and primitive aggressive aspects of the superego on the other are left relatively intact. These structures are left at a primarily introjective level of integration, with the result that primitive elements of aggression, both oral and anal, are highly susceptible to reprojection in the form of paranoid projections.

While such individuals may show a pattern of authoritarian conformity, they nonetheless see themselves as getting away with something. It is often out of this context of narcissistic grandiosity and its attendant unleashing of primitive aggressive impulses and their correlative projection to the outer world that the antisocial tendencies and conflicts with authority arise. The narcissism in such cases may take the form of the demand that recognition and reward be given them without their having to work for it or earn it, along with the resentment at the failure of the world to respond to this demand, which may then take the further form of resentment and resistance to all forms of external control.

Shame and Pathological Narcissism

Signal Affect

Shame is the direct affective expression of the underlying narcissistic deprivation or mortification. It carries the burden of sensitivity and guardedness, as though it were a vulnerable pain center which the patient needs to keep hidden at all costs.

Often the patient's resistance, which seems so intense and belabored, finally yields a relatively trivial fantasy to which the feeling of shame is attached. This terrible secret is shared with the analyst as a privileged communication. The analyst or therapist may experience a sense of disappointment, a letdown because the actuality does not measure up to the echoes of power and importance that the experience has in the patient's perspective. As Kohut (1971) has pointed out, the patient's shame is related to the discharge of relatively crude and unneutralized narcissistic exhibitionistic libido. The patient's concern is inevitably associated with his fear of ridicule and humiliation.

In following Freud's suggestion that shame, along with disgust, is one of the important inhibitory forces opposing the excessive expression of the sexual instinct, Levin (1967) has suggested that shame can function as a signal affect. Thus, it has the important function of preventing overexposure to trauma—in Levin's terms the trauma of rejection, but in terms of the present discussion, shame serves as a protection from narcissistic trauma. Trauma can take the shape of ridicule, scorn, abandonment, rejection, et cetera (Rochlin 1961; Spiegel 1966). It thus stands in opposition to the wished-for acceptance or respect, which is a component of self-esteem.

Shame is the signal affect for feelings of humiliation, inferiority, or narcissistic mortification. It can function quite directly in relation to the projective economy, since the self-exposure involved in shame must involve a perception of others perceiving the self as a failure, or regarding the self with some form of devaluation or contempt. In a derivative sense as well, shame serves as a painful affect which can in a secondary way stimulate signal anxiety, which arouses the ego to defend itself against the shame affect by repression or other defensive maneuvers.

Injured Narcissism

Although shame may arise in the course of development as a basic inner regulator of libido, its function is primarily a reflection of injured narcissism. The susceptibility to shame is undoubtedly influenced by the tendency of parents to utilize shame in the socialization of the child. Such shaming from the parents can again serve as a narcissistic trauma. Obviously, the traumatic effects of parental shaming are mitigated by a larger context of parent–child interaction and the extent to which parental shaming reflects a basically positive affection for the child.

The infantile response to parental shaming is usually in the direction of inhibition or repression. It is on this basis that some of the basic repressions which appear in adulthood become established. Thus, the influence of parental shaming on the development of character and the subsequent history of the child's capacity to reach out and express is sometimes profound. Lichtenstein (1961) has in fact related the impact of parental shaming to the acquisition of the child's identity. Quite frequently, in patients with paranoid propensities, there is a certain manifest shyness and sensitivity. Such individuals tend to keep a certain distance from others as a way of protecting themselves from the intense shame they experience under self-exposure. In many such patients, any attention from others is experienced as shameful. Even when the response of others is one of admiration or praise, these patients react with feelings of shame.

Such individuals are often acutely attuned to the potentialities of criticism from others. Frequently, when such critical attitudes are not forthcoming as expected, they then become guarded, often secretive and suspicious, with the presumption that even more dreadful criticism is being concealed. The same reactions, when generated at a slightly greater degree of intensity of shame, can easily issue into frank paranoid symptoms of ideas of reference, or a feeling that one's mind is being read, or the like.

Narcissistic Disturbance

Kinston (1983) hypothesizes that the narcissistic disturbance at the basis of shame has its origin in the movement by which the child tries to individuate in the face of parental efforts to maintain symbiosis. Responding to his own unconscious needs, the parent fails to acknowledge the child's emerging autonomy. The child's continuing dependence is required to maintain the narcissistic equilibrium of the parent, so that the child's bid for autonomy is experienced by the parent as unfeeling rejection, abandonment, or separation, which produces pain, depression, and antagonism in the parent. The child is seen in negative terms as wrong, bad, ungrateful, and rejecting. The child is caught between individuation and self-assertion on the one side, and the pull of symbiosis and the parental narcissistic need on the other.

The motif of shame and its connnection with parental attitudes is brought sharply to mind by my experience with a young woman of about 30 who came to analysis for a rather severe depression, which involved a severe impairment of self-esteem. Her chronic and recurrent expectation was that she would be criticized for whatever she did. These feelings could easily be traced to her hypercritical mother, in whose eyes this girl could do nothing right and could do nothing to demonstrate any worthwhileness. These expectations were transposed to the transference and expressed themselves in her conviction that I would be critical of her, that I would tell her she was a worthless patient who did not deserve to be analyzed, that I was sitting, waiting and watching her—letting the analytic material build up so I could then turn on her and show her how worthless and evil she was. She even felt at times that I was reading the perverse and degenerate thoughts that came into her mind and that I could feel only contempt and disgust at what I must be seeing in her. The whole of this material was underlaid quite extensively and intensively with shameful feelings.

Levels

Levin (1967) refers to two levels of shame. The first and deeper level is that of primary shame, which attaches to thoughts, feelings, and impulses which in consequence tend to be inhibited or suppressed. On a more superficial level, secondary shame is experienced as a response to the primary shame affect. The patient is in a sense ashamed of shame. On the secondary level, however, there may be efforts to conceal the shame and its related inhibitions. Individuals may be led to conform with peer-group expectations as a result of secondary shame. Thus, youths may indulge in sexual activity or take to drugs as a way of avoiding the criticism or ridicule of fellow students. The avoidance of such shaming attitudes of others may be unconsciously motivated by previous shaming experiences on an infantile level. Moreover, the absence of shame is regarded in many subcultural settings as a sign of strength or capacity, so that concealment of such shame responses becomes a necessity. This process may at times take the form of counterphobic maneuvers or attempts at excessive exposure to shame-inducing experiences.

Shame versus Guilt

Shame is often connected with or associated with guilt, but it is useful and important to keep these two signal affects differentiated:

(1) In shame, any aspect of the self, including actions, feelings, thoughts, and wishes, is compared with an idealized self-image, one that we would wish to see in ourselves and to have others see in us. Guilt sees the same aspects in relationship to a code of standards and prohibitions of what one ought to be, or what one ought to do. The emphasis of shame falls on qualities of the self, while the emphasis of guilt falls on the action character of what is done or not done.

(2) Shame is global in character in that it focuses on a wishful, ideal self-image that embraces the whole person and becomes the measure of our self-evaluation. Guilt, in contrast, is delimited and additive rather than global, focusing on specific actions and their consequences.

(3) Shame is a form of self-contempt, while guilt expresses self-hatred. This affective differentiation reflects different vicissitudes of aggression: hatred seeks to hurt and destroy; contempt seeks to eliminate something dirty or evil.

(4) In their signal functions, shame and guilt reflect different sets of instinctual wishes. Shame counters exhibitionistic and scoptophilic wishes. Guilt counters wishes to attack, hurt, and destroy. The shame experience involves the sequence of exposure, condemnation, rejection, scorn, and hiding; the guilt experience involves the sequence of attack, retaliation by punishment, atonement by pain.

(5) The element of suddenness or surprise, particularly of discovery, plays a role in shame; not so in guilt.

(6) Both affects serve protective functions; they protect the separate private self from intrusion and merger. Shame protects in the field of expressive and perceptual experience (touching, looking, exhibiting, et cetera), while guilt protects in the field of motor activity and aggression (attacking, hurting, castrating, killing, et cetera) (Wurmser 1978).

It has been observed that shame and guilt are often associated in the patient's experience. Piers and Singer (1953) refer to such complex reactions as "guilt-shame cycles." Shame is related to the frustration of narcissistic aspirations but depends for the most part on the perception of such failure on the part of others. Such attitudes can be internalized, but often the experience of shame still requires the external exposure. The intense experience of shame can lead to the disturbance of libidinal economy, so that diffusion ensues, and destructive energies are deneutralized and may be channeled via the superego against the self. When this happens, it is experienced by the subject as guilt. In such cases, the narcissistic defense takes the introjective route and gives rise to a depressive position. However, the deneutralized energy can also be directed exteriorly in the form of a blaming response. This is more typically associated with projected elements and is more characteristic of a paranoid response. The blaming operation has the advantage of helping to support and restore narcissistic equilibrium. The depressive alternative is less satisfactory in this regard.

Ego-ideal

The presumption that the affect of shame is related to the tension between ego and ego-ideal and reflects a failure on the part of the ego to live up to ego-ideal aspirations has been challenged in passing by Kohut (1971). He agrees that shame signals do play a role in maintaining and restoring homeostatic narcissistic equilibrium. But he rejects the notion that shame is a reaction of the ego to failure in fulfilling ego-ideal expectations. He observes that many shame-prone individuals do not have strong ideals but for the most part are exhibitionistic people driven by ambition. The economic imbalance which is experienced as shame is due to a flooding of the ego by unneutralized exhibitionism rather than to a comparative ego-weakness in relationship to the ego-ideal.

Narcissistic defeats for such individuals are experienced as shame, but then, more often than not, the shame is followed by envy. This combined state of shame and envy may be followed by self-destructive impulses and a feeling of guilt. But Kohut understands these not as superego attacks but as attempts by the ego to do away with the disappointing reality of failure. Self-destructive impulses are an expression of narcissistic rage. Kohut cautions that the attempt to deal with shame-prone patients therapeutically by diminishing the power of the ideal system is frequently a technical error and that success is more frequently founded on the basis of a shift in narcissism, as in a transformation of the narcissistic investment in the grandiose self to the ego-ideal system. His approach is based on the strengthening of the ego-ideal rather than on the attempt to diminish it.

Envy and Pathological Narcissism

Entitlement

Envious feelings are frequently identifiable in narcissistic patients. The paradigm is that offered by Freud, namely, that of the "exceptions" (1916). In these cases, the physical malformation serves as a narcissistic injury which allows the individual to feel deprived and correspondingly entitled to compensatory recognition or acceptance, or entitled to special considerations and benefits that others who have not suffered such deprivations are in no way entitled to. Such individuals feel they should not have to earn recognition, but it should be given to them automatically. They resent that they must work to support themselves, feeling the world somehow owes it to them to support them. They have an abiding sense of unfairness at having to face, acknowledge, and submit themselves to the restraints and limitations of an unfeeling and forbidding reality (Jacobson 1959).

Such feelings of deprivation and resentful entitlement are often bound in with penis envy in certain female patients (Freud 1916; Jacobson 1959). But if we were to consider only the genital implications and relation to castration concerns, we would miss the essential narcissistic dimension of this envy state. These feelings can also play a role in the transference. This was particularly true in one of my female patients whose narcissism was quite strongly fixated at an infantile level. At the birth of her two-years-younger brother, she felt herself deprived and cheated, no longer the center of her parents' affection and attention, and forced to take second place to her brother.

The narcissistic loss and resulting envy drove her to focus all her resentment on her brother's penis—the only obvious difference between herself and him upon which she could focus her attempts to understand why he was more important than herself. Penis envy became a pervasive aspect of her neurotic adjustment and led to highly competitive and narcissistic ambitions, which drove her to seek high academic accomplishments. When her efforts did not measure up to the level of her aspirations, she inevitably felt herself to be a failure and plunged once again into the depressive trough. Her state of mind was overshadowed by the overwhelming conviction that anyone who did not have a penis was not worth anything and could never be in a position to achieve anything significant in life.

In the transference relationship, she carried the conviction that she could improve her situation only by depending on me and keeping in my good favor. This was a direct reflection of her childhood conviction that the only way she could maintain any importance or value in her parents' eyes was by a continual attempt to please her father and keep his good favor. Pleasing her mother was not very helpful, since mother herself was unimportant. She did not have a penis.

Only late in the analysis was this patient able to express and work through some of her intense envious feelings of me. She saw me as a strong, capable, helping person and came to feel she could rely on and trust me. But beyond this capacity for trust and her therapeutic compliance, there was the conviction that she had to depend on, please, and comply with my wishes, since it was only by clinging to a powerful penis-bearing object that she could have any hope of gaining strength and stabilizing her sense of self-worth. Embedded in this was a deep and abiding sense of envy. The envy was focused on the issue of penis-power but at a deeper primitive level cloaked the primitive oral rage at having been deprived of the pleasures of mother's breast and the accompanying infantile attention and adulation.

Impediment to Treatment

Enviousness of this sort can often be an impediment to treatment. Modell (1971) points out that, while Freud had originally assumed the content of unconscious guilt feelings to be responsible for the negative therapeutic reaction, specifically the incestuous and rivalrous impulses, Modell's own experience indicates that the guilt associated with negative therapeutic reaction is related to the patient's conviction that he does not have a right to the better life that might follow the success of the analytic process. The essential element here is that of envy. Such individuals seem to suffer from a conviction that they do not have a right to such improvement and therapeutic success. A common fantasy shared by these patients is that if they were to possess something good, someone else would be deprived. Thus, therapeutic improvement as a result of successful analysis is seen by them as unacceptable, since it means they are depriving someone else of this same improvement. Modell (1971) comments:

> These individuals seemed to suffer from a particularly intense form of envy and greed, i.e., they wished to take away all that others possessed. So that in an additional sense the negative therapeutic reaction could be understood as a wish to deprive the analyst of the "good" that he possessed by virtue of his therapeutic skill. (p. 340)

A similar point has been made by Melanie Klein (1957), who considers envy one of the primary contributing factors to negative therapeutic reactions.

Modell's presumption is embedded in a narcissistic logic. The logic of narcissism states that if the subject is without a certain good, then everyone else must be in possession of it, so the subject is inferior. The patient, true to the dynamics of narcissism, is unwilling to consider the proposition in any but absolute terms. That is, if the patient is deprived to any degree, the deprivation is seen as absolute. Consequently, if the patient feels himself to be so deprived, he sees himself as having nothing and others around him as having everything. Herein lies the root of jealousy. It follows, however, that when the patient comes to acquire some good, others would thereby be deprived. Herein lies the root of a possible negative therapeutic response.

Humiliation and Pathological Narcissism

In those narcissistic disorders in which there is the fear of losing an illusion of narcissistic perfection, the loss of that perfection can be experienced as a humiliation. Rothstein (1984) links the fear of humiliation to narcissism, masochism, and sadism. Certain masochistic patients derive narcissistic pleasure from the sense of eliciting and controlling their own humiliation at the hands of a sadist. Other narcissistic patients enjoy sadistically humiliating others, just as their own humiliating superego similarly afflicts them. While masochistic patients may gain unconscious narcissistic gratification through controlling the inevitable insult, narcissistic patients may have the added fantasy that they can master the implicit danger by an active identification with the sadistic humiliator. The enactment of the humiliation of others has the added benefit of demonstrating their inherent superiority. The intrapsychic organization in such patients often reflects the internalization of humiliating introjects derived from parental models. The resulting introjective configuration contains the sadistic, masochistic, and narcissistic components derived from the object of internalization.

Narcissism and the Paranoid Process

Superiority versus Inferiority

We can link these patterns of narcissistic pathology with the elements of the paranoid process. The discussion here projects back to the earlier exposition of the narcissistic introjects (see Chapter 1). The accompany-

TABLE I. Features of Narcissistic Pathology

SUPERIOR NARCISSISTIC CONFIGURATION	INFERIOR NARCISSISTIC CONFIGURATION
Gradiosity	Depression
Entitlement	Worthlessness
Exhibitionism	Shame
Perfectionism	Defectiveness
Omnipotence	Inadequacy/Impotence
Pride	Humiliation
Elation	Diminished Self-esteem
Contempt (of other)	Envy
Superiority	Inferiority
Narcissistic Invulnerability	Narcissistic Vulnerability
Devaluation (of other)	Idealization
Self-sufficiency	Need for Admiration
Isolation	Dependence

ing table (Table I) contains the catalogue of pathological narcissistic expressions that express or reflect underlying narcissistic pathology.

The columns present the elements that constitute the general dimensions of narcissistic superiority and inferiority. These elements cluster around the motif of narcissistic excess which reflects the underlying structural organization of the narcissistic superior introject. By the same token, the cluster of features that reflect narcissistic inferiority would betoken the functioning of the narcissistic inferior introject. The rows also reflect the corresponding narcissistic elements that seem to be defensively and reciprocally connected. Thus, grandiosity is not only often a defense against an underlying depression but, when grandiosity begins to fail, the clinical consequence is usually the emergence of the underlying depression. It should also be noted that frequently in the clinical setting these features are found in a variety of combinations and overlapping interactions. The clinician is most frequently presented not with one or another of these pathological narcissistic features but with some salient combination which reflects the particular shape or quality of organization of the underlying narcissistic introjects.

Diagnosis

Debate

While the pathological narcissistic indices make an important contribution to the diagnostic process, in that they signal the operation of narcissistic dynamics and reflect the underlying structural integration along pathologically narcissistic lines, they do not dictate specific diagnostic categories. These features can span a range of intensity and pathogenicity, and thus can be found at all levels of the diagnostic spectrum, from the psychotic to the neurotic.

The diagnostic debate is represented by the respective approaches of Kernberg and Kohut. On one hand, the problem arises from the attempt to extend the analysis of borderline personality structure to include the narcissistic personalities. Kernberg, for example, sees narcissistic personalities in terms of underlying borderline features (1967), tends to emphasize the similarities of defensive organization, including the use of primitive defenses of splitting, denial, omnipotence, and idealization (1970), and in general emphasizes the common denominators, particularly in terms of narcissistic character traits and narcissistic deficits in both types of personality organization (1971).

On the other hand, Kohut (1971) describes the narcissistic personality disorders essentially as cohesive self-organizations manifesting specific archaic narcissistic configurations. He leaves open the question of vulnerability to regression, so that the actual distinction from borderline conditions is somewhat obscured, even though he asserts their differentiation from borderline states.

There is left in the relative descriptions of borderline and narcissistic personalities a considerable overlap, both in the narcissistic character-istics and in the tendency to regression, particularly to transient and partial regressions. Kernberg also remarks on the regressive potential of narcissistic personalities (1970, 1974) and makes no attempt to dis-tinguish between them on this basis. One way to summarize this problem is to say that Kernberg writes as though the diagnostic spectrum stretching between the psychoses and the neuroses were filled by nothing but forms of borderline personality, while Kohut writes as though the same diagnostic spectrum was filled with nothing but narcissistic personality forms.

Kohut does attempt to differentiate these conditions on the basis of the relative cohesion of nuclear narcissistic structure. As he sees it, the narcissistic personalities are characterized by an insecure cohesiveness of the nuclear self and self-objects, and only fleeting fragmentation. He contrasts this with borderline conditions, in which the symptomatology hides the fragmentation of nuclear narcissistic structures or in which the breakup of such structures remains an ever-present danger which can be prevented by avoiding regression-inducing narcissistic injuries—as in schizoid personalities. These intermediate conditions are again distin-guished from the frank psychoses, in which there is a permanent and protracted fragmentation of narcissistic structures and in which the symptoms openly reflect their decompensation. The discrimination between the fleeting fragmentation of the narcissistic personality and the hidden or potential breakdown of nuclear narcissistic structures in the borderline (including schizoid) conditions is difficult to grasp, if not tenuous in conceptualization (Rothstein 1979).

The upshot of the ambiguities in these approaches is that there is considerable diagnostic confusion in making appropriate discriminations between these various forms of psychopathology. In fact, Ornstein (1974) argues that Kohut's classification of the narcissistic personality disorders encompasses those conditions previously considered to be borderline or psychotic characters, and may even include some of those previously diagnosed as neurotic character or psychoneuroses.

Ornstein's (1974) suggestion that the argument may founder on the fact that it is concerned with essentially different patient populations is a cogent one and points to the possibility that part of the difficulty arises from ambiguities in diagnosis. The same point of view has been expressed by other authors as well (Spruiell 1974; Schwartz 1974; Rothstein 1979). Spruiell (1974) also observes that the narcissistic personalities described by Kernberg would seem to make up a smaller group than would those patients described by Kohut. Thus, Kohut's group of narcissistic patients may not only overlap with but also encompass those described by Kernberg.

Methodology

All forms of personality organization have their narcissistic elements which influence the form of the pathology. However, we are discussing here forms of character pathology in which the narcissistic disorder forms the central or core dimension of the patient's pathology. The wide spectrum of narcissistic pathology is not equivalent to the more restrictive diagnosis of narcissistic personality. An essential trait on which that diagnosis rests is the capacity for forming stable and at least potentially analyzable narcissistic transferences.

It has been argued that Kohut's focusing on transference phenomena as essential to the diagnosis of narcissistic personalities stands in opposition to descriptive diagnostic categories, such as those used in general psychiatry. This objection presupposes that Kohut uses no phenomenological elements in defining his categories. However, we do not observe anything in psychoanalysis that is not phenomenal. Even our judgments of transference are based on phenomenological observations of transference manifestations (behaviors or verbal reports of inner states) from which the construct "transference" can be derived.

Further, psychoanalytic observations of transference phenomena do not stand in opposition to descriptive observations, any more than psychoanalysis stands in opposition to general psychiatry. Psychoanalysis merely adds to psychiatric observations a different dimension that has to do with the fantasy-related, affective, transferential, and object-relational aspects of psychological functioning. The position taken in the present study is that psychoanalytic and psychiatric observations are complementary.

Consequently, any attempt at diagnostic differentiation, based either on behavioral description or on transference and object-relations phenomena, must remain partial and incomplete.

Modes of Investment

Rothstein (1979) has noted that attempts to develop a diagnostic classification of narcissistic personalities have involved two different modes of narcissistic investment: (1) the predominant mode of narcissistic investment in objects, and (2) the state of structural narcissistic integration within the subjective self. He notes that Kohut's emphasis on the nature of the transference phenomenon not only is not synonymous with the predominant mode of investment but is incomplete without a consideration of the structural integration of the patient's narcissism. Thus, the correlation of the predominant mode of investment of narcissism with the state of ego integration of narcissism could become a fundamental principle of diagnostic discrimination.

We would amend these observations by the further consideration that the predominant mode of narcissistic investment characterizes both the self-investment and the object-investment. This implies a more evolved concept of the development and vicissitudes of narcissism and would take into account the observations noted above regarding self-narcissism and object-narcissism (Kinston 1980, 1982). In addition, we would argue that the mode of investment is not simply an investment in the self-representation but implies narcissistic investment in the self-organization or self-structure, which underlies the representation. We would adhere to the basic principle enunciated previously that the narcissistic investment is directed to and attached to the self, rather than to its derivative representations. By the same token, narcissistic investment is not in object-representations, but, rather, in the objects. In other words, the basic intentionality of such investment is directed toward the object itself; the representation is only a medium or instrumentality which functions as a part of the capacity of the self to relate to objects (Meissner 1981b, 1985).

Phallic Narcissistic Personality

In trying to order the narcissistic personality types, Bursten (1973) has suggested that the highest level of narcissistic personality organization is found in the phallic narcissistic personality. The exhibitionism, pride in prowess, show-offishness, and often counterphobic competitiveness and risk taking in the service of narcissistic exhibitionism are quite familiar. Such individuals tend to be self-centered and have an exorbitant need for approval and admiration—particularly admiration—from others. There is often a quality of arrogance or contempt in their relationship with others which is defensive in tone and tends to mask underlying and often repressed feelings of inadequacy or inferiority.

This inner sense of inferiority often stems from a sense of shame from an underlying identification with a weak father figure compensated by the arrogant, assertive, aggressively competitive, often hypermasculine and self-glorifying facade. In other words, the unconscious shame from the fear of castration is continually denied by phallic assertiveness. This may even be accompanied by a sense of omnipotence and a feeling of invulnerability which allow such individuals to continually take risks, feeling that some miraculous fate or good luck will carry them through. Such individuals tend to have a firmly established and cohesive sense of self, which shows little tendency to regression or fragmentation.

Such individuals often seem to also have strong inner resources for maintaining their independence, and express little need for others beyone the demand for admiration and acknowledgement. The intense attachment to self-objects that may be found in other forms of narcissistic pathology is not usually apparent in these patients or is concealed behind a facade of hyperadequacy. The extent of their real dependency becomes apparent only when the love or support of such objects is lost. These personalities may have elements of grandiosity and omnipotence which reflect the persistence of the grandiose self in Kohut's terms, and there may at times be an idealization of objects which then serve as models for imitation or identification. The vulnerabilities of such personalities are generally well concealed by counterphobic and counterdependency mechanisms.

Nonetheless, they remain susceptible to the ravages of time and diminishing capacity and potency. The diminished capacity to perform with advancing age, whether sexually, physically, or intellectually, can constitute a narcissistic trauma with rather severe pathological results. The outcome is usually a depression. Kernberg (1974) has underscored the exigency for treating narcissistic disorders, particularly in view of the often severe inroads on unresolved pathological narcissism that occur during the second half of life. The titre of narcissistic supports tends to be higher in the earlier segment of life experience, during adolescence and early adulthood, and even for many narcissistic personalities during the years of adult productivity when the benefits derived from intelligence, industry, talent, and monetary or career success provide an adequate flow of narcissistic gratification. But when the aging individual turns the corner of adulthood and inevitably faces the gradual erosion of aging, illness, the loss of mental acuity and creativity, the increasing flood of separations and losses, isolation and loneliness, the internal narcissistic configurations are put under increasing stress.*

Such individuals do not generally show a dramatic regressive crisis, but under conditions of acute stress the regression may be severe and at times irreparable. One wonders, for example, whether the cases of war neurosis in which individuals seemed to suffer little or no fear or anxiety about danger prior to the traumatic event but seemed incapable of reconstituting in the usual way to pretraumatic levels of functioning were not in fact such phallic narcissistic characters. In such cases, the assault of the traumatic event on the individual's self-image would have so damaged the individual's self-image and self-esteem that they proved relatively incapable of reconstitution.† That self-image had been based on a view of themselves as fearless and as capable of withstanding any amount of stress or danger. The experience of severe anxiety would have destroyed that image and would have created an impediment to its reconstitution or effective treatment (Zetzel and Meissner 1973).

Nobel Prize Complex

There is a more subtle variant of this form of narcissistic pathology which Tartakoff (1966) describes as a variant of the apparently well adjusted, sociologically "healthy" personality. These are often academically or professionally successful individuals who are able and ambitious, often have achieved significant degrees of professional respect and recognition, but find themselves dissatisfied with their current life situations. Difficulties arise in connection with competitive feelings or competitive situations, or in their inability to gratify the needs of others

---

*See the more extensive discussion of aging and its vicissitudes in Chapter 11.

†A striking literary portrayal of just this form of narcissistic pathology is provided in the character of Marrow, the "hero" of John Hersey's *The War Lover* (1959).

in intimate human relations, with family, close friends, et cetera. Some of these individuals can recognize symptoms, usually reactive depressions, or anxiety attacks under stress, or a variety of psychosomatic symptoms. Others are essentially asymptomatic, recognize no underlying motivation for treatment, but seek analysis essentially as a way of broadening their professional training. They share the conviction that their exceptional abilities, talents, or virtues will win them success if they work properly at it. Achieving these goals or life expectations has become essential to their psychic harmony. They often experience little difficulty in life, since their abilities and endowments usually allow them to gain some narcissistic gratification and recognition from the environment, or at least to maintain the hope of fulfilling their narcissistic expectations— a hope that can receive considerable cultural and social reinforcement. It is when the reinforcements begin to fail or the expectations begin not to be met that narcissistic imbalance and symptomatic manifestations may arise.

Success in analysis is seen as a means to gratification. Active mastery of the analytic situation and the conflicts it mobilizes is a first line of defense for these patients. They treat the analysis as an adaptive task which carries the unspoken assumption that they will gain acceptance or acclaim from the analyst as a reward for their efforts. The behavior is defensive, often competitive with the analyst, with an implicit expectation of gaining a special relation with the analyst. This may be expressed in the fantasy of being a special patient, especially interesting or especially difficult, preferred to other patients, even loved—exclusively—by the analyst.

When the adaptive function of the patient's attempts to master the analytic situation is seen and understood as repetitions of previously successful endeavors, a second line of preoedipal transference emerges in the idealization of the analyst. This externalization of the ego-ideal comes closer to Kohut's (1971) notion of the idealizing parental imago. Conformity to the analyst's expectations holds the promise that the patient will be rewarded by success in the analysis and will thereby be endowed with the qualities of omnipotence and omniscience he attributes to the analyst. Such fantasies may continue to be unspoken and become a secret source of resistance. Insofar as the analyst fails to meet these narcissistic expectations, the patient's disillusionment and narcissistic rage can become intense. The "Nobel Prize complex" embraces two predominant fantasies: (1) an active grandiose fantasy of being powerful and omnipotent, and (2) a more passive fantasy of being special, chosen for special recognition by reason of exceptional talents, abilities, virtues, et cetera.

Manipulative/Exploitative Personalities

At a somewhat more pathological level, the narcissistic need expresses itself not simply in terms of the drive to gain recognition and admiration but, further, in the entitlement to use, manipulate, or exploit others for the purposes of self-aggrandisement. Bursten (1973) describes such personalities as "manipulative." His description of these personalities comes close to the description of psychopathic or antisocial personalities, and it is undeniable that the pathology may frequently take this form in more or less flagrant degree. However, the antisocial or psychopathic quality of such personalities may suggest that the pathology is more than merely narcissistic and that such personalities may be functioning at the more primitive level of borderline personalities.

Nonetheless, the contempt for others, the implicit devaluation of others as having potential value only in terms of their exploitability or manipulability in the service of self-enhancement, the high value often placed on putting something over on others or getting away with something, even though that involves practices that may be deceptive or even dishonest, all carry the stamp of the narcissistic personality and reflect the persistence of residues of the grandiose self. The exploitative form of narcissistic repair covers an underlying narcissistic vulnerability in which the self feels vulnerable to exploitation or manipulation by others and is constantly turning the tables, as it were. The inherent sense of shame, vulnerability, and worthlessness attached to this narcissistically vulnerable self-image is equivalently projected onto the victim of the subject's exploitation, so that the denial and reassurance that one's self is not really entrapped in this impoverished self-image is gained through the projection and exploitation of the victim.

In these circumstances the victim is of vital importance to the subject as a means of maintaining the subject's narcissistic equilibrium, but the victim is in no sense valued or idealized, but rather held in a devalued posture or even regarded with contempt. This contrasts with the normal narcissism in which there is little pressure to seek favor or support from, or *a fortiori* to manipulate or exploit objects. Rather, their exceptional endowment and precocity have led them to expect success and admiration, so that the need to gain or extort such narcissistic feedback from others is less. Their dependence is focused on evidence for such success and the related narcissistic gratification, with a related impairment in the capacity for meaningful love relationships.

The sense of self in more exploitative patients is relatively well established and subject to little regression, as long as the resources for continuing narcissistic repair are available. These patients maintain a sense of separateness in their relations with others and have considerable difficulty in developing meaningful or mutually gratifying relationships, since the premise of any meaningful relationship rests on the underlying narcissism, which requires that the other be put in the service of the self. When the means of narcissistic repair fail or become unavailable, such patients generally fall prey to depression. Depending on the severity of the pathology, the depression can be quite severe and even suicidal. Something similar can be seen even more dramatically in the effects of inpatient confinement and restricted mobility on criminal psychopaths (Vaillant 1975). When such patients are confined and control is established over their behavior so that flight is impossible and they are relatively immobilized, the underlying depression becomes much more clinically apparent. Such psychopathic personalities are more primitive than exploitative narcissistic personalities and fall within the borderline spectrum (Meissner 1984a).

Primitive Narcissistic Personalities

At even more pathological levels, however, the narcissism becomes even more needy, clinging, and demanding. There is a heightened need to be given to, supported, and taken care of that reflects a sense of peremptory and uncompromising entitlement. The neediness for such input from others may be so profound as to take on a symbiotic quality, so that these individuals often become involved in intensely dependent and needy relationships with the significant others in their lives. Frequently, such involvements have a highly ambivalent, hostile-dependent quality, since the object is never quite capable of satisfying the patient's narcissistic demand and expectation. Such individuals are constantly exposed to the threat of disappointment and frustration, feeling deprived and often desperate. In such states, they can become sullen and pouting, even whining and complaining, in their attempts to wheedle the necessary response from the important other.

As with all narcissistic personalities, there is in these individuals as well a capacity for charm, the ability to entertain, flatter, and influence others. But the quality of this activity is quite different from that in the phallic narcissist, for whom the objective is gaining admiration, or from that in the more exploitative narcissistic personality, for whom the objective is putting the other in the service of his own narcissistic objectives. In these more severely disturbed narcissistic patients, the objectives are much more in the line of drawing others onto the position of giving, supporting, taking care of, or otherwise filling up the intense neediness and deprived emptiness of these patients. Consequently, the quality of behavior in such individuals is intensely oral and has been aptly characterized by Bursten (1973) as "craving."

Vulnerability/Grandiosity

At all levels of narcissistic pathology, there are degrees of both narcissistic vulnerability and grandiosity. These qualities are inherently linked and are never found in isolation. Frequently, one or more dimensions may be found as explicit or conscious manifestations of the narcissistic personality, but even in such cases the correlative aspect of the narcissistic pathology can be found on further clinical investigation. Thus, the phallic or exploitative narcissistic character who displays his vanity and grandiosity in a variety of public ways can be found to carry a concealed core of narcissistic vulnerability and feelings of inferiority, shame, weakness, and susceptibility. Similarly, on closer evaluation, the clinging, dependent, needy, and demanding type of the more primitive narcissistic character will be found to be concealing a core of grandiosity. This core underlies the infantile expectations and extreme sense of entitlement which make them feel that they have a right to demand concern, care, and attention from others, often to the point of considerable self-sacrifice and disadvantage or detriment to the other. This same grandiosity also expresses itself in the sulking, pouting, whining, and demanding quality of efforts to gain narcissistic supplies.

There is often an implicit supposition that others owe it to the subject to make up for the deprivation and deficits that he feels he has suffered at the hands of depriving others and for which he feels expiation is owed to him. The obligation falls upon others, therefore, to make up this deficit and to exercise themselves to undo the wrongs that have been done to the subject, rather than the subject taking upon himself the responsibility for dealing with his own difficulties. This goes along with a general blaming tendency in such individuals which tends to lay the responsibility for the individual's difficulties at someone else's door—frequently, that of parents or other caretakers, but not infrequently that of other family members, friends, employers, coworkers, et cetera. This tendency in its more extreme forms may take a paranoid expression. As we have noted elsewhere (Meissner 1977, 1978b), the narcissistic pathology forms a substantial part of the core of paranoia.*

---

*See the extended discussion of the role of narcissism in paranoid psychopathology in Chapter 6.

Narcissistic Transferences

Kohut (1971) has emphasized, as the predominant characteristic of narcissistic personalities, the formation of cohesive narcissistic configurations around which the personality organization takes shape. These configurations on the objective side involve the idealized parent imago, and on the subjective side the grandiose self. These relatively stable configurations are cathected with narcissistic libido, either idealizing or grandiose-exhibitionistic, and manifest themselves in various forms of object relations and in analytic transferences.

Idealizing Transferences

The therapeutic activation of the omnipotent and idealized object leads to the formation of an idealizing transference in which residues of the lost infantile experience of narcissistic perfection are restored by assigning it to a transitional object, the idealized parent imago. Thus, all power and strength are attributed to this idealized object, so that the subject feels empty and powerless when separated from it. Consequently, he must bend every effort to maintain contact and union with this object. The continuing contact and union with an idealized object seems to characterize one of Reich's (1953) forms quite adequately. The second form, however, is unable to sustain a consistent object attachment and vacillates quickly between narcissistic configurations, between infatuation and contempt, idealization and devaluation. This instability and the defects of object constancy give rise to an as-if quality and suggest that such narcissistic attachments are essentially borderline.

Such idealizing transferences can reactivate archaic narcissistic states which stem from one or other multiple levels of development. These may include primitive mergings of the self with an idealized maternal imago or may reflect later developmental traumata which produce specific narcissistic fixations. Such traumata or narcissistic disappointments may create impediments in the development of the child's idealization, or may contaminate or undo insecurely established idealizations which may interfere with the idealizations of objects. This may result, by failure of internalizations, in insufficient idealization of the superego and secondary structural deficits resulting from fixations on the narcissistic aspects of preoedipal and oedipal objects. Kohut (1971) notes:

> Persons who have suffered such traumas are (as adolescents and adults) forever attempting to achieve a union with the idealized

object since, in view of their specific structural defect (the insufficient idealization of their superego), their narcissistic equilibrium is safeguarded only through the interest, the responses, and the approval of present-day (i.e., currently active) replicas of the traumatically lost self-object. (p. 55)

These varieties of pathogenic narcissistic fixation give rise to differentiable transferences. Certain varieties of idealizing transference reflect the disturbance of later stages of the development of the idealized parent imago, particularly at the time of introjection of the idealized object in the formation of the ego-ideal. More archaic forms of narcissistic idealization may express themselves in global, mystical, or even religious concerns associated with awe-inspiring qualities that do not seem to emanate from a clearly delimited, single admired figure. While such primitive idealizing elements tend to be more diffuse and vague, particularly when merged with elements of the grandiose self, the special bond and the idealizing attachment to the analyst is never in doubt. In such cases, the restored narcissistic equilibrium is experienced as a sense of omnipotence and omniscience, along with feelings of esthetic and moral perfection. These feelings are maintained as long as the patient can feel that he is united and sustained by the idealized analyst. Along with this, there is a diminution of the symptomatology of the narcissistic imbalance, particularly affecting the diffused depression, disturbed work capacity, irritability, feelings of shame or inferiority, hypochondriacal preoccupations, et cetera. The establishment of union with the idealized object also minimizes the threat of further narcissistic regression, perhaps to even more archaic precursors of the idealized parent imago (Kohut 1971). The narcissistic dynamics in the Wolf Man's case seem to have followed such a pattern (Meissner 1977).*

Mirror Transferences

In some individuals the narcissistic fixation leads to the development of the grandiose self. The reactivation in analysis of the grandiose self provides the basis for the formation of mirror transferences. Kohut (1971) has described three forms:

The cohesive therapeutic reactivation of the grandiose self in analysis occurs in three forms: these relate to specific stages of development of this psychological structure to which pathogno-

---

*See the discussion of the Wolf Man's narcissism in Chapter 4.

monic therapeutic regression has led: (1) the archaic *merger through the extension of the grandiose self*; (2) a less archaic form which will be called *alter-ego transference* or *twinship*; and (3) a still less archaic form which will be referred to as *mirror transference* in the narrower sense. (p. 114)

In the most primitive merger form of mirror transference, the analyst is experienced only as an extension of the subject's grandiose self. Consequently, he becomes the repository of the grandiosity and exhibitionism of the patient's grandiose self. Kohut uses such terms as "merger" or "symbiosis" to describe this extension but reminds us that what is at issue here is not merger with an idealized object but, rather, merger achieved by a regressive diffusion of the borders of the self to embrace the analyst, who is then experienced as united to the grandiose self. The analogy to the adult experience of cathexis of one's own body or mind reflects the kind of unquestioned control or dominance that the grandiose self expects to exert over the invested object.

With such patients, the analyst may find himself forced to resist the oppressive tyranny with which the patient seeks to control him (Kohut 1971). The quality of this merging and extension of the grandiose self seems to eliminate the object as such and to make it simply a reflection of the self. Consequently, merging of this nature must be regarded as severely regressive and comes closer to the modalities of incorporation that we have described elsewhere (Meissner 1971b, 1979a). To this extent, they may be regarded as psychotic in character, or at least regressively borderline.

At a somewhat less primitive level of organization, the activation of the grandiose self leads to the narcissistic object being experienced as similar to and, to that extent, a reflection of the grandiose self. In this variant, the object as such is preserved but is modified by the subject's perception of it to suit the subject's narcissistic needs. This form of transference is referred to as alter-ego or twinship transference. Clinically, dreams or fantasies referring to such an alter-ego or twinship relationship with the analyst may be explicit. The patient assumes "that the analyst is either like him or similar to him, or that the analyst's psychological makeup is like, or is similar to that of the patient" (Kohut 1971, p. 115). In this type of transference, then, the reality of the analyst is preserved, but it is modified after the fashion of a transitional object by a projection of some aspects of the patient's grandiose self onto the analyst.

The most mature and most developed form of the mirror transference experiences the analyst as a separate person but nonetheless one who becomes important to the patient and is accepted by him only to the degree that he is responsive to the narcissistic needs of the reactivated grandiose self. Kohut appeals here to the model of the gleam in the mother's eye which responds to and mirrors the child's exhibitionism. In this way, the mother participates in and reinforces the child's narcissistic pleasure in himself. Thus, in this strictest sense of the mirror transference, the analyst's function becomes one of admiring and reflecting the grandiosity and exhibitionism of the patient. This need on the part of the patient may also take a more subtle form in which the patient seeks such admiration and confirmation from the analyst but constantly acts in a way that reflects the fear of not getting it. Consequently, the patient becomes extremely resistant out of a fear that the revelation of less than ideal impulses, fantasies, or wishes may deprive him of the analyst's admiring eye. For such patients, the grandiose self is not so much confirmed as maintained intact behind a highly defensive facade. The analyst runs the risk of becoming a threat to the vulnerability of the grandiose self and may even be seen in persecutory or paranoid forms of transferential distortion.

Diagnostic Implications

Kohut assumes that where the "archaic" narcissistic configurations or their transferential expressions are identifiable, one is dealing by definition with narcissistic personality disorders as such. This may be one source of diagnostic confusion, since both narcissistic configurations can be found expressed in varying degrees and modalities, not only in the lower levels of pathological organization, even the psychotic, but also at higher levels of organization, in relatively well organized, more or less neurotic personalities. Such an assumption would presume that wherever the idealized imago or grandiose self is identifiable, one is dealing with a narcissistic personality. It seems more reasonable from our perspective to view Kohut's formulations as fundamental forms of pathological narcissistic organization that can be found expressed at many different levels of pathology and character structure. Consequently, one can view the narcissistic personality structure as having one or both of these configurations as predominant parts, but the diagnostic formulation does not simply rest on the identification of these configurations. It must include other factors as well.

Self-cohesion

One of the primary aspects of narcissistic personality organization, and a significant dimension of its diagnosis, is the element of self-cohesion.

Kohut emphasizes that these patients have developmentally attained the stage of cohesive self-organization, and that it is by reason of the attainment of such stable and cohesive psychic organization that they are capable of establishing stable narcissistic transferences. Moreover, Ornstein (1974) has emphasized that the establishment and maintenance of a cohesive self is a sine qua non for psychoanalysis and lays the ground of possibility for the formation of narcissistic transferences. Bursten (1978) marks this relatively greater degree of self-cohesion as a central characteristic of the narcissistic personality organization. He writes:

> People with narcissistic personality types have a firmer sense of self. Generally, they confirm their sense of self more easily. Kohut (1971) indicates that they have a more cohesive self and are less vulnerable to fragmentation. However, the confirmers utilized in the maintenance of this cohesive sense of self give them their typical narcissistic stamp; they are self-oriented. (p. 18)

Not only has Kohut (1971) emphasized this cohesiveness of the structure and functioning of the self in such narcissistic personalities but he has also emphasized this as a discriminating factor from primitive borderline or psychotic forms of organization.

Therapy of Narcissistic Disorders

I will add some observations on the treatment of narcissistic personalities and narcissistic psychopathology more generally. The subject is large and complicated, so I can offer no more than a rudimentary schema. My objective is to focus some of the aspects of narcissistic pathology in terms of the paranoid process and to suggest the ways in which the basic schema generated by the paranoid process can be applied to the treatment of narcissistic issues. The following observations provide an elaboration of the psychotherapeutic approach and schema already developed (see Chapter 3).

Difficulties of the Therapeutic Alliance

The therapeutic alliance is absolutely essential for any degree or kind of meaningful therapy to take place. But difficulties in the forming and maintaining of a therapeutic alliance occur from the very beginning of the therapeutic process with narcissistic patients, and often remain a problem throughout the greater part of the therapy. Narcissistic patients do not bring to the therapeutic encounter a well-developed or evolved capacity for entering a therapeutic alliance. Their difficulties have a very special quality, which emerges from their narcissistic pathology.

But if there is to be therapy at all, it must begin somewhere. Urged by whatever internal distress or by whatever extrinsic circumstances or forces, the patient comes to the therapeutic enounter, usually with his narcissistic defenses raised—with his dukes up, as it were. The very need to turn for help to a therapist and to seek treatment may constitute a severe narcissistic insult. Nonetheless, the patient must be willing to mitigate his defensiveness and to overcome his resistance to a sufficient degree to allow him to come to a therapist and to engage in the therapeutic process.

Narcissistic Alliance

This initial and partial therapeutic rapport, which allows the patient to modify his narcissistic defensive organization to include the possiblility of a helping relationship to the therapist, is the narcissistic alliance (Meissner 1981b). Such an engagement with the therapist, however minimal, requires a degree of trust in the therapist as a helping figure who at least has the potential of offering the patient relief from distress. The trust takes the form of a basic willingness to accept the competence of the healer. If the narcissistic alliance is successful, it allows the patient to introduce the therapist into his defensive alignment as a potential resource for redressing the patient's uncomfortable narcissistic disequilibrium and sense of narcissistic vulnerability.

However, at the very beginning of treatment, when the archaic narcissistic elements play a dominant role in the personality organization, the capacity for even a narcissistic alliance may be seriously impaired. The imperious demands of the grandiose self or the pressures to maintain narcissistic equilibrium by attachment to an idealized object (Kohut 1971) may impede even the first steps toward a narcissistic alliance. The pathology of the grandiose self has a poor capacity to tolerate dependence on a helping object; by the same token, the need for an idealized object carries with it such magical and illusory expectations that a potential alliance may be subverted and overwhelmed by the patient's narcissistic and defensive needs. Often the therapist is in a position, in the beginning of the treatment process, of having to settle for whatever degree of narcissistic alliance the patient's injured naracissism will allow, or at times even has to do some preliminary work to make it possible for even a minimal narcissistic alliance to emerge.

The narcissistic needs and illusory expectations that lie behind the narcissistic alliance tend to remain as persistent qualities in the therapeutic relationship. As the therapeutic alliance advances and evolves, the persistence of such needs in subtle and varied forms can continually erode the therapeutic alliance and bring it into the service of pathogenic narcissistic needs. Consequently, at no point in the therapeutic process does the focus on the therapeutic alliance and its narcissistic impediments recede into the background. Moreover, this segment of the therapeutic or analytic work can assume primary and central importance for the therapeutic outcome.

Transference Distortions

Narcissistic Introjects

The narcissistic transferences are forms of preoedipal narcissistic transference, which derive from and are an expression of the dynamics and organization of the underlying narcissistic introjects. The idealization involves a projection of narcissistic elements from the introjective configuration onto the figure of the analyst. Correspondingly, the grandiose self is organized around the superior narcissistic introject as its core component. The mirror transferences, by and large, serve the function of bringing the object to the service of the narcissistic needs of the grandiose self: whether in the more archaic and primitive form of merging (by extension of the grandiose self), or in the less archaic form of a twinship (alter-ego) transference, or in the more mature form, the mirror transference in its narrower sense (in which the analyst is experienced as separate but valued by the patient only insofar as he responds to and serves the reactivated needs of the grandiose self).

Devaluation

The basic narcissistic dynamic will express itself, depending on the case, with varying degrees of intensity or totality. The degrees of idealization may wax and wane during the analytic work. By the same token, the degrees of mirroring may vary. In both cases, the narcissistic dynamic may be accompanied by forms of devaluation. In the case of idealization, the extent to which the idealization may or may not be accompanied by a devaluation of the patient's self can vary considerably, but almost inevitably at some point in the course of the analytic work the aspects of the self-devaluing component will become manifest. In terms of the paranoid process, this is not an unexpected result, insofar as the projection of elements of the narcissistically superior introject means that the inferior narcissistic introject remains internally operative.

Consequently, to the extent that idealization of the external object takes place, we would expect a corresponding degree of self-devaluation, diminished self-esteem, and even depression.

In the mirroring transference, however, the devaluation tends to be of the object. Insofar as the object is put in the service of and subjugated to the narcissistic needs of the patient, the way is open to a corresponding degree of devaluation of the object based on projection of the inferior narcissistic introjective components. Seen in this perspective the narcissistic transferences provide a projective matrix within which the dynamics and patterns of organization of the narcissistic introjects are displayed and can become readily available for therapeutic processing. It is as though the narcissistic material is brought into the analytic or therapeutic interaction in a vivid, reactivated, and vital form in which both analyst/therapist and patient are participants. Thus, the transference matrix provides the most immediate, vivid, and powerful field of observation of these narcissistic vicissitudes and often can provide the medium for the most effective and telling therapeutic interventions.

Clarification of the Introjects

To return to the psychotherapeutic schema (Chapter 3), the clarification of the introjects has a certain priority. In working with the patient's narcissistic material, the therapist is listening for the derivatives of both the superior and the inferior narcissistic introjects. His primary task is the amplification of this introjective material on both sides of the narcissistic polarity, so that an increasingly elaborate and concise picture is gained of the manner and style in which these introjective components permeate the individual's life experience and express themselves in a variety of contexts. When the therapist is hearing about the aspects of the patient's sense of inferiority and inadequacy, his sense of shamefulness and worthlessness, his fears of humiliation, of envy and vulnerability, the therapist's primary task is to listen with understanding, empathy, and acceptance. He wants to give as much room as is necessary for the patient to develop and explore this side of his feelings about his impoverished and narcissistically depleted self. When the opposite configuration begins to show itself in terms of the patient's sense of entitlement, perfectionism, his exhibitionistic impulses or wishes, his wish for admiration, then the superior narcissistic configuration is on display, and the therapist's aim is again to provide an ample space within which the patient can explore these parts of his inner self-organization.

It is at this juncture that some of Kohut's cautions are well taken. Most therapists do not have a great deal of difficulty in gaining empathic access to and acceptance of the patient's narcissistically inferior feelings and attitudes. Even this, however, is not always easy, since there may be difficulties in given therapists in tolerating the patient's painful, often self-pitying depression, but generally the capacity to tolerate such affects is a working part of the therapeutic armamentarium. Kohut cautions rather against the tendency to react to the patient's grandiosity and sense of narcissistic superiority, particularly insofar as it may be accompanined by attempts to devalue the analyst. The same tolerance and empathic acceptance that one extends to the narcissistically inferior side should be extended to the narcissistically superior side, however strong the temptation may be to react to it or to try to do something with it by way of therapeutic intervention (clarification, interpretation, et cetera).

Part of the process of clarification of the introjects has to do with their display in the transference interaction. Part of the clarifying process is to link the aspects of both superior and inferior narcissistic introjects as discovered in the other aspects of the therapeutic work with the patterns that emerge in the transference interaction, since they derive from a common root. The recognition and acknowledgment of these patterns in the ongoing interaction with the therapist can often carry with them a powerful impression and add conviction and vividness to the basic patterns.

Therapeutic Strategy

But there is more to be done than offering the patient acceptance and empathic understanding of his narcissistic needs. At this point the consideration would diverge from Kohut's perspective and move beyond it. As the respective introjective configurations are progressively clarified and defined, the question arises as to what can be done with them therapeutically. To begin with, there is little to be done with the superior narcissistic configuration. It is to be allowed to expand and emerge so that its various configurations and emphases can be adequately delineated. As this process is evolving, the therapist is carefully noting and identifying the defensive aspects of this superior configuration. The defense, however, does not have the same focus as that described by Kernberg (1974), which seems more appropriate to the dynamics of borderline personalities (Meissner 1984a). While we would agree with Kernberg that the grandiose self is indeed in large measure a pathological formation, we would not completely agree that in all cases of narcissistic personalities the defensive aspects of the grandiose self are directed against underlying oral aggression and envy. This certainly is a part of the picture in more primitively organized (borderline) personalities but does not tend to be the dominant configuration in narcisssistic personalities. The defense is rather against the components of the opposite narcissistic introjective configuration, that is, against the inferior configuration. The grandiosity and other elements of narcissistic superiority are maintained to defend against the shame, worthlessness, depression, envy, and inferiority of the opposite narcissistic configuration. The therapist can listen to the patient's material which contains such narcissistically superior elements and learn in what manner and to what extent these components serve an important defensive and narcissistically equilibrating function.

The more successful therapeutic task arises when the narcissistically inferior components become available for processing. It is then that the therapist will want to establish an accepting, understanding, and empathically attuned bond with this aspect of the patient's personality. The processing of the narcissistically inferior components leads to both an increased understanding of their connection with narcissistically defensive attitudes, and to an increased questioning of the origins of and reasons behind these narcissistically impoverished feelings. Gradually, the opposite components of narcissistic grandiosity and superiority can be brought into focus and understood in terms of their defensive function.

The strategy I am describing here is analogous to the approach to paranoid patients (who form an extreme form of narcissistic pathology).* In the treatment of paranoid patients, the strategy dictated by the paranoid process is not that of a frontal attack on the patient's delusional system or feelings of grandiosity but, rather, an empathic contact and understanding of the patient's sense of weakness, impotence, vulnerability, and victimization—what we have called the "soft underbelly" of the paranoid system. As the elements of that soft underbelly are gradually worked through, understood, and resolved, the paranoid defense crumbles and evaporates simply because there is no longer any need for it. Something similar is in question in dealing with patients with narcissistic pathology. The preferred strategy is not to attack the narcissistically superior aspect of the patient's pathology in any sense, but to after a fashion "handle it with kid gloves." Any attempt to intrude on, manipulate, or modify the patient's narcissistically defensive stance can only have the results of increasing the titre of narcissistic embattlement, and undermining any opportunity for strengthening the

---

*For an extended discussion of the treatment of paranoid patients, see Chapter 7.

therapeutic alliance and gaining a foothold that will give promise of therapeutic modification. If the therapist can ally himself with the narcissistically inferior side of the patient and can put himself in understanding, accepting, and empathic contact with the patient's sense of shamefulness, enviousness, worthlessness, inferiority, and so on, the chances for therapeutic amelioration are considerably enhanced.

Shame

For example, shame is one of the primary signal affects of the narcissistically inferior introject. As Kinston (1983) points out, the shame-prone individual is often caught between the dilemma of defensive shamelessness or shameful hiding. Such patients can create a wide variety of devices for hiding their inner sense of shamefulness and inadequacy from the therapist. The move toward shamelessness and unfeeling isolation is a retreat to the protective confines of the isolated and self-sufficient grandiose self. Such patients must ultimately be brought into contact with their underlying feelings of shame (Morrison 1984).

The alleviation of shame ultimately depends on acceptance of the self, not only by others but by the self. In therapy the process starts with acceptance of the patient's narcissistically inferior sense of himself by the therapist. The therapist, however, does not lose sight of the fact that the patient's shameful posture rests on an underlying narcissistic dynamic that reflects a failure on the part of the real self of the patient to attain the narcissistically invested demands of the ideal self (Morrison 1983), so that the patient is left with a subjective sense of inner defectiveness and inadequacy. In other words, the shame experience is in some sense defending against underlying narcissistic and exhibitionistic wishes to be admired and praised. Following the dictates of pathological narcissism, particularly the law of the all or nothing, for such patients not to receive the expected and demanded degree of acknowledgment, admiration, and praise is to be inadequate and shameful. For such patients, there is no middle ground. To be ordinary, or average, or "good enough" is not acceptable.

Care must be taken in the exposure of this narcissistically vulnerable and inadequate aspect of the patient. If such exposure is undertaken too rapidly or intrusively, the patient may respond with a heightened titre of narcissistic demand and narcissistic rage. Proneness to shame is accompanied by an exquisite sensitivity to any implications of narcissistic affront or devaluation. It is only when the patients achieve a degree of sufficient trust in the analytic interaction that they begin to reveal the underlying sense of narcissistic vulnerability and their intense needs to protect and shield themselves from external view. These concealed narcissistic wishes, which reflect the dynamics of the superior narcissistic configuration, can be brought into focus, dealt with, and integrated only to the extent that they have been accepted and adequately processed. Because of the reciprocal linkage between these various aspects of the patient's narcissistic pathology, to a certain extent their processing takes place along parallel paths. The patient will not be able to resolve his envy of others until he has reached a point at which he is able to accept that what he has is good enough, that he can get along very well with that, and that not having something that others may possess is in no way a deprivation or defeat for him.

Transference Neurosis

As the components of the narcissistic configuration become increasingly identifiable in the patient's life experience and attitudes, the same elements enter into the therapeutic relationship and come to express themselves in the transference neurosis. The degree to and pace at which this occurs will vary considerably from patient to patient, but as this progression takes place the therapist will begin the task of identifying the component elements with the patient. In the idealizing transference, the qualities of narcissistic perfection and superiority are attributed to the therapist/analyst; correspondingly, the aspects of narcissistic inferiority are attributed to the self. The therapist must be alert to this self-devaluation and its implications. The idealization is best accepted and tolerated without comment or attempt at correction in the first instance. The therapist must not lose sight, however, of the related and often hidden or implicit self-devaluation. The decision as to when to move to the objective of gaining greater clarification of the narcissistic introjective configurations is a matter of clininical acumen. The analyst would have to feel that the idealizing transference had been relatively securely established without excessive threat to the patient's narcissistic vulnerability, and that the therapeutic alliance had evolved to the point at which the next step in the process could be usefully undertaken.

The mirror transference, in contrast, represents the attempt to preserve the original infantile narcissism by way of its concentration upon a grandiose self. To the extent that all power and perfection are assigned to the grandiose self, this introjective movement is accompanied by a projection of all imperfections, particularly the aspects of the inferior narcissistic configuration, to the outside. In the respective forms of the mirror transference (see pp. 194 to 196), the patient's effort is directed to enlisting the object in the service of sustaining and supporting the grandiose self. As with the idealizing transference, the emergence of and reactivation of the grandiose self within the mirror transference must be accepted and tolerated. The task here is even more onerous for the therapist, insofar as the emergence of the grandiose self is inevitably accompanied by the devaluation of the object. If the elements of the narcissistic superior configuration are allowed to emerge into the light of day and to unveil themselves, they not only carry with them important communications about the patient's inner world but they inevitably bring with them the bits and pieces of the other side of the narcissistic configuration, that against which the patient's grandiosity and superiority act as a defense.

Efforts on the part of the therapist to engage with and work on aspects of the patient's grandiosity are bound to prove relatively unsuccessful and ineffective. Rather, the therapeutic task is to try to gain access to the elements of narcissistic inferiority. To the extent that these can be focused, explored, and understood in the complexity of their origins and motivations, the narcissistic defenses will yield, and the supporting substructures of the narcissistic superiority and grandiosity will crumble. The implications of this approach, therefore, stand in stark opposition to the theoretical emphasis in Kohut's (1971) approach. One might almost say that Kohut proposes his theory of a normal path of narcissistic development that includes both idealization and the development of the grandiose self as a necessary prop to his insistence on the clinical importance of the therapist's acceptance of and empathic tolerance for these narcissistic elements. The position taken here would rather emphasize the importance of such empathic acceptance within its appropriate and limited focus, but would insist that the narcissistic configurations are in essence pathological and that they function in reciprocal, defensive relationship. Whatever side of the narcissistic configuration dominates the clinical picture, it maintains itself by defensive pressures against the opposite narcissistic configuration. This is the essential understanding and insight that governs the strategy of clinical intervention in these cases.

Countertransference Vicissitudes

In connection with the vicissitudes of the narcissistic transferences, it follows that the analyst's countertransference reaction bears particular weight in effecting a therapeutic outcome. The universal experience with such narcissistic patients is that the countertransference pressures are unremitting and constant. The emergence of narcissistic transferences creates a situation in which the analyst's own narcissism is put under constant pressure and assault. The reactivation of the grandiose self often results in the heightening of narcissistic resistances. Some patients will find it necessary to defeat the analyst at his own game. They cannot abide the notion that their own improvement or gaining of a higher level of satisfaction and effectiveness could be due to the effort of some other individual. Such patients are afflicted with the basic envy of the analyst and all that he possesses in terms of knowledge, power, and status. They find it necessary to deny any dependency in the relationship and to expunge any feelings of affection, admiration, or respect from the relationship. They may seek to devalue the analytic process and to deny their own emotional experience, particularly when feelings of attachment and dependency arise. The denial of the separateness and the difference from themselves of the analyst is a part of this picture and may be reflected in varying degrees of merger, twinship, or mirroring. Both the intense envy of the analyst, and the need to defeat him and destroy the analytic process place the analyst in an extremely difficult position in which his own narcissism, his identity as an analyst and a healer, are jeopardized. There is a constant pressure for the analyst to respond by devaluing the patient, countering the narcissistic assault by a counterattack that will defeat the patient's narcissism, feeling that the patient is unanalyzable, or even more subtly moving too quickly and directly or even objectively to confront the patient's grandiosity and make correct but ill-timed interpretations calculated to modify the patient's narcissistic position.

The patient's attempts to idealize the therapist create a different pattern of narcissistic pressures, since they may play into the analyst's or therapist's own unresolved narcissistic needs and propensities for narcissistic enhancement. If the therapist's own grandiosity and the components of the grandiose self have not been adequately integrated and resolved, the therapist remains vulnerable to these countertransference risks.

From the point of view of the paranoid process, these countertransference vicissitudes reflect the interaction of projections and introjections operating between patient and therapist. The induction of a countertransference response on the part of the therapist or analyst is set up by the projection on the part of the patient of some part of the narcissistic configuration. In the case of idealizations, that projected element tends to derive from the superior narcissistic introject, and on the part of the mirroring process the projections tend to come from the inferior narcissistic configuration, while the superior narcissistic elements are introjectively maintained in the grandiose self.

Pressures are thereby created for the therapist to internalize the projective content and to be drawn affectively into the corresponding narcissistically inferior or superior position. The therapist is drawn toward responding to the patient's idealization by taking on more of a narcissistically invested and important role. He may find himself giving advice, taking over areas of the patient's responsibility, imposing interpretations or observations on the patient, and in the extreme acting the role of the all-knowing, all-caring, all-giving, omnipotent therapist. He may also be drawn into responding to the inherent demands of the mirroring process, in subtle ways supporting or bolstering the patient's grandiosity, or responding to the implicit projective pressures by feeling somehow diminished, unimportant, ineffective, worthless, envious in one or other regard of the patient, and so forth.

The Role of Internalizations

Projection/Introjection

The role of internalizations may be the most central and significant component of the therapeutic process in dealing with this form of psychopathology. The emergence of the transference/countertransference interaction is based on the interplay of projective and introjective processes. The patient's projection of narcissistic components onto the transitional object created within the context of the relationship with the analyst is the basis for the transference. The therapist's or analyst's corresponding introjection of that transitional projective content and his internal processing of it provides the basis for the countertransference. The resulting process of mutually interacting projections and introjections tends to metabolize the projective content.

Various authors have attempted to describe this process in metaphoric terms—we can think of Winnicott's (1960b) metaphor of maternal "holding" and Bion's (1984) metaphor of the "container." For example, the patient projects idealized elements onto the figure of the analyst. The analyst comfortably and congenially accepts this projection, easily assimilates it, and integrates it with the ongoing flow of his responsiveness to the patient. In the face of the patient's idealization, he remains unconflicted and comfortable both with the idealization and with his own inherent limitations. As long as he is able to avoid the countertransference traps, his response to the patient is not that of an idealized superior or omnipotent object. Rather, it is that of an ordinary human being who remains interested, respectful, and appropriately committed to the patient and his welfare. What is reflected back to the patient from this idealization is not a sense of devaluation, contempt, or trivializing disregard of the patient. Such a response would play out the counter-transference paradigm and would reinforce the corresponding feelings in the patient of narcissistic inferiority, unimportance, inadequacy, and even shame. Rather, the patient receives from the therapist a sense of his own value in the therapist's eyes, and a projective content that would call for a different affective response from the patient, namely, one of greater equality, balance, mutual involvement, and collaboration.

While the process can work in contexts of transient transference/countertransference interaction, even within limited time segments of the therapeutic involvement, the same processes actually play themselves out over much broader time frames. The patient's need to idealize the therapist is constantly eroded by the flow of realistic impressions, gathered over long periods of therapeutic interaction, of the failings, human limitations, and inadequacies of the therapist. The patient must ultimately integrate this flow of awareness into his assessment of the stature and narcissistically invested superiority of his therapist. The pervasive fact in a good therapeutic relationship is that the idealized object is not at all discomforted, conflicted, troubled, or unsettled by his own obvious weakness and limitations. He is comfortably and easily able to assimilate and integrate these into his overall functioning and suffers no deficit of self-esteem when these shortcomings are brought home to him.

Corrective Effects

The patient learns within this context that it is possible to be competent, effective, and have a meaningful place in the world and in human affairs without having to scale the heights of grandiosity and perfection. He learns that there is such a thing as being good enough, that to be imperfect and limited does not necessarily imply worthlessness and shamefulness. In the ongoing interplay of projections and introjections, these gradual modifications of what is internalized from the analytic relationship by the patient take on a different quality, in which the narcissistic titre is modified, in which the pressure of narcissistic demands is shifted off the extreme basis that underlies the patient's psychopathology to a more moderate middle ground which allows for the emergence and development of meaningful ideals, values, and ambitions.

From Transference to Therapeutic Alliance

These modifications take place within the transference/countertransference interaction, which provides the matrix for the interplay of introjections and projections. However, there is another important dimension of the analytic process, which plays itself out in the context of the therapeutic alliance. The processes of identification are carried on in parallel with the introjective elements we have been discussing. The capacity for meaningful and constructive identifications becomes more available as the transference vicissitudes are gradually worked through and resolved. As the pathogenic narcissistic configurations give way to more moderate and realistic forms of narcissistic self-investment, the path is open for the emergence of more meaningful and selective identifications, which tend to be based in the alliance segment of the analytic process (Meissner 1981b).

As the transference elements are resolved, more and more of the therapeutic interaction tends to be based on meaningfully emergent alliance factors. The therapist or analyst emerges more clearly and decisively as an object for meaningful identification. The entire process takes place on an unconscious level, although in transient and partial ways the effects or consequences of the process may rise to a level of conscious awareness for either analyst or patient. There is nothing that either analyst or patient can do that will foster or facilitate these important identifications beyond the effort to work in an effective, meaningful, and therapeutically useful manner in the therapy itself. At no point does it serve the therapeutic process or the patient for the therapist to propose himself as an object for identification in any sense. This would indeed reflect the analyst's failure to avoid the narcissistic countertransference trap of narcissistic superiority.

But in fact the therapist does serve in meaningful ways as such a model, and from time to time the patient's wishes to be like the analyst or the patient's experience of finding himself responding to situations with attitudes, thoughts, or feelings that he links with the figure of the analyst become grist for the therapeutic mill. The therapist's task is neither to encourage nor discourage such identifications but to allow them to follow their natural course unimpeded by countertransference interferences. To the extent that this task can be realized, the patient's identifications become selective, differentiated, and autonomous, and reflect a pattern of self-generative creativity and expression that is authentically the patient's own and becomes the basis for the integration of an authentic and purposeful sense of self. Such an integration owes nothing to the analyst beyond the unconscious seeding of an intrapsychic process leading to increasing autonomy and integration of the patient's own self as a by-product of the analytic effort.

Part Three

Psychotherapy of the
Paranoid Patient

Chapter Six

Diagnosis

The intent of this chapter is to apply the psychotherapeutic schema developed in Chapter 2 to the treatment of patients with frank paranoid psychopathology. We will take up the question of paranoid characteristics and the diagnosis of paranoid and related conditions and then consider the issues related to the psychotherapy of these patients in greater detail.

Paranoid Characteristics

The first question we must ask is, "What does a paranoid individual look like?" What are the characteristics that allow us to identify an individual as suffering from paranoid pathology? From one point of view, the question is easy to answer, insofar as the paranoid manifestations are often dramatic and striking, but in another sense the answer is difficult, since these same characteristics tend to shade off into various grades of expression that might easily be found in a relatively normal population. We can speak of a paranoid style, a manner of construction of life experience and an organization of the perception of reality which permit a partial testing and validation of the subject's experience, but which at the same time involve distortions in the individual's reality experience. The paranoid state of mind can be seen as an organization of coherent beliefs which allows the individual to interpret and organize his reality to serve certain adaptive needs. The manner in which the individual organizes his experience serves specific defensive needs, particularly in defending against underlying anxiety or depression.

Blaming Tendency

One dominant characteristic of the paranoid style is the tendency to displace responsibility from oneself to others. In this sense, the paranoid sees difficulties not in terms of internal conflict or inadequacies but, rather, in terms of forces and external influences that cause him difficulties. Instead of blaming himself as a depressive individual might, the paranoid blames others for his unhappiness. By this means the individual avoids the self-blame that is so painful and threatening, while at the same time allowing him to maintain a certain measure of self-esteem and self-justification. The blaming maneuver allows the paranoid individual to feel that his own behavior, feelings, or beliefs are indeed right, true, and good, so that others who do not see things his way or do not agree with his view of reality may be regarded as wrong, stupid, devious, or even malicious.

Suspiciousness

The trait of suspiciousness is pervasive in paranoid personalities. Paranoid suspiciousness and guardedness serve an important self-protective function and allow the individual to preserve the rightness of his interpretation of reality. Paranoid suspiciousness is usually quite insistent in its effort to assimilate the available data in reality into the paranoid beliefs. This is not intellectual curiosity but a constant pressure which requires that the data of reality be modified, distorted, or reinterpreted to make them consistent with the paranoid beliefs. Clinically, paranoid patients are quite resistant to any attempts at clarification, testing of reality, or interpretation that are not consistent with their paranoid convictions. Any such efforts on the part of therapists serve only to cast the therapist in the role of one who seeks to attack the paranoid patient at the point of his greatest vulnerability.

Grandiosity

Paranoid grandiosity is a general feature of paranoid states, but the intensity and degree of pathological distortion involved in the grandiosity are subject to considerable variability. Freud noted the role of grandiosity in paranoid states in helping to preserve the individual's self-esteem. The paranoid retreat to grandiosity not only involves a denial and a distortion of the perception of reality, and particularly of the individual's own inadequacies or limitations, but also serves as a basis for assertion of his own specialness and rightness.

Delusions

In its most pathological form, paranoid grandiosity expresses itself in terms of delusions of an identity that is special, extraordinary, unique. Psychotically paranoid individuals may identify themselves with important historical or religious figures: Jesus, the Blessed Virgin, one of the saints, or important political and public figures. The grandiosity, however, can be seen in more subtle forms, as, for example, in ideas of reference in which the patient is convinced that others are watching him and thinking things about him (usually uncomplimentary things, accusing him of certain sins and particularly of homosexuality). Such ideas may take an even more elaborate form, as when the patient is convinced that he is the object of a far-flung and complicated plot involving Communists or Nazis, the CIA or the FBI, even a far-flung international conspiracy. Hitler's delusions about a worldwide Jewish conspiracy are a well-known example. In such delusions, the patient becomes the focus for intense interest and conspiratorial effort on the part of many individuals, a position which makes him or her someone of considerable importance and interest to others—even though that interest be malicious and destructive.

Paranoid delusions and the individual's conviction of their reality are remarkably strong and unyielding, particularly when the illness has progressed to a psychotic level. Paranoid patients are highly sensitive to any hostility, impatience, or irritation that may come their way, especially when their behavior or the stubbornness of their beliefs may accomplish little more than to elicit such reactions from people around them. Thus, paranoid individuals are unable to modify their beliefs in response to their ongoing experience of reality. But, as Freud points out, the delusional beliefs are usually not without a basis in reality, the so-called "kernel of truth" which gives the paranoid individual sufficient ground to cling to his beliefs. The paranoid conviction may also be based on a set of psychological pressures which make any admission of error or any yielding in one's conviction somehow threatening or painful. The admission of error or inconsistency in the patient's theoretical formulation means that he must also admit some sense of personal defect.

Paranoid Pseudocommunity

The last characteristic of paranoid individuals we will discuss is what has come to be known as the "paranoid pseudocommunity" (Cameron 1959). As the patient's delusion evolves and becomes more consolidated, ideas of reference or persecution may be referred to nonspecific groups or to isolated individuals, but these delusions gradually become organized into perception of a more unified and broadly extended conspiracy which aims to work some harm against the patient. Thus, the patient creates an imaginary organization composed of real and imagined persons who he represents as united in conspiracy to carry out some malicious action against himself. The formation of the pseudo-community marks a final crystallization of a paranoid psychosis.

Diagnosis

It may help at this point to review the diagnostic categories pertaining to paranoia as contained in the Diagnostic and Statistical Manual of the APA (DSM-III). The predominant feature of paranoid disorders in this classification is persistent persecutory delusions, or delusions of jealousy. These delusions may be simple or elaborate but usually involve a single theme or a series of connected themes as, for example, being the object of a conspiracy, being cheated or spied upon, being followed by suspicious individuals, being threatened by persecutors, being poisoned or drugged, or feeling maliciously maligned, harassed, or obstructed in the attainment of long-term goals. In such individuals, even small slights may be exaggerated out of all proportion and become the nucleus of a delusional system. Delusions of jealousy may occur without any clear persecutory theme. In such cases, without any basis or relevant evidence, a spouse will become convinced that his or her mate has become unfaithful. The offended spouse will then begin to collect small bits of "evidence" to bolster a delusional case.

The paranoid syndromes may be associated with anger and resentment which can escalate to frank physical violence at times. Ideas of reference are common and are often accompanied by tendencies toward social isolation, seclusiveness, or behavioral eccentricity.

The Pathology of Paranoia

The recognition and diagnostic categorization of paranoid conditions is not clinically difficult. There is general agreement as to what constitute identifiable paranoid symptoms. But historically, consensus as to the meaning of and the relevant diagnostic configurations in which such paranoid manifestations have occurred has been somewhat elusive. The modern history of the problem can be traced from the nineteenth century, particularly in the work of Heinroth, who emphasized the notion of paranoia as a form of mental derangement, predominantly affecting the intellect and understanding rather than the will or affects. The question remained whether paranoia should be counted as a persistent and chronic condition in its own right or whether it should be included among the psychotic conditions that tended to follow a deteriorating course, terminating in dementia. Kahlbaum, for example, regarded paranoia as a form of delusional illness, characterized by persecutory or grandiose thoughts, that tended to be relatively stable and showed little or no signs of progressive deterioration.

It was only at the turn of the century that any extensive degree of clarity or definition was brought to this confusing situation. The psychiatric world of the period was dominated by the thinking of Kraepelin, who was able to establish the validity of the descriptive approach in psychiatry and particularly contributed a descriptive definition of paranoia. Kraepelin regarded the ultimately deteriorating diseases as forms of dementia praecox and drew a distinction between dementia paranoides and paranoia itself. Patients who were simply paranoid were defined as those who had relatively systematized delusions without hallucinations, whose course did not lead to dementia, and whose personality functioning remained otherwise intact. Kraepelin also described an intermediate group, which he called the paraphrenias, in which relatively systematized delusions and hallucinations were found but which did not seem to pass through the stages of deterioration that Kraepelin identified with dementia praecox.

Kraepelin's conception of paranoia brought a certain degree of diagnostic clarity to this situation. He observed that cases of paranoia were characterized by prominent delusions, which were often the only symptomatic expression of the disease. He described these cases as developing a chronic, stable system of delusions without any accompanying disorders of thought, will, or action. But even in Kraepelin's approach it proved difficult to hold closely to the constraints of this definition. A close examination of Kraepelin's cases reveals that many of them in fact belong to other clinical groupings, including various forms of dementia praecox, manic-depressive psychosis, and chronic alcoholic delusional conditions. It was because of this difficulty that Kraepelin later weeded out the cases that did not seem to conform to his definition and grouped them under the closely-related heading of the paraphrenias. The residual cases, in which pure delusional distortion was the more or less monosymptomatic expression of the disease, he regarded as the true paranoias.

Along with this diagnostic crystallization there were emerging controversies over the nature of the disorder. One group saw the difficulty as primarily affective (Kleist), while others argued that the disturbance was essentially intellectual or that the emotional disturbance was not the primary cause (Krafft-Ebing, Bleuler). Bleuler regarded paranoia as a psychosis in which some complex of ideas or a group of such complexes is associated with powerful emotions, so that any thinking related to this complex is powerfully determined by the affects instead of by facts or logic. Bleuler called such thinking "autistic." The persistence of this tendency gives rise to errors so that, whenever anything in the individual's experience arouses these associations, the errors are perpetuated and extended into delusions which become persistent and tend to elaborate themselves. Only the thoughts and feelings of the patients which relate to this particular complex can be said to be abnormal. There is no dementia and no other psychotic symptoms. Abbott (1914) noted in this connection that such autistic formations and delusions may be found in other forms of psychosis but also may be identified in relatively normal phenomena such as daydreaming or social or religious prejudices. He noted in passing Freud's recent (1911) account of the Schreber case, but adhering to the Kraepelinian line he discounted it by reason of the fact that the case was not one of true paranoia but, rather, of paranoid dementia—what we would term a paranoid schizophrenia in contemporaty categories.

The Kraepelinian preoccupation with differentiating a clear-cut diagnostic category has given way to greater uncertainty as to whether such a category of true or pure paranoia does in fact exist. Harry Stack Sullivan was wont to say that in every schizophrenic there are paranoid elements and that in every paranoid, if one looked carefully and deeply enough, there are elements of schizophrenia. Consequently, we are much inclined to accept Freud's interpretation of the Schreber case, for example, as having more general applicability to the understanding of paranoid phenomena. In addition, there is a greater realization that the paranoid symptom complex may express itself in a wide variety of clinical contexts and that these manifestations of paranoid disturbance share certain identifiable characteristics.

Along with this diagnostic flexibility and diffusion, there has also been a shift from the descriptive preoccupation of an earlier day to a greater concern with the understanding of developmental and defensive aspects of paranoid mechanisms. Abbot (1914) notes the shift from a descriptive to an interpretive approach as a result of the Freudian influence. He commented:

> Symptoms, symptom-pictures, even diseases and disease-processes, are being thrust into the background, while the mechanisms of the origin and development of the content of

thinking and feeling, and the interpretation and explanation of symptoms, are coming into the foreground. Make-up or personality and individual experiences assume increased value and importance. (p. 31)

Abbot thus cast a glance down the long road toward the present, which has tended to lead away from the descriptive preoccupations of a more or less Kraepelinian perspective toward a deeper concern with the understanding of mechanisms and processes, with their genesis and function, which characterizes our contemporary viewpoint.

Psychosis

An important discrimination must be made between psychotic forms of paranoia and paranoid schizophrenia. Paranoid symptoms are often a prominent part of schizophrenic illness and take the form of persecutory or grandiose delusions, or hallucinations with persecutory or grandiose content. Delusions of jealousy may also occur in schizophrenic patients. However, paranoid schizophrenic patients also show the stigmata of the schizophrenic process, which may manifest itself in a variety of disorganized symptoms, such as an unusual degree of agitation, anger, argumentativeness, violence, or feelings of fearfulness and terror, along with concerns about autonomy, gender identity, and sexual preference.

On the psychotic level, the inner world of the paranoid patient is plagued by the fragmentation and fusion of intrapsychic representations, regressive symbiotic needs, and precarious ego functioning reflecting incomplete resolution of separation-individuation. Issues of engulfment and enslavement are compounded with fantasies of fusion or annihilation. Paranoid fears of invasion or engulfment are mingled paradoxically with fears of abandonment, desertion, or betrayal, jeopardizing both true intimacy and separation (Blum 1981).

Besides the paranoid psychosis, the DSM-III describes two other forms of paranoid illness, namely, the shared paranoid disorder and the paranoid state. In the shared paranoid disorder, the delusional system develops as the result of a close relationship with another person who already has an established paranoid psychosis. Usually, when the second individual can be separated from the individual with the primary disease, the former's delusional beliefs diminish or disappear. Such shared delusional systems at times may involve more than one person. This phenomenon may be at work in some religious cults, for example. In contrast, the paranoid state is a more or less acute condition that arises as a result of some recent traumatic change in the individual's living or work situation. Such paranoid states usually occur with a relatively sudden onset but are time-limited and rarely become chronic. Such states may occur in recent immigrants or refugees (Grinberg and Grinberg 1983), in prisoners of war, in military inductees, or even in young people or college students who leave home for the first time.

Paranoid Personality

The paranoid style may also be expressed in the form of a personality disorder, that is, a form of personality organization in which the paranoid features have become embedded as a long-standing and relatively consistent fashion of dealing with reality and personal relationships. In the paranoid personality, the suspiciousness and lack of trust found in other forms of paranoia become pervasive and long-standing characteristics. These individuals are usually hypersensitive and easily feel slighted or offended. They are constantly scanning the environment for even minimal clues that may serve to validate their prejudicial ideas. They have a limited range of affective experience, and generally feel little in the way of anxiety or depression. Such persons are incapable of accepting blame and avoid it under any circumstances in whatever way possible, even when blame may be warranted.

Putting such individuals in a new set of circumstances presents them with an intense challenge. They are forced to intensely survey the new context for the available clues that will confirm their attitudes and biases. The selection and emphasis of such confirming details invariably make it impossible for them to appreciate the broader meaningfulness of a given context and the modifying or countervailing aspects of the broader picture. It is by no means surprising that their ultimate conclusion proves to be exactly what they expected and were looking for in the first place.

Paranoid individuals are generally argumentative and easily aroused to agitated contentiousness. They are experts in making mountains out of molehills. To others, they may appear tense, anxious, guarded, even devious, sensitive to any least innuendo or any perceived hostility, and ready at a moment's notice to counterattack. They are ready at all points to criticize and devalue others, but any criticism of them is simply unacceptable. In their relationship with others, they seem cold or unfeeling, lacking any sense of humor or spontaneity.

Paranoid individuals may often be seen as energetic, ambitious, hard-working, and competent. Generally, they tend to be intelligent and intellectual, but they are often also hostile, stubborn, and rigid. They tend to be inflexible in their judgments and unwilling to compromise.

The capacity for intimacy is severely limited, since the capacity for trust is at best fragile. They have an excessive need to be self-sufficient, with an exaggerated sense of their own self-importance, such that participation in group activities is either uncongenial or threatening.

In contrast to the paranoid psychotic, the paranoid personality retains many areas of intact functioning and is able to preserve relatively cohesive object relationships, although object constancy is lacking or fragile within the persecutory relationship. As Blum (1981) notes, the system of narcissistic grandiosity and the persecutory relation act to preserve the connection with the inconstant narcissistic object. This sets the stage for expectations and/or convictions of antagonism, betrayal, infidelity, and conspiracy. The outcome is often hate and rage directed at the disappointing object or its substitutes. The object is kept under a cloud of suspicion and distrust. There is a pervasive need to search out and maintain connection with the object, to seek the persecution of the hurtful, inconstant, and betraying narcissistic object.

It can readily be seen that the characteristics of paranoid person-alities may be found in varying degrees in a great many people. As Blum (1981) comments:

> This disposition for the use of projection, particularly the pro-jection of aggression, criticism, and reproach is potentially present in everyone. Others may be blamed for any disappointment, injury, or transgression, and unacceptable impulses are external-ized. (p. 790)

The diagnosis, therefore, can be made only when there is a cluster of such characteristics and when the level of difficulty they create in the patient's life becomes sufficiently maladaptive or disruptive. The diagnostic problem, however, is that such paranoid traits may be manifested in minor degrees in a significant portion of the normal population. Consequently, drawing the line between pathology and normality is sometimes a considerable problem. Paranoid manifesta-tions are frequently quite subtle and form a relatively hidden or latent portion of the patient's personality that emerges only under special circumstances or stresses, or after lengthy periods of treatment.

Paranoid Traits

Centrality

A number of indexes might reflect the subtle and more or less minimal operation of paranoid factors and may serve as clues for an underlying but as yet not readily identifiable paranoid illness, or may reflect minimal levels of a paranoid personality style that has not yet reached pathological proportions. One such indicator of the paranoid process is the notion of "centrality." This is the quality of the patient's thinking that places him in the center of interest or attention from other people. The feelings of core vulnerability may find subtle expression in the individual's feelings of being impinged on by outside forces, of a sense of being a passive recipient of external influences over which he feels he has little or no control.

Hypersensitivity

Hypersensitivity is another subtle indicator. The individual may seem more than usually reactive to comments or opinions of other people; there are often feelings of being slighted, wronged, or mistreated. Such sensitivity is not uncommon within the normal spectrum of behaviors and may often have reasonable justification in reality. When individuals present a facade of excessive self-sufficiency, one can sense beneath it an underlying sense of vulnerability which is being defended against and countered by the hyperadequate facade. Both the hypersensitivity and the hyperadequacy reflect different aspects of the patient's underlying vulnerability. The characteristic preoccupation with hidden meanings reflects the same underlying issues. In terms of the inherent dynamics of the paranoid position, things cannot be taken at face value, but the hidden, subtle, and fragmentary implications must be exposed in order that the patient's experience be consistent with his paranoid view of reality. The meanings which are thus divined behind the apparent data of reality are always overladen with threat, harm, or deleterious implication for the paranoid individual.

Autonomy

Another subtle and pervasive concern of paranoid individuals is that over autonomy. This may take various forms, often subtle, such as a fear of loss of control. But often the concerns may be expressed in avoidances, or even unexpressed and silent inner reservations that resist the suspected attempts at influence or persuasion on the part of others. Paranoid autonomy is a threatened and fragile autonomy.

Externalization

We have previously noted the tendency to blaming in paranoid individuals, but this characteristic may also be subtle. It is closely related to the tendency to externalize, that is, to formulate and understand problems and difficulties in terms of external circumstances, forces, events, persons, et cetera, rather than in terms of one's own internal difficulties or limitations.

Inadequacy

Feelings of inadequacy or deficiency are pervasive in paranoid individuals. They may take the form of complaints about being too short or too tall, or of concern about genital size or adequacy, or they may take a more diffuse and nonspecific form, as in concerns about being somehow different. Some paranoid individuals will express feelings of being an outsider, of not being part of the social, political, or cultural contexts in which they live.

Authority

The whole question of authority relations is particularly problematic. Individuals with a paranoid predisposition tend to be excessively concerned with problems of power and powerlessness. These concerns may be expressed in a form of personality functioning that is described as authoritarian. Such individuals tend to be conventional, that is, rigidly adhering to conventional middle-class values; they tend to have a submissive and uncritical attitude toward the idealized moral authorities in any social group. They tend to be extremely sensitive to and reactive against anyone who would violate conventional values, and they tend to adopt excessively punitive responses to such violations. Their thinking tends to be cast in more or less rigid categories, tending toward superstition and stereotypical thinking. They are occupied with issues of control, power-submission, and strength-weakness, and have a strong tendency to identify with figures seen as powerful and influential. Conflicts and concerns over domination and enslavement are prominent and recurrent. Such individuals tend to have a generalized hostile attitude, seeing the environment as hostile and threatening, and expressing the belief that, unless control and rigid constraints are maintained, dreadful or destructive consequences will follow. Projection in such individuals is a major form of defense.

These attitudes can find ready application in religious contexts. They can be reflected in excessively rigid and dogmatic stances, in prejudicial attitudes toward other religious groups, in moral rigidities and stereotypical thinking, in rigid and unthinking adherence to authoritative moral directives, and in forms of superstition and fanatical investment. Any authority figure may become the object of such authoritarian attitudes and may well experience passivity and willing compliance with any directive or pronouncement he might make. The wise boss, leader, pastor, teacher, or even therapist knows that such superficial compliance may well be accompanied by its underlying measure of rebellion. These attitudes and feelings are all too familiar in the psychoanalytic consulting room.

To the clinical psychiatrist, all of these indexes may suggest the first stirrings or the minimal reflections of an underlying process. But in the broader nonclinical context, these same indexes are the stuff of everyday human experience.

Related Conditions

Envy and Jealousy

This statement receives considerable reinforcement from a consideration of certain pathological conditions that may not be explicitly paranoid but are nonetheless closely related to paranoia. The first of these are envy and jealousy. Such feelings are relatively common in human relationships. Early views of envy and jealousy connected them with an inner sense of deficiency that involved feelings of self-dissatisfaction and self-criticism. Early analytic thinkers related such feelings to unconscious guilt feelings, usually relating them to unconscious oedipal wishes. The unconscious guilt created a sense of lack of self-love and self-esteem, leaving the jealous person sensitive to any criticism and excessively yearning for approval or recognition. For such individuals, the loss of love is equivalent to a loss of their own self-esteem. More recent views have emphasized the vulnerability of these individuals to recurrent losses, which may contribute to inner conflicts which can be defended against only by primitive forms of projection and denial, thus enabling the individual to avoid the intense experience of grief and rage. Jealous and envious individuals suffer from significant narcissistic vulnerability.

The continuity between states of envy and jealousy and paranoid states is not difficult to discern. Not only are the mechanisms of denial and projection at work in all these states but there is a sense of wounded narcissistic expectation and injustice which serves to displace the blame for the individual's lack or loss to another person or persons, or even to impersonal forces in the social environment. The envious person begins to feel not only that he has a right to the possession or state of well-being that he desires but that the fact that another person should possess it is equivalently an injustice that he has suffered at the hands of that other person.

The Grudge

Another state of mind that mimics aspects of paranoia is the attitude of vengeance or holding a grudge. The grudge has certain characteristics consistent with paranoia: It occurs in the context of a close, positive relationship; the degree of resentment is usually out of proportion to the wrong committed; the grudge-holder often feels urged to defend or publicize the wrong committed against him; there is a tendency to phobically avoid the object of the grudge; and finally, the thought content is usually distinctively paranoid in quality. The injury, whether real or imagined, is narcissistic, that is, an injury to self-esteem that is interpreted as a humiliation. At a greater degree of intensity, the seeking of revenge is associated with pain and rage secondary to loss. The vengeful person is unforgiving, remorseless, ruthless, and inflexible. At the extreme, the vengeful person lives with but a single object in mind: to get even. He seeks revenge against all odds, no matter what the cost, and experiences no guilt or concern for possible moral or other consequences of his revenge. The paranoid motifs of injured narcissism and victimization at the hands of persecuting objects are evident.

Prejudice

Another widespread phenomenon that reflects the continuities with paranoid dynamics is that of prejudice. Prejudice is a complex phenomenon with many intrapsychic, social, economic, and even cultural determinants. Our emphasis here is on the psychic mechanisms in prejudicial attitudes, which mimic or approximate those of paranoia. A moment's reflection on social conditions of our time brings home the realization of the multiple forms of prejudice in our society—racial, sexual, religious, economic, and cultural. Prejudicial attitudes are, for all practical purposes, endemic in the population, and given the right combination of circumstances and influences, any one of us may develop frankly prejudicial attitudes on one or other of these scores, depending on the extent to which they impinge on our own narcissistic vulnerability.

Prejudice carries with it an inherent antipathy, suggesting that it is related to underlying fear and anger and that the hostility and rejection are expressing underlying unconscious needs. Study of prejudicial attitudes has revealed the underlying projective mechanisms that contribute to the distorted perceptions and interpretations in such attitudes (Traub-Werner 1984). Prejudicial devaluations are based on underlying projections in which attributes of the subject's own personality are denied and projected onto the object of prejudice. Prejudice also serves in important ways as a defense against depression and the diminution of self-esteem (Meissner 1978b). Study of a group of veterans suffering from depressive and psychophysiological symptoms revealed feelings of hatred for enemies identified as anything foreign or nonwhite. Traub-Werner (1984) calls this form of prejudice a "facilitating defense."

Related Nonpathological Conditions

Belief Systems

There are also important contexts of human endeavor which tend to mimic aspects of the paranoid dynamics but are in themselves non-pathological, such as religious belief systems and value systems. The belief system organizes the understanding of some aspect of reality in terms of a coherent schema of explanation. The belief system requires assent not on the basis of evidence but on the basis of inner needs which the belief system satisfies and responds to. Religious belief systems answer to some of the most basic and fundamental needs and insecurities in man, including his insecurity about the meaning of life and the confrontation with death (Meissner 1984c).

Belief systems may enjoy varying degrees of closedness or openness. The more closed the belief system, the more one sees a rigidity in adherence to it, the greater becomes the insistence on maintaining the totality of the belief system with all of its parts, and the greater the degree of intolerance to other belief systems. The degree of dogmatism, or closedness, is associated with a need to adhere to the belief system as a whole. No single part can be challenged or questioned without posing a threat to the whole. The individual needs the support and security of a complete, totally integrated, unshakable, and unquestionable view of his world and its meaning. If doubt is cast on any portion, this threatens the individual's inner stability. This is the same quality of rigidity and peremptoriness that we have identified in the paranoid's need to maintain his delusional projective system.

The paranoid finds it essential to his sense of inner equilibrium to bring all data into congruence with his delusion and to maintain it even in the face of contradictory evidence. There is thus an analogy between the paranoid delusional system and belief systems, particularly religious belief systems, which involve such basic and fundamental needs. In the area of religious beliefs one finds various degrees of rigidity and dogmatism. This by no means implies that religious belief systems can be reductively regarded as equivalent to paranoid delusional systems, but it does alert the clinician, as well as the pastor, to the likelihood that religious beliefs held with excessive dogmatism, rigidity, and stereo-typical thinking can become the vehicle for underlying paranoid dynamics.

Chapter Seven

Psychotherapy of the Paranoid Patient

Treatability

Two important questions arise in the very beginning of any consideration of the treatment of paranoid patients, namely, the question of treatability and the question of clinical strategy in approaching these difficult patients. The assessment of treatability rests, in general, on the degree to which the paranoid system has become consolidated or embedded on the one hand, and on the extent and availability of the resources of the patient's ego to engage in and work through the demands of the psychotherapeutic process on the other. In these terms, some special problems arise in attempts at psychotherapeutic intervention with such patients.

The first difficulty is the apparent lack of trust. This is a pervasive problem for all paranoid patients and is more severe in those patients in whom the paranoid manifestations come to dominate the clinical picture. Suspiciousness and an inherent lack of trust become the hallmarks of paranoid psychopathology. Consequently, the issues of lack of trust and the impediments it creates to meaningful psychotherapeutic work must become issues of the highest priority in approaching the treatment of these patients.

Another problem is the characteristically fragile sense of autonomy that one often sees in paranoid patients. The fragility of the patient's autonomy and its ready susceptibility to regressive pulls may at times be less than apparent when one is dealing with the seeming rigidity of paranoid defenses, but it must be kept in mind that the intensity and apparent impenetrability of such defenses ride upon an underlying sense of exquisite vulnerability and lack of autonomy. Thus, threats to the patient's autonomy become an extremely important focus in the therapeutic work. These threats dictate certain priorities in the setting up of the therapeutic situation which can bolster the threatened autonomy of the paranoid patient, as well as providing a context within which it is no longer quite so necessary for the patient to maintain the sense of rigid and threatened pseudoautonomy that so often characterizes the clinical picture.

Third, the characteristic paranoid defense of projection presents particular problems in the therapeutic context, particularly when the projective defense may be accompanied by varying degrees of denial, or failure of reality testing. Dealing with projective defenses requires considerable skill and calls for particular therapeutic approaches that will allow the therapist to get beyond this first rank of the defensive system that the paranoid patient throws up.

Related to the problem of projection and the rigidity of the paranoid system, the issues of delusional conviction have a profound impact on the patient's pathology and pose particular problems for therapeutic intervention. When the patient's paranoid projective system has reached a level of delusional fixity and conviction that has become psychotic in proportion, it does not augur well for the prospects of therapeutic change. Delusional fixity is largely a matter of the degree to which the paranoid construction has become elaborated and consolidated. One should not presume, however, that when the paranoid construction has become delusional, or is marked by a failure of reality testing, or is accompanied by other signs of psychosis, that the delusional belief system is by that circumstance placed beyond the reach of therapeutic intervention. While the prospects for meaningful therapeutic modification are diminished, they are by no means eliminated. Therapists are often taken by surprise by the extent to which unalterable psychotic convictions can suddenly yield in the face of therapeutic efforts.

Evaluation

The treatability of paranoid patients depends on the diagnostic evaluation. Patients who manifest more or less transient paranoid reactions in the face of particular kinds of stress or regressive pulls would seem to be good prospects for therapeutic intervention. Such is often the case in patients of a more primitive narcissistic or borderline personality structure, in whom the vulnerability to regressive pulls and the degree of regressive potential may be relatively high; such patients often will produce a form of paranoid reaction in regressive crises.* Also, patients who may be characterized as having a paranoid personality disorder are relatively amenable to meaningful psychotherapeutic work. The paranoid attitudes in such patients usually do not attain the level of severe fixity, and their otherwise substantial ego resources augur well for a meaningful therapeutic outcome.

The greater difficulties arise in those patients in whom the paranoid manifestations are built into an otherwise psychotic personality structure. Patients who have transient or episodic psychotic episodes may be treatable in terms of the paranoid dynamics, but the clinical picture is contaminated by the degree of the underlying psychosis. Often, paranoid schizophrenics can be worked with in meaningful terms, particularly when they operate at levels of better compensation and have available a degree of ego capacity that allows them to participate in therapeutic work. However, they often experience a recrudescence of paranoid thoughts and attitudes in periods of relative psychotic decompensation.

We are left, then, with the hard-core, usually chronically psychotic and delusional patients, in whom the paranoid delusional system has a high degree of conviction and fixity, accompanied by elements of psychotic denial and the loss of a capacity for reality testing. The therapist who undertakes the treatment of these patients must be able to play the long shot, realizing the difficulties and dangers of any therapeutic endeavors with them but holding to a rock-bottom optimism that a way may be found to help the patient to alleviate the stigmata of this severe, chronic, and incapacitating disease.

Psychotherapeutic Process

The schema we are proposing deliberately shifts the emphasis from the patient's projective system, with its inherent distortions, to the underlying introjective configuration. The strategy deals with the projective system as a source of information about and a reflection of the underlying introjective configuration from which it derives. The strategy is to bypass rather than to confront, challenge, or test the patient's

---

*See the discussion of these forms of psychopathology in Chapter 4 as well as in Meissner 1984a.

projective system, whether it qualifies as delusional or not. The intention, therefore, is ultimately to undermine the projective system, but with the immediate purpose of allowing the therapeutic work to bring into focus and to begin to deal with the underlying introjective organization.

To this extent, the strategy dictated by the paranoid process would differ considerably from more traditional approaches which focus primarily on the paranoid defensive system, and test and correct the patient's reality distortions. In the present approach, the projective system is viewed as a symptomatic expression of the underlying disorder, located in the pathogenic organization of the patient's core introjects. The rationale is that by focusing, articulating, and bringing to increasing awareness the nature of the patient's introjective configuration, the ground is prepared for the modification and therapeutic change of the introjects, whereby the secondary symptomatic elaboration will be undermined and dispensed with.

Depressive Shift(s)

The second aspect of this overall strategy is to facilitate a shift from paranoid defenses to a more depressive position. The logic of this shift is that as the paranoid defenses, including the projective system, are gradually undermined and surrendered, the underlying depressive core of the patient's illness, specifically related to the more narcissistic and vulnerable aspects of his self-organization, becomes apparent and opens the way to a potentially successful therapeutic intervention. In these terms, the depression is more therapeutically workable and offers the potentiality for more meaningful therapeutic change than the more resistive paranoid stance. The psychotherapeutic schema that follows has a twofold purpose: building up the resources of the patient to engage meaningfully in the psychotherapeutic work, and following a tactic of gradual undermining and circumventing of the paranoid defensive system to allow for meaningful engagement with and resolution of the underlying pathogenic introjective configuration.

Establishing the Therapeutic Alliance

While the therapeutic alliance is the sine qua non for any effective therapy, and the establishing and maintaining of a therapeutic alliance must be a matter of high priority, not only in the beginning of the therapeutic process but throughout its full extent, it is obvious that with paranoid patients the therapeutic alliance is placed in considerable jeopardy. The major impediments to the therapeutic alliance are the patient's lack of capacity for trust and the precarious state of the patient's autonomy, both of which are essential ingredients in the evolution of a meaningful therapeutic alliance.

Despite the obvious difficulties and the inherent precariousness of any therapeutic alliance with paranoid patients, the case is not hopeless. With most paranoid patients, the therapist immediately encounters a facade of suspiciousness, guardedness, and secretiveness. While the patient's defenses may be in a state of hypermobilization due to the circumstances which may have brought him to therapy and because of the inherent threats posed by the threatening relationship to the therapist, it is important to remember that the paranoid patient who comes into psychotherapy is there because his paranoia is failing him. The patient is in therapy because of the failure of his paranoid defenses, which leaves him in a condition of heightened vulnerability and susceptibility to the resulting affective turmoil, whether that be predominantly depressive or anxious or some combination of the two. Implicitly, then, the patient must seek help. The acknowledgment of the need for help and the willingness to seek it thus provide a first important breach in the paranoid defensive system. Despite the patient's pathology, we can infer that there is something in the patient that in fact seeks and may indeed find security and comfort in the therapeutic alliance.

If the patient is brought to and forced to undergo therapy by external pressures of various kinds, then the situation becomes extremely difficult. Not only is the patient basically unwilling to undergo treatment but he is inclined often to perceive these pressures as persecutory delusions, and is only too likely to see the therapist as a malign collaborating agent. The likelihood of the therapist's being able to establish a meaningful therapeutic alliance in the face of the countervailing forces is not very great.

The Therapeutic Contract

Several aspects of the therapist's approach to the patient can, if not overcome these difficulties, at least minimize their interference with therapeutic work. We would emphasize in this context the importance of the therapeutic contract. The therapeutic contract is a complex arrangement which sets the conditions for any therapeutic work and establishes the terms on which both patient and therapist enter the therapeutic relationship. Once an adequate evaluation has been made and a preliminary diagnosis arrived at, patient and therapist must reach an agreement that they will continue with a course of therapy. The therapist's attitude in conducting these arrangements is important; dealings with the patient should be open, frank, honest, and should bear the stamp of unwavering consistency. The therapist's outlook in discussing arrangements with the patient should not be too eager, enthusiastic, or positive. A noncommittal and reserved attitude is in order. Glover's (1955) excellent phrase "noncommittal receptivity" comes to mind.

In these early negotiations, it is desirable that the therapist direct the burden of initiative, the primary motivation for undertaking the therapy, and the fundamental undertaking of responsibility for the therapeutic effort to rest with the patient. If the therapist is more motivated for the therapy than the patient, or if the therapist takes too much responsibility for the course of the therapeutic work and for its outcome, the therapeutic alliance has gotten off on the wrong foot. The therapist promises very little, if possible nothing, expresses his willingness to work with the patient but puts the burden of responsibility for the therapeutic work on the patient. The therapist is there only to help the patient in this undertaking, to understand the patient's difficulties and to participate in the patient's efforts to reach some understanding and resolution of his problems. The specific arrangements of the therapeutic contract include matters such as where and when the meetings will be held, the duration and frequency of them, arrangements regarding the billing and payment of fees, and a clear understanding of the patient's responsibility for coming to the therapeutic hours, for coming to them on time, and particularly for bringing and presenting to the therapist the material on which they will work during the course of the therapy.

Paranoid patients are not often willing participants in this process. Their suspiciousness and guardedness often make it difficult for them to enter into any meaningful agreement with a stranger. But the therapist's frank and open manner, businesslike approach to the discussion of specific details without any attempt at concealment or obfuscation, is often reassuring and allows the patient to take the risk that is involved in making such agreements. There is an important metacommunication to the patient that has to do with the establishing of perhaps the most basic principle on which the therapeutic relationship and the therapeutic work proceed: the principle of the patient's freedom of involvement in therapy. The therapist's matter-of-factness, objectivity, and unwillingness to take inappropriate responsibility for the course and direction of the therapeutic work, the therapist's statement of the patient's responsibilities and working performance in the therapy, all bespeak and reinforce the underlying principle of the patient's free involvement in the therapy.

Another contractual arrangement that strengthens the therapy is the understanding that the patient is to be charged for missed appointments. Whatever the specific arrangements a given therapist may prefer in setting up such a requirement, the central message is that it guarantees the patient's freedom of choice in undertaking the therapeutic work at all points. When he has paid for the hour, he is free to use it as he chooses. He is free to come or not to come. He is free to come on time or not. He is free to come and use the hour as he sees fit—even if that means that he chooses to come and spend the hour in total silence. The arrangement creates a situation in which the therapist is paid for his time and thus is not treated punitively by the patient, nor is he placed in a position of being victimized by the patient's whims or ambivalences. Thus, the patient does not harm the therapist by choosing not to make use of an appointment but only shortchanges himself. This important aspect of the therapeutic contract undercuts the potentiality for a variety of countertransference reactions that would in fact be deleterious to the therapeutic work. The therapist does not have to feel resentful, or feel financially cheated by the patient's behavior; he can be free to deal with the patient's behavior in more therapeutically productive terms.

Testing

A good paranoid patient can be counted on to test these arrangements in a variety of ways and usually to a considerable extent. He is basically unable to trust the therapist to stick by the contractual arrangements, and at the same time he cannot believe that the therapist is willing and able to grant him the degree of autonomy that is implicit in such arrangements. It is important that the therapist keep firmly and consistently to these contractual arrangements. Therapists who disregard or undervalue such contractual arrangements find themselves getting into difficulties with the patient that frequently only intensify the patient's paranoid defenses and ultimately prove disruptive to the therapy. It is useful in such contexts for the therapist to keep in mind the basic principles which are built into the contractual arrangements, since these arrangements have meaning only insofar as they implement and foster the basic principles.

Confidentiality

While staunch adherence to the requirements of confidentiality is essential for meaningful therapy with any patient, it becomes a matter of special necessity with the paranoid patient. The matter of confidentiality should be taken as a matter of course and not, in the beginning of the therapeutic work, made a focus for explicit concern or discussion by the therapist. The therapist should focus upon the actual implementation of clear and unequivocal arrangements for the preservation of confidentiality. If, however, the patient should bring the matter up, as is often the case, the therapist should be prepared to discuss every and all aspects of the arrangements for preserving confidentiality. The therapist should be specific about records that are to be kept and communications that are to be made to outside persons or agencies, and about any ways in which the patient's material is to be used. For example, therapists in training will often present patient material to supervisors. The nature and purpose of this communication can be openly discussed with the patient. It does not serve the patient well and is a violation of the right to privacy of the supervisor to identify the supervisor.

Extreme care needs to be exercised with regard to extratherapeutic communications about the patient, so that as little room as possible is given to the propensity of the paranoid patient to become suspicious or to feel that his confidentiality, which assumes a major place in therapy, may be violated. The two usual channels of such communications are telephone and letter. My own practice when a request for information about any patient comes over the telephone is to stop the requester short and to make the following statement: "I am sorry, but it is not my policy to give out any information over the telephone about any patient past, present, or future. If you feel that you have a legitimate request about an individual patient, please put that request in a letter, specifying what information and for what purposes you are requesting it, and we will do our best to respond." Any legitimate requesters for information about the patient, as, for example, from insurance companies, will readily accept and cooperate in such a process.

The only exception I personally make to this rule about communication over the telephone is when a colleague calls who is known to me and who presents a legitimate claim for information about a patient whom I may have seen or whose treatment I may have supervised. Even in such a context, however, any therapist must exercise good judgment as to what information can be appropriately communicated about the patient for the legitimate clinical needs that are being met. Not all information about the patient is either necessary or pertinent to such requests, and a certain screening should be imposed that allows for sufficient pertinent information to be provided but protects other areas of the patient's privacy and confidentiality.

When a letter arrives requesting information about a patient from a legitimate source, I undertake to write a letter in reply in the presence of and with the collaboration of the patient. Only that information is put in the letter which meets with the consent of the patient. When the substance of the letter is written out in longhand, I turn it over to the patient for his perusal and approval. When the content of the letter has met the patient's approval, in a subsequent meeting the final typed copy of the letter is handed to the patient as yet unsigned. When the patient has read and approved of this final version, I sign the letter and hand the unsealed envelope to the patient. The final steps of actually sealing the envelope and putting it in the mailbox are left to the patient. There is no step in the preparation and sending of such a letter to which the patient is not privy and over which he does not have complete control and power of decision. Without making an explicit issue of confidentiality, the carrying out of such a procedure is immensely relieving and reassuring to the paranoid patient.

Trust

The element of trust is basic to the forming of a therapeutic alliance. Patients come because they are in distress or pain, or because they realize that they are suffering from a condition that places them at significant risk. There is a certain fundamental trust that they place in the therapist as a helping figure, presuming that something can be done by the therapist to help them obtain the relief they seek. The process of coming to a physician and submitting oneself to the physician's care implies a basic willingness to accept the competence and capacity of the physician to cure.

There is both a rational and an irrational side to this willingness (Greenson 1967). The reasonable component has to do with the physician's training, knowledge, experience, and competence, as well as with the objective necessity for medical intervention. The irrational component, however, embraces a number of factors, including symbolic elements, sometimes magical expectations, superstitious beliefs, pre-formed transference elements, wishes, and narcissistic defenses, as well as the basic capacity for entrusting oneself to the care of another human being.

Narcissistic Alliance

Following Mehlman's (1976) clarifying suggestions, a critical element in this context is that, in a situation of presumed narcissistic vulnerability, the patient moves to include the relationship to the therapist in the armamentarium of narcissistically protective elements used to guard a fragile sense of self. That quality, which enables the patient to reorganize the narcissistic defensive organization to include the therapeutic relationship, has been described in terms of "basic trust" (Zetzel 1970). Mehlman (1976) describes the initial therapeutic rapport as a "narcissistic alliance" which is rooted in basic trust. In her original discussion of the therapeutic alliance, Zetzel links the elements of basic trust to the successful negotiation of the early maternal one-to-one object relationship, in much the same terms as Erikson (1963).

Here a basic discrimination must be made. The patient must carry into the treatment context a capacity for narcissistic alliance. If, however, archaic narcissistic elements dominate the personality, this capacity may be seriously impaired. Such patients may be so involved in the demands of the grandiose self or the need to maintain narcissistic equilibrium by attachment to an idealized object (Kohut 1971) that even the first step of the narcissistic alliance becomes problematic. The grandiosity of the self cannot tolerate any dependence on the helping object, or the need for an idealized object generates such magical and illusory expectations that an effective alliance is subverted and brought into the service of the patient's narcissistic needs (Meissner 1977). These patients lack the capacity to form a narcissistic alliance and are deficient in basic trust. Analysis with such patients is either impossible or can be done only with limited goals. In some cases, however, psychotherapy may sufficiently modify the patient's narcissism to permit a narcissistic alliance to emerge.

This first trusting rapport or narcissistic alliance provides the basic root out of which the therapeutic alliance will develop. The nourishing of these rudiments of the therapeutic alliance depends in large part on the empathic and intuitive responsiveness of the analyst from the very beginning of contact with the patient. Zetzel's description of this process in terms of the working through of primitive one-to-one issues in relationship with primary objects is very much to the point, since the model of that early parental interaction is operative from the onset of the therapeutic interaction.

The patient's willingness to include the therapeutic relationship in his narcissistic defensive organization must be responded to by the therapist in a way that is sensitive to the areas of narcissistic vulnerability, minimizes anxiety, and shores up the patient's faltering narcissism. Commenting on this process, Mehlman (1976) observes that to establish reasonable rapport, the therapist must allow the patient's willingness to trust or nonrational positive motivations to exist. The appeal to reason will only aggravate the situation. The therapist's contribution is to determine the locus of the immediate narcissistic crisis and to address it, intuitively or cognitively. He thus avoids adding to the patient's fright and so diminishes it that the patient can include him irrationally as part of his adaptive-defensive system.

Secondary Trust

In keeping with the overall epigenetic frame of reference, it should be noted that the individual elements of the schema may also have their own describable ontogeny. Mehlman (1976), for instance, has described a form of secondary trust, different from basic trust, in which, after the establishment of basic trust, a certain state of openness is maintained with the parents. According to Mehlman: "Secondary trust has to do with the willingness to cede over to the parental object some of those adaptive and defensive ego functions that would otherwise represent a *closed* system of previously internalized archaic parental images irrespective of their quality" (pp. 23–24). Thus, the element of trust can be seen to have its own relatively independent ontogeny which reflects specific vicissitudes in the child's developmental experience.

This is paralleled in the analytic process. If the narcissistic alliance requires the operation of basic trust, then the subsequent elaboration of the therapeutic alliance also requires trust, but it requires a more specifically evolved form of trust to sustain its functioning. In other words, as the therapeutic alliance emerges out of the narcissistic alliance, the element of trust undergoes a corresponding development. It does not lose contact with its roots in basic trust; rather, it goes through a progressive differentiation which maintains the rudiments of basic trust but organizes them in a form of secondary elaboration which, in turn, becomes more developed in the manner of its functioning and structure. This form of secondary trust is operative in a genuine therapeutic alliance. The failure of secondary trust or premature closure limits both the possibility of subsequent development (for instance of the superego) and the capacity for a genuine therapeutic alliance. The therapeutic alliance is a late development in a relatively mature system and no longer subject only to primitive object relationships. The primitive attachment to the parental object to avoid this progression represents an avoidance of closure (e.g., resolution of an oedipal crisis), and limits the possibility of a genuine therapeutic alliance.

As Mehlman (1976) comments: "The development of trust, then, has its ontogeny, just as does narcissism. Basic trust would seem to be a necessary antecedent to the earlier establishment of sufficient object relationship to enable these early ego introjects to take place at all. *Secondary* trust or its failure has to do with the subsequent traumata that necessitate the child's becoming his own parent far too early and is probably a great deal of what we struggle with in developing a therapeutic as opposed to a purely narcissistic alliance" (p. 24).

A transition, however, must be made from this initial level of naracissistic defensive alliance to a genuine therapeutic alliance. The critical element is the transformation of basic trust into a more elaborated and secure sense of secondary trust. What makes this transition possible is the empathic responsiveness of the analyst, who senses the locus of the patient's narcissistic vulnerability and provides sufficient support and reassurance for the patient to enter more deeply into the relationship without the threat of further narcissistic injury. It is at this critical juncture that the characteristics and sensitive empathic response of the analyst play a key role (Greenson 1960; Olinick 1975; Poland 1975; Schafer 1959).

Autonomy

To the extent that the patient is able to resolve and integrate the issues of trust, he is capable of moving on to a stage of emergent autonomy. Within the framework of a positive trusting relationship with the analyst, the patient begins to test out areas of autonomous functioning within the analysis. The ontogeny of autonomy within the analytic process is a subject worthy of study itself, and little or no attention has been paid to it. Perhaps the most pertinent work in this area is the contribution of object-relations theorists dealing with the progression in the analytic work from dependence to independence (Winnicott 1965). The analogy to the toddler's testing of autonomy is also relevant here.

The emergence of autonomy within the analysis implies that the patient is ready, able, and willing to enter into the work of the analysis and to take responsibility for it. This is quite different from the earlier attitude of trusting reliance and dependence. The emergence of autonomy implies that the patient is an active agent and a vital force in the work of the analysis. It is in this context that the patient takes responsibility for making the appointment times, paying his bills, producing material and working productively within the analytic hours, reporting dreams, and so on.

The process of establishing and maintaining autonomy is a delicate one and requires careful attuning on the part of the analyst to the needs of the patient. The analyst must respect the patient's emerging autonomy and not subvert it with implicit demands for analytic subservience or compliance. The line between signs of the patient's resistance, which need to be analyzed, interpreted, and effectively diminished, and aspects of the patient's growing autonomy, which need to be supported and sustained, is often a difficult one to draw. Within a given analytic context, the patient's missing a therapy hour may express important resistances, but it may also indicate an emerging autonomy. The therapist must take a careful reading of the state of the patient's defenses, the status of the alliance, and the level to which the analysis has advanced, and must situate the patient's behavior within the complex context of the overall analytic progression.

The emergence of genuine autonomy allows for the acceptance and acknowledgment of autonomy in others. Thus, it is important for the fostering of the patient's autonomy that the therapist's own autonomy be genuine and well integrated. The critical issue is the extent to which the patient's modified dependence and emerging independence are a source of stress or difficulty for the analyst. It is altogether too easy to interfere with and truncate the patient's growing autonomy. This difficulty is inherent in the parent–child relationship. A parent's insistence on conformity and compliance, for example, can undermine and diminish the child's beginning efforts at autonomy. Similarly, in the analysis, an excessive quickness to interpret on the analyst's part can effectively take the play away from the patient and deprive him of an area of hesitantly emerging autonomous functioning.

Any deviation from genuine autonomy in the direction of excess or deficit will have its effects on the analytic process. If the patient prematurely and excessively asserts independence of the analyst, the alliance is disrupted, and one can presume that this retreat to hyper-independence is serving defensive needs. On the other hand, if the patient is overly compliant and fails to exercise his independent judgment at the appropriate phase of the analytic process, the alliance also suffers. Thus, at a certain phase in the development of the therapeutic alliance an appropriate balance between the relative autonomies of the patient and the therapist must be obtained for the effective progression of the analytic work. A patient may come to the threshold of a more autonomous relationship to the analyst and may then retreat to an earlier position of accepting trustfulness and noncon-fronting dependence. Clearly, such a retreat is defensively motivated and forms a type of resistance within the alliance.

Defining the Projective System

Purpose

The first step in identifying the content and structure of the patient's pathology is defining the projective system. The projective system, compounded out of projective elements elaborated in terms of the paranoid construction, serves as a sustaining and meaningful matrix within which the projective elements can be reinforced and gain a sense of validation and purposeful integration. The necessity for this elaboration comes from the fact that the projections themselves are intimately related to the internal economy of the introjects and serve to buffer and prolong the organization of the introjects themselves. Consequently, the projective system itself is of little consequence or interest, except insofar as it contributes to this defensive organization and serves the inner purposes of the integration of the patient's self. Dealing with the projective system, then, is really a means to the end, namely, the end of identifying and coming to know the patient's introjective configuration and the manner in which it is elaborated and developed.

For the most part, paranoid patients, in a context of a somewhat trusting alliance, are more or less willing to share their projective system with the therapist—usually focusing on their phobic or persecutory anxieties. In many paranoid personalities, the projective system has a ring of plausibility and, given a few key interpretations or assumptions on the part of the patient, hangs together with consistent logic. In sicker patients, the projective system may contain delusional elements, which reflect elements of denial and the weakening of reality testing to such an extent that the process must be regarded as psychotic. Often, where a basis of trust is not adequate and the therapeutic relationship is contaminated by paranoid transference distortions, the patient will make efforts to conceal the projective system either entirely or in part. The suspiciousness and guardedness of such patients makes any attempt on the part of the therapist to find out about the projective system frustrating. Such attempts tend to run in the face of the patient's defensive system and serve only to reinforce it.

Focus

The therapist's best tactics at this juncture are to adopt a posture of patient and sympathetic listening and to learn something about the patient's projective system that ultimately will be useful in the further therapeutic work. The therapist's interest in the projective system is rather secondary, insofar as the system is a vehicle to understanding more about the dynamics and organization of the patient's inner psychic life. Therefore, the therapist listens in order to learn: his listening is empathic without being critical, challenging, or testing the patient's distortions, misperceptions, or misinterpretations against the data of reality.

The usual pattern of the projective system involves some sense of threat, persecution, devaluation, or other malignant influence directed against the patient for purposes of injury or defeat. As the therapist

·ention, in superficial terms, is focused on
projective system as the patient represents
is attentive listening with a "third ear" are
hat lie behind the projective account. He
ticularly to the sense of vulnerability,
ε, and victimization that pervades the
..ι-pervasive and constantly reiterated inner
...uιιement to this dimension of the patient's account is a
..gιιaι to the patient that the therapist not only understands in an
empathic and nonthreatening fashion, but, in addition, the therapist has
no intention of attacking, criticizing, or devaluing him on account of
these fears and weaknesses.

Intentionality

We have used the term "defining" to describe the intentionality at this
point in the process, in an attempt to convey the sense of what the
therapist is about. His purpose is to gain a descriptive account of the
patient's pathology, to set the limits of its extent and depth, and to gain
some sense of the character and significance of the elements that it
contains. In listening to the projective system, therefore, the emphasis is
on the objective account, at least in the first instance. From the vantage
point as an empathic and interested listener, the therapist can encourage
the patient to develop and enlarge the account that he is giving with
particular emphasis on concrete details and the recounting of specific
events and episodes.

For example, if a patient complains about the hostile and threatening attitudes of his fellow workers, the therapist is interested to
know more about this difficult situation and to hear from the patient
specific and detailed accounts of how fellow workers have demonstrated
this hostility and their intentions to do harm to the patient. If the
therapist's attitude in seeking such information is not confrontative or
challenging, the patient is usually willing to present the details of his
predicament and to present his story to the therapist. The very process of
reconstructing the account for a sympathetic and noncritical listener
begins the therapeutic process in the patient's own awareness. In telling
the story and elaborating on its specifics, the patient is beginning the
process of objectification that allows both the therapist and the patient
himself to express, in an inchoatively distancing fashion, the facts,
perceptions, and interpretations, and most particularly the emotional
reactions, that constitute the material basis for the patient's projective
system and his pathological reaction.

Introjective Elements

In this detailed and objectifying recounting, it is almost inevita
the patient's account not only presents elements from the pr
system itself but also includes data deriving either directly or in
from the introjective level. If the patient is describing the malicio
hostile actions of his persecutors, there is an implication of his own
of vulnerability and victimization. As the therapist listens to the ac
of these persecutors' hostility, he can usefully respond with emp
comments that convey to the patient a sense of his awareness of
patient's sense of threat, of the intensity and torment of his anxiety,
of how difficult it must have been and must be for the patient to be
object of such enmity and hostility. By the same token, and particula
where the elements of trust have found a sufficient footing, the therapi
is also liable to hear more direct representations from the level of th
patient's introjective organization. These will usually come in terms o
descriptions of how threatened, anxious, and fearful the patient may
have felt, or how vulnerable, weak, and helpless he may have felt, in the
face of the threat of his adversaries.

It is usually the case that these introjective elements, whether
conveyed directly or indirectly, have a depressive cast. They reflect the
patient's inner frailty, vulnerability, and weakness, as well as a sense of
worthlessness and shame that frequently pervades the inner world and
the self image with which these patients live. The latter elements,
reflections of the patient's narcissistic conflicts, are not frequently
brought into the picture or brought into focus in an identifiable way
with any great alacrity by paranoid patients. This is the most vulnerable
part of their pathological sense of self, the most sensitive and difficult
part of their personality organization which requires the greatest degree
of protection and defensive elaboration. The therapist, however, is
attuned to the likelihood of such introjectively derived affects, and
should not be surprised if, in the course of the patient's recounting, he
begins to hear such implications.

A further point that can be emphasized at this juncture is that the
material of the projective system, particularly the projective elements
themselves, and the derivatives of the introjective organization insofar as
they can be identified, serve as a kind of template or an "early warning
system" for the later development of transference/countertransference
interactions. What the therapist learns from defining the dimensions of
the projective system has direct implications and sets a pattern for the
interactions that will evolve in the therapeutic relationship. The manner
in which the introjective configuration plays itself out in the various

parameters of the patient's pathological interactions will likewise act as the basis for the pattern of the patient's interaction with the therapist. Not only will the introjective components play themselves out in the patient's relationship with the therapist but the projective elements will likewise find their way into the same interaction, and the therapist will find himself in terms of the developing projective transference cloaked with the same projective elements.

Testing Reality

Technique

With the progressive defining of the projective system occur the first steps toward the therapeutic impingement on the patient's delusional system. For reasons we have already discussed, it is inadvisable to confront the projective system of the paranoid patient, since at best one is rowing upstream in the face of the patient's powerful resistances, and at worst one runs the risk of placing oneself in the position of a persecuting agency.

The pertinent techniques at this stage of the therapeutic effort are the tagging of feelings and the testing of the limits of the patient's knowledge as described in Chapter 2. Both of these techniques can be judiciously introduced during the course of defining the projective system. The approach is meant to be gradual, to offer the elements of interpretation in almost subliminal doses and to only slowly build toward a more amplified interpretation. In listening to the paranoid patient's account, the therapist will inevitably hear inklings, and sometimes more than inklings, of the patient's sense of inner vulnerability, impotence, and threatened autonomy. The therapist's response to these affective elements is empathic but is also calculated to underline the feeling quality of the experience. When the patient says that he feels his life is somehow being threatened by outside forces that are out to get him, the therapist responds not to the factual content of the communication but rather to the tone of feeling. The therapist might comment empathically on how terrified or threatened the patient must feel. If the patient can admit that he feels threatened and fearful of his life, the therapist can respond empathically to that feeling and even emphasize that what the patient is expressing is a feeling.

The second technique for testing the reality of the patient's delusions is a testing of the limitations of the patient's knowledge. The projective system maintained by the patient contains in its elaboration a variety of conclusions, attitudes, convictions regarding the beliefs and intentions of others, and a host of other inferential convictions. Gradually, the therapist can begin to explore and test the basis of such convictions in the patient's experience. While a direct confrontation and challenging of the patient's conclusions or convictions will inevitably prove to be fruitless and counterproductive, the detailed exploration of the material on which the patient may base the conclusion can often reveal certain gaps and uncertainties in the patient's account. If the therapist can tactfully point out such areas of uncertainty, it can gradually be established that the patient's conclusion does not rest entirely on objective evidence but is shaped in some degree by his own subjective contribution. It is as though the patient fills in the blanks in reality with projective material derived from his own inner world. Unfortunately, one of the important blanks in our environment that requires constant filling in is the inner attitudes, thoughts, feelings, and judgments of other individuals. The degree to which such manifestations of the inner world of others can be accurately assessed and known is quite limited, so that the arena of object relationships provides a fertile field for paranoid projections.

This process was demonstrated quite vividly in a young man in his mid-twenties who came seeking help because of the total paralysis his life was in. He had had a paranoid schizophrenic episode about two years before, followed by a profound clinging depression. His life was paralyzed by fear. Everywhere he went, he met hostility; people stared at him, laughed at him, thought he was a sniveling weakling with no backbone or guts—a worthless creep. He could not shop at his local grocery because the clerk had given him a funny look, presumably thinking that he was a worthless degenerate. He fulminated against the capitalist system, social values, corporations, the American government, et cetera, because he felt victimized and impotent in his dealings with them. His posture was one of impotent rage.

It was hardly difficult to discern the dimensions of this paranoid construction and the introjective configuration from which they derived. It was only after repeated and prolonged testing of many of these situations that he was able to grasp the projective nature of his reactions and to turn his concern to an internal frame of reference. As this shift evolved, his capacity to tolerate social situations gradually increased to the point of his holding a steady job and having a sexual relationship.

As this patient strikingly dramatized, the drift in this process is toward a progressively clearer and more discrete delineation of the realm of the patient's fantasy life—both in its external and internal referents— which had functioned, in this case, by and large at an unconscious level.

The further clarification of these introjectively derived fantasy systems and their role in early object relations, as well as in any current transference relation, helps to specify the introjective configuration and progressively delineate it from reality. Further steps of the schema elaborate these aspects.

Undermining

The process of defining and gradually testing the reality of the projective system induces a gradual undermining of the projective system itself and its associated paranoid defenses. As the projective and paranoid defenses weaken and wane, the underlying affective components that are built into the organization of the introjects become more available to the patient's consciousness and find their way into increasingly direct expression. While in most patients the affective quality tends to be more or less depressive, in paranoid patients this is particularly the case. To the degree that the projective system is effectively undermined and no longer serving its defensive function, such a patient will become clinically depressed. The intensity and severity of the depression will be in direct proportion to the intensity, fixity, and extent of delusional conviction implied in the projective system. In many patients in whom the projective system has reached psychotic delusional proportions, the underlying depression can be expected to be severe, even suicidal.

Clarification of Introjects

Focus

The gradual erosion of the projective system leaves the underlying introjective configuration increasingly exposed and available for exploration and understanding. Consequently, the next item on the therapeutic agenda is the turning of therapeutic interest toward this introjective level and a gradual definition and clarification of the introjective configuration itself. The focus falls on the patient's feelings, attitudes, beliefs, and convictions about himself. Undoubtedly, this is one of the most sensitive and at times difficult phases of the work with paranoid patients. It is at this juncture that the patient's most exquisite and sensitive core vulnerabilities are exposed. The extent to which this opening up, unveiling, and clarifying of the introjective configuration in paranoid patients can be accomplished depends to a considerable degree on the extent to which the therapeutic alliance has been stabilized and on the capacity of the therapist to maintain good empathic contact with the patient.

As the shift to the introjective focus takes place, more of the content and particularly the affective resonances of the introjective configuration become available. By and large, what is thus unveiled is a sensitive depressive core to the patient's personality organization. At this level of the therapeutic work, the therapeutic task is analogous to the task presented in defining the projective system itself. In the clarification of the introjects, the therapeutic intent is not to challenge, correct, interpret, or in any way alter the introjective alignment—certainly not directly, or as a first order of business. We are much more interested in discovering what is contained in the introjective configuration, and in the process helping the patient to accomplish the same discovery. The same strategy is used as was employed in defining the projective system. We want to help the patient to amplify his account of his experience of his own inner world. Gradually, the patient's feelings about himself are drawn into increasingly well delineated and articulated terms. The patient is encouraged to fill in the picture with as much detail and concreteness as can be mustered.

Configurations

The elements that emerge from this exploration are already familiar from our discussion of the component introjective configurations that cluster around the motifs of aggression (the aggressor-introject and the victim-introject) and narcissism (the superior and inferior introjects). Because of the basic structure of the paranoid pathology, what is most readily available in this context are the more depressively toned elements, namely, victimization and inferiority. The therapeutic strategy would focus primarily on filling out the concrete details of whatever context the patient is presenting. As each such episode or context is explored and developed, the therapist is interested in helping the patient to focus and articulate the prevailing affects, here usually depressive and often having to do with motifs of weakness, vulnerability, poor self-esteem, shame, humiliation, inferiority, and the like.

As the backlog of such accounts grows in the therapeutic progression, little by little the therapist is able to establish connections between accounts, gradually drawing attention to certain motifs that seem to arise recurrently in a wide variety of contexts. The patient becomes increasingly attuned to the fact that in so many of the variant contexts of his life experience the same motifs come into play and dominate his view not only of his world but of himself. This allows for the gradual integration of the relevant introjective themes. These can be expressed in terms of the motifs of victimization and hostile or destructive aggressiveness, in aggressive terms, and in terms of the narcissistic themes of superiority and inferiority.

While the depressive aspects of the introjective configuration tend to be more readily available at this stage of the therapy, the therapist must not lose sight of the fact that the correlative configurations must also play a role in the patient's pathology. When the paranoid patient is relatively more willing to express his feelings of vulnerability and victimization, the therapist knows that the motifs of aggressiveness, power, and hostility, the hallmarks of the aggressor-introject, are also at play. These are displayed in the first instance through the projective system in the form of specific projections. However, in the course of the patient's elaboration the same elements can be identified, ultimately in terms of the introjective configuration itself. The same applies to the narcissistic elements, where the patient may be more inclined to present his feelings of shameful inferiority and humiliation, and relatively reluctant or slow to unveil his sense of entitlement, specialness, and even grandiosity.

Case

This process was very clearly manifested in the therapy of the young paranoid man described above. As the therapeutic work progressed, the patient was increasingly able to talk about his feelings of vulnerability and impotence. He would describe without much hesitation some of his paranoid experiences. Recounting experiences of walking down the street, he would describe ideas of reference in which the people passing by were looking at him and thinking what a weirdo or creep he was, how he was not worthy to even walk on the sidewalk like a normal human being, that he was homosexual, or otherwise degrading or hostile thoughts. The intensity of these ideas of reference even reached the level at which he at times would feel a sense of overwhelming panic, feeling convinced that at any moment one of the people passing him in the street would turn upon him, pull a knife on him, and stab him in the chest. Or he would fantasize that someone in the crowd would suddenly pull out a submachine gun and turn it on him, spraying him with bullets. These were not idle imaginings but were accompanied by feelings of total conviction and panic. At one point, the patient described a recent experience in which he mustered his courage to go to a downtown department store to buy a suit. He walked in the front door of the store and was suddenly overwhelmed with panic, feeling convinced that there were armed storm troopers posted around the balconies of the store with high-powered rifles trained on him, ready to gun him down. He turned and ran from the store in a total panic.

If these feelings and delusional preoccupations reflected in an intense and exquisite fashion his sense of vulnerability and victimization (the victim-introject), the patient was also able to express a different set of fantasies that came to him as he was walking down the street. He would imagine himself suddenly turning on some passerby and stabbing him— usually someone who looked particularly impressive, or expensively and well dressed. Or he would imagine himself pulling out a submachine gun and ruthlessly gunning down the people in the street, showing no mercy, taking no prisoners. In his paranoid tirades against people who were rich and successful, against corporations and professionals who made money by trading on the weakness and vulnerability of the helpless masses like himself, the patient would entertain fantasies of invading the offices of big corporate law firms and machine-gunning everyone in sight, or passing the offices of some important firm like IBM and hurling a powerful bomb through the front door. If the motifs of vulnerability and victimization were played out at levels of intense pathology in this patient, there was a proportional and parallel component of aggressive hostility and destructiveness that played itself out in equally intense and dramatic terms. This exemplifies a rule of thumb regarding the vicissitudes of such introjective components, namely, that the intensity and pathological distortion of the introjective configuration on one side of the introjective polarity is matched by the intensity and pathogenicity of its correlative configuration.

The same thing can be observed in this patient regarding the elements of pathological narcissism. The patient was primarily and for a long period of his therapy in touch with the feelings of inferiority, of worthlessness, of deep and abiding shame about himself, of humiliation, inadequacy, and inferiority. These would often form a part of the content of his paranoid convictions. He felt that people who crossed his path, whether in the street or in any other aspect of his life, not only held him in disrespect but despised him as worthless and as totally inferior. After some period of therapeutic effort, the patient was gradually able to express some of the opposite elements of this introjective polarity. He was basically a gifted and intelligent young man, but his school efforts had been paralyzed both by his narcissistic perfectionism and by the excessive demands he would put upon himself for performance, which he was never able to realize. Instead of being able to function effectively at the level which his intelligence would indicate, the patient was usually paralyzed by his inability to meet his own excessive and highly narcissistic standards. For him not to achieve at the highest level was to be a failure, to be nothing, and to be entirely worthless. He thereby condemned himself to an inexorable trap and lived under the heel of the "tyranny of narcissism."

Nonetheless, the patient's grandiosity would occasionally reveal itself. He would look at people who were professionals, doctors or lawyers or scientists, and he would complain bitterly that they were no more intelligent or knowledgeable than he was, and that in fact he knew a good deal more than most of them. The fact that despite his intelligence his efforts at schooling and generally in the work area of his life had been failures was attributed to the malignant intentions and hostility of fellow workers, employers, teachers, and others. His projective system in this sense worked as a defense against his own feelings of failure and inadequacy. Along with this, there was a frequently expressed cold hauteur, a kind of contempt for ordinary mortals, whom he regarded as if they were an inferior race of men who hardly deserved to breathe the air of the atmosphere or to walk upon the face of the earth. In his eyes, they were fit for only menial, trivial tasks. He called them slaves, peons, and it was not only the demeaning language but the utter contempt that expressed the intensity and the pathogenicity of his narcissism. All the more pervasive, in the light of these contemptuous tirades, was his feeling that fate and the conspiring opposition of others around him had forced him to function in this degraded and inferior position.

Countertransference Interaction

In delineating and formulating the introjective configuration, the therapist must be reminded that here too, as in the earlier dealings with the projective system, the elements displayed will inevitably find their way into the countertransference interaction. The classical paranoid configuration in which the patient adopts the victim position will be paralleled by the projection of the derivatives of the aggressor-introject onto the therapist. The therapist will then be seen somehow as a victimizer to the patient's victim. He will be regarded as critical, demanding, judging the patient in a variety of ways, possessing power that the patient does not have, influential, omniscient, or even hostile, depriving, and in some fashion out to hurt the patient.

The narcissistic components may play themselves out in a similar fashion. If the patient feels inferior, humiliated, or worthless in relation to the therapist, the therapist is more likely to be seen in terms of narcissistic aggrandizement and idealization. Depending on the level at which the pathology operates, it is also possible for these polarities to reverse. The patient may defensively become the aggressor and try to find ways to turn the tables and make the therapist a victim or, correspondingly, may place himself in the position of narcissistic superiority and thus devalue or humiliate the therapist. The identification of these motifs in the therapeutic interaction in terms of the interplay of transference and countertransference elements can be a crucial and extremely valuable component of the therapeutic work.

An additional important piece of work in the clarification of the introjects refers back to the technique employed in clarifying the distinction between feelings and facts. In the early stages of testing the reality of the patient's projective system, the distinguishing of matters of feeling from matters of fact had more to do with the intrinsic frame of reference within which the projective system operated. Here, however, the focus is shifted to the patient's inner world and specifically to the feelings and facts about himself. For the most part, patients are so ingrained in the tendency to base their attitudes about themselves on feelings that they forget that feelings and facts may not indeed be the same. In the young man described above, the realization that his feelings of inferiority had no relation to and were in no way identical to the facts of who and what he was gradually brought the introjective components into perspective and opened the way to a further inquiry, which made it possible to undermine and gradually dissolve the pathogenic introjective configuration. This clarification of the nature and structure of the introjects leads the way to a broader field of investigation, having to do with the derivation of the introjects and their inherent motivation. At this juncture, we can take up these questions in more detail.

Derivation of Introjects

Object Related

Following the basic psychotherapeutic schema based on the paranoid process, the clarification and focusing of the introjective configuration draws the patient and the therapeutic inquiry to inevitable questions regarding the origin and sources of the introjects. The approach to these phenomena in terms of the paranoid process proposes that the introjects themselves are forms of internalization and derive ultimately from the significant object relationships in the patient's developmental history. The primary figures in this drama are the parents, but frequently they do not form the exclusive base for these critical internalizations. Other significant individuals may play a role, including siblings, grandparents, aunts and uncles, or other significant family figures. There may, on occasion, also be components derived from other important figures in the patient's life, particularly where there is a history of a broken family and the emergence on the child's horizon of other important influential figures, for example, a stepmother or stepfather. Even foster parents can, at times, play a role.

Several important emphases can be made about these internalizations. First, the patterning of the introjection may not always be apparent to more superficial observation. The internalization is based on and derived from the introjective configurations embedded in the personality structure of the objects, rather than their more superficial behaviors or patterns of adjustment. The patterns of introjective organization are at work in the objects of internalization, with their inherent patterns of defensive organization and polarization. The child may resonate with, assimilate, and internalize aspects of the parents' introjective organizations in terms of the specific reference points of victimization, aggression, superiority, or inferiority. The mother who views herself as inadequate and worthless as a woman conveys to her child a model for internalization that carries with it these devaluing components. The child may then internalize the more victimized and inferior qualities of the maternal object.

A second point to be emphasized is that the process of internalization is not a mechanical, automatic stamping of an object-relational impression on the malleable childhood psyche. It is a process which calls into play certain mechanisms and shaping propensities within the child's self. Thus, internalizations are never simply translations of object qualities into the child's internal world but, rather, undergo a process of selection, modification, and amalgamation as dictated by the internal vicissitudes of the child's psychic life. The shape and the dimensions of the introjective configurations within the child may take in and synthesize, in terms dictated by the defensive pressures, elements from a number of objects. The formation of a victim-introject may derive ultimately from more than one object.

Family System

In paranoid patients, for example, these critical pathogenic introjections tend not to derive exclusively from one or the other parental figure. That is to say, the aggressor-introject is not based exclusively on the internalization of the aggressive aspects of one parent, nor are the components of the victim-introject derived exclusively from the other parent. The family background of such patients frequently manifests patterns of sadomasochistic interaction, patterns of victimization and victimizing, that operate in reciprocal ways. If a father, for example, is the brutal aggressor towards a masochistically victimized and martyred mother, there are also ways in which the mother surreptitiously turns the tables on her husband and makes him the victim of her hostile aggressiveness. The child in such contexts will build into his own introjective structure the aggressive elements derived from both parental figures in a synthesis that carries the stamp of his own personality integration. By the same token, the victim components will be derived in the same complex fashion.

It is important to keep in mind, in the context of exploring these relationships and their implications, that while the introjective components may indeed derive from particular object relationships and their interaction, these relationships exist within the matrix of a complex family emotional system, which underlies and often shapes these patterns of interaction and transaction (Meissner 1978a, b). These family systems, in which paranoid patients experience their development and within which their psychic lives are molded and shaped, often have a paranoid tinge that may or may not express itself from time to time in forms of paranoid interaction. However, they usually can be found to express and embody more or less subtle prejudicial attitudes that reflect the relatively nonpathological operation of the paranoid process in the family system. There may even be a perception of the world and reality as aggressively threatening and destructive, such that the only safe harbor of love and security is within the confines of the family. Such families may follow a pattern of social isolation and exclusiveness, often tinged with strong narcissistic components reflecting feelings of embattled superiority, but such prejudicial attitudes may also lurk behind a facade of social agreeableness and adaptivity.

The therapist must be aware of the manner in which such patterns can assert themselves within the family system. Part of the therapeutic task is to help the patient tease out these elements and to gradually come to some understanding of how they played themselves out in the family relationships, and particularly of how they came to shape and influence his own psychological development. This part of the process serves to reinforce the therapeutic gains previously made and helps the patient to appreciate that the patterns that he has discovered in his own inner world, the structure of his own introjective organization, arose as the result of certain identifiable influences that have both a history and a pattern of motivation. This discovery is both illuminating and reassuring, in that it carries with it the suggestion that if the shaping of the patient's critical internalizations was based on particular motivations and influences, then there is a possibility for reexamining and reopening the introjective configuration for possible modification.

At times, the details of the patient's developmental history that permit some deeper understanding of the influences that played a role in personality development are not available, or at least not available in a form that allows for this kind of insightful processing. Almost inevitably, in the process of clarification of the patient's introjects, these elements play themselves out within the transference interaction. The therapist can make the theoretically based presumption that the patterns which are identifiable in the transference context are reflecting patterns that may have arisen within the context of the family system and its interaction. In almost all patients who get this far in the therapeutic work, there is enough material available to at least attempt the beginnings of a genetic reconstruction.

Motivation of the Introjects

Self-motivation

When we enter the world of the introjects, we encounter a unique realm of specific motivation. We run up against the enigmatic and sometimes elusive question of why an individual shapes the particular view of himself that he does. The sense of self is fashioned out of the underlying introjective configuration, so that the question ultimately resolves itself into one of the inherent motivation involved in the forming and maintaining of those introjects.

It is important to emphasize that we are dealing with a distinct and unique set of motivational factors in this respect. Traditional psycho-analytic theory more or less contented itself with the issues of extrinsic, object-related motivation. To a certain extent, the emergence of a psychology of the self within psychoanalysis has altered that picture and has necessitated consideration of an alternate, often complementary, and at times even contradictory set of motivations that is involved in the organization, maintenance, and perseverence of the self. While these inner motivations play an essential role in all forms of psychopathology, their role in paranoid disorders is particularly acute. We have already discussed the manner in which the paranoid patient seems to center his inner world around the victim-introject with all of its connotations and implications. The aggressive elements are consequently projected away in varying degrees of externalization and in the most extreme forms of paranoid expression are transformed into persecutory objects or other persecutory elaborations. The vicissitudes of narcissism in paranoid pathology are not so clearly etched, sometimes displaying the aspects of narcissistic inferiority and at other times, usually in the more disturbed expressions of paranoid psychopathology, displaying the superior configuration.

Victim-Introject

The elements of victimization played themselves out graphically and dramatically in the famous Schreber case.* For Schreber, the internal introjective configuration was amalgamated out of introjections of the sadistic, harsh, punitive, hostilely destructive, and rigidly demanding father on the one hand, and of the depressive, masochistic, and victimized image of the mother on the other.

The basic pathology described so graphically in the *Memoirs* constitutes a playing out and playing off each other of these respective introjects. The childhood persecution is played out again on a grander and more elaborate scale, first of all in the persecution at the hands of the esteemed physician Flechsig, and ultimately by Schreber's enlistment in the grandiose scheme of the divine purposes. Running in tandem with this persecutory projection, however, and playing an essential role in sustaining and preserving it, is the persistent identification with the victimized mother. The elements of this introjection, which plays such a vital role in the dynamic underpinnings of the delusions system, are graphically displayed in the transformation into a woman. Both of these aspects of the introjective economy and their embellishment in the delusional system have significant involvement and motivational rooting in the underlying narcissistic needs that remain substantially unresolved and unfufilled.

What becomes central in the paranoid pathology, then, is the organization of the introjects. What must not be missed, however, is the way the patient's organization of introjects is linked with and derives from the patterning of parental projections within the family system. The evident link between Schreber's introjects and the persecutory treatment he received at the hands of the father dramatically exemplifies this process. The father's attack on his son was substantially an attempt to subdue those projective elements of his own sadistic and destructive nature that had been imposed on the figure of his son. Consequently,

---

*See the extended discussion of the Schreber case in Chapter 3.

the interlocking of the parental projection with the child's internalization provides the matrix out of which the paranoid process derives.

The introjective process plays itself out on the mother's side as well. It has been our consistent clinical experience with other paranoid patients that the child's interaction with the mother carries the mother's implicit conviction that the child is somehow defective, weak, and inadequate. Again, it is the mother's own feelings of weakness, inadequacy, vulnerability, helplessness, and castrated inferiority that are projected onto the child and subsequently introjected by the child.

Self-Organization

We have discussed the dynamic relation between the projective system and the organization of the introjects, but there is also an adaptive aspect that deserves consideration. The adaptive aspect of the projective system has to do with the organization and maintenance of a sense of self. The child's emerging sense of self is structured and organized around the core introjects that are derived from paternal figures. In the normal course of development, these introjects are relatively nonambivalent and allow for two important developmental progressions. The first is the induction of identifications, which serves to consolidate the ego capacities and to provide for the stabilization and consolidation of autonomous ego functions. The second is the elaboration of a matrix of object relations, within which the developing ego finds a degree of recognition, acceptance, belonging, and meaningful relatedness which sustains and nourishes the emerging sense of self that is so closely linked to the achievement of individuality. In the developmental matrix provided by the family of the paranoid patient, this essential object-matrix is distorted. The relationships with the primary objects are intensely ambivalent and overridden with destructive and hostile aggressive impulses. Both the induction of effective ego identifications and the elaboration of a matrix of meaningful belongingness for shaping and sustaining the integrity of the self are undermined.

The sense of self, which is shaped around the pathogenic and highly ambivalent introjects, is highly susceptible to regressive pulls and to a variety of drive-derivative influences. Building further on the projective influences, the impaired ego erects a system of substitute object relatedness that provides a distorted matrix within which the pathological sense can integrate itself and find a relative degree of meaningful relatedness. We can speak of the process as one of pathological identity formation analogous to the process of relatively normal identity formation, through which the emergent sense of identity defines and articulates itself in relation to a system of real objects and a more elaborate social and cultural framework.

False Self

The sense of self that is formed within this system of pseudobelonging and quasi-meaningful relationships is close to what Winnicott (1965) has described as the "false self." The false self is organized internally around the core of ambivalent and pathological introjects. The establishing and sustaining of the false self, however, cannot take place in an object vacuum. The ego must defensively and derivatively form a meaningful matrix in relation to which the false self can function and fulfill the essential adaptive needs. The core element in this paranoid system is the organization of the sense of (false) self around the core victim-introject— so that victimhood becomes the basis and the motive of the substitutive object involvement. For Schreber, the need for victimhood, along with the narcissistically driven need for acknowledgment and recognition in terms of compensatory grandiosity, were aptly resolved in his special redeeming relation to the father god. It was here that he found that degree of meaningful belonging and purposeful existence needed to sustain and nourish the narcissistic needs of his deprived and depleted victim-self. The organization of this system of substitute belonging and meaningful relatedness calls into play the basic mechanisms of the paranoid process—projection and paranoid construction (Meissner 1978b). The intensity, distortion, and degree of delusional pathology reflect the underlying primitiveness, narcissistic intensity, and pathological ambivalence of the introjects from which the projections derive.

Intrinsic Motivation

It becomes increasingly clear regarding the intrinsic motivation of the introjective configuration, which is reflected in the sometimes powerful clinging on the part of the patient to the elements of the introjective configuration, particularly in the case of paranoid patients to the victim-introject, that the motivational components are both objective and subjective. Due to the contexts of derivation, the motivations built into the introjective configuration can reflect the basic motivational components involved in the object relationship of origin. Thus, the adoption of the victim-position may reflect the quality of the relationship to the original object. In the case of Schreber, for example, his adherence to the victim-position may reflect important components of his relationship to his victimizing father.

But by the same token, the tie to the object may take the form of an internalization, that is, by way of the introjection from the object. In Schreber's case, this would have led to an identification with the victim based on the introjection of Schreber's suffering and victimized mother. Thus, Schreber is both victim to his father and identified with the victim in his mother; however, as the case history reveals, he had also internalized the aggressive, sadistic, and destructive aspects of his father, and these elements provide the basis for his persecutory delusions.

The motivations that lie on the subjective side of this dichotomy are tied up with the maintenance and preservation of the individual's sense of self. Here, the motivations are both narcissistic and nonnarcissistic. They are narcissistic to the extent that the self has built into it certain structures that derive from the residues of archaic narcissism. As Kohut (1971) has described these, they embrace aspects of both the grandiose self and the idealized parental imago. The narcissistic investment, therefore, would reflect the compensatory pressures that arise in the face of narcissistic vulnerabilities and the threats to narcissistic integrity. Obviously, these components could operate at a variety of levels of intensity. When the narcissistic residues are more structuralized, internalized, and effectively integrated with the rest of the psychic organization, these essentially defensive pressures are correspondingly modified and the resultant structural organization is more adaptive and less pathological. At a higher developmental and structural level, therefore, the integration of the ego-ideal with other superego and ego components can provide the elements of much stronger and functional psychic apparatus. When the narcissistic residues remain more infantile, more pathological, and less well integrated with the rest of the psychic structures, the defensive pressures are increased, and the narcissistic investment in maintaining the archaic residues of narcissistic grandiosity and omnipotence play a much larger role in the patient's pathology. These latter formations are more explicitly identifiable in terms of the narcissistic introjective configurations, both superior and inferior, that we have already described.

The motivation for maintaining the self-configuration can be nonnarcissistic as well. Here, the approach dictated in terms of the paranoid process would differ radically from a Kohutian frame of reference, in that the self is viewed as an overriding structural organization which embraces not only narcissistic determinants but other instinctual as well as noninstinctual determinants (Meissner 1981c, d).

The power of this intrinsic or subjective motivation should not be underestimated, since it often provides the most vigorous and vital resistance to therapeutic efforts with paranoid patients. It seems paradoxical that anyone would invest so strongly in maintaining a pathological sense of self, but the issues here can indeed be survival issues and involve motives which lie close to the core of the patient's existence. In attacking and undermining these motivations, we are attacking the very core of the patient's sense of his own being. He has no other meaning or sense of self than that which is tied up in his attachment to the pathogenic configurations. For the paranoid patient, it is this exquisite sense of himself as a victim—as victimized, vulnerable, and attacked—that gives meaning and sustenance to his existence.

It is perhaps this aspect of the motivational configuration that gives some credibility to the familiar clinical phenomenon of delusional fixity, that is, the degree of conviction and unalterability that the patient's delusional beliefs often acquire. It is not a matter of commitment to the external frame of reference or the external conditions or causes that are involved in the delusional beliefs but, rather, a matter of maintaining the inner sense of self, the configuration of introjects to which the projective system is ordered as a sustaining and reinforcing matrix. In this sense, then, to paraphrase Erikson's comments about negative identity, it is better to be a victim than to be nothing at all.

The Mourning of Infantile Attachments

The uncovering and exploration of these hidden motivations, as well as of the derivation of the introjects as previously discussed, open the way to the resignation of the attachment to these introjective configurations and a consequent process of mourning. The mourning process involves a sense of loss and a detachment from the objects of loss. For the paranoid patient, this involves a gradual mourning of the attachments to the original objects from whom the introjective configurations derived, as well as a working through of the internalizations, particularly the core introjections, that serve as the basis for the patient's pathogenic introjective configuration. At one level, therefore, the mourning process takes place in the context of object attachments, that is, the attachments to specific objects and the corresponding object relationships. But the mourning process must also take place in the internal domain with regard to the introjects themselves.

The loss here is not simply the loss of something extrinsic to one's self; rather, it is the loss of one's self or, more precisely, of one's sense of one's self. The patient gradually comes to terms with the realization that to exist does not necessarily mean to exist as a victim. The mourning requires a surrendering and a resolution of a sense of identity based on pathological introjects, particularly, in the present instance, the victim-introject. But in the process, the patient is called upon to allow for the emergence of a different, a more adapted, a more meaningful and nonpathological identity that finds its roots in some other context, some other framework of meaningful belonging and significance.

There is a monumental risk involved in this process, one that frightens and paralyzes patients. The risk must be taken, however, if the patient is ever to find his way out of the labyrinthian entanglement of his own inner world and to strike out in a new direction, seeking to find a new way of being, a new way of living, even a new way of feeling and thinking. His task is to seek and to establish a new sense of identity, but the process is fraught with dangers and risks. The therapist's task is in the first instance to acknowledge the patient's fears and apprehensions and recognize with the patient the realistic risks involved. These most often have to do with issues of narcissistic vulnerability in the paranoid patient, particularly the risk involved in making himself somewhat more vulnerable to narcissistic insult, criticism, or failure. In the second instance, the therapeutic task is to foster, support, and facilitate those impulses of the patient toward increased psychic growth and toward the establishment of a more meaningfully functional, competent, and autonomous ego.

The Emergence of
Transference Dependence

The process of the resolution and mourning of infantile attachments is accompanied in paranoid patients, as in other forms of pathology, by a replacement of these infantile attachments by dependence on the therapist. The infantile objects and attachments are not initially surrendered but, rather, are translated into or substituted for by the attachment within the transference. This deepening and intensifying of the transference neurosis in paranoid patients is accompanied by an increased sense of vulnerability and inadequacy, expressions of the dynamic patterns involved in the inferior and the victim-introjects.

The intensification of these dynamic patterns may be followed compensatorily and defensively by an increased titre of aggression and elements of narcissistic superiority, reflecting a resort to the elements of the superior and aggressor-introjects in an attempt to regain both aggressive and narcissistic equilibrium. The intensification of these pathogenic patterns may express itself within the therapeutic relationship by affective withdrawal, a retreat to isolated self-sufficiency in relationship to the therapist, a turning to patterns of devaluation and distancing in the therapeutic relationship, or the adoption of a facade of pseudoautonomy. Thus, in the face of the inevitable mourning of the attachments to infantile objects and to the introjects, and in the face of the corresponding emergence of intensified dependence within the transference, the paranoid dynamics are remobilized and find expression in transient forms of pathogenic distortion of the therapeutic process. The therapist should not mistake this transient reactive pattern as regressive or as signaling the undoing of the achievements of the therapy. Rather, it is an expectable and even necessary part of the therapeutic process, which must be worked through and resolved in its own terms, specifically in terms of the issues of the mourning of previous pathogenic commitments and the resolution of current transference dependence, thus allowing for more effective and meaningful internalization of the therapeutic relationship and of the therapist as a meaningful object in the patient's experience.

Transference Resolution

The final stages of the therapeutic process involve the mourning of the attachment to the therapist himself. The previous attachments to infantile objects, and commitment to introjective configurations, were loosened and resolved through displacement to the therapeutic relationship; thus, the dissolution of that very relationship, the surrendering of attachment, and the loss of the object of therapeutic dependence now pose a significant hurdle in the patient's progress.

This aspect of the psychotherapeutic schema forms the core of the work of termination. At this point in the therapeutic effort, work with paranoid patients is substantially the same as that with all patients who have come to a point of productive and meaningful termination. One can view this part of the therapeutic work from any number of vantage points, but one that we find useful is that of the therapeutic alliance. In a sense, as the mourning process holds sway, and as the attachment to and dependence on the therapist are gradually resolved, it is in terms of the development of alliance that this process takes place. Consequently, in this phase of the therapeutic work considerable effort is directed toward developing and reinforcing the autonomy, initiative, and industry of the patient within the therapeutic context. These emphases dictate certain technical approaches, which serve to mobilize these resources of the patient's ego, even as the process of resolution and separation is evolving with increasing intensity and intent.

Patients who can in some meaningful degree carry through these final pieces of therapeutic work have a chance to complete the work of termination and to evolve in the course of it, particularly through crucial therapeutic identifications, a new sense of identity which allows them to leave behind the pathological residues. The capacity to accomplish this task is not a matter of whether the patient is paranoid or not. It is rather a matter of the level of personality organization and functioning. The capacity of the patient to internalize, which is the crucial determinant in this closing stage of any piece of meaningful therapeutic work, does not hinge on whether the patient is paranoid but, rather, on the level of primitive structural organization on which the paranoid process works. The more primitive the level of structural organization, the greater difficulty patients have in accomplishing such internalization.

By the end of a lengthy course of psychotherapy, in which enough has been accomplished to undertake the work of termination, the therapist is more than likely to be in a fairly comfortable position to pass judgment on this issue. If his feeling is that the patient has sufficient internal resources and ego capacity to accomplish the work of termination and to entertain the possibility of meaningful internalization, a classical termination can be attempted. The termination can be approached in terms of setting an appropriate date for termination of the therapy and working toward that final goal in a process which has an intentionally determinant endpoint and thereby mobilizes the mechanisms of loss, separation, and mourning that are inevitably involved in any meaningful termination. The alternative is to adopt a strategy of attenuation in which the therapeutic relationship is gradually diminished over a period of time, leaving the process open-ended, so that even when meetings between therapist and patient are scheduled only at rare and extended intervals, the therapeutic relationship is left intact and the therapeutic process in fact continues without termination.

Part Four

The Paranoid Process
in Clinical Contexts

Chapter Eight

Adolescence and the Paranoid Process

The transition to the adolescent phase of development involves a recrudescence of instinctual pressures. This regressive moment in adolescent development reactivates and intensifies the functioning of basic mechanisms of introjection and projection that are in large measure responsible for the reworking of personality configurations characterizing this period. Thus, the paranoid process has a particular and special role to play in working through the vicissitudes of adolescence.

This chapter will focus on the paranoid process in adolescent development, particularly on the interaction of projection and introjection. These elements will be examined in the case history of a patient who demonstrated these phenomena in an extreme pathological form. The discussion will lead to some conclusions regarding therapeutic intervention.

The Adolescent Period

Projective Shift

The shift in the use of projection from latency to early adolescence has been described by Sarnoff (1972) as a shift from projection associated with repression in the earlier phase to projection associated with denial in the later phase. He also notes that the latter form of projection is equivalent to the forms of projection and displacement frequently involved in paranoid conditions. In contrast, projection associated with repression follows more closely the pattern of phobia formation. In this sense, the progression to early adolescent development marks a definite shift in the direction of a more characteristically paranoid style of defensive projection.

This shift in projection parallels a transition of the primary role of defense, from that of fantasy and symptom formation to that of the testing of fantasy against reality in establishing object relations. It also parallels the partial dissolution and opening up of the superego to cultural influences. In other terms, there is identifiable a shift from id projections to superego projections. As Sarnoff (1972) notes:

> Through projection the superego is externalized. The child who attributes her [sic] formerly internalized commands to a peer or teacher stands the chance of acquiring an externalized ego ideal, with characteristics of the ego ideal of the new object. With reinternalization of the ego ideal (the projection-reinternalization is a dynamic, ongoing series of events) modifications of the superego take place. (p. 521)

Instinctual Drives

The transition to adolescence brings changes in bodily growth and an upsurge of instinctual pressures, so that adolescence involves a reopening and a reworking of earlier developmental conflicts and fixations. Relatively subtle and transient cathectic shifts in the closing stages of the latency period tend to anticipate the more marked upheaval of adolescence. The preadolescent typically forms close and somewhat idealized friendships with same-sex peers. This reflects an intensification of already established latency patterns. The capacity, which is often developed in the latency period, for sustaining sublimated interests and work habits seems to become more fluid and variable. There is a confused and somewhat conflicted searching for different interests, goals, and sources of involvement, which reflects an underlying sense of dissatisfaction. These transitional shifts signal the onset of a developmental phase which promises to be considerably more active and tumultuous than the relative quiescence of the latency period (Blos 1962).

The upsurge of instinctual drive intensity at the onset of adolescence obviously presents the ego with a problem. Mastery of these instinctual drives and their derivatives is one of the major developmental tasks of adolescence. As a result of these increased drive pressures, there is induced a regression in ego functioning that serves to reactivate basic unresolved conflicts from earlier developmental levels. The developing ego is thus presented with the necessity of and the opportunity for reworking some of these underlying conflicts in a more thoroughgoing and definitive way. The opportunity arises to undo earlier developmental defects and consequently to remodel the psychic apparatus in more effective and positively constructive ways. This implies the opportunity for new and more meaningful identifications that can provide a major direction and organization for these remodeling processes.

Narcissism

The adolescent's withdrawal from dependence on the familiar objects of childhood leads to a narcissistic overvaluation of the self. The adolescent becomes increasingly aware of his inner processes. He becomes self-absorbed, self-centered, and self-concerned. This may lead to a narcissistic withdrawal and disturbance of reality testing. The adolescent often resorts to narcissistic defenses to defend against the disappointment and disillusionment of his meager position in reality. He may find it difficult to give up the gratifying parent on whom he has come to depend—especially if that parent has been overly protecting and solicitous—and to face his own limitations and inadequacies. He may be afraid to take responsibility for his own abilities and their consequences—as well as to be faced with the demands of adult responsibility.

With the induced narcissistic regression, the intensity of narcissistic needs increases. This leaves the adolescent self more susceptible to narcissistic injury and disillusionment. It also provides another important source for the mobilization of introjection-projection, specifically as narcissistic defenses. Thus, introjection and projection come into operation to sustain the threatened sense of self and preserve its threatened integrity. The regressive activation of introjection-projection tends to regressively intensify cathexis of and attachment to parental objects.

Adolescent Paranoia

Separation

If the sense of identity requires and builds itself in relationship to a sense of communion and belonging with both significant objects and a context of belonging, it is also true that an important element in the maintaining and functioning of the sense of identity is its capacity to tolerate a separation from the same significant objects. Modell (1968) discusses this important developmental attainment in the following terms:

It is a fact that those individuals who have the capacity to accept the separateness of objects are those that have a distinct, at least in part, beloved sense of self. If one can be a loving parent to oneself, one can more readily accept the separateness of objects. This is a momentous step in psychic development. (p. 59)

The capacity to tolerate the separateness of significant objects is a correlative of the capacity to tolerate painful reality. It is only on this basis that a mature capacity for realistic object relations can be established and sustained. The mature sense of self, the fully developed sense of identity, then, is correlated with the capacity to recognize and accept the identity of others and the ability to come to terms with and acknowledge the separateness and the autonomy of those others. Where there is an intolerance for such separateness, there develops an inner need to incorporate the object within the limits of one's own self or to extend the orbit of one's self to encompass that object. This incorporating or extending is accomplished through defensively toned uses of projection and introjection. When a relationship is contaminated with introjective components, the object begins to be regarded as somehow belonging to the self—the sort of self-object relationships to which Kohut's (1971) considerations of narcissism address themselves.

It can be quickly seen that in these terms we are dealing with an extension of the concerns of individuation and separation that have been an integral part of the developmental process from the beginning of the child's experience. But we need to go a step further. We would contend not only that development and maintenance of the sense of identity require a capacity for the toleration of the separateness of objects but that an integral part of the process is the active separation out from and over against such objects. We are consequently, bringing into focus the obverse of the concerns for relatedness and belonging. If the processes underlying and building a sense of inner integrity and belonging can be seen in terms of their contribution to the process of identity formation, they must also be seen as functioning reciprocally with other processes which serve to separate the emerging identity from and place it over against other objects and contexts—literally defining the emerging sense of identity in terms of such opposition. We are talking here about the need for an enemy.

Need for Enemy

The subject of a need for an enemy is one which I find rather distressing. It is painful to reckon with the possibility that the very mechanisms which we have been at pains to define as substantially contributing to and sustaining the sense of identity are also intrinsically related to a process which serves to separate that identity out from others and to set it in basic opposition to them. But I find myself forced to this consideration. As Blum (1981) has noted, some degree of hate can be regarded as an ubiquitous phenomenon, particularly the need for a safe target for hostile and hateful affects in the interest of maintaining psychic equilibrium. This need is especially noteworthy in adolescents. The basic dilemma, the difficult task which is imposed upon the adolescent by the exigencies of development is that he articulate a sense of himself and integrate that sense with a specifically defined social unit, a community which organizes and expresses itself with specifically defined limits and internally generated and specific criteria of belonging and sharing of values.

Community

However, as Erikson (1959) points out, the integration is a function of *mutual* recognition and acceptance. The community may feel recognized by the emerging individual who is ready to seek recognition and acceptance from it. It can also feel rejected by those more alienated individuals who reject it, rebel against it, or simply seem not to care about it. If the community responds to the former with acceptance—thus promoting participation and integration—it can also withhold its acceptance from the latter. This creates a paranoid impasse—a standoff of mutual rejection. The individual and the community become enemies. The paranoid process requires the individual to seek affiliation with other groupings—often countercultural subgroupings—or, failing that, to construct a more decisively pathological paranoid system.

The defining of self and the articulating of its relationship with the community—both under conditions of mutual rejection and under conditions of acceptance—are achieved in part through a setting of the self over against other communities, other groupings, other contexts of belonging which are defined in terms of their exclusiveness from the initial social grouping and in terms of their opposition in beliefs, values, attitudes, et cetera.

The community which the adolescent shapes about himself is built around a core of inherent values and attitudes but is likewise set in opposition to other such groupings. The adolescent in our society delineates and articulates his sense of identity through participating in certain groupings. He envisions himself as sharing certain affiliations with different such groupings. Thus, he envisions himself as an

American citizen, or as Jewish, or as Republican, or in terms of professional affiliations as a psychiatrist, or perhaps as a psychologist, or perhaps as a carpenter, or perhaps as a truck driver.

Each of these affiliations makes a contribution which can be differentiated from others and can be set in opposition to them. Moreover, when conflicts and matters of interest and advantage bring these issues to the fore, feelings and attitudes can be generated which regard the outgroup specifically and concretely as the enemy of the ingroup. One can observe this phenomenon occurring with varying degrees of intensity and even pathological distortion in the events which form the fabric of our common social experience.

Paranoid propensities make a significant contribution to the forming of ingroups within which the sense of identity can articulate itself and maintain significant contexts of belonging and sharing which serve to sustain and confirm the inner sense of individual identity. The important tasks confronting the adolescent have to do precisely with his articulating his sense of self in terms of these complex social groupings— that is to say, an integral part of the forming of an identity is the acquiring of a sense of belonging to certain specified ingroups, thereby defining oneself as opposed to and separated from other social and cultural groupings which constitute the outgroups.

The phenomenon is applicable to social and cultural groupings, but it also has relevance in terms of the very personalized and individualized articulation of the sense of self as separate from and over against other selves. In a certain necessary sense, an important task of adolescent development is that the adolescent set himself apart from and position himself in opposition to his parents or other significant caretaking figures. The adolescent revolt against parental restrictions cannot be seen simply in pathological terms but must also be seen as a way of making a significant contribution to the adolescent attainment of identity. This also applies to the adolescent exigency to revolt against all forms of authority.

Paranoid Mechanisms

These considerations lead us to suggest a process of "adolescent paranoia." We are suggesting that adolescent paranoia is based on the working out of the specifically paranoid mechanisms we have been discussing—projection, introjection, and the paranoid construction— and that it provides an essential aspect of the process of achieving a sense of identity. We are suggesting further that even though these mechanisms are a continuation of developmental vicissitudes, in the adolescent period they assume a specifically paranoid quality—more akin to the paranoid manifestations found in the context of clinical psychopathology.

The adolescent unavoidably sees himself as the victim of parental restraints and restrictions. He must also to some extent see himself as the victim of social pressures and cultural constraints, which require him to integrate himself with the society around him in terms of certain standards of behavior and values. It is the working of this adolescent process and its attendant persecutory anxieties which contribute significantly to the tumultuousness, the anxieties, and the rebellious turmoil that we have come to associate so explicitly with adolescence. It is important, however, not to lose sight of the fact that such deviant and rebellious expressions—marked by the usual accompaniments of paranoid distortions, such as extreme narcissism, defensiveness, rebelliousness, hostility, and destructive potentiality—are at the same time an expression of important developmental functions operating in the service of establishing and consolidating a sense of identity.

Alienation and the Paranoid Process

Identity

The problem of alienation can be articulated as a problem of identity—particularly identity in its extrinsic frame of reference as expressing the relatedness of the individual to his social and cultural matrix. The pathology of alienation is basically a pathology of the self. The focusing of the problem of alienation was stimulated by the social and cultural emphases of neo-Freudian theorists—particularly Horney and Fromm. However, as a result of the emergence and development of analytic ego psychology, the relationship between man's intrapsychic life and the familial, social, and cultural contexts in which he develops and functions has undergone a profound reconsideration. In this more extended understanding of man's psychic development and structure, it has become possible to rethink neo-Freudian contributions and to integrate them meaningfully with the main body of analytic understanding.

Horney related the problem of alienation to the disparity between the idealized self and the real self. Because of the neurotic failure to measure up to the ideal, the neurotic hates himself—hates his own limitations and inadequacies. This self-hate expresses itself in relentless demands on oneself, repeated self-accusations, self-devaluation, forms of self-torment, and self-destructive behavior. In its extreme forms, such alienation can take the form of amnesia and loss of a sense of reality and of depersonalization. But more pervasively, alienation can take the form of a feeling of numbness and remoteness. The individual tends to become more impersonal in all his dealings. He loses a sense of responsibility for himself and for the direction of his life and activity. His continual sense of disappointment with himself and his interaction with his environment leads to a gradual disowning of his real self and a retreat into an ineffectual style of life (Horney 1950). One of the serious questions that confronts us is the extent to which this pattern of life experience is emerging as a cultural type. The line between psychopathology and cultural maladaptation becomes thin and highly permeable. Alienation in its many guises and "formes frustes" may well have permeated our society to such an extent that it can no longer be regarded as deviant or pathological in the usual sense.

Anomie

The problem of alienation, therefore, focuses psychiatric concern on the interface between intrapsychic dynamics and the social and cultural processes which surround the individual and inevitably influence his development and capacity to function. Alienation becomes a sort of middle ground on which psychiatric concern mingles with and to some extent overlaps with the concern of more social approaches to human behavior. The concept of alienation thus carries an implicit reference to the social context which continually influences the individual and with which he is in constant interaction. Alienation is an alienation from something that is around and outside the individual. One of the most valuable insights of modern social science is that patterns of deviant behavior are not merely the product of disordered intrapsychic processes or impediments of development—although these play an unquestioned and critical role—but that the organization of social structures and social processes within which the individual functions also has a determinate influence on the patterns of individual adaptation.

The interrelation between social anomie and psychological alienation is complex. The cultural disparity involved in anomie has its psychological counterpart in the disorganization and inner conflicts of values of the individual. The basic question is how intrapsychic and social processes influence each other in the complex process of value formation and value change. Merton (1957) has suggested that the organization of our contemporary culture, with its emphasis on material wealth and competitiveness, creates a certain strain toward anomie. The shift of cultural emphasis from the satisfactions involved in competitive effort to an almost exclusive concern with the outcome—in terms of measurable criteria of wealth and power—tends to create a stress on the regulatory structures and an attenuation of institutional controls. Cultural and personal values are undermined, and calculations of personal advantage and risks of punishment become the main regulatory resource. This social strain toward anomie can be paralleled by a failure of internalization processes and a regression from internalized sources of regulation to a more primitive and externalized reliance on external rewards and punishments, on directives and prohibitions of external authorities. The social strain toward anomie is paralleled by an inner strain toward extremes of conformity or rebellion.

Alienation Syndrome

The alienation syndrome has been described primarily within the adolescent and postadolescent group. The elements of the syndrome include a basic sense of loneliness—the feeling that one somehow does not belong, is not a part of things, is not in the mainstream of life and interests that surround one. There is a sense of estrangement and a chronic sense of frustration. The alienated person carries with him a continual sense of opposition between his own wishes and desires and the wishes and desires of those around him—with the additional feeling that his wishes, desires, and ambitions are actively being denied by others. He lives in a chronic state of disappointment—others are continually letting him down, disappointing his expectations, frustrating his designs, pressuring him to conform to their wishes and desires. His disappointment and chronic frustration produce an inner state of unrelenting anger that serves to isolate and estrange him further. Occasionally, the anger will erupt in destructive outbursts that leave him even less satisfied and further disappointed.

An important element in the syndrome is the alienated person's sense of continuing frustration. He carries within him a chronic despair—a sense of hopelessness and helplessness which he sees as unremitting. When this sense of hopelessness dominates the picture, alienation tends to take the drop-out, give-up form of retreatism. The individual may resort to any number of pathological forms of behavior to alleviate his sense of inner frustration, including alcohol, drugs, or other forms of escape. Much of what we have seen over the years in the skid-row phenomenon and much of what we are seeing on the contemporary drug scene has this quality of frustrated retreatism. When the sense of frustrated rage dominates the picture, however, we are much

more likely to see its manifestations in rebellious behavior of one kind or
other. The sense of helplessness and the sense of smoldering rage can
easily coexist in the same individual—so that the helpless victim may
find himself striking out in impotent rage from time to time.

Rejection of Values

A central element of the alienation syndrome is the rejection of or the
conflict over social values. The alienation syndrome lies at the interface
between the person and social processes. This raises a problem in
differential diagnosis. Psychiatrists have tended to see the clinical
manifestations of the alienation syndrome more in terms of the
parameters of inner psychic dysfunction and less in terms of the social
parameters. Thus, the alienation syndrome is usually described in terms
of some form of character pathology, or in terms of its narcissistic
aspects, or in terms of its depressive aspects.

But the associated estrangement reflects a more basic rejection of
values which the society embodies and implicitly requires that these
patients accept. Their rejection of these values may leave them in a
relatively valueless vacuum—or they may actively foster divergent values
which they oppose to the prevailing values of the culture. Or there may
arise an inner conflict between partially accepted values of the general
culture and partially accepted values of a divergent nature. The
alienation syndrome adds specifically to these other well-known clinical
pictures the aspect of value conflict and a tendency to reject the accepted
cultural value system of society.

The rebellious expression of the alienation syndrome is characterized by the formulation or acceptance of a divergent set of values. Often,
this takes place in conjunction with a group of likeminded individuals
who can share the same set of deviant values. It should be noted that the
term"deviant" in this context does not have the connotation of better or
worse, but simply emphasizes that the values of the subgroup stand
somehow in opposition to those of the general culture. Such value-
oriented subgroupings are alienated from the larger social group but
may be quite unified within themselves. This allows the alienated
individual to achieve a compensatory sense of belonging. This compensatory aspect of group formation is a significant part of the motivation
behind adolescent gangs and the youth movement in general. The value
deviance can be focused and expressed in almost any aspect of
behavior—clothing, hair styles, sexual mores, language, expression of
values, attitudes, beliefs, et cetera.

The important dimension of this value divergence is not so much the formation of new and constructive and meaningful values. Rather, the emphasis in the alienation syndrome falls on the rejection and, in the rebellious extreme, on the overthrow of preexisting values. Divergent alienated groups seize on any ideology or formulation of divergent attitudes to express their rejection. Often, in the service of frustrated and impotent rage, the objective seems to be to find the most extreme form of articulation of values that might fly in the face of the prevailing social values. Thus, rebellious groups spout the most extreme socialist and communist rhetoric. They also have a need to question, challenge, and confront social institutions and practices on all levels.

Portrait of a Young Rebel:
A Case of Adolescent Alienation

I would like to offer some reflections on my experience with a young man who was in psychotherapy for nearly three years. This particular patient provides an unusual opportunity for exploring a crucial issue in our professional attempts to help many of the disturbed younger people in our society; namely, that of the difficult interplay between the patient's distorted perceptions of the world around him and the pathological and destructive elements that persist in the social environment. The patient's paranoid perceptions are driven by inner subjective needs, but to what extent are these perceptions reflected and verified by external processes? What problems does the overlap between inner perceptions and external realities create for the psychotherapist in carrying out his professional effort?

Present Illness

My first contact with Jerry took place when he was brought by the police to our hospital. He had been found disrupting traffic by standing in the middle of a large highway, brandishing a crowbar, shouting at the drivers and threatening to smash their cars with the crowbar if they tried to pass him. At the time of his arrival he was quite agitated, disorganized, somewhat confused, and delusional. He was plainly in the throes of a schizophrenic decompensation.

In discussing Jerry's difficulties, I will look briefly at the latter course of his illness, then go back to look at his family background and earlier history. Later, I will consider some of my experience during the course of approximately three years of his therapy.

Recent History

It turned out that Jerry's hospitalization was not his first. His psychiatric history had started several years before when he was in the army and had to be hospitalized for a psychotic break. Jerry had matriculated at a large eastern university, where he spent a year that was unhappy, lonely, and only moderately successful academically. He had felt isolated from his fellow students and unable to make any substantial friendships. He decided at the end of the year to interrupt his schooling and to enlist in the army. He was assigned to a computer training program.

The army did not prove to be a hospitable environment for him. The discipline and impersonality of army life were difficult for him to accept. He again found it difficult to make friends—particularly since he looked down on the other men as intellectually and educationally inferior. He had particular difficulty adapting to army discipline, which he found arbitrary, cold, excessively demanding, humiliating, and completely unresponsive to his personal needs and wishes. He became increasingly despondent. As an escape he contacted some of his college friends who were involved in the drug scene and had them send him a supply of LSD. He had occasionally dropped acid at college without any bad effects.

Jerry began to feel that the army was trying to destroy him and ruin his mind. He became quite suspicious and began to think that the instructors in the computer program were plotting against him. At this point one of the instructors wrote on the blackboard "LSD," for "least significant denominator," but Jerry took this to mean that he was under surveillance for possessing LSD. He rushed to his locker and ingested the whole supply. A bad trip ensued, complete with florid delusions of paranoid quality and thoughts that the army was controlling his mind by means of computers. He was briefly hospitalized, rather quickly recompensated, and was given a medical discharge.

He returned to college, where he again found himself isolated and having great difficulties relating to fellow students. He became heavily involved in radical student politics. He was troubled by feelings of loneliness and estrangement, feelings that people were out to get him, feelings that people were staring at him or talking about him. Involvement in radical politics served a double purpose: it enabled him to share a common interest with other somewhat estranged and angry students, and it served as a channel for the rage he felt toward the establishment.

He developed his skills at haranguing groups and at organizing political activities. He finally ran for a major school office on the radical ticket. He poured all of his energy and enthusiasm into the campaign, only to be defeated.

The loss was a severe narcissistic blow and proved to be one of the precipitants of his decompensation. A second important precipitant was the disruption of his relationship with his girlfriend. He had become very dependently attached to her, and they had been living and sleeping together for several months. She finally decided that he was too unstable for any serious relationship and broke it off. He was crushed, hurt, disappointed, enraged, and felt betrayed. Coming on the heels of his election loss, he felt that there was a conspiracy on the part of the school to "get" him because of his radical political views.

As the end of the school year drew near, Jerry's psychosis grew more apparent. He attended a national student conference where he became so disruptive that he had to be taken out of the meeting. He was convinced that the meeting was being controlled by the CIA and was determined to disrupt it. He interrupted the proceedings by shouting obscenities, breaking into the discussions with angry and provocative political harangues against the establishment, against then-President Nixon, against the war in Vietnam, against the draft, et cetera. He remained in this state for several more weeks, living in a commune with a group of fellow student radicals who more or less protected him.

Then one evening he took it into his head to go out and try to cross a nearby highway. He felt that the traffic was preventing his crossing the busy highway and was thereby infringing on his constitutional rights. The relentless metal machines bearing down on him, uncaringly forcing him aside without any consideration of his needs or wishes, represented the cold, uncaring, heartless, and indifferent establishment that made decisions about his life and forced him to do things he did not want to do—without consulting him in any way or taking his personal needs into account. He felt an intense rage against this impersonal and indifferent imposition from above, and a powerful wish to strike out against it and destroy it.

Family Background

The roots of such attitudes and feelings were not difficult to find. Jerry's family had not been a very happy one. Jerry's mother is a rather affected, labile, narcissistic, very demanding, and probably borderline woman. From almost the day of her marriage she started drinking. She has been a chronic alcoholic for years and bears a number of the physical stigmata of alcoholism. His father is a trim, graying, pinstriped business executive. He was pleasant and proper but kept a disconcerting distance at all times. Jerry's parents did not get along at all. The marriage was torn by conflict and bitterness on the part of both parents. Father responded by a pattern of emotional and physical withdrawal. He would get up early in the morning and leave the house before the mother got out of bed. He would not return home until late in the evening.

The split between the parents and the father's withdrawal created other problems. Jerry was drawn much closer to his mother. She seemed to take out her frustrations and needs on him. She would be perfectionistically demanding—and never seemed satisfied with his performance. She would easily become impatient and irritated at him, and would beat him in sadistic fury. He recalled episodes when his mother would attack him seemingly without reason and would keep hitting him, knocking him down, and demanding that he stand up again and "take it like a man"—whereupon she would knock him down again. At other times, she was overly affectionate and would embrace and fondle him in a manner that was physically intimate and sexually seductive. Jerry could never figure his mother out—never knew what to expect from her. He also resented the fact that his father seemed so distant and uninvolved. He felt that his mother's problems were related to her relationship with his father, and he resented the fact that his father allowed her treatment of him to go on and did not protect him from his mother. In time, Jerry had two younger brothers, but he remained mother's favorite, the one whom she treated with excessive affection as well as with often brutal beatings.

One of the important themes of Jerry's childhood was his continual longing for closeness with his father—a longing that was always frustrated. He hardly saw his father during the week. The family never ate together; father would come home late and the children were not allowed to disturb him while he ate dinner. By then, it was usually time for them to go to bed. If father was home, he would usually want to read the paper and was not interested in spending time with Jerry. The father also demonstrated a remarkable capacity for detachment and denial. Even in the face of Jerry's severe decompensation, he seemed incapable of recognizing or admitting that there was any problem in the family, or that he might have had any part in it. For years, he blandly denied any problems on the part of his wife—even when the evidence of her progressive alcoholism was overwhelming. This was one of the counts of Jerry's rage at him—that he could ignore the self-destructive course his mother was on and refuse to do anything about it.

Early Difficulties

Jerry was a shy and lonely child. He complained that they lived in a remote suburban area where there were few friends he could play with, and those who were there he could not get along with. He was a fearful child, with a number of severe childhood phobias and given to severe nightmares. Nightmares were a persistent feature of his experience. His dreams were filled with scenes of bloody murder and destruction. He frequently experienced a typical incubus nightmare—feeling a heavy weight on his chest, paralyzing him and crushing him and preventing him from breathing.

The basic difficulties in Jerry's situation were reinforced by the pattern of the succeeding years. The father's job required frequent changes of locale, every year or so. Jerry felt there was never any time when he could really settle in and make friends. As soon as he started to make friends, his family would move again. When he was old enough, his father decided to send him to prep school in England. The father defended his decision on the basis of Jerry's educational needs but when pressed finally admitted that he felt that Jerry's involvement with his mother was unhealthy and that he felt it would be better if Jerry could escape from her. The other two brothers stayed with the family.

Jerry experienced this as an abandonment and a rejection. This feeling was reinforced by the fact that the family never visited him, that he often would not receive any presents or communications on special occasions like birthdays or holidays, that usually his father prevented him from visiting his family because of the expense. Jerry hated the school situation. He resented the harsh discipline, the intense competitiveness among the boys, the fact that they made fun of him because he was a Yank and poked fun at his mannerisms and speech, the fact that he could not make friends, et cetera. He felt lonely, isolated, hurt, abandoned, unwanted, and unloved. He reacted with angry withdrawal and rebelliousness. He was constantly fighting with the other boys and getting into trouble with the school authorities.

He was finally sent back to the United States to complete his high school education. Father thought it would be good for him to go to the same prep school that father had attended. Jerry became more of a discipline problem. His marks were also very poor, and at the end of a year the school requested that he not return. He then went to live with his father's sister, who was a very cold, demanding, and ungiving person. She made demands on Jerry that he resented, and he felt that she exploited him to do work for her. He experienced all these years as a punitive exile from his family. He bitterly resented the fact that he was forced to endure all this while his brothers could be with the family. He had lost out in the sibling rivalry—and had been rejected by his parents, particularly his father.

The Money Issue

An important aspect of Jerry's difficulties had to do with money. Father had always made a big thing of money, constantly complaining that the family was spending too much and living beyond their means. His rationalization for not visiting Jerry and for not letting Jerry come home more often had always been money. For most of his time away from home, Jerry had lived frugally, always deeply concerned yet resentful about the lack of money. Since his return to school from the army, he had lived at a bare subsistence level—spending less than a dollar a day, living commune style with fellow students, eating poorly and cheaply— but steadfastly refusing to ask his father for more money. He felt that his father would only hold it against him. Money was also an issue in his illness; father would complain about the hospital bills and insist that Jerry get out of the hospital. When Jerry got such letters, he would invariably regress noticeably and become more psychotic—until we were able to find out that he had received such a letter and we were able to discuss it.

Jerry's resentments about money were deep, especially since money served as the basis for his father's rationalizations for so much that Jerry was bitter about. Gradually, he was able to accept the view that he had some right to help and support from his father. He came to see that even though his father complained about money, the family lived comfortably in a well-to-do suburban area, Jerry's mother consumed large amounts of alcohol that cost a significant amount of money, and his father could afford little indulgences like vacation trips and a sailboat. It was interesting that Jerry could displace his resentful feelings to surrogate objects and could rationalize stealing, cheating, and "ripping off" against them but that he had great difficulty in coming to accept even reasonable demands on his father for money.

It was clear that these experiences reinforced his deep ambivalence toward both parents. His love for mother was contaminated by the threatening aspects of her seductiveness and overly possessive control— not to mention her sadistic punishment, which he so often felt was capricious and unmerited. He had a deep, if continually frustrated, longing for closeness to his father. But he was enraged at father's continuing indifference and cold distancing, even as he was enraged at his father's apparently blind indifference and refusal to do anything about not only his own difficulties but his mother's problems as well.

Adolescent Alienation

Jerry's case exemplifies many of the pathological features of adolescent alienation. Alienation is a frequent and familiar part of the picture presented by adolescents in our culture. Adolescence is a developmental period of regressive disorganization, hopefully followed by a progressive reorganization, of the personality. This developmental progression allows the child to pass through the physical and inner psychic changes that are required for him to begin to approach his definitive role and position in adult society. But the adolescent is not really a part of that society—he is only potentially a part. He will be able to integrate himself with the adult world only by forming himself to fit adult roles and by demonstrating to the adult community that he is ready and capable of fulfilling them. Only then can the adult community recognize and receive him. During the period of adolescent development, however, he remains outside looking in. There is a sense of estrangement which is embedded in the adolescent experience in our culture (Berman 1970). It is an expression of what we have already described as "adolescent paranoia."

Depression

Helene Deutsch (1967) has pointed out the frequency of depressive affects in many adolescents. For many adolescents, adolescence is a traumatic period in their lives. They are confronted by the demands of reality, by performance standards, by adult competition for positions, awards, et cetera, which is often intense, and by an increasing realization of their own limitations. A crucial aspect of the child's capacity to adapt is related to the issue of narcissism. Promising children often come to the adolescent challenge with narcissistic dreams of accomplishment and glory—dreams that may have been fostered and prolonged by their parents, most often the mother. Thus, the infantile narcissism with its dreams, expectations, and sense of entitlement is often prolonged into adolescence—and the inevitable disappointment becomes traumatic. An increase of narcissism is quite characteristic of adolescence anyway, but these particularly narcissistic adolescents were raised in an atmosphere of expectation—generated by their mother's excessive investment in them, in the hope that they would one day compensate for the mother's own sense of disappointment and frustration. We can hear the echoes of this theme in the highly conflictual relationship between Jerry and his mother—her demandingness and perfectionism, alternating with abusive and punitive rejection.

Devaluation of the Father

With this basically narcissistic picture, alienated adolescents show an added feature. The narcissistic investment from the mother tends to undermine the position of the father as a model for identification. The mother's disappointment is often intensified by the failure of the father to measure up to her standards. The father is thus devalued. The child who is caught up in this process must therefore devalue the father in order to share the mother's dream and to gain her approval. He too devalues and rejects the father, and this devaluation is intensified during the adolescent period. The father is seen as weak, debased, worthless, insignificant, inconsequential. At a deeper level, the adolescent boy's resentment against the father is often due to the fact that the father is too weak to protect him from an often ambivalent dependency on his mother, as well as from an incestuous involvement with her. This underlying devaluation of the father often erupts in adolescence—even though it may have been there since earliest childhood. It becomes extended to the entire world of adults, adult standards, and adult institutions. The adolescent rage against society and its values and its institutions can be rooted in a rage against the devalued father and all he stands for.

But the devaluation of the father does not erase the underlying idealization of the father and the unremitting longing for closeness, approval, and acceptance from the father. Regardless of the hostility toward and undermining of the father in Jerry's case, there remained a wishful and unrequited longing for a father who would be better, stronger, more available, loving, and supportive. The tragedy for Jerry, as for other alienated adolescents, is that the wish is doomed to unfulfillment.

Thus, the adolescent boy stands on the threshold of a world of adult standards and expectations. But it is his father's world. The devaluation of the father and the struggle against identification with the father lead to a rejection of all social commitments, all social values, all conventional roles, all responsibilities, and many of the forms of emotional relatedness with others that form the normal fabric of society. A similar problem confronts the adolescent girl. If she idealizes her father excessively, she runs the risk of devaluing and despising her mother—

with an intensification of her penis envy and an impairment of a meaningful and constructive identification with her mother. She thus tends to rebel against any conventional forms of feminine role or status, and strives for more masculine competitiveness and forms of accomplishment. The rebellious expression of these aspects is eloquently expressed in some of the radical feminist phenomena.

Identifications

It is useful to realize that in large measure the process of alienation may serve some important developmental functions. One of the questions that the apparent increase in manifest alienation raises is the extent to which social and cultural conditions require that the forms of alienation take the patterns of expression that they do. Alienation is a feature of all adolescent development—but the reorganization of inner structures, defenses, values, and patterns of identification can be pressured into maladaptive and even pathological molds. Alienation, however, can also serve adaptive purposes in helping to achieve a necessary physical and psychic distance from parents and society, and provide a defense against painful ideas and affects associated with the disruption of cathexis to the past relationships (Berman 1970). In the normal course of things, such adaptive alienation is not extreme and is resolved into new and functional adult patterns of identification and role functioning. The extremes of alienation, however, distort the growth process and make adaptive resolutions more precarious.

Protest

The problem and the paradox of alienation are acutely focused in the use of social protest and revolutionary violence. Revolution, and the use of violence in the service of revolution, are nothing new, but they have taken on new social implications in our time. The threat of violence has become a familiar refrain from a variety of disaffected and dissatisfied subcultural groups.

The protest of students is particularly interesting in this regard. The protest of student radicals runs deep. It is a protest and a rebellion against important values that form the essential fabric of our society. However destructive and pathological the means by which some students choose to express this divergence, we miss the essential dimension if we ignore that the core issue in their dissent is a matter of values. Youth is not merely objecting to a style of life or a pattern of living in adult society—it is protesting and rebelling against the system of values that governs and guides adult society. This raises a severe problem in that adults and administrators at all levels, from the family to the larger units of social organization in educational and governmental institutions, can often discuss and debate matters of fact, but they are sometimes unable to see or find their way to debate matters of value. As a result, confrontations yield results unsatisfactory to both sides, because the real issues are never joined.

If protest and dissent have a place in social process, what about violence? Some student radicals are committed to violence. The rhetoric of this subgroup proclaims that social injustice is too deeply rooted to try to reform our social institutions. They view social institutions as based on the exploitation of the many in the interest of the few. Such institutions are seen as unjust and evil, as controlled by a concern for nothing but money and power—and as an evil to be destroyed. These few see no possibility for reform or change from within. The only effective means for getting rid of such evil and oppressive institutions and the values that govern them is believed to be violent overthrow and destruction.

Idealism

Behind this current of discontent and dissatisfaction lies a strong ideologically colored commitment to a form of utopian idealism. Erikson (1964) has taught us that ideological commitment is a necessary ingredient in the growth of youth to maturity. But ideology can be put in the service of inner growth and the confirmation of cultural integration, or it can be put in the service of infantile needs and the dynamisms of alienation (Meissner 1978b). Social idealism has served as an inspiration for human social and political aspirations for centuries. But utopian ideals can also represent the prolongation of infantile narcissism and wishes. They can come to embody infantile wishes to receive unconditional love, protection, care, and freedom from those powerful sources that represent the omnipotent parents. It was such powerful infantile yearnings that motivated Jerry's paranoid rebellion. They may also represent the opposite and equally unrealizable wish to obtain such omnipotence for oneself.

For some of today's more fanatical youth, the utopian wish must be responded to and fulfilled immediately—without delay, planning, consideration, reflection, or questioning. They have no patience for the slow process of cultural change; they cannot wait for the plodding deliberation and interaction of positions and interests that constitute the political process; they demonstrate little capacity for toleration of delay and postponement of gratification of their wishes and demands. Their rejection of social values and the intensity of their rage lead them to believe that the solution to their frustration lies in the destruction of whatever opposes their demands. The supposition is that if one destroys what one believes to be evil, good will automatically spring up in its place. In the impulsiveness of their inner needs and their external demands, they ignore and bypass the essential nature of social and cultural processes (Greenacre 1970).

The frustration and denial of such pressing inner demands and of the deeper narcissistic expectations that so often lie beneath them lead to a sense of inner disappointment and rage. We have seen how the sense of powerlessness, worthlessness, meaninglessness, and social and self-estrangement can easily lead to the expression of frustrated rage. Increasing evidence suggests that much violent confrontation is produced by a relatively small group of alienated individuals who are acting out their infantile needs and wishes in immature ways—lashing out with destructive rage and without any constructive plan or purpose. There is no doubt that deeply unconscious, irrational, and infantile wishes are frequently rationalized under the guise of social idealism and that the frustration of such wishes can lie at the heart of the pressure for violent social reorganization. But the analysis of inner psychodynamics does not explain away the need for nor substitute for social change. The infantile needs and behavior of a few radicals do not obliterate the need for social change or the conditions in our society that make such change desirable or necessary.

Complementarity Model of Psychosocial Interaction

We have been presenting a consideration of the complex interaction of psychopathological and social variables. Jerry's story represents a case of student activism and "New Left" radicalism which carries clear pathological roots in childhood experience and in the continuing sense of frustration and rejection on the part of parental figures. The argument to this point has emphasized that despite the obvious elements of displacement and projection from infantile levels of conflict and ambivalence, understanding student radicalism in exclusively these terms can be misleading. It is clear that the social context and the interactional processes involved in it contribute significantly to the emerging pattern of deviant behavior.

For therapists to approach such problems with a one-sided model rooted in psychopathology only would seem to reflect certain political prejudices, which would tend to prejudge deviant behavior as pathological and to prejudge the social context as above reproach. From this point of view, the charge so often leveled at psychiatry of getting the patient to conform to the norms of society may be justified. But the situation is obviously more complex and calls for a more complex analysis as the basis for psychotherapeutic understanding.

The dialectic of polar positions has been sketched quite effectively by Fried (1970). The psychodynamic position accounts for psychopathology on the basis of unresolved conflicts which involve intrapsychic forces—e.g., impulses and defenses—in relation to significant objects. This approach does not exclude but, rather, leaves open the question of the influence of social relationships and processes. Individual differences in the ego's capacity to relate to and adapt to reality are related to individual selection, rather than to systematic differentiation of social influences and patterns. The social approach does not exclude motivation but sees it as derived from social interactions and forces. The respective orientations are not only tenable but can be seen in complementary perspective.

In terms of Jerry's experience and that of a significant proportion of young rebels, the displacement of inner conflicts and intensely ambivalent relations with significant objects (parents) onto social structures at a university or government level is reinforced and complemented by elements of dehumanizing detachment and uncaring impersonalization, bureaucratic rigidity, authoritarian and repressive attitudes, and morally inconsistent and exploitative approaches. Jerry's projections were met and validated to a significant degree by the public situations in which he found himself impelled to protest. Thus, what can from one point of view be identified as psychopathology must to some extent be regarded as legitimate social protest from another perspective. Conversely, one might wonder whether—if social institutions did not so often operate in ways that correspond to and validate the projections of the young—the opportunities and stimulation for rebellious attitudes among society's younger members would be as frequent or intense.

The Therapeutic Process and Therapeutic Issues

Hospitalization

All of these issues were alive and active in the course of Jerry's psychotherapy. The treatment course was difficult and problematic. On his initial evaluation he was suspicious and guarded, agitated and confused, obviously psychotic. His mind was filled with ideas that he later described as "freaky"—that the world was under attack by hostile extraterrestrial forces, that the world was threatened with chaos and destruction, with powerful forces vying with each other for control. His behavior at that point was quite paranoid.

At the beginning of his hospitalization, he was quite angry, hostile, and resistive to treatment. He would break out in angry tirades, proclaiming a radical socialist philosophy and damning all the forces of the political establishment. Several times he violently disrupted patient community meetings with wild, angry, foot-stomping harangues against the doctors who were trying to subjugate and control the patients' minds, and against the hospital administration, urging the patients to revolt. One of these outbursts was culminated by his smashing a chair to the floor and breaking it. This behavior was quite disturbing to other patients and had to be restrained. Gradually he began to respond to high doses of phenothiazines and became less disruptive. He then entered a long period of depression and despondency that lasted for several months. His thought processes remained obviously, though moderately, disorganized for several weeks.

Psychotherapy

His psychotherapy hours were at first consumed by seemingly endless tirades. He fulminated against the government, against the war, against the draft, against the President, against the school administration— against any expression of or representation of authority. The tirades always had the same themes: that those who exercise power are cold, indifferent, and uncaring; that they make decisions that affect the lives of helpless individuals without any concern for or interest in what the feelings and wishes of those individuals might be. These complaints were accompanied by feelings of intense rage and bitterness; it almost seemed at times as though he were going to literally explode. His vituperations were expressed in the most extreme and destructive terms. His rhetoric was cast in the most extreme radical and revolutionary terms. He saw no other alternatives but that the present political system and the economic structure that went with it should be destroyed. Any tactic, any device, any course of destructive action that interfered with and served to cripple or destroy the operation of this heinous system was, therefore, praise-worthy and good. Any system that so subjugated and destroyed human beings was hateful and worthy only to be destroyed. Not to work for its destruction was itself a crime. Any action taken to destroy it was an act of heroic rebellion.

Hour after hour, Jerry would proclaim the rights of the down-trodden and the underprivileged: students, blacks, Puerto Ricans, women, et cetera. Every episode that suggested actions of powerful figures to take advantage of or control the lives of people became the starting point for an angry tirade. Any decision or implementation of policy in the university, any action of the government, any statement by a public official, would serve to trigger an angry outburst. There seemed to be no end to his bitterness and furious rage—and no end of subjects and targets against which he could launch it. During this period there were several student riots and strikes at the university, each of which provoked long tirades. In most of these he actively participated. The sight of his friends being arrested and dragged off to jail was intolerable to him. When the tragic events took place at Kent State and at Jackson State, his rage was nearly psychotic.

Gradually, the scope of the therapy widened. In the face of these tirades I could do nothing but wait and listen. The waiting and listening were difficult because the tirades seemed so endless and so incredibly repetitious. Little by little, however, I began to hear more of his resentments against his parents. With some encouragement, he began increasingly to move back and forth between his current resentments and the resentments he had felt as a child against his parents. At one crucial juncture, I pointed out to him that the language and the themes of his tirades against society and its structures were quite similar to the complaints he launched against his parents, and particularly against his father; namely, that they were cold and indifferent, that they exercised control over his life in a way that seemed to have no concern for his individual needs and wants, and that he felt himself to be helpless and victimized in the face of their control.

The revelation was shocking and disturbing to him. His therapy turned much more to a problematic process of trying to disengage his infantile displacements from the real concerns that confronted him in his present experience. The realization that the intensity of his political concerns might in part reflect infantile frustrations and rage served to severely threaten his sense of political commitment. Outside of his political commitment and his idealized picture of himself as the courageous revolutionary struggling for the rights of the humiliated and downtrodden against the hateful forces of imperious, capitalist subjuga-tion, there was little with which he could sustain his sense of self-esteem and self-respect. To have that brought into question was disturbing indeed.

My tactic therapeutically was one of avoiding any questioning or confronting. I encouraged him to explore and examine his feelings and thoughts. We both began to see that the intensity of his rage was often disproportionate. We recognized that it was usually triggered when he suffered some disappointment, and that the frequency and intensity of his disappointment was correlated with the level of his expectations. Over and over again, he generated excessive expectations which were doomed to frustration or disappointment, which then allowed him to burst forth in frustrated rage.

One graphic event occurred which demonstrated his self-destructiveness and the consequences of his infantile rage. He became enraged about something one night and smashed his fist against the wall. He succeeded only in fracturing a metacarpal and came into my office the next day sheepishly sporting a cast on his hand. We discussed the blind anger of his lashing out, how his rage made him want to lash out blindly, but that he usually ended up being only destructive and self-defeating through such lashing out. There was a strong wish in him to be constructive, to be able to act effectively, to bring about realistic and effective changes in the evils of society he saw around him. The infantile rage made him want to lash out at the wall and destroy it, rather than to find out how to work his way around it and be able to achieve what he wanted. The dawning realization of the destructiveness of his infantile rage brought complications for him. He increasingly saw the radical activities of his fellow students as self-destructive and self-defeating; so many of them were freaking out or dropping out, and their tactics were so ineffective and were not really changing anything. He found himself increasingly alienated from them.

The difficulty was put in vivid terms. Surrendering his infantile rage and approaching the real problems of society would seem to require that he become more mature and realistic in his approach. He would have to come to terms with the means that society proposes for inner change. That might mean directing himself toward getting an education—perhaps a law degree—and thus meant for him the postponement of goals, the adoption of a strategy of indirect action and delay, the commitment of himself to hard work and discipline to achieve these goals. He spoke admiringly of people like Saul Alinsky and Ralph Nader as examples of men who found more effective ways of generating change. But the threat was then that he might be "co-opted" by the system—that he might succumb to the lure of middle-class values that his parents stood for. In the face of this possibility, he could not bring himself to accept a job in any corporation, nor could he commit himself to any idea of further education. His skills permitted him employment in only relatively menial and trivial jobs, and this only compounded and intensified his rage and resentment against the system. It was extremely difficult for him to recognize or accept his own self-defeating role in this; he preferred to blame the system that put him in this position.

His relationship to me was ambivalent. He came to see me as a sympathetic and understanding person with whom he could share his concerns without any fear of retaliation or consequences. Despite his many maneuvers to get me to take a position or to oppose him, I consistently resisted this ploy, and continually reinforced and supported his capacity for reaching his own conclusions and for taking responsibility for them. Throughout the therapy, he had difficulty in coming to trust me. The fact was that he did trust me to a considerable degree, but it was against his principles to admit that an "establishment type" could be trusted and confided in. But I became for him the father that he had longed for and had never had.

Projective Distortions

It was quite clear that Jerry's pathology was largely, but not exclusively, focused in the area of his political concerns and activity. It was not merely the striking parallels in his attitudes toward authority figures and his parents but the obvious projective distortions and the disproportionate intensity of his displaced rage—as well as the exaggerated and peremptory nature of his expectations—that reflected his pathology. But it was nonetheless inescapable that university administrators and government bureaucracy responded to public issues in a manner that tended to reinforce and complement elements of Jerry's projections, in such a way as to provoke similar responses in many of his peers and schoolmates and thus provide a considerable degree of consensual validation for his often extreme views.

Thus, Jerry was outraged at the Vietnam war, which he saw as engineered by warmongering and power-hungry politicians who were in cahoots with big business interests and who were carrying out the war solely in the interest of reaping profits from the war itself and of extending American economic dominion over Southeast Asia. The military-industrial-educational complex paid the price with the lives and freedom of young people who had no recourse but to flee the country and become expatriates. The draft was consequently an evil coercion and violation of basic human rights which was foisted on young men—his friends and classmates—for the most exploitative and venal of reasons. The complicity of the university in permitting ROTC and allowing Marine recruiters to come on campus was testimony to the basically corrupt intentions of that institution. It seduced students into paying exorbitant sums of money, gave them little or nothing for it, deprived and robbed them at every turn, and finally gave them a worthless piece of paper which would not even guarantee a decent job—and in fact was a liability for many more menial but also more available positions.

Sabotage

Anthony (1981) has commented on the almost deliberate and persistent effort on the part of adolescent patients to sabotage the analytic or therapeutic situation. The same issue has been observed in the treatment of early adolescent (pubertal) patients (Fraiberg 1955). The therapist must learn to adapt to the patient's needs if there is to be treatment at all. Analytic inquisitiveness or attempts at interpretation are exquisitely threatening to the highly suspicious patient, particularly in the opening phase of treatment before the issues of trust have been worked through. The adolescent is basically distrustful of all adults, and the therapist is the representative of the adult world vested with power and authority. Beyond that he is a mysterious figure, a "shrink" or "nut doctor" who has the power to declare the adolescent sick or crazy. He is therefore to be feared and avoided, and the treatment to be subverted or sabotaged at whatever cost. He becomes a hated and feared persecutor.

Suspension of Suppositions

Therapy depends closely on clinical understanding. To presume univocally that social processes function normally and provide a normal context for adaptation, in Jerry's case, would have been to distort reality and to respond in terms of idealistic—if not ideological—presumptions that could not stand up to specific inquiry. I found it necessary to suspend all such suppositions in favor of open and honest inquiry. I suspended my personal ideological persuasions (not that I minded to surrender them); in my interaction with Jerry I had to maintain the willingness to examine and question them, even as I had to acknowledge my willingness to endorse and stand by them. The basic honesty and openness required to deal with Jerry's paranoid suspiciousness and distrust demanded that I be willing to open my mind about such issues if I were to expect him to approach his own concerns with anything like an open mind.

In my own experience with Jerry and similar patients, I have found a sustained attitude of open, honest, and ruthlessly objective inquiry to be essential. One must be willing to question and hold open for investigation everything—the patient's presuppositions, attitudes, feelings, and distortions, one's own convictions, presuppositions, attitudes, and values, the suppositions and values of the social and cultural matrix within which both the patient and the therapist move and experience reality, et cetera. The inquiry must be as objective as possible—in intent if not in fact. With Jerry my tactic was at first no more than to hear out his bitter complaints and tirades. I made no objections, no attempts to correct or question his obvious distortions. I listened sympathetically and encouraged him to fill out his accounts in greater and more specific detail. From time to time—in the interests of objectivity and under- standing—I wondered aloud whether his observations were real facts or whether they were his perceptions or interpretations. Little by little, the line between fact and fantasy, between real and distorted perception, between real actions and hearsay, between data and interpretation, was more clearly drawn.

Sustaining the Inquiry

The inquiry was sustained at all levels. It was directed not only to his present concerns but to his past experience as well. What gradually came into focus was the insensitivity, stupidity, impersonal detachment, and even repressive hostility and destructiveness of persons and institutions that acted as the bearers of authority and power. It also became much clearer the degree to which the respective pathologies—the indifference, repression, detachment and denial, pathological conflicts and incapac- ities—of his parents played such a significant role in the patterning of Jerry's own unfortunate experience. It also became much clearer in time the extent to which his own excessive expectations and the intensity of his disappointment and consequent rage caused him difficulty and interfered with his capacity to function more effectively.

With increasing clarity, in many detailed areas of his experience, it gradually became possible to tease out the elements of his experience that derived from infantile conflicts and projective distortions and to separate them from the more realistic and validly questionable or objectionable aspects. Jerry slowly came to see how his inner processes and resentments actually interfered with and distorted his view of the real world and its problems. He could increasingly see such distortion as an impediment to effective action to bring about change in the world about him. He saw with increasing clarity the futility and impotence of the destructive outbursts of his fellow student radicals.

It became clear that in many instances he set the stage for his own downfall. On one occasion he was to take a final exam. When confronted with the exam, he found it too difficult. The teacher had offered the option of a 50-page paper. Jerry decided to take the option and stormed out of the exam room. He raged furiously at the heartlessness and callousness of the teacher and the university for giving such impossible exams. He was particularly bitter about the paper, since it made his studying for other exams all the more difficult. Only gradually was he able to accept his own responsibility for not studying enough—or perhaps not being as smart and quick as he might wish -and for putting himself in the position of having to do a 50-page paper. Similarly, he refused to work in the usual business settings, since he refused to be associated with the corporations that so cruelly exploited people. Consequently, he had no recourse but to take menial and poorly paying jobs, much below his level of skill and education. His bitterness could only reluctantly give way to the realization that his torment was in some degree self-imposed.

Other issues were not so simple or easy. In the face of his tirades about the war, the clarification and testing of reality was not altogether helpful. We agreed that there was much in what he saw that was unfortunate and could be honestly condemned. But we both also began to see that there was much that was uncertain and complex. In these areas, he filled in the gaps of uncertainty with his own certainties and distortions. It was not clear that the motivations and intentions behind government decisions were simply as venal and uncaring as he felt. What was clear was that the gaps were filled from his own more infantile perceptions of the inconsiderate and apparently uncaring decisions that his parents had made about him, without any consultation or consideration of his wishes and needs.

Confrontation with Reality

All of this was to be counted as therapeutic progress. It would serve me well if I could report that the further course of such inquiry led to an unequivocal therapeutic success. But I cannot. After three years of sustained work, Jerry came to the point of realizing that he was confronted with a fundamental alternative. He could yield to the demands of reality and find effective means of obtaining his ideals and objectives. But this would require discipline, hard work, hard study— and involved a risk. He might not succeed. The demanding investment might not pay off in terms of the somewhat grandiose expectations he clung to: he wanted to change the face of society to fit his somewhat utopian ideals. Reality did not offer him any assurance of success on terms that he could accept.

If, however, he clung to his infantile expectations and his rage, he could persist in his pattern of rebellious bitterness and alienation—and he could retain the omnipotent and grandiose fantasy of bringing about dramatic changes in society by means of the magic of revolutionary action. He made a clear choice. He ingested a heavy dose of mescaline, became psychotically disorganized, and was rehospitalized.

Jerry's case is illuminating both from the point of view of what contributed to its success and from the point of view of what contributed to its failure. Essential to its success were the combination of therapeutic alliance and a sustained objective inquiry. The transference was mixed, but with positive aspects outweighing the negative. He saw me as the concerned and available father whom he had always yearned for. Although long in coming about, the therapeutic alliance was firmly maintained through most of the therapy. It provided the emotional matrix within which an attitude of sustained, interested, honest, and objective inquiry could be achieved. The inquiry bore its fruits. It achieved significant therapeutic goals; but in the end, it served only to bring Jerry more fundamentally to confront the demands of reality against which he had railed from the beginning. But clearly the confrontation was different: he was no longer confronting external forces of oppression and authoritarian power; he was confronting instead the inner forces of narcissistic entitlement and infantile gratification. On these rocks the treatment foundered.

Countertransference Vicissitudes

There was more involved in it, of course. My attempts to remain neutral and objective could not be sustained in the face of his efforts to bring me into a position of authoritarian intervention against which he could rebel. He had managed this with every other person and institution with which he was involved—why should I be the exception? He became sexually involved with another female patient of mine in what I felt was a flagrant acting out of the transference. Efforts to interpret the oedipal and preoedipal aspects were ineffective. My hand was forced. I told them both that there was no question but that their relationship was destructive to their respective therapies. Although I could not tell them what to do, I made it clear that they would be faced with a choice. They would be forced to choose between each other or therapy. I did not ask them to make the choice but merely indicated that they could not avoid such a decision. The girl made a clear choice for treatment and began to cut Jerry off. Jerry was obviously angry at her and at me. I too had been callously unresponsive to his needs. I had taken away from him his woman, whom he felt he needed and desperately wanted. It was soon after this that he left town, and not long after that I was notified of his rehospitalization.

The ability of such patients to elicit and actualize the transference paradigm is one of the most problematic areas in their treatment. Glover (1955) emphasizes the necessity for dealing with the paranoid suspiciousness and distrust before making any attempt to analyze defenses or deal with the patterns of aggressor-victim (sadomasochistic) interaction. In paranoid adolescents, preoedipal issues predominate over oedipal, and the dynamics of shame, humiliation, and persecution anxiety take precedence over guilt (Anthony 1981). The patient will set repeated traps in which the trustworthiness of the therapist is tested. At each testing the ante is raised, so that ultimately the test will be failed.

As the therapy progresses, the chief task of the therapist is to avoid the patient's determined attempts to turn him into a persecutor. The therapeutic dilemma is charged and persistent: to respond to hostility with kindness or friendliness only deepens the adolescent's suspicion, and any attempt at closeness or intimacy intensifies hostility. Only when these issues have been sufficiently worked through and resolved is it possible to move on to more familiar therapeutic ground. Anthony (1981) observes that when the therapy has reached this phase

> one can begin tentatively the analytic work of retracing the course of the Oedipal situation, dealing with the sadistic type of superego that has been introjected. . . . However, work during this phase, as during all other phases, is frequently interrupted with periodic regressions during which the defense of suspiciousness returns suddenly with full force. At any one of these regressive crises, the patient is liable to break off treatment. (p. 761–762)

It is well worth bring into focus the countertransference difficulties in dealing with such treatment problems. Jerry's tirades were in varying degrees assaults on my own middle-class values. They were a constant temptation and invitation to respond defensively and to feel that I was being questioned in basic and anxiety-provoking ways. From a more therapeutic perspective, I could sense the distortion and self-destructiveness in so much that he said. My paternal and protective instincts told me to try to confront his distortions and show him the truth that constantly eluded him. But to do so, I would have to take a concrete position and would implicitly put on him the demand to comply with or rebel against it. Clearly, Jerry could not tolerate a position of relative autonomy and had to find a way to polarize our relationship into one of either compliance or rebellion. His sexual acting out served the purpose and achieved his objective. It forced me into a position which raised the threat of compliance and against which he could react with his own form of rebellion, however self-destructive and self-defeating. What is of interest here is that when he could not draw me out of my objective-neutral stance on many dimensions of my own value orientation— political, religious, et cetera—he succeeded by confronting my thera- peutic value system and violating it in such a way that I felt I had to take a position in the interest of preserving the therapeutic process. This speaks to the underlying characterological defects that remained beyond the reach of this therapy but also dramatically illuminates the crucial therapeutic issue.

Therapeutic Values

Jerry's treatment—despite its failure—could not have enjoyed any success without its sustained atmosphere of inquiry. Insofar as Jerry was capable of maintaining it, the therapy progressed. It foundered at a point where the inquiry led him to the need to surrender his infantile needs. Gedo's (1972) comment offers a pertinent warning:

> Should anyone think that the destruction of our culture can leave us unscathed in some kind of therapeutic isolation, it may also be pertinent to question Hartmann's belief that these holy wars can be kept out of our consulting rooms. . . . At any rate, times are now out of joint, and many patients whose personality structure should permit successful analysis are impossible to treat because of the content of their value systems. If these fundamental differences are not recognized, something that passes for analysis may take place without the realization that it is nothing more than a hidden argument about *Weltanschauung*. (p. 220)

Thus, the capacity to sustain objective inquiry is essential to the treatment not only of potentially analyzable patients but also of more primitive and narcissistically vulnerable patients like Jerry. But such an objective and "scientific" inquiry must be uncompromising if it is to be effective. In dealing with the revolutionarily minded and radical students who find their way into treatment, the inquiry must match the intensity of their rebellious feeling with a ruthless commitment to objectivity. The treatment process falters when the therapist is drawn away from such uncompromising objectivity, whether in the direction of unquestioning adherence to his own personal presuppositions or values or in the direction of endorsing to any degree the presuppositions or values of the patient.

Under a constant and often intense assault, the major risk is that the therapist will retreat to a more defensive position and will answer the patient's onslaught with his own face- and value-saving counterattack. Such a response is exactly what the patient's neurosis and his introjective dynamics demand—and he often will settle for no less. The therapist has no recourse but to maintain his neutrality, his "noncommittal receptivity," remaining alert to possible countertransference traps and keeping to his therapeutic role and tack. No easy feat! As Anthony (1981) observes:

> The countertransferences that come into play are doubled by the two provocative factors of adolescence and paranoia, and the analyst must remain "eternally vigilant" to his own reactions toward a damaging negative transference. As Glover (1955) puts it (and as every analyst of a paranoid patient will echo), The analysis of a paranoiac is undoubtedly the most severe test of the analyst's capacity to sustain the impact of a steady current of hostility. Only those who can withstand such hostility should undertake the analysis of persecutory anxiety (p. 762).

One must honestly and effectively leave open the possibility that the patient may choose the course of rebellion against social institutions *as a result of therapeutic progress.* Hopefully, also as a result of therapeutic progress, the rebellion can be more realistically directed and realistically implemented. If, however, the therapist loses objectivity by adhering to personal presuppositions, he runs the risk of losing trust, undermining the therapeutic alliance, and becoming identified as part of the forces of constraint and repression against which the patient's paranoia is directed. If the therapist loses objectivity by accepting or endorsing the patient's presuppositions, he runs the risk of undermining therapeutic effectiveness and eliminating the possibility of testing the patient's perceptions and attitudes in reality terms.

The direction of my argument and my experience with Jerry and similar patients is that one cannot attain or sustain the objectives of scientific and objective inquiry without supporting it by a theory of psychological and social complementarity. It is only by seeing personal pathology and social process in their overlapping and intermeshing functions that one can maintain an unprejudiced set of mind that will support the therapeutic inquiry. The therapist must be as capable of and as ready to recognize the pathological and destructive aspects of the social environment as he is ready to and capable of recognizing and acknowledging the pathological aspects of the patient's psychic functioning.

Chapter Nine

Suicide

There is perhaps no enigma more perplexing and more confounding than suicide. The motivations of the suicidal impulse have escaped our capacity to understand, and consequently frustrated our ability to predict and prevent the suicidal event. Suicide has been defined as "a human act of self-inflicted, self-intentioned cessation" (Schneidman 1973). As a human act, suicide embraces a multitude of underlying motivational states, both conscious and unconscious, and is influenced by multiple factors, both intrapsychic and psychological, which come into play and influence suicidal behavior. These states are also strongly influenced by interpersonal events, social forces, economic crises, cultural influences, and a host of other determinants which exhaust the capacity of scientific thinking to detail and integrate.

This chapter indicates a basic typology of suicidal behavior, briefly discusses the basic sociological orientations toward suicide, and then focuses on the psychoanalytic understanding of suicidal phenomena, particularly in terms of the paranoid process.

Types of Suicide

Descriptive categories of suicidal behavior have been broken down in a variety of ways. The first important distinction is that between committed suicide and attempted suicide. Committed suicide refers to one of the general recognized modes of death—natural, accidental, suicidal, or homicidal—involved in certifying actual deaths. In this usage, the term generally implies that the victim consciously intended the lethal act to result in his own death. Attempted suicide, however, is complicated by the issue of intent. Stengel (1968) defines the suicide attempt as "any nonfatal act of self-damage inflicted with a self-destructive intention, however vague and ambiguous."

A second important distinction involves the seriousness of the suicide attempt. Other than cases of successfully completed suicide, serious attempts may be regarded as those in which the individuals express a definite intention to die, but the suicide act is aborted through some unforeseen circumstance. In other, less serious attempts, such as cases in which attempters gamble with death or in which the suicidal intent is uncertain even to themselves, the act must still be regarded as serious enough to pose a definite risk to life. Even attempts that involve a minimum of suicidal intent and are carried out for consciously or unconsciously manipulative motives cannot be regarded lightly. We will return to this aspect of suicide later in regard to the question of intentionality.

Menninger (1938) also describes forms of subsuicidal phenomena: (1) chronic suicide includes asceticism, martyrdom, addiction, invalidism, and psychosis; (2) focal suicide involves acts of self-mutilation, malingering, polysurgery, multiple accidents, and impotence and frigidity; and finally, (3) organic suicide refers to the operation of psychological factors in organic disease states, particularly self-punitive, aggressive, and erotic components. Moreover, the role of self-destructive impulses in alcoholism and drug addiction, the neglect of medical care for such chronic and debilitating diseases as hypertension and diabetes, and even the role of suicidal impulses in the victims of homicides have been carefully studied.

Seen in the broader context of subsuicidal phenomena and suicidal equivalents, the incidence of suicidal behavior and of the suicidal impulse in the human race is by no means minimal, nor is its significance to be underestimated. The questions raised by this self-destructive dimension of human existence are indeed profound and perplexing. They touch on some of the most basic theological, philosophical, social, psychological, and moral questions about human nature and human existence. We can wonder indeed whether the suicidal impulse and the incidence of serious committed suicide can ever be meaningfully reduced beyond a certain level.

Recognition of Suicide Risk

The most serious psychiatric aspect of dealing with suicide is the recognition of suicidal patients and the prevention of suicidal behavior.

Freud's Views of Suicide

Accidents

As in so many other areas of psychodynamic understanding, it is Freud's thinking which has given primary direction to our understanding of the dynamics of suicide. Freud's (1901) attention was drawn in the early stages of his work to the occurrence of accidents. He suggested that these apparently accidental and unintentioned instances of self-injury are in fact manifestations of an impulse to self-punishment, which normally finds it expression in self-reproach or symptom formation but in these instances takes advantage of the external situation to bring about the injurious effect. Freud observed:

> Anyone who believes in the occurrence of half-intentional self-*injury*—if I may use a clumsy expression—would be prepared also to assume that in addition to consciously intentional suicide there is such a thing as half-intentional self-*destruction* (self-destruction with an unconscious intent), capable of making skillful use of a threat to life and of disguising it as a chance mishap. There is no need to think such self-destruction rare. For the trend to self-destruction is present to a certain degree in very many more human beings than those in whom it is carried out; self-injuries are as a rule a compromise between this instinct and the forces that are still working against it, and even where suicide actually results, the inclination to suicide will have been present for a long time before in lesser strength or in the form of an unconscious and suppressed trend. (pp. 80–81)

Freud added a further note in the analysis of the Rat-Man (1909b), in which he established that the suicidal impulse is itself a form of punishment for a murderous wish directed against an external object.

Self-destructive Sadism

These views received greater crystallization in Freud's classic paper *Mourning and Melancholia* (1917). In thinking about self-destructive sadism, Freud pondered how the ego can consent to its own destruction in the suicidal act. Freud answered that the suicidal impulse is equivalent to a turning against the self of murderous impulses originally directed against a loved object. Thus, the depressive mechanism is equivalent to a taking-in of the ambivalently cathected object in a form of internalization which represents a regression from a basically narcissistic form of object choice. Consequently, the self is the receptacle of impulses, including the destructive impulses, previously directed against the object. Subsequent to Freud's formulation, thinking about suicide was dominated by concepts of identification with the ambivalently held object, both loved and hated, and the turning of aggression against the self as a result of murderous hostility against the introjected ambivalent loved object. Suicide was thus viewed equivalently as murder turned inside out. Freud (1917) himself observed:

> The analysis of melancholia now shows that the ego can kill itself only, if owing to the return of the object-cathexis, it can treat itself as an object—if it is able to direct against itself the hostility which relates to an object and which represents the ego's original reaction to objects in the external world. (p. 252)

Thus, the suicidal impulse at one and the same time strikes a blow against the ego itself and against the loved and hated object (Freud 1917).

Freud's understanding of suicide kept pace with his evolving views on aggression. After his formulation of the death instinct (1920a), the suicidal impulse was regarded as a turning of the death instinct against the self. Freud went on to insist that such death wishes inhabit the unconscious of every human being.

Superego

The next step in the argument came with the transition to the structural theory and the crystallization of Freud's thinking about the superego (1923). Behind the phenomenon of guilt, Freud saw the sadism of the superego turned against the ego. He turned again to his original analysis of melancholia:

> If we turn to melancholia first,.we find that the excessively strong super-ego which has obtained a hold upon consciousness rages against the ego with merciless violence, as if it had taken possession of the whole of the sadism available in the person concerned. . . . What is now holding sway in the super-ego is, as it were, a pure culture of the death instinct, and in fact it often enough succeeds in driving the ego into death. (p. 53)

Freud's last statement in these matters, his unfinished *Outline* (1940), emphasized the notion of a primitive aggressiveness, a form of self-destructiveness within the human psyche. Thus, impulses to self-destruction, the death impulse, are countered and balanced by the instincts to self-preservation. When the normal constraining fusion of these instincts is undone, the defusion results in the liberation of the destructive instinct, which is then directed inward and brings about the reversal of the impulse to self-preservation, the suicidal intention. The basic Freudian notion of superego aggression directed against the self has been the predominant model for the understanding of suicidal behavior.

Sadomasochistic Derivatives

Perhaps the best-known development of Freud's view is presented by Karl Menninger in *Man Against Himself* (1938). Menninger amplifies the psychodynamics of hostility and divides the murderous wish in suicide into the wish to kill, to be killed, and to die. Gregory Zilboorg (1936, 1937) adds that not only does every suicidal case contain strong unconscious hostility but it also reflects an unusual lack of the capacity to relate to and love others. He similarly maintains that the role of the broken home in the tendency to suicide demonstrates that suicide is the result of both intrapsychic and external causal developments. The danger of suicide, or its correlative homicide, can thus be increased by a regression which activates underlying oedipal conflicts and related internalizations based on an essentially sadomasochistic relationship with the parents. The internalization of such sadomasochistic components derived from parental object relations may play a considerable role in the dynamics of suicide. Zilboorg also adds the important point that suicide is motivated by the need to oppose frustrating external forces, but even more specifically by the need to achieve immorality and thus extend the existence of the ego rather than terminate it.

Death Instinct

Some important contributions were added by Melanie Klein (1934), building on Freud's original formulations. She specifically views suicide as an expression of the death instinct turned against the introjected object. She envisions a further objective in the suicidal act, namely, unification with the loved object:

But, while in committing suicide the ego tends to murder its bad objects, in my view at the same time it also always aims at saving its loved objects, internal or external. To put it shortly: in some cases the fantasies underlying suicide aim at preserving the internalized good objects and that part of the ego which is identified with good objects, and also at destroying the other part of the ego which is identified with the bad objects and the id. Thus, the ego is enabled to become united with its loved objects. (p. 296)

Suicide in Klein's view may also take the form of an attempt to preserve the good external objects by ridding the world or the loved objects of that part of the ego identified with the bad objects and the inherent, id-related destructive instinct. Thus, the depressive suicide is an attempt to save the external loved object from the uncontrollable destructiveness of the death instinct.

Hidden Executioner

Asch (1980) delineates a specific unconscious fantasy that may be fundamental to a certain subgroup of suicides and may also represent a more general component of the unconscious factors found in a wide range of suicidal motivation. The fantasy usually occurs in response to an object loss and involves an effort to enlist or force the significant object to act as an actual or imagined executioner. The suicide becomes an attempt at restitution by means of a regressive masochistic relationship between the passive victim and the "hidden executioner." Thus, the conflict over the internalized object, which is loved both ambivalently and narcissistically, is displaced and projected in the form of the externalized executioner, while the subject himself adopts the position of the passive victim—a role that may be actively sought or defensively resisted. Thus, the suicidal act can be seen as an acting out of an unconscious fantasy in which the object tie is recaptured through a sadomasochistic regression in which the suicide can be seen as the passive victim of an externalized aggressor. This formulation is an embellishment of the older view of suicide as homicidal aggression turned against the self. Asch observes that "the final choice of act depends on whether the ultimate victim is internalized (oneself in a suicide) or externalized (the hated image displaced onto an outside person in a homicide)" (p. 54).

Passivity plays a dominant role in the fantasy. Frequently, the suicidal individual seems to insist that he be regarded as the victim of circumstances or fate. In addition to its defensive function in dealing with the vicissitudes of aggression, such passivity may also become a primitive vehicle for reestablishing the lost or threatened object relationship. Asch (1980) comments:

> The silent partner in the suicidal act derives from the object relationship that originally had been internalized. An ego ideal derived from an identification with a masochistic parent tends to perpetuate similar submissions and sufferings in order to be loved (Asch 1976). By externalizing the conflict, with re-projection of both the primitive and ego ideal elements of the superego, moral masochism is avoided. Instead of experiencing the painful affect of guilt as a result of internal conflict, the external object is allowed to attack. As we have seen, 'fate' becomes the executioner; 'death' takes over. (p. 55)

Suicide and Depression

As a consequence of Freud's earlier formulations, there was also a tendency to link suicide with the dynamics of depression, particularly in terms of the superego model. This tendency was brought into question by Edward Bibring's important study of depression (1953), in which he regards depression as an ego state in which the feeling of helplessness and hopelessness is the basic underlying dynamic.* Bibring's view does not envision depression simply as a turning of hostility against the self but, rather, as an independent primary affect. Thus, the pathogenesis of clinical depression may be independent of aggressive vicissitudes. Nonetheless, the dynamics of helplessness and hopelessness may be seen as a conscious affective correlate of the victimization that is inherent in the depressive mechanism and the suicidal act.

Subsequent studies (Gershon et al. 1968; Friedman 1970) have lent support to this view. A comparison, for example, between acutely depressed and suicidal patients suggests that manifest hostility is the most important characteristic distinguishing those attempting suicide and depressives, who are considerably more compliant and passively accepting (Weissman et al. 1973). The classic model that would lead one to expect increases in the intensity of the suicidal impulse to be accompanied by diminished hostility.

---

*See the discussion of Bibring's view in regard to the connection of depression and narcissism in Chapter 5.

The role of feelings of helplessness and hopelessness has been highlighted in the suicidal syndrome (Appelbaum 1963; Stengel 1964), but the association between suicidal behavior and depression cannot be taken as absolute. Stotland's review of the concept of helplessness (1969) defines it in terms of a cognitive schema whose basic characteristic is negative expectations about the future. This cognitive distortion results in a pessimistic or hopeless view that nothing can turn out right, important goals are unattainable, and the worst problems are incapable of solution. Other evidence (Minkoff et al. 1973) suggests that such negative expectations as a component of helplessness may be more closely related to the seriousness of suicidal intent than the depressive affect.

Psychodynamic Issues

Narcissistic Illusions

The analytic view of suicide has not been limited to the perspective of superego dynamics or the vicissitudes of depression. The differentiation of the dynamics of suicide from the dynamics of depression has found its counterparts in analytic thinking as well. In his summary statement on analytic thinking regarding suicide, Fenichel (1945) discusses two major forms of suicide dynamics: the classic model of superego aggression turned against the ego (depressive suicide), and a second form based on hopeful illusions leading to some form of alternative gratification. Thus, the aim of the suicide attempt is not destruction of the ego as a murderous equivalent but, rather, fulfillment of libidinal aims associated with the ideas of death. These hopeful fantasies may take the form of joining a lost, dead loved one, an identification with a loved, dead person, or even the longing for reunion with the mother. Such hopeful illusions may also play themselves out in depressive suicide in terms of the attainment of forgiveness and reconciliation—this representing a form of reunion with the loving protective superego, a reunion that puts an end to the inner evil and recreates the original narcissistic omnipotence of symbiotic union. Fenichel points out that such a narcissistic union with the loving superego is achieved in fact in mania, so that the manic state serves as a defense against underlying suicidal impulses.

Even in the depressive suicide there is often a double aim, of purifying the self and then uniting (reuniting) with an omnipotent or idealized love object. The depressive suicide may be preoccupied with self-critical or self-devaluing thoughts, and his aim may be partly to punish himself. But the primary goal is self-cleansing, purification, getting rid of the bad part. The suicidal act becomes an exorcism (Alvarez 1972). In this connection, Maltsberger and Buie (1980) have commented

> that suicide may occur for purposes other than punishment. There are those who are fascinated with death, who perceive it as a peaceful refuge, who see self-destruction as the transportation there. For others, death in suicide is the achievement of a magical omnipotent moment, the triumph over necessary human limitations. For most people who destroy themselves, it is probable that self-destruction is an aim, but not the total aim. The fuller, if fantastic, intention is to preserve the essence of oneself for a better life beyond the magical passage of death. (p. 61)

Regression

Subsequent literature has emphasized the libidinal and regressive aspects of suicide. The libidinal aspect and the inherent symbiotic wish in borderline personalities have been particularly emphasized (Blanck and Blanck 1974). The suicide attempt may represent a wish for fusion with the maternal breast, a wish to achieve the illusion of an objectless stage of narcissistic satisfaction. In this stage, objects are no longer needed for purposes of need satisfaction, and thus can neither be lost nor destroyed (Modell 1961). Such suicidal attempts may be associated with severe regressive states involving loss of ego boundaries and a wish for fusion with the mother (Socarides 1962). Suicidal fantasies have thus been linked to early infantile fantasies of falling asleep at the breast and seem to reflect the complex issues of union with and separation from the mother in the early undifferentiated state of object relationship (Lewin 1950).

The link between the oral triad and the regressive wish for symbiotic union with the mother has been related to the suicidal tendencies in fugue states (Luparello 1970). It may be that in some of these cases the threat of separation or abandonment gives rise to a murderous rage, so that the regressive symbiotic wish may avert this murderous impulse. This dynamic would seem to come closer to the original depressive model. A similar point was made by Pollock (1975), citing Zilboorg's (1938) earlier view that the sense of guilt which relates to the repressed wish for the death of the parents underlies and motivates the self-destructive wish for immortality—this represents a return to the earliest symbiotic state. In suicidal regression, intrapsychic structures and ego boundaries are dedifferentiated, and the suicidal victim immerses himself in a narcissistically blissful state of reunion—a form of personal utopia.

Similar motivation may express itself in the longing for death found in many older people for whom life offers more suffering and less pleasure. Loewenstein (1957) speculates that diminution of genital gratification brings about a regression to pregenital libidinal stages which carries with it the wish for reunion with the symbiotic mother. These powerful wishes for undifferentiated narcissistic symbiotic union with the archaic mother underlie the powerful wishes for union with the dead loved object and the achievement of immortality. As Pollock (1975) observes: "The merger of the grandiose self with the idealized object explains the regressive solution of re-establishing earliest narcissistic equilibrium and cohesion. Regressive merging with the god-figure results in an immortal, blissful, pregenital existence" (p. 343). In a similar case, suicide serves the function of reestablishing narcissistic equilibrium, thus contributing to the cohesiveness of the self; at a higher level of narcissistic development, however, it points toward reunion with the ego-ideal.

Hendrick (1940) presents the case of a young woman who attempted suicide as a form of regression to an erotic and idealized relationship with her brother, in which the suicide represented the fulfillment of her wish for identification with him rather than a consequence of such an identification. The brother had been an aviator-hero in the First World War who had attained his moment of highest phallic achievement in a flaming death over the fields of France. The patient's destiny was ruled by an imperative need to be like her dead hero-brother, who formed her ego-ideal since childhood. In this case, the ego-ideal was of a special type represented externally by the person of the brother. This external ego-ideal, which Hendrick (1964) refers to as a *prepuberty ego-ideal*, was a necessary component for the maintenance of the cohesion of the patient's self. Thus, "ego failure and regression to primitive and unsocializable narcissism resulted from the traumatic impact of the death (or its equivalent) of the real person who represented the ego-ideal" (p. 525).

Suicidal Intentions

In the light of such cases it becomes abundantly clear that the suicidal intention is various and variously motivated. In some cases it may express the dynamics of self-punitive, self-destructive impulses—along the lines of the more classical Freudian analysis—while in other cases it may express the deepest and most unconscious wishes and needs for narcissistic self-fulfillment and self-expression. It was Weisman (1971) who pointed out that intentionality is not equivalent to the wish to kill oneself or the suicidal intent. Motives for attempting suicide are as obscure as, if not more obscure than, motives for any behavior. The expression of suicidal intent is often a reliable clue to a high degree of lethality. But they are by no means necessarily related. More commonly, suicide attempters try to deny their wishes or to mask them by presenting their ambivalence and equivocation. Intentionality, even in the suicide act, is concerned with the organization and direction of purposeful activity. Intentionality is thus a form of consciousness by which we distinguish purposeful human activity from merely reflexive or stereo-type forms of behavior. Human intentionality is related to the capacity we possess to make sense out of our experience and the ambiguities of life. Consequently, lethal intentions must be seen as reflecting and expressing "transient belief-systems that impel people to anticipate greater pain and to terminate existence" (p. 229).

Suicidal Act

Some of the components of the acute suicidal act have been delineated by Shneidman (1976a). The elements he describes include inimicality, perturbation, constriction of intellectual focus, and the idea of cessation. The combination of these four elements constitutes an explosive mixture that requires only the merest spark to ignite it.

Inimicality translates roughly into concepts of self-hate or self-destructiveness. The suicidal state is characterized by a heightened degree of inimicality, so that the individual is more likely to perform acts that are contrary to his own best interest, or in its extreme form to become self-destructive. Often, the occurrence of loss or failure will tend to heighten the degree of inimicality and increase the tendency to self-defeating or self-destructive behavior.

Perturbation refers to a state of psychological disequilibrium, a state of inner turmoil and acute conflict. The individual is upset, anxious, depressed, or agitated. Added to the heightened degree of inimicality, acute emotional turmoil increases the potentiality for suicidal out-come.

The sense of cognitive constriction is a form of tunnel vision, a narrowing of the focus of attention, a closing off of perceptions, considerations, and alternatives. There is a constriction of memory and of associations, so that the ordinary range of attachments and in-volvements is no longer available to consciousness. The focus of attention is drawn inexorably to the unbearable emotional state and the means of escaping from it. The suicide's world view becomes closed, encapsulated, impregnable, but entirely convincing.

Cognitive Organization

The cognitive organization of the suicidal individual is marked by several characteristics that are not found in nonsuicidal individuals. The suicidal person has a much greater degree of difficulty in utilizing imaginative resources. His perceptions tend to be polarized to a much greater degree than those in any comparison groups. His thinking is more rigid and constricted, and tends to be almost exclusively focused on the present rather than the past or the future. Such individuals seem incapable of projecting an image of themselves in the future, or of imagining future circumstances of their lives. Schneidman (1976b) has described the same cognitive features in suicide notes. The suicidal individual is in a constricted frame of mind, one that would seem to make the writing of a lucid suicide note almost impossible. This may account for the fact that suicidal notes are less than satisfactory in terms of their explanatory value or their psychodynamic relevance.

Hopelessness

The phenomenon of cognitive constriction seems to be closely related to the dynamics of hopelessness in suicidal patients. In efforts to identify the relationship between suicidal intent and affects of hopelessness or depression, suicidal intent has been found to be more highly linked with hopelessness than with depression as such (Beck 1963; Wetzel et al. 1980). Man loses hope and becomes hopeless by way of defect; he withdraws from hope by a failure to wish, to desire, to have ambition, or to plan. He also becomes hopeless by way of excess, by clinging to excessive and unrealistic expectations. It is the burden of man's omnipotent expectations that prolongs his torment.

The sense of hopelessness is permeated by a sense of the impossible. The hopeless person feels that he is caught in a prison from which there is no exit. Hopelessness embraces a sense of futility and a sense of the unattainability of goals and purposes, regardless of activity. What needs to be done seems to stand beyond one's capacity to perform or achieve. The patient is trapped and checkmated. His watchword is "I can't!" His perspective of the world and of himself is immersed in impossibility.

In his hopelessness, the patient makes a basic presumption that he possesses no inner resources to bring to bear on the solution of problems or the fulfillment of wishes—or at least that his inner resources are completely inadequate. In his feelings of frustration and inadequacy, he may expect or demand that others do things for him. He may be unwilling to try but at the same time be angered and resentful that others do not respond to or satisfy his wishes. In his sense of frustrated entitlement, he may blame others for their failures and become enraged at their inability to satisfy his expectations. The shifting of blame and responsibility away from oneself and onto others is often accompanied by projections of malignant and evil intent on others, a process that can become frankly paranoid.

Negative Sense of Self

Basic to this position of hopelessness is the perception of oneself as unworthy, inadequate, unacceptable, valueless. This perception is based on a fantasy that provides an inner core of self-perception. It reflects the underlying function of a persistent and resistant introject derived from the internalization of the punitive and hostilely aggressive parent. This internalization gives the child a sense of inner evil and destructivness, and subsumes the inner instinctually derived impulses of hateful destructiveness and infantile wishes to hurt and damage.

This internalized destructiveness builds a negative sense of self that permeates the rest of the individual's life, experience, and activity. It colors all the rest and remains stubbornly resistant to any alteration by the influence of reality. One often sees clinically depressed patients who persistently maintain this view of themselves as worthless and devalued, not only in the face of a lack of confirming evidence but also in the face of overwhelming evidence to the contrary. The sense of inner conviction of worthlessness carries on independently of any influence of reality. The inner sense of evil means that the individual cannot set useful goals, has no right to hope or strive, cannot perform good acts, for what these acts produce must bear the stamp of its origin: worthlessness and evil.

Hopelessness is related to the individual's subjective estimate of the probability of achieving certain goals. Plans and goals seem to be out of joint. Goals may be striven for long after any realistic expectation of their fulfillment is past. Plans may be restricted merely to immediate short-term goals to the exclusion of any long-term purposes. The expectation of hope is that plans of action will reach and achieve anticipated goals. Hopelessness expects failure; planning is futile and meaningless. The disjunction of plans and goals and the feeling of hopelessness are most characteristically found in depressed patients. They form the central and basic theme of depression. The patients are overwhelmed with a sense of purposelessness and futility.

The depressive patient is afflicted with a sense of hopelessness and helplessness. He believes that his skills and capacities are inadequate to achieve the goals he has proposed for himself, that his failure is due to his own inner inadequacy and incompetence, and that his previous attainments or accomplishments are meaningless. He has a sense of helplessness, of dependency on others for any attainment or grat-ification, and of being foredoomed to futility in any exercise of his own resources. His incentive is lost; he sees no recourse but to give up.

The depressive patient does not surrender his goals, particularly the continuing and long-range ones. He despairs because of the disparity between aspirations and achievements and because of his sense of the unattainability of his goals. The experience of frustration and the sense of impossibility do not extinguish such long-term goals and aspirations. The depressive patient, in this view, clings to a future that is thwarted and frustrated. His belief is that his own capacities and skills are the source of any possibility of attaining such goals but that his resources are too meager for the task.

Suicidal Process

When this trio of elements—heightened inimicality, increased level of emotional perturbation, and hopeless constriction—fall into conjunc-tion, the individual is then potentially suicidal. The concept of lethality, previously discussed, indicates the active conjunction of these three elements. When the fourth element is added, the suicidal process is thrown into gear. The idea of cessation, the notion of death, that one can put an end to one's existence and thus stop the pain, provides the desperate solution to an intolerable situation. The idea of cessation becomes the solution, the way out, the resolution of an intolerable situation, and a turning point in the suicidal drama (Shneidman 1976a).

The cognitive constriction, the restriction of alternatives, and the sense of resolution and conviction involved in this process are akin to the cognitive reorganization that characterizes the paranoid construction. In the paranoid transformation, the emergence of the delusional system brings with it a sense of relief from intolerable inner tensions. It thus becomes an attempt to achieve cognitive closure and affective relief. The resolution becomes relatively single-minded and fixed (Meissner 1978b).

The cognitive structure of suicidal ideation has the same quality of relief of inner stress but fortunately usually falls short of the degree and fixity of paranoid closure.

In the light of these theoretical considerations, we can approach a clearer appreciation of the role of precipitants in the suicide act. Frequently enough, object loss of one kind or another lies behind the suicidal behavior. The loss of the object sets in motion a mourning process, which is incomplete and is prevented from moving forward to achieve detachment from the lost object. The current loss seems to revive and symbolize repressed or denied reactions to previous childhood losses.* In addition, these patients demonstrate a strong dependency on the lost object for the maintenance of narcissistic integrity and equilibrium (Dorpat 1973). Generally, suicide attempters show a higher rate of childhood separations (Levi et al. 1966) and a higher number of precipitating life events (Paykel et al. 1975). The incidence of such events in suicide attempters in the six months prior to the attempt was four times that in controls and one and a half times that in depressed patients. Precipitating life events seemed to peak in the month preceding the suicide attempt.

The dynamics of object loss and mourning as precipitating factors in suicidal behavior must be related to the problem of anniversary suicides, which take place in the period close to the anniversary of the parent's death. The incidence of such suicides far exceeds statistically expectable rates (Bunch and Barraclough 1971). Anniversary reactions must be taken as manifesting incomplete or partial mourning of the lost objects. Suicidal acts, then, can be motivated in varying degrees by the need to restore narcissistic equilibrium in the face of narcissistic loss and the need to compensate for resulting narcissistic rage and guilt (Pollock 1970).

Adolescent Suicide

Perhaps the area in which these dynamics express themselves with the greatest vividness is that of adolescent suicide. Winnicott (1971) has made some telling comments in this regard:

---

*Evidence suggests that a broken home in the suicidal patient's childhood is a significant factor. Dorpat et al. (1965) found that 50 percent of those committing and 64 percent of those attempting suicide come from broken homes. The death of a parent was the most common cause of a broken home for completed suicides, while divorce was the most common cause for attempted suicides.

If the child is to become adult, then this move is achieved over the dead body of an adult. . . . In the total unconscious fantasy belonging to growth at puberty and in adolescence, there is *the death of someone*. . . . This makes it difficult also for the individual adolescents who come with shyness to the murder and the triumph that belong to maturation at this crucial stage. The unconscious theme may become manifest as the experience of suicidal impulse, or as actual suicide. (p. 145)

Separation

Friedman et al. (1972) note that the impulse to destroy or mutilate one's own body rarely occurs before adolescence. They suggest that the changes of adolescence make it possible for these aggressive impulses to be directed against the adolescent's self in such extreme ways. One of the crucial tasks of adolescence is the detachment of the libidinal cathexis to the original object. Suicidal adolescents, however, are unable to make this detachment, have great difficulty in giving up the libidinal tie, particularly to their mothers, and react as though the breaking of this tie were an intolerable loss that could not be faced.

Instead of the normal developmental mourning process associated with adolescent movement away from parental ties, these subjects seem to develop a state more akin to melancholia (Toolan 1975). The ties to the mother are markedly ambivalent, involving intense hostile, even murderous feelings existing side by side with intense feelings of loving dependency. Thus, separation from parents, particularly the mother, seems to represent a threat to vital libidinal supplies and, I would also suggest, a threat to narcissistic integrity. The reluctance to surrender and mourn the object results in introjection, "narcissistic identification," as described by Freud (1917). Thus, the suicide attack may be seen as a hostile and destructive attack launched against the internal object, usually the internalized mother-introject.

Adolescent girls may feel a need not to give in to their mothers. Such rebelliousness may serve as a defense against regressive, often masochistic or homosexual wishes related to the mother, who is somehow seen as powerful, overwhelming, and castrating. Defensive aggression, however, in my own experience, is often related to an attempt to counter and mask the underlying feelings of dependency and longing for closeness and nurturance from the mother. Thus, even where such rebellious and aggressive attitudes are manifest, there are often identifiable elements of a strong maternal introject. This defensive aggression and the underlying aggressive wishes tend to intensify the difficulties and conflicts over aggression, a typical adolescent problem. For the young woman, the emergence of secondary sex characteristics tends to increase her implicit identification with the mother.

Internalization of Aggression

The internalization of aggression in such patients has often been noted; many suffer from depression, guilt, low self-esteem, and even psycho-somatic difficulties. However, although the tendency to introject and thus identify with the more vulnerable and weak, susceptible aspects of the parents may be less discernible, it is of no less significance in the dynamics of the suicide. This is particularly important in terms of the identification of suicidal adolescent girls with victimized, vulnerable, and castrated maternal imagos. Thus, while the suicide attempt may, from one perspective, represent an attempt to destroy one's own body as the instrument of murderous aggression, it may also represent an attempt to achieve in some maximal sense that inner vulnerability by which the adolescent feels most attuned to and identified with the parental object.

It should be remembered, however, that in the suicide act the subject is both the destructive aggressor and the passive victim. Friedman et al. (1972) suggest that such suicide attempts or self-mutilatory acts reflect the dynamics of primal-scene fantasy. As I have suggested elsewhere (1977, 1978b), although primal-scene fantasies influence to some extent, they also reflect the sadomasochistic organ-ization of introjects. Thus, primal-scene fantasies may be influenced strongly by other aspects of the sadomasochistic relationship between the parents or other aspects of the family situation.

Family Dynamics

While the dynamics of adult suicide reflect residues of family dynamics in an internalized form, it must be appreciated that suicidal dynamics in adolescents are much more immediately responsive to the ongoing patterns of influence from the adolescent's family. Adolescent suicide attempts may often come as the culmination of progressive disorgan-ization, disruption, and social maladaptation within the family (Barter et al. 1968). As Sabbath (1969) points out, the adolescent suicide is often enough an "expendable child," that is, the object of a parental wish to be rid of the child or for the child to die. In such cases, the child's growth conflicts stir unresolved adolescent conflicts in the parents themselves. Often, such children were unplanned and unwanted, and the history of ambivalence in the parent-child relationship reaches a crisis during the developmental stresses of adolescence. The parents come to regard the child's emerging sexuality and aggression as threatening to themselves and to their own marital stability, their sanity, and even their existence. Correspondingly, the parents are seen increasingly as oppressive and persecuting. The suicide becomes a matter of compliance with an implicit parental wish.

Hendin (1975b) describes similar circumstances in which the suicidal wish seems to express a compliance with parental wishes. For these adolescents death becomes a way of life. Their family milieux have been permeated with depression, and their lifelessness has been required to sustain the family emotional matrix. Hendin (1975a) observes:

> Suicide is a way of life for the many students I saw who continually killed their enthusiasm, their hope, their freedom, and finally attempted to kill themselves. It is the climax of the ongoing drama they play out with parents in which emotional death is seen as the price of domestic peace. (p. 253–254)

Obviously, similar dynamics as those previously described are operative here as well and reflect a pattern of "adolescent paranoia" (see Chapter 11). An additional note must be added that the adolescent suicide often reflects and expresses dynamics within the family such that the suicidal act alleviates an otherwise intolerable tension in the family emotional system.

Suicide and the Paranoid Process

We can connect some of these elements of the dynamics of suicide to the paranoid process (1978b).

Victim-Introject

The organization of the pathogenic introjects is central to understanding the dynamics of suicide and, in fact, underlies some of the basic dynamics of the suicidal impulse. As Maltsberger and Buie (1980) note: "Suicide is a phenomenon of disturbed internalization, an effort to cope with hostile introjects, and to cope with the absence of those comforting inner presences necessary for stability and mental quiet" (p. 61–62).

The victim-introject is one of the central and most critical components of the pathogenic organization of the self. If we return for a moment to the Freudian superego model of suicide dynamics, it is the turning of aggression against the ambivalently held and internalized object derivative that provides the basic mechanism. This makes sense in terms of the internalization of the victim aspects of the object—the victim-introject. The victim is the recipient of destructive aggression. The aggression, however, is the subject's own. When this model is transferred to the superego, the aggression in question is somehow that of the object—through identification (introjection) with the aggressor. This early model thus contains certain inconsistencies and fails to provide an adequate explanation for other aspects of the internalization.

Most current views have come to appreciate the considerable significance of narcissism in the dynamics of internalizations. Our current views would infer that the rage against the lost object reflects a narcissistic injury or trauma due to the loss. In many such cases, the object was important to the maintenance of narcissistic equilibrium and to the integrity of the affected individual. The object may have served as an idealized object—Hendrick's (1964) prepuberty ego-ideal or the other forms of idealized object described by Kohut (1971)—or, at a more primitive level, may have been required to sustain the subject's inner integrity or cohesiveness. Thus, the suicide may also reflect the need to reconstitute narcissistic integrity by reunion with the lost, but necessary, object.

In the present formulation, it is being suggested that the victim-introject expresses these dynamics. Internalization of and adherence to the victim-introject are motivated by the narcissistic need to cling to and even fuse with the object. The victim-introject is equivalently the internalization of a narcissistically invested object. The ultimate realization of the identification comes through the suicide act, by which the individual becomes the ultimate victim, thereby gaining fusion with the victim-object. The organization of the victim-introject, then, serves as the vehicle for the defensive absorption of superego aggression, of sadomasochistic introjections (particularly those underlying the dynamics of a masochistic-depressive posture), and of union or fusion with the victim-object. Thus, it is the focus for feelings of helplessness and hopelessness.

While the dynamics of the victim-introject are primarily expressible in terms of the vicissitudes of aggression, it must not be overlooked that these interactions ride on a substratum of narcissistic concerns and investments. Consequently, introjection of the victim-introject is simultaneously a matter of continuing relatedness to the needed object and maintenance of the integrity of the self. The same necessity underlies the compliance with the implicit demands of the family system. Thus, the suicide's victimization may be required for the security of the psychic integration of the parents and the equilibrium of the family system.

Aggressor-Introject

In a developmental perspective, the purpose of identification with the aggressor is to ward off aggressive impulses by externalizing them and identifying with the aggressive external source. The mechanism consequently implies the defensive ability to separate self- and object-images by projection of these aggressive drives onto external objects, while at the same time a portion of these same drives is temporarily taken into the self. Consequently, the externalization partially spares the immature and vulnerable ego from the destructive effects of unneutralized aggression. As Orgel (1974) comments in this connection:

> True morality also implies a stable retention of self-object differentiation, and maintains the object relationship even in the face of threatened aggression by the object of the self. A structured superego is, thus, a barrier against suicide, maintaining a balance between identification and projective elements compatible with normal empathy, preventing both object loss and regressive self-object fusion. (p. 531)

Orgel goes on to describe what he calls "fusion with the victim" as a regressive vicissitude of identification with the aggressor. Fusion with the victim is connected with the dynamics of the victim-introject. Where this aspect of the introjective economy is prominent, one can see the failure of the subject's capacity to maintain stable aggressive feelings toward objects. This may range all the way from simple self-assertiveness to sadomasochistic relationships to outright hatred of aggressive others. Thus, the victim-introject is the exact opposite of identification with the aggressor, although the defenses against it may take either the form of shifting to the position of the aggressor-introject itself or the form of explicitly paranoid reactions.

Thus, the internal psychic drama of suicide takes place between two psychodynamic configurations, which dominate the patient's psychic life. The patient himself becomes the passive victim of powerful forces of self-hatred and self-destructiveness. He is the victim of an internal persecutor, an alien and destructive inner presence, the hidden executioner (Asch 1980). The conflict between the passive suicide-victim and the destructive persecutor-executioner is an inherent aspect of every suicidal process. Maltsberger and Buie (1980) describe this process in the following terms:

Clinical work with suicidal patients reveals case after case in which the patient has never been able to achieve comfortable self-integration, but suffers continually a kind of divided inner life, in which the weak and helpless patient feels himself to be under constant contemptuous scrutiny of an alien yet inner presence. . . . At times this presence may become sufficiently contemptuous of the self so as to demand an execution, and the spent self may hopelessly acquiesce. (p. 63)

I have described these respective configurations in structural terms, specifically as the victim- and aggressor-introjects.

The parallels here with the dynamics of frank paranoid psychopathology are striking (Meissner 1978b; Maltsberger and Buie 1980). In paranoid conditions, the persecutory presence based on the dynamic configuration of the aggressor-introject is displaced from the self-representation and externalized as a hostile presence in the outside world. The persecutor becomes, rather than an internal presence, an external enemy or persecutory force. In the suicide, however, the aggressive content remains internally located, part of the patient's inner world, often not adequately discriminated or experienced as separate from the patient's sense of himself. In any case, both the suicidal context and the context of paranoid distortion as in a persecutory delusion carry the common motif of the wish to be rid of an intolerable part of the self. To this extent, there may be many cases of paranoid pathology in which the paranoid system serves as a defense against underlying suicidal impulses.

False-Self System

We would like to shift the ground at this point to another aspect of Winnicott's view of the development of the child. Winnicott addresses himself to the formation of what he calls a false self (1960a).* Where the dynamics we have been describing fail, the consequence is the emergence of a false self, usually based on the child's compliance as a defense against undischarged and unneutralized aggression. This forces a split in the child's emerging sense of self, between the true self and the false self, and forces the child's development in the direction of an evolving and progressively adaptive elaboration of the false self. The price is the frustration and strangling of any true worth of the inner and real sense of self.

---

*See the discussion of the false-self configuration on pp. 132–133.

The false self can be seen in part as a struggle to cope with the dangers and difficulties of the outer world. It thus serves quite specific and important defensive needs. At times, it can represent an often heroic struggle to stay alive. The price that it pays is the sacrifice of creativity, vitality, and originality to the more pressing needs for safety and ensuring external supports. If the important caretaking objects cannot tolerate and respond meaningfully and lovingly to the child's emergent aggression, the child is forced into a position of compliance and internal division which leads to the formation of the false self.

Suicidal Acting Out. The persistence of this false self can have a powerful impact in setting the stage for suicidal acting out. This implication was clearly stated by Winnicott (1971):

> One has to allow for the possibility that there cannot be a complete destruction of a human individual's capacity for creative living and that, even in the most extreme case of compliance the establishment of a false personality, hidden away somewhere there exists a secret life that is satisfactory because of its being creative or original to that human being. . . . The individual in such an extreme case would not really mind whether he or she were alive or dead. Suicide is of small importance when such a state of affairs is powerfully organized in an individual. . . . (pp. 68–69)

We are reminded at this juncture of a case in our own experience of a young woman whose early life was marked by constant rejection and devaluation from a hostile and rejecting mother. The whole pattern of her life was carried out around the internalization of that malignant and devaluing maternal figure. The patient felt that nothing was good, nothing strong, nothing worthwhile in herself. Her constant complaint was that there was no hope, no future for her, and that it would have been better had she not been born. Moreover, the whole pattern of her external life had been carried out to try to appease the mother's expectations and gain some measure of acceptance from her. She had turned to nursing as a career as a result of her mother's suggestion that she do so, since mother felt that she did not have the brains or ability for much of anything else. The false-self pattern was, of course, considerably more extensive than simply a matter of career choice. The patient reviled the whole pattern; she was disgusted and caught up in hopeless despair over almost every aspect of it. Her only alternative, as she saw it, was suicide. It seemed clear at this juncture that a suicide action on her part would have had two clear implications. First, it would have destroyed the false self built upon her lifelong compliance to her mother's wishes and her seeking her mother's acceptance; and second, it would have realized in the fullest measure the sense of victimhood that she sensed within herself and within her life experience.

Schizoid Suicide. This patient represents many of the aspects of what Guntrip, building on the basic notion of the false self, has called schizoid suicide. The schizoid suicide differs somewhat from the depressive suicide, in which the self-destructive impulse is angry and hostile. Rather, it is the result of an apathy toward real life which can be accepted no longer. There is a quiet but tenacious determination to fade from the scene and give up the struggle. The death of the false self carries with it the hope of a rebirth of what is more authentic and creative in the subject's own existence. Guntrip (1969) writes:

> Whereas in depressive suicide the driving force is anger, aggression, hate and a destructive impulse aimed at the self to divert it from the hated love-object, i.e., self-murder, schizoid suicide is at bottom a longing to escape from a situation that one just does not feel strong enough to cope with, so as in some sense to return to the womb and be reborn later with a second chance to live. (pp. 218)

In our patient, as in others of this sort, it was a rebirth with the hope of experiencing a meaningful, accepting, and loving relationship with the mother that lay at the root of these impulses. It was a relationship of loving closeness and acceptance that had been constantly desired, constantly frustrated, and never attained.

Introjective Configuration. In a more theoretical vein, the idea that we are proposing here is that the false self is in fact organized around the introjects that we have been describing. In suicidal patients, it is, in particular, the forming of a false self around a central victim-introject that forms the root and underlying motivation of the suicidal tendency. The suicidal impulse becomes the expression of the inner unneutralized and unresolved aggressive impulses which have been solidified and embedded in the dual configuration of the aggressor- and victim-introjects, and which form an essential aspect of the core of the individual's sense of self.* It is the unresolved aggression, which cannot

---

*The victim-introject thus becomes the core around which is organized a "negative identity." In discussing adolescent suicide, Erikson (1956) suggests that the "wish 'to die' is only in those rare cases a really suicidal wish, where 'to be a suicide' becomes an inescapable identity choice in itself" (p. 82).

be adequately discharged and absorbed by the significant love-objects, which must be projected onto those objects and subsequently reintrojected to become the permanent possession of the child's emerging sense of self. It is in this context that the self-hate and self-loathing of such individuals takes on a particular meaning. It not only reflects their utter sense of guilt and shame because of the inner hatefulness and evil they sense in themselves; it also reflects the unresolved and unassimilated hatred in their significant love-objects (more often unconscious than conscious).

The interplay between the dynamics of the victim-introject and victimization on the one hand, and the dynamics of hatred on the other, takes place not only in the developmental experience of the child but in the living experience of the adult. It is not merely that the suicidal patient is fixated at a point of victimization; there is also a commitment to victimization, and clinging to the victim-introject. The clinging to the victim-introject has strong narcissistic underpinnings, the discussion of which would carry us far afield. But it can be noted that this becomes a powerful force in the suicidal patient's unconscious motivation and represents a clinging to the original, intensely ambivalent object of infantile dependence. The point is that the patient's commitment to victimhood leads him to attempt to elicit and provoke the conditions of victimhood in many of his adult relationships. An understanding of these dynamics provides some insight not only into the child's developmental experience but also into the patterning of the suicidal patient's life experience, which draws him to the brink of suicidal behavior.

I can summarize and focus these conclusions no better than with a quotation from Maltsberger and Buie (1980):

Suicide can be understood as an effort to deal with the failures in internalization. The hating introject [aggressor-introject], poorly integrated and always alien in some degree, calls out for the execution of an evil self [victim-introject]. The perpetual menace of the hating introject may prompt the self to attack in order to be rid of a persecutor. Death may itself become personified as the comfort-giving mother, as may that dark oblivion which waits beyond the grave.

From life, a desert of intolerable inner loneliness and helplessness, the patient turns to death in flight from inner persecutors, in quest of rebirth into the arms of a comfort-giving mother. It is the paradox of suicide that the victim, finding inner death in life, seeks inner life in dying. (pp. 70–71)

Therapeutic Implications

If the suicidal patient carries out these dynamic processes in his living experience, it can be expected that the same dynamics can come into operation in an even more intense and provocative way in the therapeutic encounter. The patient recreates the dynamics of destructive and ambivalent impulses that were at work in the original relationship to the primary love-objects. It is essentially the undischarged and un-neutralized aggressive and destructive impulses that the patient projects onto the figure of the caring object and that are experienced then as hate.

This maneuver has the obvious advantage of unconsciously reinforcing and consolidating the patient's position as victim. The patient reacts with a sense of inner evil, worthlessness, and primitive guilt. The defensive gain through this projective maneuver is of sufficient importance to the patient who must attempt to validate it by various forms of provocative behavior. The patient will discredit, devalue, criticize, and disparage his therapist. Any sign of irritation or anger in the doctor's response will be taken as confirmation and validation of the projection. The provocations may take the form of direct physical action, involving physical assault or destruction of personal property. There may be telephone calls at particularly inconvenient times. They may take the form of mutinous rebellion and withdrawal within the therapeutic situation.

Therapist's Role

There is a constant appeal in many suicidal patients for the therapist to take responsibility for keeping the patient alive. This assumption regarding the nature of the therapeutic bond between therapist and suicidal patient is reinforced by a rather pervasive motif in the psychiatric literature, namely, the emphasis on the therapist's role in protecting the patient from his suicidal impulses. A variety of management techniques are advised (getting rid of lethal weapons, limiting prescriptions, hospitalization, surveillance by third parties, et cetera) to limit the possibility of the patient's self-harm. Techniques of intra-therapeutic manipulation are encouraged—all with the effect of reinforcing the suicidal tendency to make others responsible for keeping the suicide alive. As Hendin (1982) notes, there is no evidence that such approaches are effective in preventing actual suicides. He comments:

> In any case, it would be better for the therapist working in or out of
> a hospital to recognize that he is not likely to keep alive by

surveillance, incarceration, or any form of precaution a patient who is determined to kill himself. The best chance for helping the patient lies in understanding and helping with the problems that are making him suicidal, including most specifically the way in which he uses the threat of death. (p. 162)

Suicidal patients are unusually sensitive to anxieties stirred up in the therapist, particularly anxiety in response to the patient's threat to kill himself. They are adept at using such anxiety in a manipulative fashion and are not slow to test the therapist's mettle. Hendin (1982) observes:

If the therapist meets unreasonable demands in response to death threats, the situation usually repeats itself, with escalation of the demands and increasing angry dissatisfaction if they are not met. Unless these character attitudes and expectations of the patient are explored and understood, the therapist is liable to go into bondage to the patient, with bad results. (p. 163)

The therapist is often placed in a vulnerable position (i.e., put in the position of becoming the patient's victim) by his own unavoidable concern, his wishes to keep the patient from killing himself, and his understandable anxiety in the face of suicidal threats. If he allows himself to fall into the narcissistic illusion that he can, in fact, save the patient from suicide, or if he basically accepts the responsibility for keeping the patient alive, the probability that he will actually do so diminishes. As Hendin (1982) observes:

In fact, a major therapeutic difficulty often stems from the therapist's assumption that by simply supplying a care and concern that had been missing in the patient's life—that is, by not being rejecting—he will somehow give the patient the desire to live. Often, however, the patient's hidden agenda is an attempt to prove that nothing the therapist can do will be enough. The therapist's wish to see himself as the suicidal patient's savior will blind the therapist to the fact that the patient has cast him in the role of executioner. (pp. 171–172)

There is the abiding accusation that the therapist is inadequate, is not helpful, is doing little or nothing to alleviate the patient's pain—in general, the constant, direct, and implicit assertion of the therapist's incompetence. Thus, the resistance to any therapeutic inroads or effective progress can be quite rigid and intense and may frequently take the form of a profoundly negative therapeutic response. If we remind ourselves that the suicidal patient carries out this behavior in many facets of his life experience, it is not difficult to understand how the constant reinforcement of these dynamics can lead progressively closer to a suicidal resolution.

Countertransference Hate

The dynamics of this interaction are carefully delineated by Maltsberger and Buie (1974). They describe in some detail the patterns of defense which therapists mobilize in one or other degree to deal with the distressing experience of hatred elicited by the patient. Such counter-transference hatred may be repressed, so that the therapist finds himself daydreaming or thinking of something else besides what is happening in the therapy. He may find himself restless, bored, or drowsy. The countertransference hatred may be turned against the therapist's own self and may begin to fill him with doubts as to his capacity to help the patient; he may begin to experience feelings of guilt, degradation, and a sense of inadequacy, helplessness, and hopelessness. He may even begin to experience suicidal impulses and feelings himself. This masochistic and penitential stance on the part of the therapist further impedes any possibility of the patient's unleashing directly aggressive impulses on him and only intensifies the suicidal dynamics.

Countertransference hatred may also be turned into its opposite. The therapist finds himself preoccupied with trying to be helpful to the patient, being excessively solicitous about his welfare. There is an anxious urgency to cure and help. The therapist may be drawn into an excessive fear of the patient's suicide and resort to the excessive use of restrictions and even hospitalization when it may not particularly be called for. Such a therapist cannot take the necessary reasonable risks in dealing with the patient's impulses and rage and, in general, cannot help the patient with these feelings.

Countertransference hatred can also take the form of counter-projection onto the patient's own projective operations: "I do not wish to kill you; you wish to kill yourself." A subjective sense of anxious dread might accompany this, and the therapist might become preoccupied with fantasies about the patient's potential for acting out the suicidal impulses. Thus, the therapist may often tend to feel helpless and have considerable difficulty deciding how much of his concern comes from the objective possibilities and how much from his own hostile feelings. There are a number of risks that operate in this position. The therapist may act out his countertransference hostility by imposing unnecessary external controls such as hospitalization; these will serve to disrupt the therapeutic alliance and possibly provoke suicidal acting out. The therapist may also run the risk of failing to recognize the objective need for protective measures out of fear of such acting out. Or, the therapist may run the risk of giving up the case and rejecting the patient, feeling that the situation is hopeless when in fact it is not so. The projection may at times also take the form, "I do not wish to kill you; you wish to kill me." This may be in part a recognition of the patient's own hatred, but it runs the risk of the therapist's responding to his sense of frustration with further rejection and abandonment of the patient.

Lastly, the therapist may resort to distortion and denial of the objective reality as a way of validating the countertransference hatred. Under these circumstances, the therapist tends to devalue the patient and is prepared to see the patient as a hopeless or bad or dangerous case. He may then prematurely interrupt the therapy, transfer the patient to other therapists or other institutions, or discharge him from the protective environment of the hospital.

Maltsberger and Buie (1974) conclude their discussion of these patterns of defensive interaction in the dynamics of countertransference hate by making the following observations, which resonate strongly with the previous comments of Winnicott regarding the hatred of the mother for her child:

> The best protection from antitherapeutic acting-out is the ability to keep such impulses in consciousness. Full protection, however, requires that the therapist also gain comfort with his counter-transference hate through the process of acknowledging it, bearing it, and putting it into perspective. . . . In other words, the suicidal patient's repetition compulsion to involve others in relationships of malice and ultimately to be rejected is signaled in the therapist's countertransference hate. In time, it can be interpreted and worked at, provided the therapist, by accepting, tolerating, and containing the countertransference, does not join the patient in repeating his past instead of remembering it. (p. 632)

Case Example

These elements played themselves out in a vivid manner in a stylish woman of 50 in whom suicidal feelings persisted in an intense and agonizing manner over several years of treatment. She was the only child of well-to-do, socially prominent, but indifferent parents. The father particularly was subject to recurrent depressions and often felt suicidal. The parents were poorly matched, constantly fought, and were chronically on the brink of divorce. When the patient was 5, an older orphaned cousin was taken in by the family. The patient felt pushed aside, as if her wishes did not count—while the cousin became increasingly demanding and difficult. The cousin became an increasing source of difficulty and discord in the family, but the patient continually felt that it was her lot to act as a peacemaker between her parents and the cousin. When finally the parents had both died, the patient turned over her inheritance (a substantial amount) to the cousin on the grounds that the cousin had nothing and no one, while the patient herself could make her own way— a repetition of the childhood pattern.

This masochistic pattern of repeated victimization played itself out in recurrent contexts throughout the patient's life. In each instance, she would make a critical decision putting herself at considerable disadvantage, usually in relation to an older male figure to whom she devoted herself self-sacrificingly, and always with the feeling that she was doing the better thing and that she could take care of herself. She never married and repeatedly fended off opportunities that presented themselves. In this way, she repeatedly put herself in the position of victim, at each step building a reservoir of bitter resentment and murderous rage. In this process, she was capable of working at a high level of competence and resourcefulness. The immediate precipitant of her depression and suicidal wishes was the retirement of her boss, an older, high-level executive, who then moved out of town. The patient was offered another position but abruptly quit the company and entered her downhill course.

The oedipal components of this picture were transparent. She was once again the helpful support of a faltering father figure—her own father had been withdrawn and unable to work in his depressive periods. The patient cherished the illusion that her boss cared for her and would one day ask her to marry him. His departure and abandonment dashed her illusions, propelled her into exquisite victimization, and stirred her unconscious rage. She stopped working, spent her savings, withdrew from friends, even moved to another city. She created the circumstances of increasingly desperate victimization in every aspect of her life. She was alone, without family or friends, without work, and was inexorably eroding her financial resources. The hole she was digging was getting deeper and deeper. At this point, she entered treatment.

Gradually, in the face of considerable resistance, we were able to establish and clarify this pattern of victimization. We related it to the little girl in her who desperately sought love and caring from a good father figure (and by degrees from me as well), but who felt hurt, enraged, and abandoned when she did not receive it. The little girl responded with a sort of intrapsychic temper tantrum, turning her frustrated rage against herself and plunging herself deeper into the pit of victimization. Each stage was a renewed cry for help, which she hoped would come from her illusory father-substitute. Each disappointment reinforced her hurt, rage, and guilt. Underlying this pattern was an intense stubborn degree of primitive narcissism: the little girl demanded that her expectations be satisfied, her frustrations and deprivations made up, without any effort or responsibility on her part. Her guilt floated on an underlying stratum of envy which dictated that any good possessed by others must be seen as her deprivation (as in her childhood interaction with the cousin), along with the contradictory conviction that she deserved nothing. These opposite polarities of envious entitlement and self-deprivation are readily recognizable as expressions of pathogenic narcissism in the introjective configuration.

The patient had integrated a false-self system around a victim-introject which expressed itself in compliant submission to important figures, but whose self-sacrificing, masochistic self-denigration served only to feed the intensity of self-destructive components embedded in her aggressor-introject. The victim-introject clearly was based on the depressive, nonfunctional victim she recognized in her father, in conjunction with her somewhat masochistic, self-sacrificing mother. The victim-introject was reinforced by critical internalizations from both parents and was lived out in her pathology—particularly in her identification with her depressed, suicidal father.

The therapy turned into a saga of playing out these elements in relation to me. The invitation was constantly there to feel sorry for her, to sympathize, to try to be helpful and reassuring, to make exceptions in her treatment because she was so helpless and disadvantaged. In response to these pressures, I maintained a therapeutic middle road, being sympathetic and responsive to her pain, but yielding hardly at all from a firm therapeutic stance that insisted on exploring the dynamic aspects of her feelings; constantly focused the aspects of victimization in her behavior, her life, her therapy, her history; and insisted on the need for her to take hold, accept responsibility for her life and her behavior, and resist the regressive pulls that tempted her to give in to her suicidal impulses. My task was to constantly insist that she was not a helpless victim of the past, of her parents, of her life circumstances, or of her impulses and feelings, but that for specific reasons she chose to adopt and cling to her victimhood. Her resentment and anger at my making her responsible for what she felt and did—for undermining her victimization—had to be vigorously confronted, and the responsibility thrust back on her, without any guilt on my part.

Victim-Introject

The countertransference risks with such resistant and suicidal patients are well known to experienced therapists. The patient seems intent on defeating the therapeutic process and intent at all points on bringing the therapist's efforts to naught. In this patient, no combination of medication seemed to bring relief; any medication elicited bothersome side effects that required stopping or changing it; any interpretations or insights were accepted compliantly without apparent effect. For the therapist in such a case there is continual frustration, self-doubt, guilt, and anger. His therapeutic skills are on the line, his narcissism is under attack, his impatience and frustration are ready to shift into irritation or hopelessness regarding the patient. The interaction is set up as a constant inducement to play the counterpart to the patient's victim. This patient constantly confronted my limitations as a therapist and the inherent limitations of the therapeutic process.

The central task for the therapist is to keep these countertransference elements in constant focus so that he does not inadvertently take up the patient's invitation to reinforce the victim-introject. This calls for a consistent effort to sustain the crucial elements of the therapeutic alliance, a persistent effort to explore the dimensions of the victim-introject, particularly as they display themselves in the therapeutic interaction, and a willingness to confront the patient's unwillingness to accept responsibility for his suicidal wishes. The schema for this approach has been detailed previously (see Chapter 2).

It is particularly important in dealing with the suicidal victim-introject for the therapist *not* to take responsibility for the patient's need to kill himself; at the same time, he must accept full responsibility for helping the patient to explore, understand, and manage these impulses—even to the point of hospitalizing such a patient as a means of protecting him from these impulses when they become overwhelming. Such an approach is never easy to follow, but success lies in constant self-monitoring of inevitable deviations and a collaborative focusing of the reasons for them with the patient. This can be the most effective opportunity for clarifying the operation of the victim-introject in the therapy, with correlative therapeutic gains. As the victim-introject is gradually eroded, space should be created for a more positive organization of the patient's self—one more authentically lived and felt and more congruent with the patient's own inner purposes, rather than the fallacious dichotomies of his or her false-self organization.

It is in this fashion, however difficult it may be to attain, that the therapist undermines the dynamics of the victim-introject and avoids the reinforcement of the false-self configuration. To the extent that the therapist can acknowledge, tolerate, and deal with his own counter-transference hatred, he will not be victimized by the patient's inherently aggressive and destructive impulses. A way will be open for the patient to begin to deal with those earlier issues of identification with the aggressor which have been previously thwarted and which, in regressive fashion, have been impeded by the persistence and domination of the victim-introject.

Chapter Ten

Addiction and the Paranoid Process: Psychoanalytic Perspectives

The analytic interest in addictive phenomena has been long-standing and has contributed perhaps the most significant body of theory about addiction, specifically as a psychological condition. The history of these developments, so cogently synthesized by Yorke (1970), leaves one with a sense of disparate and fragmented approaches, reflecting the emphases of their respective authors but not yielding a more comprehensive view which is responsive to the contemporary experience of drug usage and drug dependence.

Subsequent attempts to articulate a more comprehensive view of addiction have been more satisfactory. Wurmser (1974, 1978) emphasizes the role of dispositional factors in the activation of a "narcissistic crisis." Krystal and Raskin (1970) attribute the pathogenesis of drug states to the intolerance of the ego for painful affects, particularly anxiety and depression; to the pathological vicissitudes of object- and self-representations; and finally, to the corresponding or consequent modification of consciousness introduced by drug effects.

However, a comprehensive attempt at understanding drug phenomena must also face certain specific issues. A primary question is that of diagnosis. Earlier analytic studies tended to emphasize the more primitive aspects of addictive behavior and linked addictive states more closely with the psychoses or psychoticlike conditions. Even the contemporary literature has a strong tendency to describe addictive phenomena in terms of psychotic processes, or to relate it to a psychotic potential in the patient, or, frequently, to link addictive and borderline conditions. Such formulations were most likely a by-product of the selective factors we have already mentioned, as well as of the generally limited psychiatric experience with addictive patients. The exception, as Wurmser (1978) has documented, are the compulsive addicts, who reflect various levels of primitive personality organization.

Since the availability of drugs and the phenomena of drug use and abuse have become epidemic, psychiatrists have gained a much greater appreciation for the variety of personality organizations within which drug dependence can take hold, and have become increasingly aware that the outcome of the drug dependence in any given individual may reflect the influence of external determinants in addition to intrapsychic dispositions. Consequently, the diagnostic issue remains open and controverted.

In addition, a difficult problem to sort out is that of the roles of cause and effect in producing drug dependence. This is particularly true of the psychological aspects of the problem, since the mere fact of addiction does not necessitate the conclusion that correlative psychological impediments or vulnerabilities were in fact predispositions or causal determinants of the drug dependence. The extent to which personality variables are altered, modified, or influenced by toxic pharmacological effects remains to be determined.

As our experience with drug states and the variety of conditions within which drug dependence can arise are extended, the theoretical weight of complex determinants undergoes a significant shift. The original psychoanalytic perspective on addiction derived from Freud's formulations and emphasized the role of libidinal factors—the primary addiction was masturbation. However, the varieties of drug experience have become more apparent and the fallibility of depending exclusively on intrapsychic determinants for the understanding of such phenomena has also become increasingly apparent. Increasing emphasis has been laid on the role of the environment and contextual determinants as significant in the emergence of drug dependence (Zinberg 1975). Any comprehensive theory of drug dependence requires, if not that a specific role is provided for such contextual determinants, at least that the formulation of the key variables of the theory remains open to the determining influence of such contextual and socially embedded phenomena.

An additional problem has to do with increasing sophistication in the understanding of specific pharmacological effects. Early theoretical approaches to the problem tended to consider drug dependence as a monolithic or univocal phenomenon. Thus, as Yorke (1970) has noted,

> The majority of writers do not distinguish between addiction of
> different kinds of drugs, tending to treat them as identical and

including alcoholism too as part of the same pathology—which may or may not be the case. (p. 143)

Broadening experience with a variety of types of addiction has made it increasingly probable that specific qualities of the pharmacology of addictive drugs may have to be included in the drug-dependency equation. The earlier view, for example that of Glover (1932), tended to emphasize the addictive potentiality of the patient's personality but minimized addictive potential of specific pharmacological entities. Knowledge of the pharmacology of various drugs requires that we include the specific pharmacological effects as part of the drug-dependency equation.

The Paranoid Process

The present chapter will describe the complex interaction of intrapsychic determinants, environmental and contextual variables, and specific pharmacological effects in the paranoid process (Meissner 1978b). The intention is to define the complex aspects of the problem of addiction in terms of specifiable parameters of the paranoid process, in the hope of providing a more integrative context for the understanding of drug phenomena and of evolving a more secure basis for meaningful psychotherapeutic intervention and modification of drug-dependent states.

At the heart of the etiological complex which gives rise to drug dependence and addiction lies the organization of the subject's introjects. The more primitive the organization of such introjects, the more they derive from and can reflect vicissitudes of early object relationships and related developmental difficulties, the more susceptible they are to regressive pulls, and the more the self-organization to which they are so intimately related remains relatively fragile. Consequently, the more fragile the inner organization and cohesiveness of the introjective alignment and its correlative self-organization, the more intensely and urgently the self-organization requires adjunctive stabilization from external sources.

These external sources may take a variety of forms. They may include various types of group affiliation and membership, religious dedication, intense political involvement, or clinging to various self-sustaining individual relationships (as is often the case in a highly dependent and narcissistically motivated therapeutic relationship). Or they may take the alternate expression of forms of perversion or fetishism, or the addictive form of dependence on a specific drug substance or substances. In all of thesse expressions of the underlying need for an extrinsic sustaining support for the inner fragility of the self, it is not simply the dependence on the extrinsic source that is in question, but rather the organization of the extrinsic supply and its coordination and integration with the inner needs of the self-organization through the process of projection. In all of these cases, the extrinsic source is somehow modified and transformed so that it becomes a meaningful object or object-substitute that is no longer potentially but is actually linked with the needs and deficits of the self-system. As Wurmser (1978) observes, the drug answers to

> a wish to regress to that image and feel of the self which can do and be everything, gets everything and disregards boundaries and frustrations—yet merely in illusion. It is a solution to archaic narcissistic conflicts, not to problems of creativity and identity. It is a regression in the *disservice* of the ego, freed of the controls of the ego, an illusory form of control mastery. (pp. 24–25)

Object Dependence

The quality of object relations in the drug population tends to be characterized by relative constriction and an infantile and predominantly narcissistic character—particularly noteworthy in sexual relationships, whether they be heterosexual or homosexual (Hartmann 1969). In addition to the predominance of oral narcissistic determinants, there seems to be an intense need to replace a lost object. Not only does the beginning of drug taking often follow a significant loss experience but the patient may also return to the use of drugs in the context of the loss of an object. The drug is somehow meant to replace the absent object, usually one of the parents or, in the context of treatment, the therapist (Hartmann 1969). The attempt to stabilize a relationship with a lost parental object serves as the unconscious underlying motivation of the addiction.

The addict seeks to make the drug an available object which is predictable, dependable, and always under his control—and consequently never lost (Pinderhughes 1971). For such individuals, the threat of a loss of the object constitutes a severe separation anxiety equivalent to annihilation (Krystal and Raskin 1970). Early developmental experiences with the primary object seem to have been too frustrating or too seductively gratifying, with the result that the ambivalence toward the object is intensified. Consequently, the individual has a chronically unsatisfied need for external supplies. He yearns for fusion with an allows a cessation of all inner tensions. The drug serves as ⸻ object through which fusion can be realized and the state of tensionless gratification achieved. The relation to the drug may be permeated by aggressive and sadistic components. As Glover (1932) notes, the drug may then become invested with sadistic properties that are realized only when the drug is within the body: "The situation would represent a transition between the menacing externalized sadism of a paranoid system and the actual internalized sadism of a melancholic system" (p. 207).

Under the impulse of the primitive ambivalence, there is an intense craving for reunion and fusion with the lost object, yet at the same time an impelling need for separation. The primitive drama is rehearsed over and over again but does not reach a solution. In the use of the drug, there is a repeated fusion with the lost object which can be controlled and repeatedly introjected, and thus assumes proportions far more suitable to the addictive need than less available and controllable human love objects (Krystal and Raskin 1970).

Transitional Object

In order to understand the dynamics of this interaction with the drug-object, it seems necessary to postulate that the drug functions after the manner of a transitional object. The transitional mode of experience is familiar through the work of Winnicott (1953). We can note at this juncture that the composition of the transitional object takes place through the interplay of introjective and projective processes, whereby the real external object becomes the vehicle of projective elements derived from the subject's own introjective frame of reference (Meissner 1978b). In the drug experience, the external drug substance is projectively modified by the drug-taking individual in such a fashion that the omnipotent, gratifying, narcissistically reconstituting qualities of the drug are in effect projectively derived from the subject's own inner frame of reference. It is this process that Krystal and Raskin (1970) refer to as "transsubstantiation." The transitional quality of the drug experience has been noted by Hartmann (1969), and its close relationship to fetishism noted (Berman 1972), following on the formulations of Greenacre (1969) on the connection between transitional phenomena and fetishism. The similarity to fetishism has also been noted by Wurmser (1974).

In terms of the paranoid process, these relatively primitive, narcissistically embedded, and intensely ambivalent introjects derive from early experiences in the relationships to significant objects. In the case of the highly orally contaminated and primitively ambivalent internalizations in question here, these experiences would seem to derive primarily from the relationship with the mother, although significant paternal influences cannot be excluded. The resulting introjective configuration provides the pathogenic core around which the individual's sense of self and its correlative attributes are organized.

The original introjective experience is permeated by the need to preserve some sense of availability and internal relatedness to a relatively unavailable, unresponsive, or excessively ambivalent love object. The same need persists and is reexpressed and rehearsed in the drug experience, except that in the drug experience the drug substance becomes a substitute object by reason of its integration as a transitional object through projective transformation. This transitional transformation or "transsubstantiation" of the drug substance gives it its magical power and illusory potentiality for easing inner tensions and bringing surcease and gratification to the addict's inner torment (W.A. Frosch 1970).

The Typology of Addiction

Definition of Addiction

The problem of shifting emphases and meanings is reflected in attempts to define the term "drug addiction" itself. The former tendency to emphasize the addictive aspects of the drug-dependent personality or the addictive potentiality of the drug itself have given way to more nuanced formulations which seem less decisive about these issues and more open to the complex range of possible influences. Thus, the World Health Organization in 1957 adopted the following revised definition:

> Drug addiction is a state of periodic or chronic intoxication detrimental to the individual and to society, produced by the repeated consumption of a drug (natural or synthetic). Its characteristics include: (1) an overpowering desire or need (compulsion) to continue taking the drug and to obtain it by any means; (2) a tendency to increase the dose; (3) a psychic (psychological) and sometimes a physical dependence on the effects of the drug. (Krystal and Raskin 1970, p. 10).

This delimits a broad and far-reaching field of study within which a number of important dimensions can be delineated.

Degree of Drug Usage. This parameter defines a continuum of drug usage stretching from the casual, occasional, or experimental use of drugs to compulsive drug abuse. The experimental user may take the drug out of curiosity or as a result of social pressures of various kinds, but he feels no inner compelling need for the drug effect. Such experimenters compose by far the largest group of drug users, and their drug usage does not properly fall under the rubric of addiction. Consequently, such experimental drug users can be much more readily understood on the basis of extrinsic causes and environmental determinants than in terms of any intrapsychic components. It is the compulsive addict whose drug usage is symptomatic of deeper underlying psychological problems.

Extent to which the Psychological Manifestations of Addiction are Drug Dependent as Opposed to Being Independent of Drug Effects. This relates to the necessity of distinguishing among addictions to various types of drugs (Yorke 1970). The earlier tendency to envision addictive states as more or less univocal ignored any differentiation between the respective pharmacological effects of different kinds of drugs. The question of a common set of psychological characteristics remains unresolved, but it seems clear that the view that the addictive substance is irrelevant to the addictive process (Glover 1932) is no longer tenable.

Degree of Psychopathology. Experimental findings seem to support the notion that relatively severe psychopathology is found in association with heavy drug use and sociopathy (Westermeyer and Walzer 1975). Thus, psychiatric disorder and heavy drug use often coexist, even though the causal relationship between them remains unspecified. Heavy users of even a drug of such low addictive potential as marijuana usually manifest disturbed interpersonal relationships, are frequently unemployed or underemployed (Mirin et al. 1971), and are often impaired in social functioning (Hochman and Brill 1972).

In his early paper on addiction, Rado (1933) emphasizes the basic depressive character with its associated early narcissistic vulnerability, intolerance for frustration and pain, a constant need to exchange such discomfort for an emotional "high," a lack of affectionate and meaningful object relations (which they attempt to overcome by a pseudo-closeness with other drug takers during the drug experience), and finally the use of an artificial technique to maintain self-esteem. In her study of drug-taking adolescents, Dora Hartmann (1969) observes that these characteristics apply not only to those who have become confirmed addicts but also to a certain intermediate group. She describes an experimenting group in which early object relations and ego development are not severely disturbed, who use drugs more or less out of defiance of parental authority or curiosity, and who are able to stop the drug use when this type of acting out becomes no longer necessary. However, she describes a middle group who utilize drugs as a means of maintaining self-esteem. This "artificial technique," in Rado's terms, allows them to avoid tolerating the frustrations of facing reality and to avoid the active work required to establish more mature object relations—an essential task of adolescent development. They maintain a pseudocloseness to other drug users without much emotional commitment, and sexual gratification remains on a masturbatory level.

The Question of Plasticity. This has been admirably discussed by Edwards (1974). Plasticity of any psychoactive substance refers to the degree to which the behavior produced by the substance is potentially susceptible to modification. While the notion of drug dependence generally implies loss of behavioral plasticity, it remains a significant fact that drug-dependent behavior always continues to exhibit plasticity of some degree.

Plasticity includes not only the direct influence of the drug on the organism and the plasticity of the intoxicated behavior itself but also the degree of plasticity of the drug-seeking behavior of the individual, specifically the frequency and quantity of drug use, the settings and occasions, and the degree to which he gives the drug-taking behavior priority over other activities. Both aspects of drug-related behavior are influenced and modified by environmental factors.

As Edwards points out, the failure to consider this dimension of drug dependence may have led to an excessive emphasis on the absoluteness of clinical typologies in drug studies. Thus, to the degree that alcohol-dependent behavior is plastic, it can be molded in a variety of forms in different cultures and in different personalities.

Edwards (1974) cites a body of evidence provided by MacAndrew and Edgerton (1969) regarding contrasting societies. Intoxication may be accompanied by wild acting out in one social context, whereas the same drug intoxication in another society involves no violation of social controls. Edwards concludes that "much which has been conventionally assumed to be an inevitable 'disinhibiting' pharmacological effect of alcohol stands now in need of reappraisal in the light of cultural evidence" (p. 182).

The notion of plasticity allows us to regard drug behavior as a result of a core dependence state which may be more or less plastic in its inferences. Consequently, the degree of psychopathology and the role of environmental and contextual determinants may be in some degree correlative. Not only may cultural or environmental factors modify addictive symptoms and behaviors but they may also modify the extent to which pathogenic determinants play a significant role in the addictive phenomena. Conversely, the degree of intensity of psychopathology or of compulsivity may reciprocally influence the extent to which cultural or contextual factors can exercise a plastic influence.

The Causes of Addiction

The causality of addictive states must be complex and multiply determined. Following Freud's (1895) lead, Wurmser (1974) has suggested a hierarchial ordering of causes or reasons for drug addiction or dependence. He distinguishes four types of causes: preconditions, specific causes, concurrent causes, and precipitating causes.

Preconditions are those factors without which the effect could not come about, but which are incapable of their own accord of producing the effect, regardless of the extent to which they are operative. Wurmser suggests a predispositional constellation for addiction, with the need for defense against affects and the compelling wish for regressive gratification as the most specific of these dispositional factors.

The *specific cause* is one which is always present wherever the effect is found and which is sufficient to produce the effect if it is present in the required degree or intensity, provided that the preconditions are also satisfied. The specific cause for Wurmser is a narcissistic crisis, representing a more or less acute exacerbation of an underlying narcissistic conflict involving the sudden breakdown of self-esteem and the loss of power and control in the face of external limitations. He describes the following causal constellation: the narcissistic crisis and the reactivation of archaic narcissistic conflicts lead to an affective regression that is overwhelming and total, accompanied by feelings of anger, rage, shame, guilt, boredom, loneliness, emptiness, or depression; defensive reactions (mainly splitting and denial, but also repression and other defenses) follow, partly on a psychological, partly on a pharmacological basis, this latter requiring further defensive elaboration by way of externalization and reassertion of magical (narcissistic) power in the drug, linked with archaic forms of aggression and self-destructive sadomasochism. This is possible in most cases only by superego splitting and collapse, along with the emergence of primitive superego functions (superego regression) and concomitant defenses against primitive superego aggression. This results in intense gratification of instinctual drives and resolution of the narcissistic crisis, a sense of narcissistic fulfillment, and the transient integration of a cohesive sense of self (Wurmser 1978).

The *concurrent causes* are those which are neither present in every instance nor able, regardless of degree, to produce the effect by their own power, but they nonetheless operate in conjunction with pre-conditions and specific causes to bring about the etiological configuration. Wurmser places the emphasis on cultural conflicts, particularly value conflicts relating to the limitations of human existence, the dissolution of external superego representatives, and the increasing abolition of the influence of authority and tradition. Consequently, the drug becomes the symbolic expression of liberation from authority, the symbol of protest and rebellion.

The last but not least element in the hierarchy of causes is the *precipitating cause*. It is that which completes the etiological equation and brings about the effect. The precipitating cause in Wurmser's schema is the advent of the drug as a factor of the easy availability of drugs and the social compliance with peer influence.

Drug Equation

As Hartmann (1969) has noted, none of the psychological preconditions can be taken as pathognomonic for drug users or drug addicts. The factors are not specific to drug taking and can also be found in neuroses, depression, delinquencies, and even psychoses. Consequently, the explanatory power of the drug equation must rest on the combination of the necessary, specific causes with sufficient preconditions, and this complex of causes must carry the brunt of intrapsychic explanation in the understanding of drug addiction.

Thus, a critical interface in the discussion of the causality of addictive conditions is that between the role of intrapsychic factors and the extrinsic, environmentally derived and determined causes having to do with the social and/or cultural setting within which the drug behavior takes place. As Zinberg (1975) has observed, there is a growing acceptance of the idea that an understanding of the motivation of the use of illicit drugs and their effects requires that the drug, the personality variables, and the setting must be taken into account. The specific behavior, the taking of illicit drugs, consequently cannot be removed from its social matrix.

The effects of social setting can be similarly described in the case of placebo effects, but even placebo effects are not adequately understood in terms simply of suggestive mechanisms. Rather, as Edwards (1974) suggests, the pathoplastic effect of the social setting on drug-related behavior is as complex as the cultural elements themselves and as multiply determined. The cultural control of drinking among Jews, for example, is not determined by attitudes towards alcohol alone but takes place within a general matrix of Jewish cultural attitudes, values, and aspects of self-esteem and self-image.

Family Influence

Certainly, among the environmental or contextual factors that play a significant role in determining drug behavior, the influence of the addict's family must be given a primary consideration (Wurmser 1978). Most descriptions of the families of addicts emphasize the patient's close relationship to the mother and the relative distance between the addict son and his father. The mother tends to be overprotective, controlling, and indulgent, and unconsciously strives to keep the addicted child in an infantilized position (Schwartzman 1975; Calogeras and Capp 1975). The addict and his family participate in a shared belief system that he is unable to resist drugs should he be exposed to them. This feeling of powerlessness against the effects of the drug is reinforced by family members. If the addict became abstinent, other members of the family would communicate to him their conviction that this was only temporary. This implicit belief system is powerfully reinforced by the mother's overprotectiveness, which frequently undercuts any attempts by the father to insist on any more mature or responsible behavior. Consequently, the addict is seen as inadequate by all members of the family.

The addictive behavior is a result not only of intrapsychic determinants operating within the patient but also of complex forces and influences generated within the family system which operate to reinforce the preconditions of addictive behavior and to subconsciously force the patient to maintain his addiction. Thus, the addictive behavior of the addict can often be an expression of a deeper-lying family pathology, and serves important functions in the homeostatic balancing of destructive psychic forces within the family. The contextual processes which operate as concurrent causes of addictive behavior must take into account not only the more broadly focused social and cultural influences, as I have suggested, but also the more specific and immediate forces that arise out of the subculture and dynamics of the family group.

Addictive Psychopathology

The addictive constellation of depressive, narcissistic, and aggressive elements is strongly related to suicidal dynamics* and reflects aspects of the introjective organization. Relief from such internally distressing and dysphoric affects is sought by projective resolution. This mechanism is familiar enough in cases of frank clinical paranoia in which the projection relieves the pressure on the introjective system and masks the underlying depression—the classic paradigm in cases of superego projection. In addiction, the projective resolution may be elaborated into a paranoid construction in which the addict may evolve a set of beliefs, attitudes, and values toward the world around him that portrays him as victimized and disadvantaged. The drug takes its place within this schema as projectively transformed, magically providing ease of inner distress, relieving the depressive pressure, and generally filling in for the functions of lost or yearned-for objects (usually infantile and parental).

Some evidence suggests a connection between alcoholism and depression. It has been observed that suicide attempts in alcoholics most commonly occur during periods of guilt and remorse following prolonged drinking episodes. Moreover, experimental intoxication (Tamerin and Mendelson 1969) suggests that an initial phase of euphoria is followed by an intensification of depression and anxiety. Again, the etiological sequence is obscure. Hence, whatever the function of the initial depression, the intoxication with alcohol may serve to intensify it to suicidal proportions (Mayfield and Montgomery 1972). In this connection, we can recall Menninger's notion that some forms of addiction are equivalent to chronic suicide (1938).

Drug usage may also serve as a defense against various forms of aggression. Based on his experience with narcotic addicts on methadone maintenance, Khantzian (1974) was led to hypothesize "that a significant portion of these individuals become addicted to opiates because they discover that the drug acts specifically to reverse regressive states by attenuating, and making more bearable, dysphoric feeling involving aggression, rage, and related depression" (p. 65). Dealing with such unpleasant and painful affects is facilitated by a form of "shunt" (Krystal and Raskin 1970), which devolves around defenses against the awareness of affects and the alteration of consciousness facilitated by the taking of the drug. Thus, the modification of states of consciousness through the interaction with the pharmacological effect of the drug has the primary function of modifying the experience of affects (Wurmser 1974; Galenter 1976) and the introjective configuration they reflect.

---

*See the further discussion of suicide in Chapter 9.

One of the most powerful aspects of drug-dependent behavior and the one that stamps it most peculiarly as addictive is its quality of compulsiveness. Removal of the drug of choice not only provokes severe depression, anxiety, or various forms of acting out but the drug user will resort to pharmacologically unrelated drugs or combinations of drugs quite independently of physical withdrawal. The intensity of this compulsion and the correlative need to seek relief is a measure of psychopathology (Wurmser 1974; Glover 1932).

Narcissism

One of the central themes in the understanding of addictive pathologies is the triad of regression, orality, and narcissism. This regressive triad has had a prominent role in psychoanalytic views of addiction from very early on. Freud himself noted the important role of orality in addictive states and even suggested that there may be a constitutional disposition in some cases, which links addiction with forms of oral perversion (1905). Components of oral fixation or oral regression were emphasized by Glover (1928) in the analysis of alcoholism, drug addiction, and manic-depressive insanity. Similar emphases on the roles of oral erotism, oral fixation, passive narcissistic aims, oral regression, and unresolved needs for oral dependency have been persistent motifs in the literature (Rado 1933, 1957; Fenichel 1945; Marmor 1953; Meerloo 1952; Hartmann 1969). The addictive need to restore narcissistic equilibrium through symbolic union with the maternal breast, as well as the operation of Lewin's (1946) oral triad—the wish to eat, to be eaten, and to sleep—has been emphasized (Savitt 1954, 1963; Krystal and Raskin 1970). At least some aspects of the projective transformation of the drug substance in addiction correspond to this symbolic reunion—both in terms of its oral and narcissistic dimensions and in terms of its reattachment to the lost (part-) object.

The role of archaic, omnipotent narcissism in the pathology of addiction, and the function of the drug substance in temporarily restoring narcissistic balance have been noted (Rado 1933; Hartmann 1969). Such narcissistic impairments set the stage for a vulnerability to depression, which is more or less chronic (Krystal and Raskin 1970). In the same vein, Fenichel (1945) comments on the addictive fixation to passive narcissistic aims.

The increased titre of pathogenic narcissism tends to undermine the quality and the capacity for object relations. The importance of maintaining an omnipotent narcissistic equilibrium either through the reinforcement of the grandiose self or through the idealization of an archaic self-object has been noted by Wurmser (1974). Any restrictions, limitations, or imbalance within this narcissistic configuration produce an upsurge of primitive affects. The most prominent and most destructive is the narcissistic rage, which may reach murderous or suicidal proportions. The affect of shame is connected with the failure of the self to maintain its grandiose ideal. There is also a tendency to feel a sense of hurt rejection and abandonment, which results from a falling short of the goal of total union and acceptance from the idealized object.

The role of the drug substance, particularly narcotics, lies not only in its diminishing or eliminating these troublesome affects related to the narcissistic vicissitudes but also in its redressing of the narcissistic balance. Narcissistic rage and its self-destructive and socially destructive consequences as an element in the drug experience have been described by Calogeras and Capp (1975). It is the specific narcissistic trauma combined with an underlying and more chronic narcissistic vulnerability which Wurmser (1974) describes in terms of the narcissistic crisis:

> This narcissistic crisis is thus the point at which the conflicts and defects converge with a particular external situation and with the availability of the seeming means of solution: the drug. By definition a "narcissistic crisis" would have to entail a particularly intense disappointment in others, in oneself, or both—so intense because of the exaggerated hopes, and so malignant because of its history's reaching back to very early times. (p. 840)

Amphetamine Addiction

A number of the essential aspects of the addictive process are described in Berman's (1972) account of amphetamine addiction in a young female hysteric. Her deep-seated feelings of feminine inadequacy, deficiency, worthlessness, and revulsion and shame focused on her own genitals reflected the depressive core of her introjects. This provided the basis for her pathogenic feelings about herself, which were constantly being enacted and struggled against in a variety of self-demeaning and masochistic ways, including sexual promiscuity. The patient had begun taking amphetamines for dysmenorrhea at age 13 and continued to take them as diet pills thereafter, but in increasing doses. The effects were dramatic:

> The amphetamines played a crucial role in her everyday life. She depended on them to provide the strength and energy for her flurry of activities and projects at work, to give her the vitality that

won her the reputation of "human dynamo." In her social life it
was the pill that made her vivacious, sparkling, and sexually active.
It served to defend her against the intolerable feeling of weakness
and femininity. (p. 329)

Gradually reduction of the dosage brought fears that she would
become weak, lifeless, dull, lethargic, sexually uninteresting, and
unlovable. Her view of herself was dominated by concerns of genital
inadequacy: a "deranged, globby, hairy mess." She continued to carry a
half amphetamine pill in her purse, just in case she might need a burst of
energy. When asked about this, she replied that it was a "clutch"—a slip
for "crutch." She associated "clutch" to the gearshift of a car, something
she could clutch on to. This description was accompanied by clenching
an imaginary gearshift directly over her pubic area. The fragment of pill
had been transformed into a phallic substitute, which served to
compensate for her feelings of damaged and defective femininity. The
pills were originally taken to relieve menstrual cramps (weak, sick
femininity) and later for obesity (flabby, unattractive femininity). The
pills provided a masculine sense of stamina, strength, mental acuity, and
sexual prowess. The pill became a phallic substitute representing the
father's penis and her inadequate introjection of his phallic capacities.

At a deeper level, the pill came to represent the availability of oral
supplies, like the candy she kept at her bedside, which helped defend
against primitive fears of oral abandonment. The fear of being left with
nothing was both oral and phallic. Her mother had encouraged her use
of diet pills, reviving earlier oral conflicts over diets and feelings of
deprivation. The diet pill, therefore, came to symbolize the feeding-and-
depriving mother. Berman comments:

> It was this unique quality of the drug, this lending of itself to
> objective and subjective symbolization, that facilitated its incor-
> poration into the symptom complex. Within this solitary pill
> carried inside her little purse was symbolically condensed the oral
> and phallic elements of her neurosis. It served as a mortar which
> knit these elements together, and through its profound symbolic-
> pharmacologic effects it reinforced and solidified the neurosis. (pp.
> 336–337)

A similar set of dynamics was displayed in one of my own analytic
cases, a young man who had also developed an amphetamine addiction.
The organization of this patient's introjects was dominated by his view of
himself as small, weak, vulnerable, and castrated, unable to measure up

to adult standards or to perform the tasks that adults perform. This patient's introjective organization was determined by early castration motifs reinforced by a congenital heart defect, which became a focus of obsessive concern by his anxious and possessive mother, and was finally operated on in somewhat traumatic fashion at age 5. Instead of feeling cured and well, the patient felt himself to be permanently weak and defective—even though he was strongly built and was able to engage in rather strenuous sports, particularly wrestling. But after his operation, he recalled not being able to reassure himself that the large scar across his chest would not fall open one day, leaving him vulnerable and helpless. He spent anxious hours examining it, probing it, testing it, unable to convince himself that he was whole and well.

In addition, the operation and the wound became the object of his mother's anxious preoccupation. He was the youngest of three boys by about seven years. He became her baby, and she worried about and protected him—only reinforcing his feelings of defect and inadequacy. This state of affairs was complicated by his older brothers. The oldest was a ladies' man whom the patient looked up to in admiration—in fact, they played at being father and son, a sexually proficient substitute for the patient's own father, whom he saw as weak and controlled by mother. The second brother was the family student and set a high standard of academic achievement. The patient felt that he could never match his older brothers and that he was doomed to failure sexually and academically. When he approached a sexual encounter or an academic challenge—whether an examination or writing a paper—the patient felt that he could not hope to perform without the help of his pills. The pills became the talisman of masculine strength, capacity, and proficiency. Without it, he could not hold an erection but would come in his pants like a helpless infant soiling himself. Without it, he could not perform effectively in studying for exams or writing papers.

As the analysis of these elements of his drug use proceeded, it became clear that the drug became the repository for the more masculine, aggressive, and competitive aspects of himself which he had kept repressed. For him to be strong, masculine, and aggressive would mean he would lose his mother's concerned investment in her sick baby and would also run the risk of competing with his much older, stronger, and powerful brothers. They, in turn, were displacements from the patient's more infantile view of and introjection of the father, which was denied and repressed, covered by the patient's need to devalue the real father. These elements of the patient's personality were distilled and projected into the drug, a magical substance that gave the patient the strength and capacity he had need to deny in himself. The same dynamic is observable in Berman's (1972) patient, in whom repressed and denied phallic and aggressive strivings are projected onto the drug substance, endowing it with symbolic significance and power. The drug, thus transformed, serves to redress the narcissistic vulnerabilities and deficits in both patients. In both, genital defects come to reflect and represent deeper and more pervasive defects in the patient's sense of self related to the organization of core introjects.

Ego Regression

Under the impetus of ego psychology, drug dependence and addiction have been viewed as a form of ego pathology, in which the use of the drug substance induces a specific state of ego regression (Wieder and Kaplan 1969). The continuing dependence on the drug lends to an increasing impoverishment of the ego's resources and a diminished capacity for mastery of anxiety and depression. The ego's adaptive capacity, freedom of action, and autonomy are continually undermined (Rado 1933; Hartmann 1969). Thus, the preexistent ego pathology is compounded by the regressive drug-dependent condition. Dependence on the drug allows the individual to cope with and reduce inner tension and stress in a manner in which his own psychic mechanisms are incapable of doing.

Superego Deficits

Similar structural deficits have been noted in the organization of superego and its functioning. Glover (1928) regards alcoholism as a disastrous attempt to cure the abnormalities of a primitive conscience. Similar self-destructive aspects could be found in drug addictions as well (Glover 1932). To this should be added the predominance of relatively archaic forms of shame and guilt, which may be closely linked with primitive and global fears of humiliation and revenge. The archaic superego is thus capable of considerable vindictiveness and corrupt-ibility (Wurmser 1974). There is a general deterioration of superego functioning so that drug addicts cannot be expected to follow the usual rules or codes of social behavior. The deceitfulness and exploitation of those around them is accompanied by little acceptance of responsibility and a great deal of blaming of others for their difficulties, most particularly the authorities who interfere with the availability and use of drugs (Zinberg 1975). This suspension of superego functions affects not only the prohibitive and punitive aspects of the superego but also the functions of the ego-ideal. There is an overriding lack of life-guiding values and ideals or personal myth (Wurmser 1974). The blocking of superego functions, along with the awareness of intersystemic tensions, may be one of the primary reliefs sought through the use of drugs (Krystal and Raskin 1970).

The regressive and narcissistic aspects of such primitive superego functioning recall our attention to the essentially introjective quality of superego organization and its relationship to developmental parameters. Sandler (1960) observes that the prolongation of superego dependence reflects the earlier infantile dependence of the child on his parents as the source of narcissistic gain. If such narcissistic reimbursement can be achieved elsewhere, the dependence on the superego can be abandoned. Thus, drug addiction can take the form of replacing dependence with an addiction to an external substance. In other words, if the intrapsychic organization of the addicted individual were structured around a more clearly differentiated and effectively structuralized superego, there would be no need to resort to addiction.

The Projective System

Externalization

In discussing the operation of the projective system in addictive states, we come closest to the function of the paranoid process in addictive psychopathology. The presence of paranoid traits in addictive personalities has been frequently noted and documented. There is generally a tendency to blame others, particularly authority figures, for the addict's misfortunes. There is a general attitude of suspiciousness and guardedness, and a constant complaint of being victimized, cheated, disadvantaged, and exploited. There is the repeated complaint that powerful figures, including doctors, nurses, probation officers, counselors, et cetera, are not sufficiently considerate of or helpful to the poor, disadvantaged addict.

Wurmser (1978) casts similar aspects of the addictive picture under the rubric of externalization. He regards it as a process of taking magical and omnipotent control over the uncontrollable. The fear of powerful and overwhelming affects is warded off by a magically invested substance. The externalization takes the concrete form of external blaming, which masks the underlying sense of shame, humiliation, weakness, and failure. Then, of course, external social agents and authorities respond to the addict's need for externalized enemies by punishing, prohibiting, pursuing, and persecuting, providing the aggressor for the addict's sense of victimization. The result is a paranoid projective system that has identifiable and specific defensive functions.

Paranoid Trends

Along with this series of complaints there is an overwhelming sense of self-loathing and devaluation. As Zinberg (1975) notes, the flavor and content of the productions of these patients are decidedly paranoid, yet they cannot be described as paranoid in specifically psychotic terms. It is this quality of the addictive paranoia that led Glover (1932) to describe the addictions in terms of "transitional states" rather than psychoses. Behind the argumentative, troublesome, and contentious facade erected by these patients, there lurk phobic anxieties which reflect the inner compulsion to put and keep themselves in a weak, vulnerable, and helpless position.

In this connection, Khantzian (1974) has noted the tendency for significant behavioral and psychological shifts to accompany stabilization of such patients on methadone. The patients become much quieter, less labile, and show significantly less hostile projection and paranoid reactions. However, as such patients are withdrawn from methadone support, they experience a reemergence of patterns of aggressive-impulsive outbursts, projections, paranoia, and frequently enough, patterns of psychotic thinking and behavior. These observations suggest that the drug serves to modulate or modify a more general paranoid trait.

A similar connection between drug use and paranoid manifestations has been observed in a hippie population by Seitz (1974). In these drug users, there was an initial disavowal of emotion, which was facilitated by drug use, consistent with the role of drug usage in affect defense. But Seitz also documented, with the continued use of drugs, an insidious shift from a masochistically bound aggression to a form which expressed itself in an increasing reliance on paranoid-projective mechanisms. In these cases, the resort to specifically paranoid-projective mechanisms seems to be motivated by the need to defend against an underlying depressive core. Other paranoid attitudes, particularly toward authority figures, have been defined in drug users among army personnel garrisoned in Europe (Calogeras and Capp 1975). Tendencies to blaming, irresponsibility, suspiciousness, guardedness, distrustfulness, and general projective demeanor were noted by Glover (1928). He also noted that in other forms of addiction, addictive personalities may reveal a superficial, obsessional, or hysterical layer, but that the core of the pathology rests on an underlying paranoid layer that must be resolved in order for cure to be achieved (1932).

Depressive Core

The core problem in addictive states is an underlying depressive organization with the attendant dysphoric affects of anxiety and depression, frequently accompanied by feelings of shame and doubt, based on an inner narcissistic vulnerability (Wurmser 1978). The avoidance of the core depression may take the form of a manic defense or may follow a pattern of paranoid reaction. Glover (1932) has described these patterns of resolution of underlying depression but also emphasizes that the paranoid resolution differs from that seen in clinical paranoia. In clinical paranoia, the patient is threatened by external enemies, whereas in addiction the patient uses the drug to destroy an internal enemy.*

Introjective Configuration

From the point of view of the paranoid process, we are dealing with the shifting emphases between the organization of introjects in the intrapsychic realm and the correlative projections as they affect the individual's relationship with reality. The core depression relates to the introjective configuration in which there are embedded the feelings of inner weakness, inadequacy, vulnerability, and evil. These aspects of the victim-introject are invariably accompanied by elements of sadistic destructiveness which derive from an "identification with the aggressor." At the same time, the organization of the introjects is patterned along narcissistic lines as well, so that elements of inferiority, narcissistic vulnerability, and shamefulness coexist with components of superiority, specialness, entitlement, and grandiosity.

---

*From the point of view of the tripartite theory, the superego has long been recognized as an internal persecutor. From the perspective of the paranoid process, the victim-introject is always accompanied by a correlative introjective configuration, the aggressor-introject, that may remain internalized in depressive conditions or may be externalized in more paranoid states. Thus, the aggressor-introject may be seen as providing the core of pathological superego organization, particularly in depression. The victim-introject is the necessary, if often implicit, component in such states. The use of the drug is accompanied by superego modifications, not as a pharmacological effect but as a result of projective concomitants. While superego severity may be reduced, other idealizing functions are blocked as well. Both magically powerful and sadistically destructive aspects may be projected on to the drug, reflecting the underlying introjective ambivalence. (p. 746)

When the victimized and inferior components of the introjective organization are in the ascendant, the depressive aspects of the patient's pathology predominate. Other noncompatible components (aggressive, superior) of the introjective configuration are correspondingly either repressed or externalized. It is through this projective externalization that the drug substance becomes modified, in terms of the transitional object model, into an external object which is endowed with loving and hating characteristics of one or both of the patient's parents (Glover 1932). Thus, the patient's drug usage and his psychic interaction with the drug become a sort of pseudoparanoid system.

In the case of our own analytic patient, his introjective organization was dominated by his sense of victimization and vulnerability, along with inferior dimensions of his pathological narcissism. The taking of a few amphetamine pills turned him into a phallic narcissist, gave him a sense of power and competence, and helped him to overcome his narcissistic vulnerability. These aggressive and narcissistically superior dimensions were part of his existing personality structure and were externalized, attributed to the drug, even as they were repressed and denied in himself. The projection allowed him to express what was too risky, threatening, and conflicted in his own makeup. The use of amphetamines allowed him to come closer to the effective use of his own inherent potential, even though the result had a moderately phallic and narcissistic quality. In more extreme cases, where the pathology is more primitive and the aggressive and narcissistic polarities more extreme, the drug usage may have a more pathological outcome.

Projective Defense

It should be noted that the projective device is immediately and phenomenologically intended to relieve the inner tension and pressure of the depressive system organized around the aggressively toned and narcissistically vulnerable introject. This formulation is specifically saying more and appealing to more than the notion of affect defense in the explanation of addiction. The projective device, moreover, may support a manic defense or a more specifically paranoid resolution. If the projective component transforms the drug substance into the craved, nurturing, idealized, narcissistically satisfying object, the outcome is more likely to express itself in terms of satiation and euphoric intoxication. This essentially follows the pattern of manic defense. Insofar as the projective component reflects the underlying ambivalence toward the primary objects and displaces the inner sense of evilness and sadistic destructiveness, the resolution may become more specifically paranoid. The drugs may assume either noxious or benign character-istics. Insofar as the drug interaction is derived from early and usually highly ambivalent object relationships, the drugs take on a highly ambivalent perspective. The drugs, therefore, can readily take on sadistic and destructive properties as Glover (1932) so clearly indicated.

Pharmacological Effects

The interaction between intrapsychic determinants and specific pharma-cological effects was given little serious consideration in early analytic thinking about addiction and only later has become a matter of concern. The general tenor of analytic thinking about drug effects was set by Rado's (1933, p. 2) early observation that "not the toxic agent, but the impulse to use it makes an addict of a given individuality." This emphasis reflected the insistence that the compulsive and addictive aspects of drug-dependent behavior were a reflection of inner psycho-pathology. Thus, Glover (1932) emphasized the tendency to compulsive addiction even to inert substances and his conclusion that, in fact, any substance could function as a drug given the proper psychic conditions. He described these as "psychic addictions." Similarly, Wurmser (1974) commented on the tendency for compulsive drug users to substitute other symptoms when the drug effect of choice is suspended, or frequently to replace the unavailable drug with a completely unrelated drug substance. He concludes that the compulsive drug use must be regarded as one symptom, along with others which express an under-lying pathological disturbance. Consequently, it is not the withdrawal from drugs that presents the most difficult problem with such patients, but rather the coping with the patient's emotional need to use a drug, in fact to use any drug or any other equally harmful external means to find relief from inner tension.

In general, this analytically sanctioned approach tends to minimize the specific effects produced by the pharmacological actions of the drug itself. However, in terms of the operation of the paranoid process, it seems more reasonable to suggest, following the transitional object model, that the projective element which derives from the inner introjective frame of reference combines with specific qualities in the drug substance and its proper pharmacology to produce the peculiarly illusory and magical effect attributed to the drug. This symbolic interaction has been articulated by Wieder and Kaplan (1969). The drug's influence is mediated through its psychodynamic meaning and pharmacological properties. The symbolic significance attaches not only to the drug itself, which may represent an object or part-object, but also to the act of using it and to its physiological concomitants.

This pharmacogenic effect represents diffuse, direct, and indirect physiological modifications, which are expressed psychically as modifications of the personality structure. Whatever the individual psychopathology, a given drug in sufficient dosage will produce a specific state of intoxication. However, the personality structure determines the individual's reaction to this pharmacogenic effect. Wieder and Kaplan comment: "When an individual finds an agent that chemically facilitates his preexisting preferential mode of conflict solution, it becomes his drug of choice" (p. 429). The drug becomes a pharmacological key that fits the psychological lock and unlocks the special satisfaction of intoxication that gives rise to the craving for the substance that produces it (Wieder and Kaplan 1974). The same characteristic of pharmacogenic effects has been described by Edwards (1974) in terms of the modification of drug effects by pathoplastic environmental and personality factors.

Such effects are not random events or the products of chance selection. They are rather specifically determined (and specific) outcomes. Besides the operation of intrapsychic dispositions, other peripheral factors play a significant role in the production of specific pharmacogenic effects as, for example, the dosage, the route of administration, the immediate environmental setting within which the drug is being taken, and even the broader setting of cultural and social attitudes, prohibitions, and actions which sets the frame of reference within which the drug behavior takes place.

The chronic need for certain pharmacogenic effects may derive from developmental and structural defects in the individual personality. Developmental defects stemming from identifiable levels of psychological development may play a role in the determination of the symbolic equation involved in drug taking. It should be noted, however, that this aspect of the equation does not dictate that the craving should be directed to a single drug substance or that it should not tolerate significant degrees of plasticity or modifiability. It is frequent enough that drug users will experiment with a variety of drugs and then focus on one particular drug to satisfy their craving. However, this may also result in the use of a combination of drug substances to achieve similar effects. Thus, shifts from one preferred addictive drug to another or from one combination to another combination may reflect shifts in the underlying psychodynamic configuration, which would make different pharmacogenic effects necessary. As Wieder and Kaplan (1969) point out, such a shift may have considerable significance for therapeutic interventions.

Interactions

Certain pharmacological actions of different drug classes can contribute
to the complex psychopharmacological interaction we are describing,
insofar as pharmacological effects may answer different kinds of psychic
needs and/or may provide a more or less available matrix for projective
modification. The psychotomimetic or hallucinogenic drugs produce
striking alterations in perception, mood, time sense, and sense of self.
There is a loss of the normal sense of boundaries of the self and the
object world, with subjective experiences of fusion and merger with lost
or yearned-for objects. The psychedelic drugs likewise counter the state
of emptiness, boredom, disillusionment, loneliness, and meaninglessness so often found in addiction-prone personalities. The drug induces
an illusion of meaning and value, that the self is mystically expansive and
grandiose, and that the patient's environment is impregnated with
cosmic significances.

   The narcotics, including opium and its derivatives as well as some of
the synthetic narcotics, produce a state of quiet lethargy and diminished
engagement with external reality (Weider and Kaplan 1969). Addicts
frequently report a subjective sense of a calming and stabilizing action of
the drug (Khantzian 1974). There is an effect of anesthesia and analgesia
in which affective pain is blocked and consciousness reduced (Krystal
and Raskin 1970). Frosch (1970) and Wieder and Kaplan (1969)
emphasize a state of blissful satiation which can lead to the hyper-
cathecting of fantasies of omnipotence, magical wish fulfillment, and
self-sufficiency. Khantzian (1974) feels that the narcotic effect helps to
counter and attenuate the dysphoria arising from intense feelings of
aggression, rage, and depression. The drug provides a sense of
protection, union, heightened self-esteem and self-control (Wurmser
1978).

   In addition, Wurmser (1974) has noted the capacity of both the
sedative-hypnotic drugs, such as the barbiturates, and the narcotics to
calm intense feelings of rage, pain, and loneliness, as well as the anxieties
related to these affects. Humiliation, shame, and rage call for powerful
defenses rooted in partial or total depersonalization or derealization,
defenses that are reinforced by these drugs. The self is deadened,
numbed, and estranged (Wurmser 1978).

   The stimulant or energizing drugs, including the amphetamines,
methadrine, and cocaine, seem to increase awareness of drive feelings
and impulse strength, diminish the awareness of fatigue, and lead to a
feeling of assertiveness, self-esteem, and increased frustration tolerance.
They induce a restless form of activity which seems to serve the denial of

passivity (Wieder and Kaplan 1969). They also seem to provide a sense of aggressive mastery, control, invincibility, and even grandeur (Hendin 1974a; Wurmser 1978). This effect serves to bolster defenses against underlying depression or more general feelings of unworthiness and weakness (Wurmser 1974, 1978). The sense of active mastery has likewise been observed by Frosch (1970).

The energizing and activating quality of the amphetamines and related drugs serves to counter and to bolster the defense against the passivity and vulnerability of depression. The individual using such drugs may prefer to tolerate the excitement, anxiety, agitation, or hypomania rather than to be afflicted by depression, passivity, or boredom. The hyperalertness and activity associated with the drug have been compared to a manic defense against depression (Krystal and Raskin 1970). Nonetheless, it should be remembered that the abuse of these drugs can produce a paranoidlike state that has been analogized to paranoid schizophrenia. In terms of our understanding of the mechanism of the paranoid process, we can suggest that the activating and energizing properties of these drugs serve to shift the balance in the intrapsychic economy from the predominance of introjective components to a defensive mobilization of projective functions. The predominance of aggressively toned and narcissistically embedded introjects underlies the pathology of depression. The shift to a more active alignment would allow for the mobilization of projective defenses and a consequent mitigation of the depressive posture and its associated affects. These features of the effects of amphetamines and their interplay with the depressive alignment of the introjects have been graphically described in Berman's (1972) case of amphetamine addiction.

Both alcohol and marijuana seem to have similar effects in low doses, diminishing defenses against drive and impulse discharge (Wieder and Kaplan 1969). In light to moderate doses, both alcohol and the barbiturates seem to release inhibitions, probably as a result of a release of higher central nervous system regulatory centers. Both alcohol and the sedative drugs serve to relieve internal distressful states associated with anxiety and conflicts (Khantzian 1975). With both alcohol and marijuana perceptual acuity is accentuated, the subject becomes hyperactive and overtalkative, he is frequently impressed with his profound thoughts and depth of feeling, he experiences changes in time sense and body image, and he may act out sexual and hostile impulses.

The proposition being advanced here is that, in keeping with the operations of the paranoid process, different drug substances have specifiable pharmacological effects which are susceptible of plasticity or modification by a variety of influences, coming either from the external frame of reference within which the drug is administered or from the internal psychic dispositions of the individual taking the drug. Our hypothesis is that the qualities and circumstances of the drug use provide a vehicle for the specific projective elements which are generated in and derive from the subject's intrapsychic frame of reference. The projective process does not commandeer the drug substance and bring it into the service of intrapsychic needs in any absolute or apodictic sense. The drug substance, in combination with the attendant circumstances of its administration and application, must provide a suitable substrate which allows the drug to be conjoined with the individual's projective elaboration. Consequently, in each case of addiction there is a specificity of drug preference which is based on the ultimate fit between the subjective needs and the pharmacologic properties of the drug, and the extent to which they can be successfully amalgamated to meet the inner needs of the drug-taking individual.

The Paranoid Process and the Drug Equation

It remains, finally, to relate the various parameters of the drug problem to the perspective provided by the paranoid process (Meissner 1971b, 1978b). The paranoid process may provide a frame of reference within which disparate aspects of the complex variables which interact and contribute to the phenomenon of drug dependence may find their appropriate location and expression. The derivation from the introjects makes it possible for the projective content to express and fulfill precisely those complementary elements which the self requires in order to maintain its internal stability. In the addictive process, the drug substance is subjectively modified by projective components and thereby acquires transitional illusory properties which often have a magical or mystical quality. The drug substance by this transitional transformation (or transubstantiation) comes to substitute for or replace a significant self-sustaining object relationship which the self has lost in some psychically significant manner. From this point of view, the compulsiveness of the drug taking and the drug behavior is dependent not simply on the physiologically habituating or addicting qualities of the drug itself but on the necessity of the drug intake for the maintenance of the stability and coherence of the self. In most addict subjects, the intensity of the threat and the severe anxiety associated with it operate at a level of severe or primitive separation anxiety or even more ominously at a level of annihilation anxiety.

The elaboration of the transitional object–drug substance in this manner is not simply a matter of the transformation 'of an external substance by a projective distortion. The inherent pharmacological properties of the drug substance itself contribute to this process in one or another degree. The drug taker experiments with a variety of drugs or combination of drugs until he finds that proper mix which sufficiently modifies his inner state of affective disorganization or turmoil (Wieder and Kaplan 1969). The question, then, is more or less one of what particular effect or combination of effects the drugs provide which answers to the subjective need of the drug-taking individual so they can usefully become the vehicle for and perhaps the stimulus of the essential self-sustaining projections. These transitional and projective integrations may have any of a variety of dynamic significances, depending on the quality of the projection, the portion of the introjective matrix from which it derives, and ultimately the pathogenic object relationship which it revives and replaces.

Paranoid Construction

There is the question of the influence of extrinsic modifying components on the process we have been describing. A critical component of the paranoid process is that aspect which we have come to refer to as the "paranoid construction" (Meissner 1978b). The paranoid construction, varying in degree in relationship to a variety of extrinsic social, cultural, or even political factors, plays a role in drug dependence. Projective transformation of the drug substance cannot simply stand alone; rather, the phenomenon and the experience of the taking of the drug must be embedded in a broader sustaining matrix. It is this aspect of the drug experience and the operation of the paranoid process which gives rise to the frequently observed phenomenon of the drug subculture and the often paranoid opposition which is directed against the surrounding society and particularly the authority figures within that society.

Thus, the drug taker may in fact develop a fairly elaborate paranoid system, which has the implicit purpose (in part) of sustaining the drug culture, along with its inherent values and convictions, and which gives the taking of the drug and the individual addict's relationship to the drug substance a specific sustaining context and meaningfulness. The paranoid construction serves as a sustaining frame of reference within which the projections are continually validated and sustained, so that as an ultimate motivating focus for the entire process, the inner coherence and stability of the pathogenic introjective organization can be maintained.

Extrinsic forces within the social matrix can contribute to and interact with this process in different ways. As Wurmser (1978) comments, the public and legislative furor over the use of narcotics and marijuana "has a strong ring of *projection*: an emotional outrage about an outer target, a 'scapegoat,' ... with all the falsifications and exaggerations, the rage and collusion going with such a projection" (p. 19). Thus, prohibitive laws or strict legal reinforcement or condemnatory social attitudes can contribute to a sustaining matrix within which the paranoid quality of this construction and its inherent projective elements can find meaningful integration and convincing support. Whatever adaptive qualities this resolution may have, it unavoidably involves a pathological dependence on the drug. In the most primitively organized personalities, functioning on a psychotic or borderline level, the drug addiction may serve as a form of particularized or delimited paranoia which may allow relatively autonomous functioning in other areas of the individual's experience. Such individuals, however, remain at risk in view of the well-known tendency for such paranoid systems to generalize.

I am suggesting that these elements are at play in every instance of drug addiction. One does not need to demonstrate severe psychopathology in order to understand the phenomenon of drug addiction. It is entirely conceivable that an individual may turn to the use of drugs in an addictive fashion in order to answer specific internal psychic needs, having to do with the temporary sustaining of the sense of self and its inherent narcissistic organization and equilibrium. It is also readily understandable that, given a shift in circumstances and surrounding influences, some individuals might find the dependence on the drug no longer functional. It is likewise easier to understand within this perspective the effectiveness of religious conversion or meditative techniques in replacing dependence on drugs (Carrington and Ephron 1975). These alternate contexts provide a variant expression of the paranoid process which may in a significant number of cases satisfy the inner needs of the subject and serve to sustain a sense of meaningful belonging, participation, and self-cohesiveness.

Finally, with reference to Wurmser's (1974) etiological schema, we can say that the introjective organization is the necessary precondition without which the effect of drug dependence would never come about, although it can never of itself produce that effect. The specific cause, which is never missing and which might itself in sufficient intensity bring about the effect, is the narcissistic crisis or more specifically the threat to the organization, stability, or cohesion of the self which demands the resolution provided by the paranoid process. The concurrent causes, which do not produce the effect but exert their influence along with the preconditions and the specific cause, are the external factors relating to social and cultural conditions and their effects. And finally, the precipitating cause is the availability of the drug itself. The final outcome or specific effect of the etiological equation is the organization of the specific paranoid system, which involves the drug substance as transitional object, the purpose and objective of the entire system being the organization, maintenance, or sustaining of the individual's self-system.

Therapeutic Implications

While the emphasis in this chapter has not been therapeutic, some tentative suggestions for the psychotherapy of addictive states can be drawn from the present formulations. Our intention has been to propose that the explanatory schema of the paranoid process provides a sufficiently flexible frame of reference for the understanding of a number of aspects of addiction. Recognizing the often confusing heterogeneity of drug-related conditions, our intent here was to provide an account of the core psychological elements that enter into a wide variety of addictive forms.

The therapeutic line of approach this suggests runs from a careful exploration of these projective aspects to a clarification and illumination of the underlying introjective organization. The therapeutic work, therefore, entails a clear delineation of the projective dimension and its unequivocal connection with the patient's introjects. In cases of addiction, this would require a careful exploration in detail and an understanding of the meaning of the drug, a systematic uncovering of its projective elements, and a linking of these elements with the introjects. In the case of amphetamine addiction referred to, the patient was unable to surrender his dependence on the drug until he was able to give up his attachment to his introjects. The drug dependence in his case was secondary; the real addiction was to the introjects. As long as he clung to his invested position as weak, vulnerable, incompetent baby, his need for the drug was too powerful. Only when he realized that the magical significance of the drug was a reflection of something that he denied in himself, and that he no longer needed to deny that more aggressive side of himself, could he give the drug up. The essential connection was the recognition and acceptance of the aggressive, powerful, and narcissistically grandiose elements projected onto the drug as deriving from and reflecting a part of the patient's own self-image.

Such patients are usually quite in touch with one side of the introjective configuration, as was this patient, but quite resistant to acceptance of the other side. In this patient, the more aggressive and grandiose side of his character was revealed in active fantasy and dream life in which he was from time to time the powerful aggressor, the seducer of women who could at his will be forced into a variety of perverse sexual acts even against their will. It was this repressed, denied, and threatening part of himself that he invested in the drug, so that it became a magical transforming substance that made it possible for him to write his papers, perform well academically, and even to become potent and phallically competent in bed. Acceptance of this side of himself was threatening precisely because it entailed surrender of the protective and gratifying position of being his mother's special baby, and beckoned him to join the adult world of striving, competition, challenge, and the dual risks of failure and success. Remaining the special baby absolved him from the responsibility for his own limitations and failures, even as the ascription of power and competence to the drug absolved him of the consequences of his more adult performance.

Prognosis

Prognosis of any therapeutic endeavor with compulsive and severely addicted personalities has to be guarded at best, but where there is a solid core of ego strengths (as demonstrated in a capacity for responsibility and commitment to work and marriage), the prospects are improved. The more primitive the personality structure, the more the features of a lower-order borderline organization predominate (Meissner 1984a), the more guarded the prognosis. Positive collaboration from the family may help, but continued enmeshment in the family emotional system, such that basic defensive patterns of denial and externalization (projection) are sustained and reinforced, can defeat therapeutic efforts. A solid marital relation with a nondrug-taking spouse is a positive indicator; a drug-taking spouse is bad news. The presence of children in the family helps. As Wurmser (1978) notes, "Our best successes (including withdrawal from methadone) were with patients who had a spouse, one or several children, a deep sense of commitment to them, and a challenging, fulfilling type of work" (p. 283).

The addictive experience is obviously heterogeneous, complex, and reflects the dynamics peculiar to the individual subject. Therapeutic approaches to the management of drug problems frequently require difficult regimens of detoxification and drug regulation and/or substitution. Our concern in the present effort has not extended to these pharmacological aspects, except to suggest that there is an important interaction between the pharmacological properties and action of specific drugs and the individual dynamics of the drug taker. Our emphasis here has been on the psychological aspects of addiction and correlative psychotherapeutic issues. An important question remains as to the extent to which drug problems can be approached psychotherapeutically. The inference from the preceding discussion must be that any meaningful approach to treatment of drug problems must rely on an effective integration of pharmacological management and psychotherapeutic intervention. The better our understanding of these respective parameters of the problem of drug dependence and of their interaction, the greater the promise of effective treatment. Hopefully, the paranoid process may provide at least one available schema for such understanding.

Chapter Eleven

Aging and the Paranoid Process

The psychology of the aging process is complex and involves a multiplicity of sociological, economic, cultural, and environmental variables, as well as important aspects of the inner psychic dynamics and functioning of the individual. We will take it as a starting point, then, that the study of the psychology of the aging process cannot take place in a vacuum, that the influences on the aging process derive from the intrapsychic world as well as from the external world of social and environmental influences. Consequently, any model which claims to encompass these complex variables must attempt to show not only the intrapsychic changes and developments associated with the aging process but also the manner in which external influences affecting the life circumstances and the context of experience of the aging individual play a role in modifying the internal psychic process.

The Aging Process

This chapter will focus on the complex interaction of intrapsychic determinants and social, environmental, and contextual variables in terms of an overriding framework provided by the paranoid process. We will examine aspects of the aging process which may serve as the basis for normal aging or play a role in the development of pathology in the aging individual, and attempt to delineate the manner in which such internal and external influences interact with the paranoid process in a constant process of modifying and shaping the inner psychic world of the aging individual. We will then turn our attention to more pathological

manifestations that take place in the context of aging, with the objective
of deepening our understanding of the operation and influence of
aspects of the aging process in the genesis of various forms of
psychopathology. Here again, we will focus on the factors associated with
aging, their influence on the emergence of pathogenic configurations,
and on the role of such intrapsychic configurations themselves in
shaping the course of the development of such pathology. I will
conclude by attempting to develop some of the implications of this
approach for therapeutic intervention with older patients.

Research

The aging process has been an object of intensive study for some years
now but has been subject to certain catastrophic bias on the part of
psychiatrists and psychoanalysts (Gutmann 1981). The experience of
such students of the aging process is affected by a sampling error: their
focus tends to fall on hospitalized or institutionalized elder patients
rather than on the aging population that is still able to maintain itself in
the community. (Most aging individuals can maintain themselves in a
relatively stable manner over long periods of time, and it is only when
the more acute and rapid deterioration in physical, mental, and
emotional functioning associated with the terminal phase of life begins
that they come to the attention of mental health professionals.) There is a
consequent tendency to overgeneralize on the basis of clinical experience to the larger population of aging individuals. In effect, the terminal
phase of life, facing the prospect of death, becomes the model for the
later stages of life and leads to a view of old age cast predominantly in
terms of loss.

    The tendency of such a view may be to overlook important strengths
in the aging individual. We often assume, for example, that the elderly
are relatively debilitated by multiple losses suffered through the deaths
of close family and friends. Emphasis on the pain of loss and mourning,
however, may overlook the particular resilience of the elderly in the face
of death and loss. Death may have become a familiar experience to the
older individual and may lack the sense of intensity or shock experienced
by the young. At the same time, the experience of aging may call forth
creative capacities and resources in the elderly that enable them to more
effectively deal with the ravages of time.

Change

Undoubtedly, one of the significant challenges in the aging process is the
need to adapt to change. Biological and physiological changes inex-

passive and affiliative, and even nurturant, women tend to become more individualistic, egocentric, and even aggressive.

Some years ago, Neugarten (1964) advanced the hypothesis that aging is associated with relatively independent processes of internal change which first precede and then run parallel with social and adaptational changes. The individual, according to this theory, would move from a sense of active mastery of the environment to a more passive and adaptive stance and then to one in which inner psychological experiences become more gratifying than those involving relationships with others and with external contexts. But even here, the external social conditions seem to explain a good deal more of the variation in adjustment than the mere fact of chronological age.

Shifts can also be identified in changing patterns of motivation during the life course. Kohlen (1959) has described two contrasting motivational tendencies: expansion and restriction. The need for expansion, in the sense of increasing achievement, sense of significance, and recognition, dominates in the early years, while restriction comes to the fore in the later years. Expansion and restriction play themselves out throughout the life course, but the needs for continuing self-esteem and the means for satisfying them vary throughout life. As one advances in age, the titre of life disruptions and crises increases. While such changes may elicit a mourning reaction, the result need not be incapacitating, particularly if positive, restitutive processes can be set in motion. Successful adjustment in old age is more likely when the individual possesses a positive self-image and identification, is able to keep busy, can occupy significant interpersonal roles, and maintains a variety of social contacts and activities.

Values

In addition, there have been described shifts in value orientations between middle and old age. Erikson (1959) originally suggested such shifts in terms of the movement from generativity, which was characteristic of middle age, to ego integrity, which became predominant in the later stages of life. Erikson characterized this in terms of the capacity to accept one's own life as having been inevitable, appropriate, and meaningful, and opposed this to the sense of despair, which manifested itself primarily in terms of the fear of death.

A further differentiation of this approach was offered by Peck (1955). He described the predominant values of middle age as follows: (1) the value of wisdom over physical powers, consistent with the decline in physical capacity with age; (2) an emphasis on socializing in preference to sexualizing human relationships, again consistent with the impact of biological changes; (3) the value of cathectic flexibility over cathectic impoverishment, emphasizing the adaptive importance of the ability to develop new emotional investments in people and objects as the changing patterns of life and loss evolve; and (4) the value of mental flexibility over mental rigidity, emphasizing the need for cognitive adaptability in addition to emotional adaptability.

There is a shift in this schema from the values of middle age to those of old age, here enlarging on Erikson's notion of ego integrity versus despair. The values include: (1) ego differentiation in preference to work-role preoccupation, emphasizing the need to develop a sense of value of one's self for what one is rather than for what one does in the work situation and other life roles; (2) bodily transcendence as against bodily preoccupation, emphasizing the importance of the achievement of sufficient ego autonomy from physical constraints and limitations; and finally (3) ego transcendence as against ego preoccupation, particularly coming to terms with the idea of one's own death and a sense of acceptance and satisfaction with the life one has lived and the heritage one leaves behind.

Loss

Loss is an inevitable part of life, and in later life the pace of loss increases, as does its psychic meaning. The losses affect nearly every facet of the individual's life experience. There are material losses connected with diminished income; there are personal and interpersonal losses involving the deaths of friends, relatives, and the more casual acquaintances who form the context of one's daily life. There are losses in one's professional and occupational roles, and even of one's role within the family constellation. The family constellation itself is evolving and changing, losing members through death or relocation and adding members through birth and adoption.

There are even physiological changes which alter the individual's relationship to his environment and create a loss of contact or attunement to which the older person must continually adapt. Such changes include perceptual changes, related to the diminished capacity of vision and hearing particularly, as well as changes in motor capacity—both strength and fine-motor ability—which affect the individual's capacity to manipulate and deal with his environment. Consequently, there is a significant reduction in both the quality and quantity of information input and a reduced capacity to respond quickly and effectively, especially in the performance of complex tasks. Thus, the sensory motor performance of the elderly person tends to be limited by the reduced capacity of central processing mechanisms, putting a limit on the capacity for achievement within any given time span. Older individuals can compensate for this deficit by taking a longer time for learning or task performance; but if the increase in time is not available, there is an inevitable decrement in the accuracy of performance, particularly when continuous or coordinated series of movements are called for (Campbell 1974).

In addition to the effects of such natural decrements in function and capacity, there are also negative cultural expectations which create a stereotypical role or status into which the elderly person is forced by social pressure (Campbell 1974). Modern industrial cultures, particularly the highly success- and achievement-oriented American culture, define success in terms of money, activity, and youth. The failure of older individuals to measure up to such implicit standards tends to create a negative self-image and constitues a self-fulfilling prophecy for the elderly. Zinberg (1976) has described the process in relationship to sexual activity in the following terms:

> Although careful studies in this area have made it clear that such convictions are based not on physiology but on a legacy of Western puritanism, the prophecy of a decline in sexual activity in the aged is often self-fulfilling. Many older people accept the cultural stereotype and unconsciously inhibit their sexual activities and, more basically, their desires. (pp. 131–132)

Butler and Lewis (1973) have described the losses and significant changes affecting the experience and adaptation of the elderly in terms of external factors and intrinsic factors. The external factors include personal losses of loved and significant persons, socioeconomic adversities, undesired retirement, cultural devaluations producing feelings of uselessness and forced isolation, and social segregation. The internal factors include items such as personality organization, physical illness affecting both brain function and perceptual capacity, age-specific changes in bodily size and appearance (thus affecting the organization and integration of the body image), diminished capacity to respond quickly and understand readily, and, finally, experiences of body dissolution and approaching death. There is an increasing loss of physical energy, mental acuity, humor, and a sense of freedom and autonomy. There is a shift from being an active participant in life to being a passive spectator. Under the pressure of such losses, the individual becomes increasingly apprehensive and psychically debilitated. Complaints of depression, fatigue, or sleeplessness can create further isolation and make interactions with the elderly person increasingly discomforting for children and friends, leading to avoidance and gradual isolation. There is often a feeling of rage and a sense of betrayal at one's failing body, one's family, and one's fate. The gradual imposition of restrictions in diet, drinking, activities, and mobility imposes a further stressful burden and a sense of frustration that seem to make life hardly worth living.

Rochlin (1965) has emphasized the role of impoverishment in the aging process. Aging differs from preceding periods of development in that the conflicts or their residues in the last phase of life are experienced less in terms of loss with subsequent restitution than as loss and consequent impoverishment. Moreover, the sense of impoverishment comes to play an increasingly dominant and definitive role as the aging process advances.

Mourning

Such losses carry with them their inevitable burden of mourning. Pollock (1978, 1981) has described the cycle of loss and restitution in terms of a "mourning-liberation process." In his view, normal aging involves a continual mourning process which allows the individual to work through the painful detachment of libido from the earlier phases of the life cycle, so that energy is released for investment in creative potentialities in the present. He describes four possible outcomes of the mourning-liberation process:

1. Successfully completing the process, leading to greater freedom to follow newer creative paths.
2. Arrests in the development of the mourning process, requiring special therapeutic intervention so that the process can continue to develop in a normal fashion.
3. Fixation at various points in the mourning process; regression to these points can result when later stresses put strain on the integrative capacity of the organism.
4. Pathological mourning with development of abnormalities and serious difficulties.

Pollack (1981) comments:

In order to age successfully, the individual should be capable of mourning past states of self-organization, of reorganizing the reality of what is no more, and of successfully accepting present and future realities. Unsuccessful and pathological aging may be reflective of unsuccessful mourning-liberation processes and so constitutes a basis for aging or developmental pathology or deviance. (p. 582)

Narcissistic Loss

A critical variable is that having to do with the narcissistic vicissitudes of old age. As I see it, the basic problem of aging is that of narcissistic loss. The losses associated with advancing age form a type of narcissistic assault. As Rochlin (1965) writes:

> The greatest test of narcissism is aging or old age. All that has come to represent value and with which narcissism has long been associated is jeopardized by growing old. The skills, mastery, and powers, all painfully acquired, which provided gratification as they functioned to effect adaptation, wane in the last phase of life. One's resources, energies, adaptability, and functions, the intimacies of relationships upon which one depended, family and friends, are continually depleted and lost. The longer one lives (as the longer one gambles), the more regularly one loses. Aging is an assault upon narcissism. Just as in early life the precariousness of existence is made clear to the child, so the friability of what is valued is made plain to the aging. Narcissism, therefore, has no less a role in aging than it had in the years before. (pp. 377–378)

Such narcissistic traumata are accompanied by an increase in the titre of unresolved narcissistic needs. Along with this, there is also an increase in the level of aggression and aggressive conflicts. This includes what Kohut (1972) has described as "narcissistic rage." In addition, narcissistic trauma can produce depression, along with heightened anxiety, increased propensity for guilt, loss of hope, and diminution of the capacity for restitution. Such narcissistic depletion may also result in the development of paranoid trends as a defense against narcissistic loss, eventuating in forms of criticism, blaming, increasing disengagement, and even paranoid projection (Meissner 1978b). It is in these terms that we can think of the problems of the "generation gap" as an expression of these trends.

Perhaps the greatest loss of all is the encroaching deprivation and the ultimate narcissistic trauma of death. This raises the specter of loss without the concomitant elements of restitution. Here Rochlin's (1965) words are again to the point:

> Aging is the only phase of human development which is characteristically, generally, and regularly resisted. The resistance to aging reveals an awareness that impoverishment well under-

stood in advance leads to the end of life. . . . Life is made more
precarious, when it nears its end, by the replacement of a promise
of restitution with the disquiet of impoverishment, to which, in
some cases, the danger of deprivation is added. (pp. 365–366)

In terms of the relation of social factors to such inner deprivations,
one might speculate about the ways in which society deprives older
people of the promise of restitution. This certainly applies to the means
society makes available for such restitution, even in the basic material
terms of financial security and a reasonably secure, comfortable life.
Another form of deprivation stems from our society's value systems,
which tend to deprive people of the restitutive resources of religious
belief systems. Such systems, particularly those having to do with life
after death and the promised rewards for religious fidelity in the next
life, serve as a powerful resource for restoring and recovering the
potential trauma of narcissistic loss in death. Insofar as society undermines and deprives people of the resource without effectively replacing
it, it compounds the damage.

It would be totally incorrect to assume that, in addressing a theory
of narcissism in this context, we would be opting for a form of totally
internalized and self-involuted understanding. Narcissism has to do with
the integration and cohesion of the self, and the self can be defined and
maintained only in its relation to, as well as its distinction from, others. A
theory of narcissistic loss in old age must explain how social influences
both impinge on and undermine the capacity for adaptive reaction in the
aged, as well as the ways in which social functions and structures can
provide the restitutive aspects of narcissistic equilibrium.

The Pathology of Aging

Much of our discussion to this point has dealt with aspects of the aging
process that might be considered relatively normal, or at least need not
necessarily lend themselves to pathological deviation. At this point,
however, we can turn our attention more specifically to forms of
psychopathology associated with aging. For the most part, the distinction
between normal aging processes and the more deviant manifestations of
psychopathology is clear enough, but there are also times when it
becomes difficult to make a clear distinction.

There is in fact no clear line of demarcation that can be drawn
between normal functioning and the deviation brought about by disease.

The transition is gradual from one to the other, and we reach a consensus that the picture presented to us is pathological only when it exceeds a certain degree of deviation. But the extent of that degree can be relative, depending on the extent of the patient's own tolerance or defenses against deviant functioning, and on the tolerance of the social milieu in which the patient lives for whatever deviation may be involved. In the case of psychological disorder, the judgment of society plays a crucial role in the determination of what is acceptable and what becomes labeled as sickness (Campbell 1974).

Developmental Perspective

As is clear from our previous discussion, the symptomatic picture which every older patient presents is a by-product of internal structural changes brought about in his central nervous system by the aging process itself, and the pattern of social changes that take place around him, including not only social attitudes and expectations but also changes in family relationships, the loss of loved ones, changes in lifestyle and security as a result of retirement, et cetera. Moreover, as Gutmann (1981) has emphasized, it is often helpful to understand the psychopathology of later life from a developmental perspective rather than from a perspective that is exclusively deprivational.

The pathology that develops in the elderly individual may not always represent merely regression in the face of irreversible losses but may also reflect the emergence of a significant developmental potential that has not found an appropriate response in a receptive environment. Thus, from the point of view of pathological deviation, the paraphrenia of old age may be seen as a form of regressive defense against the rage at the losses and disappointments of life; but from the point of view of developmental process, it may also reflect an underlying need to give meaning, context, and organization to the changing context of life experience. As Gutmann observes:

> When the older person's capacity to grasp the underlying pattern, the structures that lie behind appearances, meets a sponsoring psycho-social ecology, this capacity emerges in its matured form as wisdom; when there is no culture to recognize, value, and sponsor the emerging potential, it may come under the sway of the pathological rather than the mature sectors of the personality, to emerge as paranoia. (p. 495)

Much of the symptomatology and deviant behavior seen clinically in older patients is equivalently an attempt to deal with shifts in sexual role functioning and to regain in some degree the narcissistic equilibrium that has been thrown off stride by a variety of losses and narcissistic incursions. In terms of the shifts from activity to passivity and their connotations for the maintenance of sexual identity, the recourse to alcohol may become a vehicle for the attempt to compensate for lost potency and power. Alcohol, as a source of instant machismo and of release from inhibitions of aggression, becomes almost a metaphor for masculine power. At the same time, it satisfies regressive oral needs so that in the course of the same drinking bout the alcoholic may be both an omnipotent superman and an impotent infant (Gutmann 1981).

Psychosomatic symptoms, including heart attacks, which are epidemic in the aging population, may also serve as a channel for dealing with passivity in ways that are socially acceptable. One can be passive and dependent on the hospital or doctor, whereas such dependency would be intolerable otherwise. The spirit is willing, but the flesh is weak. It is not the patient who is weak and asking for help but his damaged body that is weak, dependent, feminine. For others, however, it is denial that plays the dominant part in their illness. These may well be the type A personalities (Friedman and Rosenman 1974), who do not tolerate the changes of the aging process but drive themselves to a premature heart attack. The correlations between type A characteristics and coronary heart disease begin to weaken around the age of 50, when many such driven, hypermasculine men begin to accept the inherent duality of their own psychic organization. Others, however, increase the tempo of their masculine striving, constantly seeking for new conquests and new antagonists. They deny any passive wishes and project the responsibility for them onto the objects of those wishes. Similarly, divorce in the aging population may have its source not only in the male's seeking for new virility but also in his seeking for a way to externalize emerging passivity in a newly found object, who can become the receptacle for the projection of feminine wishes. The aging wife, who has in turn become more autonomous and assertive, is thus discarded in favor of a more dependent, adoring, and younger woman.

For the woman, the aging process carries its burden of liability as well. The most frequent label is depression, usually associated with loss. The patient is suffering from the loss of procreative functions through menopause, from the empty nest, from her husband's distance and disinterest, or from the pain of widowhood. But the losses are not merely external; they touch the inner core of her sense of herself and inflict a narcissistic wound that is reflected in the loss of self-esteem.

If there are men who find it difficult to tolerate the increase in their own inherent femininity, there are also women who have the same difficulty with their own increasing masculinity. They are threatened by the developmental shifts in sex roles between themselves and their husbands, and are conflicted and frightened by their own aggression. They fear that their growing independence and assertiveness will render them somehow less feminine, less desirable. They may try to live out their aggressiveness vicariously through their husbands or children, or look to the husband to control these aggressive impulses. If the husband becomes sick or dies, the problem is exacerbated. They accuse themselves of having caused their husband's death and punish themselves through the depression for their unconscious guilt. Their depression is compounded not only of the loss of the loved object but also of the upsurge of unacceptable aggressive and hostile parts of themselves.

Dementia

Whatever the form of psychopathology presenting in the aging or elderly individual, the psychiatrist must keep in mind the sometimes pervasive influence of organic factors in the production of symptoms. The symptoms of senile dementia are usually insidious in onset, but may erupt in an acute delirium with restlessness and even auditory and visual hallucinations, and sometimes paranoid suspiciousness leading to violent outbursts. The patient is usually left with a dementia that is more severe than was previously suspected. Perceptual functions and the capacity for memory registration are impaired early in the process of deterioration, and cognitive functions are generally deficient. The patient begins to have difficulty remembering—first, recent events, then names, then the names of objects. He becomes confused about time and space and may be increasingly unable to differentiate between reality and fantasy, between facts and imaginings, and between perceptions and hallucinations.

The dementia may often have a strong depressive coloring, which makes for diagnostic difficulties. It is crucial in the evaluation of such patients to be able to discriminate between a true dementia and a senile depression. Of patients who become so demented, most will show a picture of simple dementia; but about 20 percent will develop a predominantly paranoid symptomatology, and another 10 percent will develop predominantly affective symptoms (Campbell 1974). There is also a risk that the elderly depressed patient may be misdiagnosed as having a form of dementia. Depression is usually accompanied with a slowing of psychomotor processes; but when the patient is over 65, this may be perceived as cognitive deterioration and the diagnosis of dementia made without paying adequate attention to the underlying depression (Weinberg 1980).

The misdiagnosis of a functional depressive disorder as an organic dementia is a frequent occurrence, as Wells (1978, 1982) has pointed out. The diagnosis is particularly difficult where depression is found in patients who also suffer from cognitive impairments. Apparently, the greater the degree of cognitive impairment, the less the likelihood of a coexisting depression; and by the same token, there tends to be a higher titre of depression in mildly impaired patients (Reifler et al. 1982).

Wells (1978) has also described a syndrome of depressive pseudo-dementia in which patients with a functional psychiatric disorder present symptoms and findings closely resembling those of dementia. Other work has emphasized the complexity of the differential diagnosis by reason of the fact that depressive pseudodementia may be accompanied by profound cognitive impairment without necessarily being true dementia. However, the depressive syndrome may also occur in the context of a true dementia, which may further compound the difficulties of diagnosis (McAllister and Price 1982).

Depression

One of the most frequent forms of mental disturbance found in the elderly is depression. Depression may present with frank clinical symptoms and findings, but it may also occur in more latent forms, preventing both the patient and the doctor from readily recognizing it as such. It may also appear in various disguises, as in, for example, the form of hypochondriacal symptoms or psychosomatic difficulties, or may be a component, as we have suggested, of an organic brain syndrome. In elderly people, more often than not, the depression is not simply a form of sadness or unhappiness but involves painful feelings of dejection and diminished self-esteem; cognitive deficits, which may manifest themselves in a slowing of thinking, of obsessive ruminations about various wrongdoings or about death; and alternations in psycho-motor activity, usually in the form of retardation, but also at times expressing themselves in restlessness, pacing, and agitation.

At times, depressions can take a simple retarded form, with a combination of symptoms including hypochondriacal concerns, consti-pation, insomnia, abulia, and a general slowing of reactions and thinking, which may at times be mistaken for organic confusion. When the depression takes an agitated form, it tends to be precipitated by some crisis arising from a significant loss or from the alteration of the individual's life situation due to, for example, the death of a spouse or a close friend, the discovery of a life-threatening illness, or the loss of some significant status or role. In the face of inevitable losses, the older patient feels deserted and rejected, which leads to the loss of self-respect and self-esteem, compounded by the sense of helplessness and worthlessness. The increased incidence of alcoholism in old age may also be related to depression, the drinking serving to conceal the loss of self-esteem. Drinking to excess may in fact be the only obvious symptom of an underlying depression.

In addition to the depressions described, Cath (1967) has described a syndrome of depletion, which is marked by the failure of the ability to restore losses and declining capacity. In this depletion syndrome, self-reproach is rare and the other mechanisms of depression are not predominant features. While in depression ego functioning is impaired and self-esteem lowered, narcissistic aims are neither changed nor given up. In depletion, however, these narcissistically invested aims are progressively surrendered, and self-reproach is lacking. Early in depletion, there may be experiences of isolation of thought and affect, ego splitting, depersonalization, and ruminations about the past. Ego functions are gradually impaired and superego functions disrupted, so that guilt is minimized. If the depletion process can be reversed, the first sign of improvement may be seen in a regained capacity on the part of the individual to become depressed. The notion of depletion lies very close to the problem of impoverishment as described by Rochlin (1965) (see pp. 374–376).

The depression may follow a fairly predictable course. There may be vague and disquieting notions of self-blame, which gradually evolve into a conviction that earlier pecadillos or failings are responsible for the feelings. The patient will ruminate about events in his past life in a relentless search for failings or sins that suddenly assume an importance which is quite out of proportion to their real significance. The patient becomes obsessed with guilt for his supposed misdeeds or even simply bad thoughts. He seeks ways to atone for his sins and to expiate his guilt, usually in an unsuccessful attempt to undo his imagined wrongs.

Some patients will express their inner feelings of worthlessness in the form of complaints of a lack of material worth. Despite adequate savings or an adequate retirement income, they will become convinced that they are in fact poor, have no money, cannot afford to buy anything, particularly for themselves, and cannot even afford treatment. Other patients will become obsessed with the idea of death, brooding about the time they may have left in their lives, and moodily pondering how and when they will die. Guilt and depression tend to deepen remorselessly, so that the patient feels trapped, helpless, and hopeless. He may even begin to think of suicide as the only escape from his misery. The suicide then may become an appropriate punishment for the evil of his imagined misdeeds. Such suicidal thoughts must be taken seriously, since the likelihood of successful suicide increases with age.

From the point of view of the paranoid process, the various forms of depression are a predictable outcome of the patterns of change and loss that are built into the aging process. As we have seen, aging carries with it not only internal changes, in the loss of various physical and psychic capacities, but also inevitable alterations in social role and functioning, in status, and in the patterns of involvement with one's environment. While the manner and degree of such disengagement on the part of older people seems to be a matter of considerable individual variation, a critical variable remains: the degree of narcissistic vulnerability in the individual's personality structure, and the residual capacity that he or she may possess for organizing and implementing restitutive resources, so that some meaningful degree of narcissistic balance can be reconstituted. Thus, the forces that are involved in the aging process, which drive the narcissistic balance toward narcissistic loss and depletion, and inflict traumatic injury on the individual's narcissistic vulnerability, tend to work in a direction of a depressive outcome, insofar as narcissistically valid and operative restitutional resources are not available.

The other motif that plays itself out as a recurrent theme in the aging process is that of victimization. If the sense of increasing victimization is not in some degree countered by a capacity for assertive and effective action, by a sense of retaining a measure of environmental control and mastery, the sequel will follow its inevitable course toward increasing depression and the expression of the dynamics inherent in the victim-introject. Consequently, what is clearly expressed in the pathology of depression is a realignment of the introjective configurations, both narcissistic and aggressive, to bring the elements of narcissistic vulnerability and inferiority, as well as those of helplessness and victimization, to the fore. Thus, the victim-introject and the inferior narcissistic introject come to dominate the inner organization of the personality structure.

Case History

There are often interesting complications that work themselves out in the evolution of this sequence. A case from my own experience may help to illustrate some of these points. The patient first came to therapy in her early 70s with a complaint of an increasingly severe depression, accompanied by a loss of appetite and a refusal to eat that was becoming a matter of significant concern for her family. At the time of our first visit, there had been a weight loss of some 15 pounds. The patient began by focusing on her agonizing feelings of guilt but found it difficult to share what the guilt feelings were about. She was desperately fearful that I would be disapproving or condemning of her actions, a reaction that she would have found devastating. After some reassurance, she finally took the plunge and began to tell about some of the pecadillos in her early life, going back to her teen-age years, when she had been the object of occasional sexual advances on the part of older men. It seemed clear that in her depressive ruminations she had fastened upon these early events as being the central sin around which she organized the belief that her life was a failure, that she was condemned to the everlasting torment of hell, and upon which she fastened the full force of her guilt feelings.

In exploring these episodes, it became clear that they were relatively innocent in nature, involved little more than petting, and in none of them had the sexual activity ever progressed to actual intercourse. One such event stood out with particular vividness. As a young girl, she had been befriended by a young couple whom she often visited. One night she had joined them for dinner, and a particularly violent storm began to rage outside, so that the couple urged her to spend the night with them. In the middle of the night, the husband got into bed with her and began to fondle her and touch her genitals. She was terrified, and felt torn between her fear that he might assault her sexually and her dread of what might happen if she protested. She was afraid that the wife would wake up and discover what was happening and that she would be the cause of the breakup of their marriage. The husband finally gave up and went back to his own bed, but the patient spent the rest of the night sleepless, obsessing and worrying about what had happened. By the time morning came, she felt riddled with guilt; and when the wife cooked a lovely breakfast, she found herself completely unable to eat.

When I asked the patient when her depression and her difficulties in eating had begun, she replied that it had been about two years prior to her coming to see me. When I inquired what was happening at the time, she said that shortly before that her husband, who was several years her senior, had had an operation for an enlarged prostate. It came out that, as part of the sequelae of the operation, the husband was impotent and that ever since then he had not approached his wife sexually and had resisted any occasion on which they might have had sexual activity. The patient felt rejected, abandoned, and unloved.

The next piece of the puzzle to emerge, prompted by the obvious question as to what might underlie her vulnerability to such feelings of rejection and abandonment, was the fact that her own parents had died within months of each other when she was quite young. They were apparently carried off by one of the virulent influenza epidemics that swept the country at a time when the patient would have been only about 5 or 6 years of age. She recalled that the family was broken up and that all of the children were put out to live in other people's homes. It was clear that the loss, the sense of abandonment, and the unsatisfied yearning of a small child for love, affection, and protection had left their lasting scars.

The early loss left the patient with an unsatisfied yearning for closeness, affection, and love. She felt that her experience of living in a foster home had provided her with little of that, even though her foster parents were decent people and provided her with adequate food and clothing. But the love and cherishing that she felt would have been hers through her own parents were never compensated. As the young girl carried these pressing needs into her adolescent experience, they began to find some satisfaction, but in the context of sexual involvement. The sense of sinfulness and guilt became associated with the satisfaction of these underlying affectional needs. When these same needs were once again stirred by her husband's withdrawal and impotence, the same feelings of guilt and self-accusation once again rose to the surface, along with the resurgence of her frustrated longings for love and affection, and carried with them the same symptom that she had experienced in one of the most crucial of the guilt-inducing events from the past, namely, an inability to eat. The failure to eat thus served a twofold purpose: the first as a punishment for her wishes for love and affection, which in part she saw as sinful and guilty, the second of gaining her an increased titre of concern, attention, and expressions of affection from a variety of people in her environment.

The key figure from whom she sought attention and affection in the here and now, however, was her husband. Because of his own inhibitions and conflicts and his feelings that, because of his impotence, he was no longer a worthy sexual companion to his wife and would be unable to satisfy her, the response from him that she desired was not immediately forthcoming. After the pieces of the picture had been put together and the patient began to have some insight into the underlying roots of her symptoms, it took some further encouragement and discussion about the ways in which she could take a more active role in engaging her husband in expressions of affection and even sexual involvement, even if he were unable to have an erection and to complete the sexual act.

The patient had to work through some of her own inhibitions in initiating such sexual activity, in coming to accept and integrate her own sexual wishes and desires, and in finding ways to initiate more meaningful contacts with her husband. As these various aspects of the treatment program gradually took effect, the depression lifted, the patient became happy and contented, her appetite returned, and she began to put on some of the weight she had lost. And as a final footnote, for those who do not believe that brief psychotherapy can be successfully accomplished with elderly patients, the whole thing from first visit to last took only eight sessions.

The Paranoid Process

What seems evident is that the sense of loss and abandonment that came as the result of the unfortunate and nearly concurrent deaths of her parents and a subsequent farming out to relatively cold and unaffectionate foster parents had an impact on the inner organization of this patient's introjective configuration. There was a deep sense of herself as unloved and unlovable, a vulnerability to rejection and abandonment, a sense of shame and worthlessness—all reverberating with the implications of both the victim-introject and the narcissistically inferior introject. These played themselves out in the patient's adult illness.

We can also surmise that the more repressed elements of entitlement, and even of aggressive wishes that came too close to realization for an oedipal-aged child in the closely linked deaths of both mother and father, were also at work, but in highly repressed and relatively unavailable form. While this patient had managed to keep things in relatively good balance during a long and successful life as a married woman, wife, and mother, it was the gradual ebbing away of the supports for her narcissistic integrity that left her vulnerable to the critical loss of love and affection in her husband's withdrawal. Her children had grown up and left home. While she was relatively well preserved, she had nonetheless lost the bloom of youthful beauty and physical attractiveness; and these losses all contributed to the increasing instability and fragility of her narcissistic equilibrium.

Paranoid Illnesses

The other major form of pathology that one sees in old age is that of paranoia. Gitelson (1948) has observed that, as elderly people become more and more isolated, they tend increasingly to become sensitive to slights from others. This is related to the increase in narcissistic vulnerability and the increasing sense of a lack of meaningfulness or significance in their interactions with others. Thus, older persons may withdraw from such interactions with others and may become increasingly preoccupied with the past, when their lives were more meaningful and self-esteem was better supported. When such individuals feel that their prerogatives are not being adequately acknowledged, they become resentful and querulous. Their sensitivity may become heightened to the point of frank paranoia.

Gitelson cites the case of a man who had been an insatiable go-getter, the characteristic type A personality, who had spent a lifetime successfully overcoming obstacles and was suddenly incapacitated by a coronary occlusion. He had made a reasonable recovery physically, but the final outcome was one of bitterness and angry resentment, accompanied by paranoid ideas. The facts that he had been forced to slow down and that during his absence, occasioned by his illness, his business had been carried on quite successfully by a younger associate were difficult for him to tolerate. His delusion took the form of a conviction that his business associate and his doctors had plotted together in a conspiracy to remove him from the business. He was convinced that he was not really as ill as he had been told. The paranoid stance allowed him to preserve his sense of status and self-esteem and to preserve the style of hostile competitiveness that had begun in his earlier rivalries with his younger brothers. He could not tolerate the sense of inner helplessness and vulnerability that would have made him incapable of carrying on the competition and of winning out over his younger rivals.

Late Paraphrenia. Frank paranoid disorders are fairly frequent among the elderly. Roth (1955) used the term "late paraphrenia" to describe paranoid disorders in elderly patients in whom there are no signs of organic deficit or primary affective disease. The diagnosis does not include late manifestations of schizophrenia or schizophreniform psychoses, even when these develop in relatively older patients. About 10 percent of psychiatric admissions over age 60 receive this diagnosis. The age of onset tends to be from 55 on, with an average age of 70. The onset is usually insidious and is found much more frequently in women. Both males and females are more likely never to have been married. About a third of these patients have severe defects in hearing or vision (Kay and Roth 1961). Hearing losses later in life tend to be relatively gradual, and the connection with paranoid reactions is often observed. It may be that in the face of a gradually increasing hearing deficit, of which the individual is unaware, paranoid thinking emerges as a cognitive attempt to organize and explain the gaps that are left by not being able to hear what people are saying. However, the paranoid tendency is more often an extension and exacerbation of underlying character structure, which may have been manifested in earlier life by a variety of schizoid and paranoid traits.

The paraphrenic condition itself tends to develop rapidly, and the patient moves from a state of moderate suspiciousness, mistrust, and distortion to a full-blown paranoid state with highly developed delusions and a projective system. The delusions may be persecutory in form—the patient may suspect his family or friends of trying to steal his property or to get rid of him in some fashion—or they may be predominantly erotic in form, with delusional convictions that some other person is madly in love with him, even though the object of this infatuation may be someone the patient has never met. Often, the object is a popular or prominent political or entertainment personality. In other respects, the condition is quite similar to other familiar forms of paranoid psychosis.

Treatment

The views toward psychological treatment of elderly patients have certainly changed radically in the last half century since Freud (1933) voiced his opinion that the psychical rigidity associated with age would limit the therapeutic effectiveness of psychoanalysis. In subsequent years, a number of authors have pointed out that therapeutic work with patients in advanced age groups was not only possible but potentially quite successful. Even in the 1970s, King (1974, 1980), Sandler (1978), and Shainess (1979) all reported on the successful undertaking of psychoanalysis with patients in the older age brackets. There are even indications that, even when organic deterioration is found in the clinical picture, ego functions may be lost, but they do not remain unavailable forever. Given the possibility of appropriate psychotherapeutic intervention, function may indeed be recovered (Grunes 1981).

Elderly patients in fact bring certain elements to the therapeutic situation that may serve to promote the therapeutic work. While they may fear the illness that may limit or terminate their lives, they also bring a hope that the physician will be able to help. Frequently enough, in the contexts of loneliness and isolation from which so many older people suffer, they bring an intense desire for meaningful human context and attention. As King pointed out, elderly patients often come to treatment because of the increasing awareness of changes in their lives and the way in which the aging process affects their physical, psychological, and social well-being. For them, aging is a threatening prospect and brings with it fears of fragmentation or disintegration and death. But these threats to older patients bring a sense of dynamic and urgent necessity to their involvement in analytic treatment, and this motivation facilitates the establishment and consolidation of an effective therapeutic alliance that promotes and facilitates the therapeutic work.

Narcissistic Vulnerabilities

But the narcissistic vulnerabilities that underlie the patient's pathology also create difficulties in the treatment process. The sense of narcissistic vulnerability and depletion is the core issue that the psychotherapy and/ or psychoanalysis of the elderly patient must address. The sense of defeat, hopelessness, shame, impoverishment, and self-depletion are generally at the heart of the matter. The depletion in the sense of self, the gradual retrenchment from lifelong ideals, ambitions, and hopes, carry with them a burden of despair, disillusion, and diminished self-esteem. The patient's overburdening sense of depletion and shame must be recognized and accepted. If, in the face of the common paranoid propensity in the elderly, the sense of inner shame and narcissistic vulnerability is hidden or masked, it must be listened for, sought out, empathically and sensitively elicited. From our present perspective, this approach is equivalent to the gradual focusing and descriptive artic- ulation of the narcissistic introjective configuration which is central to the treatment of all forms of narcissistic pathology.

Pathogenic Introjections

The approach to psychopathology from the perspective of the paranoid process would envision part of the patient's difficulty as the recrudes- cence and reactivation of pathogenic introjections, which then give rise to various forms of phenomenological disorder. According to the basic paradigms of depressive and paranoid illness, the depressed patient finds himself increasingly victimized and his narcissistic supports increasingly undermined, so that the aspects of the victim-introject and the narcissistically inferior introject come to play the dominant role in his evolving sense of himself. As these introjective elements come to dominate the organization of his inner world, they express themselves inevitably in the form of depressive psychopathology.

The paranoid patient, by the same token, finds himself also to be subject to the vicissitudes of increasing loss of control over his interaction with his environment, increasing passivity, and increasing incapacity for self-assertion and mastery over events and circumstances of his life. He too becomes increasingly a victim and finds himself increasingly deprived of the sources of narcissistic reinforcement and gratification. Unlike the depressive patient, however, he counters this trend by mobilizing essentially narcissistic defenses, dealing with underlying aggressive impulses by their externalization and displacement to persecutory objects, and countering the undermining of narcissistic integrity by a resort to feelings of superiority and even grandiosity. Clinically, one often finds that elder depressed patients become paranoid as their disease process continues. This is not surprising in view of the underlying structure of the introjective components.

It should be noted that while most severe forms of paranoid pathology—for example, the late paraphrenias—are not very frequent in occurrence, nonetheless, minor and relatively less intense manifestations of paranoid activity can be found quite widely distributed in elderly patients with emotional difficulties. Even in depressed patients, there may be signs of sensitivity, suspiciousness, and guardedness of minor degree but nonetheless conveying an unmistakably paranoid flavor. The therapeutic direction in such cases seeks to help the patient to redress the imbalance that has been created by this pathological configuration and to help the patient both to feel less victimized and to bring back toward a state of better narcissistic equilibrium his sense of narcissistic vulnerability and depletion.

Reminiscence plays an important role in such work, insofar as it enables the patient to rescue the people, places, and circumstances of his life from insignificance. The ability to express feelings and memories, to engage in the therapeutic work, helps patients feel more in control, bolsters their sense of effective capacity, and fosters an increasing self-esteem. Patients who are caught in the grip of pathogenic introjects often interpret or view factors in their experience in a distorted fashion, which serves to reinforce the pathogenic introjective configurations. While the patient may indeed be victimized by the aging process and the losses and constraints it imposes on him, he may not be as victimized as he feels. The patient similarly may feel humiliated and narcissistically depleted, but a renewed focus on the resources that remain available to him and on the factors that might sustain his sense of self-regard and significance may help to redress the narcissistic imbalance.

Transference and Countertransference

As in all therapeutic endeavors, transference and countertransference play a central role. It is sometimes difficult for the therapist to conceive how an elderly patient in his seventies or eighties can relate to a much younger therapist in terms of transference elements that might derive from the patient's relationship with his own parents. But, as King (1980) has observed, elderly patients may function within several different time-scales. Besides the chronological, the biological, and the psychological time-scales, the time-scale of the unconscious is paradoxically unconscious. The analyst may in fact be experienced as any significant figure from the elderly patient's past. By the same token, the patient may relate to a younger therapist in the form of "son" or "daughter" transference, in which the therapist becomes the understanding, interested, trustworthy, and supportive younger one to whom the older person looks for support, help, and protection. The ability of the patient to share these needs and concerns in the relationship, without having them ignored or dismissed, is an important contributing element.

The manner of the transference and its meaning on whatever level can be analyzed and understood in helpful ways. The patient may bring to the transference relationship a sense of helplessness and dependency which reflects the dynamics of the underlying victim-introject. The therapist's manner of dealing with such dependence, of helping the patient to understand its origins and its effect in his current difficulties, helps the patient to gain a greater sense of autonomy and capacity for self-understanding and self-help.

Countertransference also plays its part. A younger therapist may have difficulties in relating in a therapeutic manner to someone who is old enough to be his own parent or grandparent. The therapist must be concerned about the residues of his own parental transferences, the residuals of ambivalence or dependency conflicts that may derive from his own relationship with his parents, and the extent to which such unresolved conflictual elements in the transference serve only to contaminate the therapeutic relationship and undermine the alliance with the elderly patient.

By the same token, the therapist must take counsel with respect to his own prejudicial attitudes toward elderly patients and the extent to which he may or may not share, even implicitly, in commonly held negative social stereotypes of the elderly. Suppositions, for example, that the elderly patient is relatively helpless or weak, or that he may be incapable of gaining effective and meaningful insight into the therapy, not only can subvert the therapeutic work but also tend to reinforce the pathogenic picture of himself that the elderly patient tends to bring to the therapy in the first place.

References

Abbott, E.S. (1914). What is paranoia? *American Journal of Insanity* 71:29–40.

Abraham, K. (1924). A short study of the development of the libido. In *Selected Papers*, ed. D. Bryan and A. Strachey, pp. 478–501. New York: Basic Books.

Adler, G. (1979). The myth of the alliance with borderline patients. *American Journal of Psychiatry* 136:642–645.

———(1985). *Borderline Psychopathology and Its Treatment*. New York: Jason Aronson.

Adler, G., and Buie, Jr., D.H. (1972). The misuses of confrontation with borderline patients. *International Journal of Psychoanalytic Psychotherapy* 1:109–120.

Alexander, F. (1935). The problem of psychoanalytic technique. *Psychoanalytic Quarterly* 3:588–611.

———(1950). Analysis of the therapeutic factors in psychoanalytic treatment. *Psychoanalytic Quarterly* 19:482–500.

Allen, T.E. (1967). Suicidal impulse in depression and paranoia. *International Journal of Psycho-Analysis* 48:433–438.

Allport, T.W. (1958). *The Nature of Prejudice*. Garden City, NY: Doubleday.

Alvarez, A. (1972). *The Savage God*. New York: Random House.

Anastasi, A. (1974). Individual differences in aging. In *Aging: Its Challenge to the Individual and to Society*, ed. W.C. Bier, S.J., pp. 84–95. New York: Fordham University Press.

Andreasen, N.J., and Powers, P.S. (1974). Overinclusive thinking in mania and schizophrenia. *British Journal of Psychiatry* 125:452–456.

Anthony, E.J. (1981). The paranoid adolescent as viewed through psychoanalysis. *Journal of the American Psychoanalytic Association* 29:745–787.

Apfelbaum, B. (1966). Ego psychology: a critique of the structural approach to psychoanalytic theory. *International Journal of Psycho-Analysis* 47:451–475.

Appelbaum, S. A. (1963). The problem-solving aspect of suicide. *Journal of Projective Techniques and Personality Assessment* 27:259–268.

Aronson, G. (1977). Defence and deficit models: Their influence on therapy of schizophrenia. *International Journal of Psycho-Analysis* 58:11–16.

Aronson, M.L. (1964). A study of the Freudian theory of paranoia by means of the Rorschach test. In *Psychopathology: A Source Book*, eds. C.F. Reed, I.E. Alexander, and S.S. Tomkins, pp. 370–387. New York: Wiley.

Asch, S. S. (1976). Varieties of negative therapeutic reaction and problems of technique. *Journal of the American Psychoanalytic Association* 24:383–407.

———(1980). Suicide and the hidden executioner. *International Review of Psycho-Analysis* 7:51–60.

Bak, R. (1946). Masochism in paranoia. *Psychoanalytic Quarterly* 15:285–301.

Balint, M. (1950). Changing therapeutical aims and techniques in psychoanalysis. *International Journal of Psycho-Analysis* 31:117–124.

———(1968). *The Basic Fault*. London: Tavistock.

Barter, J. T., Swaback, D. O., and Todd, D. (1968). Adolescent suicide attempts: a follow-up study of hospitalized patients. *Archives of General Psychiatry* 19:523–527.

Beall, L. (1969). The dynamics of suicide: a review of the literature: 1897–1965. *Bulletin of Suicidology* March, pp. 2–16.

Beck, A. T. (1963). Thinking and depression: I. Idiosyncratic content and cognitive distortions. *Archives of General Psychiatry* 9:342–335.

Beres, D. (1971). Ego autonomy and ego pathology. *Psychoanalytic Study of the Child* 26:3–24.

Berezin, M. (1969). Sex and old age: a review of the literature. *Journal of Geriatric Psychiatry* 2:131–149.

———(1978). The elderly person. In *The Harvard Guide to Modern Psychiatry*, ed. A.M. Nicholi, pp. 541–564. Cambridge: Harvard University Press.

Berman, L. E. A. (1972). The role of amphetamine in a case of hysteria. *Journal of the American Psychoanalytic Association* 20:325–340.

Berman, S. (1970). Alienation: an essential process of the psychology of adolescence. *Journal of the Academy of Child Psychiatry* 9:233–250.

Bibring, E. (1953). The mechanism of depression. In *Affective Disorders*, ed. P. Greenacre, pp. 13–48. New York: International Universities Press.

Bier, S. J., W. C., ed. (1974). *Aging: Its Challenge to the Individual and to Society*. New York: Fordham University Press.

Bion, W.R. (1984). *Learning from Experience*. New York: Jason Aronson.

Blanck, G., and Blanck, R. (1974). *Ego Psychology: Theory and Practice*. New York: International Universities Press.

Blos, P. (1962). *On Adolescence: A Psychoanalytic Interpretation*. New York: Free Press.

Blum, H.P. (1972). Psychoanalytic understanding and psychotherapy of borderline regression. *International Journal of Psychoanalytic Psychotherapy* 1:46–60.

———(1974). The borderline childhood of the Wolf Man. *Journal of the American Psychoanalytic Association* 22:721–742.

———(1981). Object constancy and paranoid conspiracy. *Journal of the American Psychoanalytic Association* 29:789–813.

Botwinick, J. (1970). Geropsychology. *Annual Review of Psychology* 21:239–272.

Bouvet, M. (1958). Technical variation and the concept of distance. *International Journal of Psycho-Analysis* 39:211–221.

Breuer, J., and Freud, S. (1893–1985). Studies on hysteria. *Standard Edition* 2. London: Hogarth Press, 1955.

Brody, E.B. (1960). Borderline state, character disorder, and psychotic manifestations: some conceptual formulations. *Psychiatry*, 23:75–80.

Broen, Jr., W.E. (1966). Response disorganization and breadth of observation in schizophrenia. *Psychological Review* 73:579–585.

Broen, Jr., W.E., and Storms, L.J. (1966). Lawful disorganization: the process underlying a schizophrenic syndrome. *Psychological Review* 73:265–279.

Brunswick, R.M. (1928). A supplement to Freud's "History of an Infantile Neurosis." In *The Wolf Man by the Wolf Man*, ed. M. Gardiner, pp. 263–307. New York: Basic Books, 1971.

Buie, Jr., D.H., and Adler, G. (1972). The uses of confrontation with borderline patients. *International Journal of Psychoanalytic Psychotherapy* 1:90–106.

Bunch, J., and Barraclough, B. (1971). The influence of parental death and anniversaries upon suicide dates. *British Journal of Psychiatry* 118:621–626.

Bursten, B. (1973). Some narcissistic personality types. *International Journal of Psycho-Analysis* 54:287–300.

———(1978). A diagnostic framework. *International Review of Psycho-Analysis* 5:15–31.

Butler, R., and Lewis, M. (1973). *Aging and Mental Health: Positive Psychosocial Approaches*. St. Louis: Mosby.

Bychowski, G. (1953). The problem of latent psychosis. *Journal of the American Psychoanalytic Association* 1:484–503.

———(1966). Patterns of anger. *The Psychoanalytic Study of the Child* 21:172–192.

———(1967). Archaic object and alienation. *International Journal of Psycho-Analysis* 48:384–393.

Calogeras, R. C., and Capp, N. M. (1975). Drug use and aggression. *Bulletin of the Menninger Clinic* 39:329–344.

Cameron, N. (1959). Paranoid conditions and paranoia. In *American Handbook of Psychiatry. Volume I*, ed. S. Arieti, pp. 508–539. New York: Basic Books.

Cameron, N.S. (1951). Perceptual organization and behavior pathology. In *Perception: An Approach to Personality*, eds. R. R. Blake and G. V. Ramsey. New York: Ronald.

Campbell, R. J. (1974). Psychopathology of aging. In *Aging: Its Challenge to the Individual and to Society*, ed. W. C. Bier, S. J., pp. 96–116. New York: Fordham University Press.

Carr, A. C. (1963). Observations on paranoia and their relationship to the Schreber case. *International Journal of Psycho-Analysis* 44:195–200.

Carrington, P., and Ephron, H. S. (1975). Meditation as an adjunct to psychotherapy. In *New Dimensions in Psychiatry: A World View*, ed. S. Arieti, pp. 261–291. New York: Wiley.

Cath, S. H. (1967). Some dynamics of middle and later years: a study of depletion and restitution. In *Geriatric Psychiatry: Grief, Loss and Emotional Disorders in the Aging Process*, ed. M. A. Berezin and S. H. Cath, pp. 21–72. New York: International Universities Press.

Chapman, L. J., and Chapman, J. P. (1973). *Disordered Thought in Schizophrenia*. New York: Appleton-Century-Crofts.

Cohen, N. A. (1982). On loneliness and the aging process. *International Journal of Psycho-Analysis* 63:149–155.

Collum, J. M. (1972). Identity diffusion and the borderline maneuver. *Comprehensive Psychiatry* 13:179–184.

Corwin, H. (1972). The scope of therapeutic confrontation from routine to heroic. *International Journal of Psychoanalytic Psychotherapy* 1:68–89.

Crawford, M. P. (1971). Retirement and disengagement. *Human Relations* 24:255–278.

Cromwell, R. (1975). Assessment of schizophrenia. *Annual Review of Psychology* 26:593–619.

Cumming, E. (1963). New thoughts on the theory of disengagement. *International Social Science Journal* 15:377–393.

Cumming, E., and Henry, W. E. (1961). *Growing Old: The Process of Disengagement*. New York: Basic Books.

De Angelis, G. G. (1975). Theoretical and clinical approaches to the treatment of drug addiction: with special considerations for the adolescent drug abuser. *Journal of Psychedelic Drugs* 7:187–202.

de Busscher, J. (1963). Le theme de l'inceste dans les psychoses paranoides. *Acta Neurologica et Psychiatrica Belgica* 63:862–891.

Depue, R. A., and Woodburn, L. (1975). Disappearance of paranoid symptoms with chronicity. *Journal of Abnormal Psychology* 84:84–86.

Deutsch, H. (1942). Some forms of emotional disturbances and their relationship to schizophrenia. In *Neuroses and Character Types*, pp. 262–286. New York: International Universities Press, 1965.

_____(1967) *Selected Problems of Adolescence*. New York: International Universities Press.

Dickes, R. (1974). The concepts of borderline states: an alternative proposal. *International Journal of Psychoanalytic Psychotherapy* 3:1–27.

Dorpat, T. L. (1973). Suicide, loss, and mourning. *Life-Threatening Behavior* 3:213–224.

Dorpat, T. L., Jackson, J. K., and Ripley, H. S. (1965). Broken homes and attempted and completed suicide. *Archives of General Psychiatry* 12:213–216.

Douglas, J. (1968). *The Social Meanings of Suicide*. Princeton: Princeton University Press.

Durkheim, E. (1897). *Suicide: A Study in Suicidology*. Glencoe, IL: Free Press, 1951.

Edelheit, H. (1974). Crucifixion fantasies and their relation to the primal scene. *International Journal of Psycho-Analysis* 55:193–199.

Edwards, G. (1974). Drugs, drug dependence and the concept of plasticity. *Quarterly Journal of Studies on Alcohol* 35:176–195.

Eissler, K. R. (1958). Remarks on some variations in psychoanalytic technique. *International Journal of Psycho-Analysis* 39:222–229.

Erikson, E. H. (1956). The problem of ego identity. *Journal of the American Psychoanalytic Association* 4:56–121.

_____(1959). *Identity and the Life Cycle*. New York: International Universities Press.

_____(1963). *Childhood and Society*. New York: Norton.

_____(1964). *Insight and Responsibility*. New York: Norton.

Evans, J. R., Goldstein, M. J., and Rodnick, E. H. (1973). Premorbid adjustment, paranoid diagnosis, and remission. *Archives of General Psychiatry* 28:666–672.

Faberow, N. L., and Shneidman, E. S. (1961). *The Cry for Help*. New York: McGraw-Hill.

Fairbairn, W. R. D. (1958). On the nature and aims of psycho-analytic treatment. *International Journal of Psycho-Analysis* 39:374-385.

Fenichel, O. (1945). *The Psychoanalytic Theory of Neurosis*. New York: Norton.

Ferenczi, S., and Rank, O. (1923). *The Development of Psychoanalysis*. New York: Dover, 1956.

Foulds, G. A., and Owen, A. (1963). Are paranoids schizophrenics? *British Journal of Psychiatry* 109:674-679.

Fraiberg, S. (1955). Some considerations in the introduction to therapy in puberty. *The Psychoanalytic Study of the Child* 10:264-286.

Franco, E. A., and Malgaro, P. W. (1977). The relationship of A-B, field dependency, and emotional openness in paranoid and nonparanoid schizophrenics. *Journal of Clinical Psychology* 33:39-42.

Frederick, C. J., Resnick, H. L. P., and Wittlin, B. J. (1973). Self-destructive aspects of hard core addiction. *Archives of General Psychiatry* 28:579-585.

Freud, A. (1936). *The Ego and the Mechanisms of Defense. The Writings of Anna Freud, 2*. New York: International Universities Press, 1966.

Freud, S. (1887-1902). *The Origins of Psychoanalysis*. New York: Basic Books, 1954.

———(1888). Preface to the translation of Bernheim's *Suggestion. Standard Edition* 1:71-87. London: Hogarth Press, 1966.

———(1892-1893). A case of successful treatment by hypnosis. *Standard Edition* 1:115-128. London: Hogarth Press, 1966.

———(1892-1899). Extracts from the Fliess papers. *Standard Edition* 1:175-280. London: Hogarth Press, 1966.

———(1893-1895). Studies on hysteria. *Standard Edition* 2. London: Hogarth Press, 1955.

———(1895). A reply to criticism of my paper on anxiety neurosis. *Standard Edition* 3:123-139. London: Hogarth Press, 1962.

———(1896). Further remarks on the neuro-psychoses of defence. *Standard Edition* 3:157-185. London: Hogarth Press, 1962.

———(1900). The interpretation of dreams. *Standard Edition* 4 and 5. London: Hogarth Press, 1955.

———(1901). The psychopathology of everyday life. *Standard Edition* 6. London: Hogarth Press, 1960.

———(1904). Freud's psycho-analytic procedure. *Standard Edition* 7:247-254. London: Hogarth Press, 1953.

———(1905). Three essays on the theory of sexuality. *Standard Edition* 7:123-245. London: Hogarth Press, 1953.

———(1908). Hysterical phantasies and their relation to bisexuality. *Standard Edition* 9:155-166. London: Hogarth Press, 1959.

_____(1909a). Analysis of a phobia in a five-year-old boy. *Standard Edition* 10:1–149. London: Hogarth Press, 1957.

_____(1909b). Notes upon a case of obsessional neurosis. *Standard Edition* 10:153–318. London: Hogarth Press, 1957.

_____(1911). Psycho-analytic notes on an autobiographic account of a case of paranoia (dementia paranoides). *Standard Edition* 12:1–82. London: Hogarth Press, 1958.

_____(1911–15). Papers on technique. *Standard Edition* 12:85–171. London: Hogarth Press, 1958.

_____(1914a). On the history of the psychoanalytic movement. *Standard Edition* 14:1–66. London: Hogarth Press, 1957.

_____(1914b). On narcissism. *Standard Edition* 14:67–102. London: Hogarth Press, 1957.

_____(1916). Some character-types met with in psycho-analytic work. *Standard Edition* 14:309–333. London: Hogarth Press, 1957.

_____(1916–1917). Introductory lectures on psycho-analysis. *Standard Edition* 15 and 16. London: Hogarth Press, 1963.

_____(1917). Mourning and melancholia. *Standard Edition* 14:237–260. London: Hogarth Press, 1957.

_____(1918). From the history of an infantile neurosis. *Standard Edition* 17:1–122. London: Hogarth Press, 1957.

_____(1919). "A child is being beaten": A contribution to the study of the origin of sexual perversions. *Standard Edition* 17:175–204. London: Hogarth Press, 1957.

_____(1920a). Beyond the pleasure principle. *Standard Edition* 18:3–66. London: Hogarth Press, 1957.

_____(1920b). The psychogenesis of a case of homosexuality in a woman. *Standard Edition* 18:146–174. London: Hogarth Press, 1957.

_____(1922). Some neurotic mechanisms in jealousy, paranoia, and homosexuality. *Standard Edition* 18:221–232. London: Hogarth Press, 1955.

_____(1923). The ego and the id. *Standard Edition* 19:1–66. London: Hogarth Press, 1961.

_____(1930). Civilisation and its discontents. *Standard Edition* 21:57–145. London: Hogarth Press, 1961.

_____(1931). Female sexuality. *Standard Edition* 21:221–243. London: Hogarth Press, 1961.

_____(1933). New introductory lectures on psychoanalysis. *Standard Edition* 22:1–182. London: Hogarth Press, 1964.

_____(1937). Analysis terminable and interminable. *Standard Edition* 23:209–253. London: Hogarth Press, 1964.

———(1940) An outline of psychoanalysis. *Standard Edition* 23: 141–208. London: Hogarth Press, 1964.

Fried, M. (1970). Social problems and psychopathology. In *Social Psychology and Mental Health*, eds. H. Wechsler, L. Solomon, and B. M. Kramer, pp. 625–651. New York: Holt, Rinehart and Winston.

Friedman, A. S. (1970). Hostility factors and clinical improvement in depressed patients. *Archives of General Psychiatry* 23:524–537.

Friedman, M., Glasser, M., Laufer, E., Laufer, M., and Wohl, M. (1972). Attempted suicide and self-mutilation in adolescence: some observations from a psychoanalytic research project. *International Journal of Psycho-Analysis* 53:179–183.

Friedman, M. and Rosenman, R.H., (1974). Type A Behavior and your Heart. Greenwich, CT: Fawcett Publications.

Frijling-Schreuder, E. C. M. (1969). Borderline states in children. *The Psychoanalytic Study of the Child* 24:307–327.

Frosch, J. (1967a). Delusional fixity, sense of conviction, and the psychotic conflict. *International Journal of Psycho-Analysis* 48:475–495.

———(1967b). Severe regressive states during analysis: introduction. *Journal of the American Psychoanalytic Association* 15:491–507.

———(1970). Psychoanalytic considerations of the psychotic character. *Journal of the American Psychoanalytic Association* 18:24–50.

———(1983). *The Psychotic Process*. New York: International Universities Press.

Frosch, W. A. (1970). Psychoanalytic evaluation of addiction and habituation (Panel report). *Journal of the American Psychoanalytic Association* 18:209–218.

Galanter, M. (1976). The "intoxication state of consciousness": a model for alcohol and drug abuse. *American Journal of Psychiatry* 133:635–640.

Gardiner, M. M., ed. (1971). *The Wolf Man by the Wolf Man*. New York: Basic Books.

———(1983). The Wolf Man's last years. *Journal of the American Psychoanalytic Association* 31:867–897.

Gardner, G. (1931). Evidences of homosexuality in one hundred twenty unanalyzed cases with paranoid content. *Psychoanalytic Review* 18:57–61.

Gedo, J. E. (1972). The dream of reason produces monsters. *Journal of the American Psychoanalytic Association* 20:199–223.

Gedo, J. E., and Goldberg, A. (1973). *Models of the Mind: A Psychoanalytic Theory*. Chicago: University of Chicago Press.

Gerard, D. L., and Kornetsky, C. (1954). A social and psychiatric study of adolescent opiate addicts. *Psychoanalytic Quarterly* 28:113–115.

Gershon, E. S., Gromer, M., and Klerman, G. L. (1968). Hostility and depression. *Psychiatry* 31:224–235.

Gill, M. M. (1963). *Topography and Systems in Psychoanalytic Theory. Psychological Issues*, Monograph 10. New York: International Universities Press.

———, ed.(1967). *The Collected Papers of David Rapaport*. New York: Basic Books.

Giovacchini, P. I. (1972). Technical difficulties in treating some characterological disorders: countertransference problems. *International Journal of Psychoanalytic Psychotherapy* 1:112–128.

Gitelson, M. (1984). The emotional problems of elderly people. In *Psychoanalysis: Science and Profession*, pp. 115–141. New York: International Universities Press, 1973.

Glover, E. (1928). The etiology of alcoholism. In *On the Early Development of the Mind*, pp. 81–90. New York: International Universities Press, 1956.

———(1932). On the etiology of drug-addiction. In *On the Early Development of the Mind*, pp. 187–215. New York: International Universities Press, 1956.

———(1955). *The Technique of Psychoanalysis*. New York: International Universities Press.

Goldstein, M., Held, J., and Cromwell, R. (1968). Premorbid adjustment and paranoid-nonparanoid status in schizophrenia. *Psychological Bulletin* 70:382–386.

Goldstein, M. J., and Jones, J. E. (1977). Adolescent and familial precursors of borderline and schizophrenic conditions. In *Borderline Personality Disorders: The Concept, the Syndrome, the Patient*, ed. P. Hartocollis, pp. 213–229. New York: International Universities Press.

Greenacre, P. (1969). The fetish and the transitional object. *The Psychoanalytic Study of the Child* 24:144–163.

———(1970). Youth, growth and violence. *The Psychoanalytic Study of the Child* 25:340–359.

Greenson, R. R. (1965). The working alliance and the transference neurosis. *Psychoanalytic Quarterly* 34:155–181.

———(1967). *The Technique and Practice of Psychoanalysis*. Vol. 1. New York: International Universities Press.

Greenson, R. R., and Wexler, M. (1969). The non-transference relationship in the psychoanalytic situation. *International Journal of Psycho-Analysis* 50:27–39.

Greenspan, S. I., and Pollock, G. H., eds. (1981). *The Course of Life: Psychoanalytic Contributions Toward Understanding Personality Development*.

III. Adulthood and the Aging Process. Adelphi, MD: Mental Health Study Center, NIMH.

Grinberg, L., and Grinberg, R. (1984). A psychoanalytic study of migration: its normal and pathological aspects. *Journal of the American Psychoanalytic Association* 32:13–38.

Grinker, R. R., Werble, B., and Drye, R. C. (1968). *The Borderline Syndrome: A Behavioral Study of Ego Functions.* New York: Basic Books.

Grotstein, J. S. (1977a). The psychoanalytic concept of schizophrenia: I. the dilemma. *International Journal of Psycho-Analysis* 58:403–425.

———(1977b). The psychoanalytic concept of schizophrenia: II. reconciliation. *International Journal of Psycho-Analysis* 58:427–452.

Grunes, J. M. (1981). Reminiscences, regression, and empathy—a psychotherapeutic approach to the impaired elderly. In *The Course of Life: Psychoanalytic Contributions Toward Understanding Personality Development. III. Adulthood and the Aging Process*, eds. S. I. Greenspan and G. H. Pollock, pp. 545–548. Adelphi, MD: Mental Health Study Center, NIMH.

Guarner, E. (1966). Psychodynamic aspects of drug experience. *British Journal of Medical Psychology* 39:157–162.

Gunderson, J. G., and Singer, M. T. (1975). Defining borderline patients: an overview. *American Journal of Psychiatry* 132:1–10.

Guntrip, H. (1969). *Schizoid Phenomena, Object Relations and the Self.* New York: International Universities Press.

———(1973). *Psychoanalytic Theory, Therapy, and the Self.* New York: Basic Books.

Gutmann, D. L. (1981). Psychoanalysis and aging: a developmental view. In *The Course of Life: Psychoanalytic Contributions Toward Understanding Personality Development. III. Adulthood and the Aging Process*, eds. S. I. Greenspan and G. H. Pollock, pp. 489–517. Adelphi, MD: Mental Health Study Center, NIMH.

Hamilton, E., and Cairns, H., eds. (1961). *The Collected Dialogues of Plato.* Princeton: Princeton University Press.

Hamlin, R. M., and Lorr, M. (1971). Differentiation of normals, neurotics, paranoids, and nonparanoids. *Journal of Abnormal Psychology* 77:90–96.

Harrow, M., Himmelhoch, J., Tucker, G., Hersh, J., and Quinlan, D. (1972). Overinclusive thinking in acute schizophrenic patients. *Journal of Abnormal Psychology* 79:161–168.

Harrow, M., Harkavy, K., Bromet, E., and Tucker, G. J. (1973). A longitudinal study of schizophrenic thinking. *Archives of General Psychiatry* 28:179–182.

Hartmann, D. (1969). A study of drug-taking adolescents. *ThePsychoanalytic Study of the Child* 24:384-398.

Hartmann, H. (1950). Comments on the psychoanalytic theory of the ego. In *Essays on Ego Psychology*, pp. 113-141. New York: International Universities Press, 1964.

———(1951). Technical implications of ego psychology. *Essays on Ego Psychology*, pp. 142-154. New York: International Universities Press, 1964.

Hendin, H. (1974a). Students on amphetamines. *Journal of Nervous and Mental Disease* 158:255-267.

———(1974b). Students on heroin. *Journal of Nervous and Mental Diseases* 158:240-255.

———(1975a). *The Age of Sensation: A Psychoanalytic Exploration*. New York: Norton.

———(1975b). Student suicide: death as a life style. *Journal of Nervous and Mental Diseases* 160:204-219.

———(1982). *Suicide in America*. New York: Norton.

Hendrick, I. (1940). Suicide as wish-fulfillment. *Psychiatric Quarterly* 14:30-42.

———(1964). Narcissism and the prepuberty ego-ideal. *Journal of the American Psychoanalytic Association* 12:522-528.

Hersey, J. (1959). *The War Lover*. New York: Knopf.

Hesselbach, C. F. (1962). Superego regression in paranoia. *Psychoanalytic Quarterly* 31:341-350.

Hochman, J. S., and Brill, N. I. (1972). Chronic marijuana use and psychosocial adaptation. *American Journal of Psychiatry* 130:132-140.

Horney, K. (1950). *Neurosis and Human Growth*. New York: Norton.

Jacobson, E. (1959). The "exceptions": an elaboration of Freud's character study. *The Psychoanalytic Study of the Child* 14:135-154.

———(1961). Adolescent moods and the remodeling of psychic structure in adolescence. *The Psychoanalytic Study of the Child* 16:164-183.

———(1964). *The Self and the Object World*. New York: International Universities Press.

———(1971). *Depression: Comparative Studies of Normal, Neurotic, and Psychotic Conditions*. New York: International Universities Press.

Jaffe, D. S. (1968). The mechanism of projection: its dual role in object relations. *International Journal of Psycho-Analysis*, 49:662-677.

Joffe, W. G., and Sandler, J. (1967). Some conceptual problems involved in the consideration of disorders of narcissism. *Journal of Child Psychotherapy* 2:56-66.

Johannsen, W., Friedman, S., Leitschuh, T., and Ammons, H. (1963). A study of certain schizophrenic dimensions and their relationship to double alternative learning. *Journal of Consulting Psychology* 27:375–382.

Jones, E. (1955). *Sigmund Freud: His Life and Work*, Vol. 2. New York: Basic Books.

Kendler, K. S., and Tsuang, M. T. (1981). Nosology of paranoid schizophrenia and other paranoid psychoses. *Schizophrenia Bulletin* 7:594–610.

Kanzer, M. (1972). Review of *The Wolf Man by the Wolf Man. International Journal of Psycho-Analysis* 53:419–411.

Katan, M. (1950). Schreber's hallucinations about the "little men." *International Journal of Psycho-Analysis* 31:32–35.

———(1952). Further remarks about Schreber's hallucinations *International Journal of Psycho-Analysis* 33:429–432.

Kay, D. W. K., and Roth, M. (1961). Environmental and hereditary factors in the schizophrenia of old age ("late paraphrenia") and their bearing on the general problem of causation in schizophrenia. *Journal of Mental Science* 107:649–686.

Kendler, K. S., and Tsuang, M. T. (1981). Nosology of paranoid schizophrenia and other paranoid psychoses. *Schizophrenia Bulletin* 7:594–610.

Kernberg, O. (1966). Structural derivatives of object relationships. *International Journal of Psycho-Analysis* 47:236–253.

———(1967). Borderline personality organization. *Journal of the American Psychoanalytic Association* 15:641–685.

———(1969). A contribution to the ego-psychological critique of the Kleinian school. *International Journal of Psycho-Analysis* 50:317–333.

———(1970). A psychoanalytic classification of character pathology. *Journal of the American Psychoanalytic Association* 18:800–822.

———(1971). Prognostic considerations regarding borderline personality organization. *Journal of the American Psychoanalytic Association* 19:595–635.

———(1974). Contrasting viewpoints regarding the nature and psychoanalytic treatment of narcissistic personalities: A preliminary communication. *Journal of the American Psychoanalytic Association* 22:255–267.

Khantzian, E.J. (1974). Opiate addiction: a critique of theory and some implications for treatment. *American Journal of Psychotherapy* 28:59–70.

———(1975). Self-selection and progression in drug dependence. *Psychiatry Digest* 36:19–22.

Krystal, H., and Raskin, H. A. (1970). *Drug Dependence: Aspects of Ego Function*. Detroit: Wayne State Unviersity Press.

Laing, R.D. (1965). *The Divided Self*. Baltimore: Penguin Books.

Langs, R. J. (1973). *The Technique of Psychoanalytic Psychotherapy*. Vol. 1. New York: Jason Aronson.

———(1974). *The Technique of Psychoanalytic Psychotherapy*. Vol. 2. New York: Jason Aronson.

Larson, C., and Nyman, G. (1973). Differential fertility in schizophrenia. *Acta Psychiatrica Scandinavia* 49:272-280.

Lawton, M. P. (1974). Psychology of aging. In *Aging: Its Challenge to the Individual and Society*, ed. W. C. Bier, S. J., pp. 73-83.

Levi, D. L., Fales, C. H., Stein, M., and Sharp, V. H. (1966). Separation and attempted suicide. *Archives of General Psychiatry* 15:158-164.

Levin, D. C. (1969). The self: a contribution to its place in theory and technique. *International Journal of Psycho-Analysis* 50:41-51.

Levin, S. (1967). Some metapsychological considerations on the differentiation between shame and guilt. *International Journal of Psycho-Analysis* 48:267-276.

Lewin, B. D. (1946). Sleep, the mouth, and the dream screen. In *Selected Writings of Bertram D. Lewin*, ed. J. A. Arlow, pp. 87-110. New York: Psychoanalytic Quarterly, 1973.

———(1950). *The Psychoanalysis of Elation*. New York: Norton.

Lewis, A. (1970). Paranoia and paranoid: A historical perspective. *Psychological Medicine* 1:2-12.

Lichtenstein, H. (1961). Identity and sexuality: a study of their interrelationship in man. *Journal of the American Psychoanalytic Association* 9:179-260.

Lidz, T., Fleck, S., and Cornelison, A. R. (1965). *Schizophrenia and the Family*. New York: International Universities Press.

Litman, R. E. (1975). The assessment of suicidality. In *Consultation-Liaison Psychiatry*, ed. R. O. Pasnau, pp. 227-236. New York: Grune and Stratton.

Loewald, H. W. (1960). On the therapeutic action of psychoanalysis. *International Journal of Psycho-Analysis* 41:16-33.

———(1962). Internalization, separation, mourning, and the superego. *Psychoanalytic Quarterly* 31:483-504.

Loewenstein, R. M. (1951). The problem of interpretation. *Psychoanalytic Quarterly* 20:1-14.

———(1954). Some remarks on defenses, autonomous ego and psychoanalytic technique. *International Journal of Psycho-Analysis* 35:188-193.

King, P. (1974). Notes on the psychoanalysis of older patients—reappraisal of the potentialities for change during the second half of life. *Journal of Analytic Psychology* 19:22-37.

_____(1980). The life cycle as indicated by the nature of the transference in the psychoanalysis of the middle-aged and elderly. *International Journal of Psycho-Analysis* 61:153:160.

Kinston, W. (1980). A theoretical and technical approach to narcissistic disturbance. *International Journal of Psycho-Analysis* 61:383-394.

_____(1982). An intrapsychic developmental schema for narcissistic disturbance. *International Review of Psycho-Analysis* 9:253-261.

_____(1983). A theoretical context for shame. *International Journal of Psycho-Analysis* 64:213-226.

Klaf, F. S., and Davis, C. A. (1960). Homosexuality and paranoid schizophrenia: A survey of 150 cases and controls. *American Journal of Psychiatry* 116:1070-1075.

Klein, H., and Horowitz, W. (1949). Psychosexual factors in the paranoid phenomenon. *American Journal of Psychiatry* 105:697-701.

Klein, M. (1934). A contribution to the psychogenesis of manic-depressive states. In *Contributions to Psycho-Analysis: 1921-1945*, pp. 232-310. New York: McGraw-Hill, 1964.

_____(1940). Mourning and its relation to manic-depressive states. *Contributions to Psycho-Analysis: 1921-1945*, pp. 311-338. New York: McGraw-Hill, 1964.

_____(1957). *Envy and Gratitude*. London: Travistock.

_____(1960). *The Psychoanalysis of Children*. New York: Grove Press.

Knight, R. P. (1940). The relationship of latent homosexuality to the mechanism of paranoid delusions. *Bulletin of the Menninger Clinic* 4:149-159.

Kohlen, R. (1959). Aging life-adjustment. In *The Handbook of Aging and the Individual*, ed. J. Birren, pp. 852-897. Chicago: University of Chicago Press.

Kohut, H. (1971). *The Analysis of the Self*. New York: International Universities Press.

_____(1972). Thoughts on narcissism and narcissistic rage. *The Psychoanalytic Study of the Child* 27:360-400.

_____(1977). *The Restoration of the Self*. New York: International Universities Press.

Kris, E. (1951). Ego psychology and interpretation in psychoanalytic therapy. *Pscyhoanalytic Quarterly* 20:15-30.

Krohn, A. (1974). Borderline "empathy" and differentiation of object representations: A contribution to the psychology of object relations. *International Journal of Psychoanalytic Psychotherapy* 3:142-165.

_____(1957). A contribution to the psycho-analytic theory of masochism. *Journal of the American Psychoanalytic Association* 5:197–234.

_____(1958). Remarks on some variations in psycho-analytic technique. *International Journal of Psycho-Analysis* 39:202–210.

London, N. (1973a). An essay on psychoanalytic theory: two theories of schizophrenia. I. Review and critical assessment of the development of the two theories. *International Journal of Psycho-Analysis* 54:169–178.

_____(1973b). An essay on psychoanalytic theory: two theories of schizophrenia. II. Discussion and restatement of the specific theory of schizophrenia. *International Journal of Psycho-Analysis* 54:179–193.

Lorr, M., Klett, C. J., and Cave, R. (1967). Higher-level psychotic syndromes. *Journal of Abnormal Psychology* 72:74–77.

Luparello, T. J. (1970). Features of fugue: a unified hypothesis of regression. *Journal of the American Psychoanalytic Association* 18:379–398.

MacAlpine, I. (1950). The development of the transference. *Psychoanalytic Quarterly* 19:501–539.

MacAlpine, I., and Hunter, R. A. (1953). The Schreber case: a contribution to schizophrenia, hypochondria, and psychosomatic symptom formation. *Psychoanalytic Quarterly* 22:328–371.

MacAndrew, E., and Edgerton, R. B. (1969). *Drunken Comportment: A Social Explanation*. Chicago: Aldine.

Maddox, G. L. (1963). Activity and morale: a longitudinal study of selected elderly subjects. *Social Forces* 42:195–205.

Maenchen, A. (1968). Object cathexis in a borderline twin. *The Psychoanalytic Study of the Child* 23:438–456.

Magaro, P. A. (1981). The paranoid and the schizophrenic: The case for distinct cognitive style. *Schizophrenia Bulletin* 7:632–661.

Magaro, P. A., and McDowell, D. J. (1981). The paranoid and the schizophrenic: the case for separate diagnostic categories. Unpublished manuscript.

Mahler, M. S., Pine, F., and Bergmann, A. (1975). *The Psychological Birth of the Human Infant*. New York: International Universities Press.

Maltsberger, J. T., and Buie, D. H. (1974). Countertransference hate in the treatment of suicidal patients. *Archives of General Psychiatry* 30:625–633.

_____(1980). The devices of suicide: revenge, riddance, and rebirth. *International Review of Psycho-Analysis* 7:61–72.

Marmor, J. (1953). Orality in the hysterical personality. *Journal of the American Psychoanalytic Association* 1:656–671.

Masterson, J. F. (1972). *Treatment of the Borderline Adolsecent: A Developmental Approach*. New York: Wiley.

Masud R.Khan, M. (1972). The finding and becoming of self. *International Journal of Psychoanalytic Psychotherapy* 1:97–111.

Mayfield, D., and Montgomery, D. (1972). Alcoholism, alcohol intoxication, and suicide attempts. *Archives of General Psychiatry* 27:349–353.

McAllister, T. W., and Price, T. R. P. (1982). Severe depressive pseudodementia with and without dementia. *American Journal of Psychiatry* 139:626–629.

McCabe, M. S., Fowler, R. C., Cadoret, R. J., and Winokur, G. (1971). Family differences in schizophrenia with good and poor prognosis. *Psychological Medicine* 1:326–332.

McDevitt, J. B. (1975). Separation-individuation and object constancy. *Journal of the American Psychoanalytic Association* 23:713–742.

McDowell, D., Reynolds, B., and Magaro, P. (1975). The integration defect in paranoid and nonparanoid schizophrenia. *Journal of Abnormal Psychology* 84:629–636.

Meerloo, J. A. M. (1952). Artificial ecstasy: a study of the psychosomatic aspect of drug addiction. *Journal of Nervous and Mental Diseases* 115:246–266.

Mehlman, R. D. (1976). Transference mobilization, transference resolution, and the narcissistic alliance. Presented to the Boston Psychoanalytic Society, Feb. 25.

Meissner, S. J., W. W. (1970) Notes on identification. I. Origins in Freud. *Psychoanalytic Quarterly* 39:563–589.

———(1971a). Freud's methodology. *Journal of the American Psychoanalytic Association* 19:265–309.

———(1971b). Notes on identification. II. Clarification of related concepts. *Psychoanalytic Quarterly* 40:277–302.

———(1972a). Alienation in psychiatric perspective. In *Alienation: Plight of Modern Man?*, ed. W. C. Bier, S. J., pp. 62–81. New York: Fordham University Press.

———(1972b). Notes on identification. III. The concept of identification. *Psychoanalytic Quarterly* 41:224–260.

———(1974a). Correlative aspects of introjective and projective mechanisms. *American Journal of Psychiatry* 131:176–180.

———(1974b). Differentiation and integration of learning and identification in the developmental process. *Annual of Psychoanalysis* 2:181–196.

———(1974c). The role of imitative social learning in identificatory processes. *Journal of the American Psychoanalytic Association* 22:512–536.

_____(1976a). New horizons in metapsychology: view and review (Panel Report). *Journal of the American Psychoanalytic Association* 24:161–180.

_____(1976b). Psychotherapeutic schema based on the paranoid process. *International Journal of Psychoanalytic Psychotherapy* 5:87–114.

_____(1977). The Wolf-Man and the paranoid process. *Annual of Psychoanalysis* 5:23–74.

_____(1978a). The conceptualization of marriage and family dynamics from a psychoanalytic perspective. In *Marriage and Marital Therapy: Psychoanalytic, Behavioral and Systems Theory Perspectives*, eds. T. J. Paolino and B. S. McGrady, pp. 25–88. New York: Brunner/Mazel.

_____(1978b). *The Paranoid Process*. New York: Jason Aronson.

_____(1979a). Internalization and object relations. *Journal of the American Psychoanalytic Association* 27:345–360.

_____(1979b). Threats to confidentiality. *Psychiatric Annals* 9:54–71.

_____(1980a). The problem of internalization and structure formation. *International Journal of Psycho-Analysis* 61:237–248.

_____(1980b). Theories of personality and psychopathology: classical psychoanalysis. In *Comprehensive Textbook Psychiatry, III*, eds. H. I. Kaplan, A. M. Freedman, and B. J. Sadock, pp. 631–728. Baltimore/London: Williams & Wilkins.

_____(1981a). Genetic aspects of the borderline conditions. *Psychoanalytic Review* 68:219–241.

_____(1981b). *Internalization in Psychoanalysis*. Psychological Issues, Monograph 50. New York: International Universities Press.

_____(1981c). A note on narcissism. *Psychoanalytic Quarterly* 50:77–89.

_____(1981d). Notes on the psychoanalytic psychology of the self. *Psychoanalytic Inquiry* 1(2):233–248.

_____(1981e). The schizophrenic and the paranoid process. *Schizophrenic Bulletin* 7(4):611–631.

_____(1982–1983). Notes on countertransference in borderline conditions. *International Journal of Psychoanalytic Psychotherapy* 9:89–124.

_____(1984a). *The Borderline Spectrum: Differential Diagnosis and Developmental Issues*. New York: Jason Aronson.

_____(1984b). Models in the mind: the role of theory in the psychoanalytic process. *Psychoanalytic Inquiry* 4:5–32.

_____(1984c). *Psychoanalysis and Religious Experience*. New Haven: Yale University Press.

_____(1985). Can psychoanalysis find its self? *Journal of the American Psychoanalytic Association*.

Menninger, K. A. (1938). *Man Against Himself*. New York: Harcourt Brace.

Merton, R. K. (1957). *Social Theory and Social Structure*. New York: Free Press.

Miller, A. (1979). Depression and grandiosity as related forms of narcissistic disturbances. *International Review of Psycho-Analysis* 6:61–76.

Miller, C. (1941). The paranoid syndrome. *Archives of Neurology and Psychiatry* 45:953–963.

Minkoff, K., Bergman, E., Beck, A. T., and Beck, R. (1973). Hopelessness, depression, and attempted suicide. *American Journal of Psychiatry* 130:455–459.

Mirin, S. M., Shapiro, L. M., Meyer, R. E., Pillard, R. C., and Fischer, S. (1971). Casual versus heavy use of marijuana: a redefinition of the marijuana problem. *American Journal of Psychiatry* 127:1134–1140.

Modell, A. H. (1961). Denial and the sense of separateness. *Journal of the American Psychoanalytic Association* 9:533–547.

_____(1968). *Object Love and Reality*. New York: International Universities Press.

_____(1971). The origin of certain forms of preoedipal guilt and the implications for a psychoanalytic theory of affects. *International Journal of Psycho-Analysis* 52:337–346.

_____(1975). A narcissistic defense against affects and the illusion of self-sufficiency. *International Journal of Psycho-Analysis* 56:275–282.

_____(1985). *Psychoanalysis in a New Context*. New York: International Universities Press.

Modlin, H. C. (1963). Psychodynamics and management of paranoid states in women. *Archives of General Psychiatry* 8:262–268.

Monti, M. R. (1981). Scienza, paranoia, pseudoscienza. *Rivista di Storia delle Idee* 1:395–424.

Morrison, A. P. (1983). Shame, ideal self and narcissism. *Contemporary Psychoanalysis* 19:295–318.

_____(1984). Working with shame in psychoanalytic therapy. *Journal of the American Psychoanalytic Association* 32:479–505.

Munschauer, C. A. (1976). Patterns of thought disorder: an application of signal detection theory to errors of overinclusion and overexclusion in schizophrenics, manics, and other psychopathological groups. Unpublished Dissertation, State University of New York at Buffalo.

Nacht, S. (1958). Variations in technique. *International Journal of Psycho-Analysis* 39:235–237.

Neale, J. M., Kopfstein, J. H., and Levine, A. J. (1972). Premorbid adjustment and paranoid status in schizophrenia: varying assessment techniques and the influence of chronicity. *Proceedings of the 80th Annual Convention of the American Psychological Association* 7:321–322. (Summary)

Neufeld, R. W. J. (1977). Components of processing deficit among paranoid and nonparanoid schizophrenics. *Journal of Abnormal Psychology* 86:60–64.

———(1978). The nature of deficit among paranoid and nonparanoid schizophrenics in the interpretation of sentences: an information processing approach. *Journal of Clinical Psychology* 34:333–339.

Neugarten, B., in collaboration with H. Berkowitz, W. J. Crotty, W. Gruen, D. L. Gutmann, M. I. Lubin, D. L. Miller, R. F. Peck, J. L. Rosen, A. Shulsin, S. S. Tobin, and with the editorial assistance of J. M. Falk (1964). *Personality in Middle and Late Life*. New York: Atherton.

Neugarten, B., and Havighurst, R. J. (1969). *Adjustment to Retirement: A Cross National Study*. Assen: Van Gorcum.

Niederland, W. G. (1951). Three notes on the Schreber case. *Psychoanalytic Quarterly* 20:579–591.

———(1959). Father and son. *Psychoanalytic Quarterly* 28:151–169.

———(1960). The miracled-up world of Schreber's childhood. *Psychoanalytic Quarterly* 29:301–304.

———(1963). Further data and memorabilia pertaining to the Schreber case. *International Journal of Psycho-Analysis* 44:201–207.

———(1968). Schreber and Flechsig: a further contribution to the "kernel of truth" in Schreber's delusional system. *Journal of the American Psychoanalytic Association* 16:740–749.

———(1974). *The Schreber Case: Psychoanalytic Profile of a Paranoid Personality*. New York: Quadrangle.

Nunberg, H. (1952). Discussion of M. Katan's paper on Schreber's hallucinations. *International Journal of Psycho-Analysis* 33:454–456.

Nydes, J. (1963). The paranoid-masochistic character. *Psychoanalytic Review* 50:215–251.

Offenkranz, W., and Tobin, A. (1973). Problems of the therapeutic alliance: Freud and the Wolf Man. *International Journal of Psycho-Analysis* 54:75–78.

Olinick, S. J. (1975). On empathic perception and the problems of reporting psychoanalytic processes. *International Journal of Psycho-Analysis* 56:147–154.

Orgel, S. (1974). Fusion with the victim and suicide. *International Journal of Psycho-Analysis* 55:531–538.

Ornstein, P. H. (1974). On narcissism: beyond the introduction, highlights of Heinz Kohut's contributions to the psychoanalytic treatment of narcissistic personality disorders. *Annual of Psychoanalysis* 2:127–149.

Ovesey, L. (1954). The homosexual conflict: an adaptational analysis. *Psychiatry* 17:243–250.

———(1955a). The pseudo-homosexual anxiety. *Psychiatry* 17:17–25.

———(1955b). Pseudo-homosexuality, the paranoid mechanism and paranoia. *Psychiatry* 18:163–173.

Paykel, E. S., Prusoff, B. A., and Myers, J. K. (1975). Suicide attempts and recent life events: a controlled comparison. *Archives of General Psychiatry* 32:327–333.

Peck, R. (1955). Psychological developments in the second half of life. In *Psychological Aspects of Aging*, ed. J. E. Anderson, pp. 42–53. Washington: American Psychological Association.

Piers, G., and Singer, M. B. (1953). *Shame and Guilt: A Psychoanalytic and a Cultural Study*. Springfield, IL: Thomas.

Pinderhughes, C. A. (1971). Somatic, psychic, and social sequelae of loss. *Journal of the American Psychoanalytic Association* 19:670–696.

Pine, F. (1974). On the concept of "borderline" in children: a clinical essay. *Psychoanalytic Study of the Child* 29:341–368.

Planansky, K., and Johnston, R. (1962). Incidents and relationship of homosexual and paranoid features in schizophrenia. *Journal of Mental Science* 108:604–615.

Poland, W. S. (1975). Tact as a psychoanalytic function. *International Journal of Psycho-Analysis* 56:155–162.

Polatin, P. (1975). Psychotic disorders: paranoid states. In *Comprehensive Textbook of Psychiatry, II*, eds. A. M. Freedman, H. I. Kaplan, and B. J. Sadock, pp. 992–1002. Baltimore: Williams and Wilkins.

Pollock, G. H. (1970). Anniversary reactions, trauma and mourning. *Psychoanalytic Quarterly* 39:347–371.

———(1975). On mourning, immortality, and utopia. *Journal of the American Psychoanalytic Association* 23:334–362.

———(1978). Process and affect: mourning and grief. *International Journal of Psycho-Analysis* 59:255–276.

———(1981). Aging or aged: development or pathology. In *The Course of Life: Psychoanalytic Contributions Toward Understanding Personality De-*

velopment III: Adulthood and the Aging Process, eds. S. I. Greenspan and G. H. Pollock, pp. 549–585. Adelphi, MD: Mental Health Study Center, NIMH.

Radford, P., Wiseberg, S., and Yorke, C. (1972). A study of "main-line" heroin addiction: a preliminary report. *The Psychoanalytic Study of the Child* 27:156–180.

Rado, S. (1933). Psychoanalysis of pharmacothymia. *Psychoanalytic Quarterly* 2:1–23.

——(1957). Narcotic bondage: a general theory of the dependence on narcotic drugs. *American Journal of Psychiatry* 114:165–170.

Rapaport, D. (1967). The theory of ego autonomy. In *The Collected Papers of David Rapaport*, ed. M. M. Gill, pp. 722–744. New York: Basic Books.

Reich, W. (1933). *Character Analysis*, 3rd ed. New York: Farrar, Straus and Giroux, 1949.

——(1953). Narcissistic object choice in women. *Journal of the American Psychoanalytic Association* 1:22–44.

——(1958). A special variation of technique. *International Journal of Psycho-Analysis* 39:230–234.

——(1960). Pathological forms of self-esteem regulation. *The Psycho-analytic Study of the Child* 15:215–232.

Reich, W. (1976). The schizophrenic spectrum: a genetic concept. *Journal of Nervous and Mental Diseases* 162:3–12.

Reifler, B. V., Larson, E., and Hanley, R. (1982). Coexistence of cognitive impairment and depression in geriatric outpatients. *American Journal of Psychiatry* 139:623–626.

Robbins, M. D. (1976). Borderline personality organization: the need for a new theory. *Journal of the American Psychoanalytic Association* 24:831–853.

Rochlin, G. (1961). The dread of abandonment: a contribution to the etiology of the loss complex and to depression. *The Psychoanalytic Study of the Child* 16:451–470.

——(1965). *Griefs and Discontents: The Forces of Change*. Boston: Little, Brown.

——(1973). *Man's Aggression: The Defense of the Self*. Boston: Gambit Press.

Rose, A. M. (1964). A current theoretical issue in social gerontology. *The Gerontologist* 4:46–50.

Rosenfeld, H. (1960). On drug addiction. *International Journal of Psycho-Analysis* 41:467–475.

Rosenfeld, S. K., and Sprince, M. P. (1963). An attempt to formulate the meaning of the concept "borderline." *The Psychoanalytic Study of the Child* 18:603–635.

Ross, M. B., and Magaro, P. A. (1976). Cognitive differentiation between paranoid and nonparanoid schizophrenics. *Psychological Reports* 38:991–994.

Roth, M. (1955). The natural history of mental disorder in old age. *Journal of Mental Science*, 101:281–301.

Rothstein, A. (1979). An exploration of the diagnostic term "narcissistic personality disorder." *Journal of the American Psychoanalytic Association* 27:893–912.

———(1984). Fear of humiliation. *Journal of the American Psychoanalytic Association* 32:99–116.

Sabbath, J. C. (1969). The suicidal adolescent—the expendable child. *Journal of the American Academy of Child Psychiatry* 8:272–285.

Salzman, L. (1960). Paranoid states: theory and therapy. *Archives of General Psychiatry* 2:679–693.

Sandler, A. (1978). Problems in the psychoanalysis of an aging narcissistic patient. *Journal of Geriatric Psychiatry* 11:5–36.

Sandler, J. (1960). On the concept of the superego. *The Psychoanalytic Study of the Child* 15:128–162.

Sanes, J. and Zigler, E. (1971). Premorbid social competence in schizophrenia. *Journal of Abnormal Psychology* 78:140–144.

Sarnoff, C. A. (1972). The vicissitudes of projection during an analysis encompassing late latency to early adolescence. *International Journal of Psycho-Analysis* 53:515–522.

Savitt, R. (1954). Extramural psychoanalytic treatment of a case of neurotic addiction. *Journal of the American Psychoanalytic Association* 2:494–502.

———. (1963). Psychoanalytic studies on addiction: ego structure in narcotic addiction. *Psychoanalytic Quarterly* 32:43–57.

Schafer, R. (1959). Generative empathy in the treatment situation. *Psychoanalytic Quarterly* 28:342–373.

———. (1968a). *Aspects of Internalization*. New York: International Universities Press.

———. (1968b). On the theoretical and technical conceptualization of activity and passivity. *Psychoanalytic Quarterly* 37:173–198.

Schatzman, M. (1971). Paranoia or persecution: the case of Schreber. *Family Process* 10:177–212.

Schmideberg, M. (1931). A contribution to the psychology of persecuting ideas and delusions. *International Journal of Psycho-Analysis* 50:317–333.

Schreber, D. P. (1955). *Memoirs of My Nervous Illness*, trans. and ed. I. MacAlpine and R. A. Hunter. Cambridge, MA: Bentley.

Schwartz, D. A. (1963). A review of the "paranoid" concept. *Archives of General Psychiatry* 8:349–361.

———. (1964). The paranoid-depressive existential continuum. *Psychiatric Quarterly* 38:690–706.

Schwartz, L. (1974). Narcissistic personality disorders—a clinical discussion. *Journal of the American Psychoanalytic Association* 22:292–306.

Schwartzman, J. (1975). The addict, abstinence, and the family. *American Journal of Psychiatry* 132:154–157.

Searles, H. F. (1965). *Collected Papers on Schizophrenia and Related Subjects*. New York: International Universities Press.

Segal, H. (1964). *Introduction to the Work of Melanie Klein*. London: Heinemann.

Seitz, P. (1974). "Reality is a stone-cold drag": psychoanalytic observations of hippies, with a selected list and annotated index of references on adolescent problems. *Annual of Psychoanalysis* 2:387–415.

Shainess, N. (1979). Analyzability and capacity for change in middle life. *Journal of the Amerian Academy of Psychoanalysis* 7:385–404.

Shakow, D. (1962). Segmental set: a theory of the formal psychological deficit in schizophrenia. *Archives of General Psychiatry* 6:1–17.

Shapiro, D. (1965). *Neurotic Styles*. New York: Basic Books.

Shengold, L. (1974). The metaphor of the mirror. *Journal of the American Psychoanalytic Association*. 22:97–115.

Schneidman, E. S. (1969). Suicide, lethality and the psychological autopsy. In *Aspects of Depression*, ed. E. S. Shneidman and M. Ortega, pp. 225–250. Boston: Little, Brown.

———. (1973). Suicide notes reconsidered. *Psychiatry* 36:379–394.

———. (1976a). A psychologic theory of suicide. *Psychiatric Annals* 6:620–626.

———. (ed.) (1976b). *Suicidology: Contemporary Developments*. New York: Grune and Stratton.

Shneidman, E. S. and Faberow, N. L. (1957). Clues to suicide. In *Clues to Suicide*, eds. E. S. Shneidman and N. L. Faberow, pp. 3–10. New York: McGraw-Hill.

Sifneos, P. E. (1966). Manipulative suicide. *Psychiatric Quarterly* 40:525–537.

Socarides, C. W. (1962). Theoretical and clinical aspects of overt female homosexuality (Panel Report). *Journal of the American Psychoanalytic Association* 10:579–592.

Spence, D. P. (1982). *Narrative Truth and Historical Truth*. New York: Norton.

Spiegel, L. A. (1966). Affects in relation to self and object: a model for the derivation of desire, longing, pain, anxiety, humiliation, and shame. *The Psychoanalytic Study of the Child* 21:69–92.

Spruiell, V. (1974). Theories of treatment of narcissistic personalities. *Journal of the American Psychoanalytic Association* 22:268–278.

Stengel, E. (1964). *Suicide and Attempted Suicide*. Baltimore: Penguin.

———. (1968). Attempted suicides. In *Suicidal Behaviors: Diagnosis and Management*, ed. H. L. C. Resnick. pp. 171–189. Boston: Little, Brown.

Stokes, R. G., and Maddox, G. L. (1967). Some social factors on retirement adaptation. *Journal of Gerontology* 22:329–333.

Stone, L. (1961). *The Psychoanalytic Situation*. New York: International Universities Press.

Stone, M. (1980). *The Borderline Syndromes: Constitution, Personality, and Adaptation*. New York: McGraw-Hill.

Stotland, E. (1969). *The Psychology of Hope*. San Francisco: Jossey-Bass.

Strachey, J. (1969). The nature of the therapeutic action of psychoanalysis. *International Journal of Psycho-Analysis* 50:275–291.

Strauss, M. E., Sirotkin, R. A., and Grisell, J. (1974). Length of hospitalization and rate of readmission of paranoid and non-paranoid schizophrenics. *Journal of Consulting and Clinical Psychology* 42:105–110.

Sullivan, H. S. (1953). *Conceptions of Modern Psychiatry*. New York: Norton.

———. (1956). *Clinical Studies in Psychiatry*. New York: Norton.

Szasz, T. S. (1958). The role of the counterphobic mechanism in addiction. *Journal of the American Psychoanalytic Association*. 6:309–325.

Tamerin, J., and Mendelsohn, J. (1969). The psychic dynamics of chronic inebriation: observations of alcoholics during the process of drinking in an experimental group setting. *American Journal of Psychiatry* 125:886–899.

Tartakoff, H. H. (1966). The normal personality in our culture and the Nobel Prize complex. In *Psychoanalysis—A General Psychology*, eds. R. M. Loewenstein, L. M. Newman, M. Schur, and A. J. Solnit, pp. 222–252. New York: International Universities Press.

Tarter, R. E., and Perley, R. N. (1975). Clinical and perceptual characteristics of paranoids and paranoid schizophrenics. *Journal of Clinical Psychology* 31:42–44.

Toolan, J. M. (1975). Suicide in children and adolescents. *American Journal of Psychotherapy* 29:339–344.

Traub-Werner, D. (1984) Towards a theory of prejudice. *International Review of Psycho-Analysis* 11:407–412.

Tsuang, M. T., Fowler, R. C., Cadoret, R. J., and Monnelly, E. (1974). Schizophrenia among first-degree relatives of paranoid and non-paranoid schizophrenics. *Comprehensive Psychiatry* 15:295–307.

Vaillant, G. E. (1966a). A 12-year follow-up of New York narcotic addicts. I. *American Journal of Psychiatry* 122: 727–737.

————. (1966b). A 12-year follow-up of New York narcotic addicts. III. *Archives of General Psychiatry* 15:599–609.

————. (1975). Sociopathy as a human process: a viewpoint. *Archives of General Psychiatry* 32:178–183.

Walters, O. S. (1955). A methodological critique of Freud's Schreber analysis. *Psychoanalytic Review* 42:321–342.

Weinberg, J. (1980). Geriatric psychiatry. In *Comprehensive Textbook of Psychiatry, III*, pp. 3024–3042, eds. H. I. Kaplan, A. M. Freedman, and B. J. Sadock. Baltimore: Williams and Wilkins.

Weiner, H. (1980). Schizophrenia: Etiology. In *Comprehensive Textbook of Psychiatry, III*, eds. H. I. Kaplan, A. M. Freedman, and B. J. Sadock, pp. 1121–1152. Baltimore: Williams and Wilkins.

Weisman, A. D. (1971). Is suicide a disease? *Life-Threatening Behavior* 1:219–231.

Weissman, M., Fox, K., and Klerman, G. L. (1973). Hostility and depression associated with suicide attempts. *American Journal of Psychiatry* 130:450–455.

Wells, C. E. (1978). Geriatric organic psychoses. *Psychiatric Annals* 8:466–478.

————. (1982). Refinements in the diagnosis of dementia. *American Journal of Psychiatry* 139:621–622.

Westermeyer, J., and Walzer, V. (1975). Sociopathy and drug use in a young psychiatric population. *Diseases of the Nervous System* 36:673–677.

Wetzel, R. D., Margulies, T., Davis, R., and Karam, E. (1980). Hopelessness, depression, and suicide intent. *Journal of Clinical Psychiatry* 41:159–160.

White, R. B. (1961). The mother conflict in Schreber's psychosis. *International Journal of Psycho-Analysis* 43:55–73.

————. (1963). The Schreber case reconsidered in the light of psychosexual concepts. *International Journal of Psycho-Analysis* 44:213–221.

Wieder, H. and Kaplan, E. H. (1969). Drug use in adolescents:

Psychodynamic meaning and pharmacogenic effect. *The Psycho-analytic Study of the Child* 24:399–431.

Wieder, H., and Kaplan, E. H. (1974). *Drugs Don't Take People, People Take Drugs*. Secaucus, NJ: L. Stuart.

Winnicott, D. W. (1947). Hate in the countertransference. In *Collected Papers: Through Pediatrics to Psychoanalysis*. New York: Basic Books, 1958.

———. (1953). Transitional objects and transitional phenomena. In *Playing and Reality*, pp. 1–25. New York: Basic Books, 1965.

———. (1960a). Ego distortion in terms of true and false self. In *The Maturational Processes and the Facilitating Environment*, pp. 140–152. New York: International Universities Press, 1965.

———. (1960b). The theory of the parent-infant relationship. In *The Maturational Processes and the Facilitating Environment*, pp. 37–65. New York: International Universities Press, 1965.

———. (1963). Psychiatric disorder in terms of infantile maturational processes. In *The Maturational Processes and the Facilitating Environment*, pp. 230–241. New York: International Universities Press, 1965.

Winokur, G., Morrison, J., Clancy, J., and Crowe, R. (1974). Iowa 500: the clinical and genetic distinction of hebephrenic and paranoid schizophrenia. *Journal of Nervous and Mental Diseases* 159:12–19.

Winokur, G. (1975). Paranoid vs. hebephrenic schizophrenia: Clinical and familial (genetic) heterogeneity. *Psychopharmacology Communications* 1:567–577.

Witkin, H. A., Lewis, H. B., Hertzman, M., Machover, K., Meissner, P. B., and Wapner, S. (1954). *Personality Through Perception*. New York: Harper.

Wurmser, L. (1974). Psychoanalytic considerations of the etiology of compulsive drug use. *Journal of the American Psychoanalytic Association* 22:820–843.

———. (1978). *The Hidden Dimension*. New York: Jason Aronson.

Wynne, L., Ryckoff, I., Day, J., and Hirsch, S. (1958). Pseudomutuality in the family relations of schizophrenics. *Psychiatry* 21:205–220.

Yorke, C. (1970). A critical review of some psychoanalytic literature on drug addiction. *British Journal of Medical Psychology* 43:141–184.

Zetzel, E. R. (1956a). Concept and content in psychoanalytic theory. In *The Capacity for Emotional Growth*, pp. 115–138. New York: International Universities Press, 1970.

———. (1956b). The concept of transference. In *The Capacity For Emotional Growth*, pp. 168–181. New York: International Universities Press, 1970.

_____. (1958). Therapeutic alliance in the analysis of hysteria. In *The Capacity for Emotional Growth*, pp. 182–196. New York: International Universities Press, 1970.

_____. (1971). A developmental approach to the borderline patient. *American Journal of Psychiatry* 127:867–871.

Zetzel, E. R., and Meissner, S. J., W. W. (1973). *Basic Concepts of Psychoanalytic Psychiatry*. New York: Basic Books.

Zigler, E., and Levine, J. (1973). Premorbid adjustment and paranoid-nonparanoid status in schizophrenia: a further investigation. *Journal of Abnormal Psychology* 82:189–199.

Zigler, E., Levine, J., and Zigler, B. (1976). The relation between premorbid competence and paranoid-nonparanoid status in schizophrenia: a methodological and theoretical critique. *Psychological Bulletin* 83:303–313.

_____. (1977). Premorbid social competence and paranoid-nonparanoid status in female schizophrenic patients. *Journal of Nervous and Mental Diseases* 164:333–339.

Zilboorg, G. (1936). Suicide among civilized and primitive races. *American Journal of Psychiatry* 92:1347–1369.

_____. (1937). Considerations on suicide with particular reference to that of the young. *American Journal of Orthopsychiatry* 7:15–31.

_____. (1938). The sense of immortality. *Psychoanalytic Quarterly* 7:171–199.

Zinberg, N. E. (1975). Addiction and ego function. *The Psychoanalytic Study of the Child* 30:567–588.

_____. (1976). Social learning and self-image in aging. *Journal of Geriatric Psychiatry* 9:131–150.

Index